PAST IMPERFECT
alternative essays in American history

EDITED BY

BLANCHE WIESEN COOK
John Jay College, C.U.N.Y.

ALICE KESSLER HARRIS
Hofstra University

RONALD RADOSH
Queensborough Community College, C.U.N.Y.

ALFRED A. KNOPF   NEW YORK

PAST
IMPERFECT
alternative essays in American history

from colonial times to the civil war

volume I

Copyright © 1973 by Alfred A. Knopf, Inc.

Library of Congress Cataloging in Publication Data

Cook, Blanche Wiesen, comp.
    Past imperfect: alternative essays in American history

    Includes bibliographies.
    CONTENTS: v. 1. From colonial times to the Civil War.—v. 2. From Reconstruction to the present.
    1. United States—History—Essays. 2. United States—Social conditions—Essays. I. Harris, Alice Kessler, joint comp. II. Radosh, Ronald, joint comp. III. Title.
E178.6.C68   973   72-5167
ISBN 0-394-31693-2 (v. 1)

Designed by James M. Wall

Cover designed by Batten, Friedman, and Kveloff

Manufactured in the United States of America

First Edition

987654321

acknowledgments

The preparation of this book has been a cooperative venture. We want particularly to thank the following people: Charles B. Forcey read the outline in an early stage; Gerald E. Markowitz, Allen Davis, Milton Mankoff, and Herbert G. Gutman read the entire manuscript and made valuable contributions throughout; Eli Faber, Jesse Lemisch, and Jacques Marchand provided fruitful suggestions for the colonial section. We are especially grateful to Clare Coss whose insights extended our vision at critical points.

We would also like to thank Ilona Harris and Katherine Welch who cut and pasted, and Laura and Daniel Radosh.

This cooperative effort would not have worked without the critiques and ideas as well as the unfailing good humor provided by our editors Arthur Strimling and Elaine Rosenberg.

contents

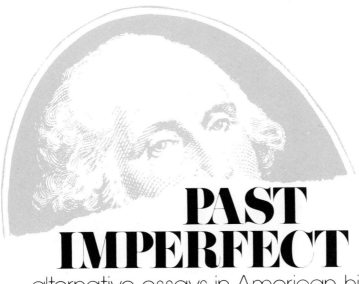

PAST
IMPERFECT
alternative essays in American history

introduction

Today, more than ever before, we hear students ask, "Why study history?" For some historians the answer has always been clear: history helps us to understand the living. Marc Bloch, an eminent medievalist who studied the daily lives of people under feudalism, wrote that "common sense dictates that we no longer avoid" the issues raised by the present. For Bloch, "understanding the living was the master quality of the historian." When, for example, he went with Henri Pirenne, another medievalist, to visit Stockholm, of all the sights in the ancient capital Pirenne wanted to see the new city hall first. Pirenne explained to Bloch that if he "were an antiquarian he would have eyes only for the old stuff." But, he said, "I am an historian, and therefore I love life."

For those who love life our world presents many challenges. Human history is the history of man's failure to achieve a decent society. While it has involved scientific discoveries, creative achievements, and humanistic pursuits, it has also consisted of oppression, war, and the poverty of most of humanity.

As we approach the end of the twentieth century, scientists and humanists who survey our planet have concluded that human life may disappear with us. Many scientists who have traveled around the earth searching for answers about the future have returned with dire predictions of imminent disaster. We have, they insist, depleted our natural resources and polluted our water and air to such a degree that we may have destroyed the wellsprings of our own lives. The violence we traffic in with each other is reflected in the violence that has been done to our planet.

A study of history will not provide the blueprints by which to build a truly humane society. But we cannot prepare for the future without perceiving accurately the world we have made—as well as the means we have used to make it and the reasons for selecting those particular means. In order not to be imprisoned by the patterns of the past we must attempt to understand them.

A knowledge of American history makes it possible to understand the present conditions of our nation and enables us to think about appropriate and possible alternatives. But the traditional study of history has worked to blind us to the realities of the present and to the dynamics by which we have gotten there. Ours has been presented as a history of heroes and leaders who, it would appear, have had a basically agreeable constituency, and no worthy opposition. The role of the ordinary citizen, the history of oppressed minorities, and the nature of the power structure have been omitted from our textbooks which have been written to serve an established system and inflate its myths. And, in the classroom, history is still largely dulled and obscured by people who remain unwilling not only to answer important questions but even to ask them.

The people who have recorded our past have ranged from those who have idealized American democracy to those who have doubted its very existence. In the early twentieth century some progressive historians explored areas of the past that revealed conflict at all levels of society. The questions they raised were quickly submerged during World War II when the calls for unity demanded a glorification of our past. The "consensus" school of traditional or mainstream American historiography that emerged then dominated the dis-cipline between World War II and the war in Indochina. It held that the United States was a melting pot of harmony and happiness where the privileged classes and institutions of feudal Europe never existed and where, as a result, conflict and violence were always and would forever be avoided by democratic consensus.

Historians such as Louis Hartz, Daniel Boorstin, and Oscar Handlin begin with the assumption that America is basically a good, liberal, and benevolent nation, in which resources are widely shared, decisions are made pragmatically, and access to power is available to all who strive for it. They tend to see America as a society in which social mobility minimizes class distinctions. They believe that all Americans participate in this liberal vision and that the ideology and actions of the nation's leaders represent the thinking of all classes and groups. These historians have concluded that not only does democracy work but that its institutions must be protected. As a result, they see dissent as merely disruptive and rival ideologies as temporary aberrations in an otherwise united nation. Divisive elements such as racism, sexism, and nativism rarely appear in their books. On the contrary, they celebrate a faith in the postulated freedoms of our founding fathers. For many, recent history has not only toppled that faith, it has also revealed that traditional or mainstream interpretations of history have served to obscure the very real tensions that have existed from the beginning.

Unlike their mainstream colleagues who see our history as the unfolding of the American dream, radical historians argue that our society was never based on the belief that democracy and equality were synonymous. That assumption was made possible by historians who systematically ignored both the divisive aspects of our past and the victims of its ideological assumptions. If they had focused on America's divided and violent reality instead of on its mythical harmonies, it is not impossible that our recent past might have been different. Radical historians see the origins of events not only in the social, economic, and political situation, but also in the motives of that class which owns the nation's corporations and governs the state. These motives are generally not to be found in its public statements but are camouflaged behind the rhetoric of equal opportunity. The ability of this class to prevail, frequently despite inimical conditions and public opposition, must be examined. Moreover, radical historians do not limit their attention to the operations of political and economic leaders but look to people at all levels and conditions of life for the impact and origins of events.

Traditionally, in periods of crisis some historians have emerged to reassess and to rewrite history. And, for a time, they are called radical historians. When, for example, Marc Bloch wrote about history from a Nazi concentration camp, his writing was influenced by his politics, his religion, and the invasion of his country.* In the United States, progressive historians such as Carl Becker, James Harvey Robinson, and Charles Beard responded to the political activities and "muckraking" of social reformers that revealed poverty, racism, and the rampant power of corporations. Unable to explain present conditions in terms of what had been previously written about life in the United States, these progressive historians began to explore the discrepancy between the rhetoric of the past and the realities of their present. The most recent stimulus to reassess

*Born of Jewish parents in Lyon, Marc Bloch was active in the French Resistance. In 1944 he was captured by the Germans, tortured, and executed. His last book, The Historian's Craft, was written during the war and published posthumously by Alfred A. Knopf in 1953.

American history grew out of the civil rights movement in the late 1950s and early 1960s. Nothing that we had learned about our past could explain the bitter racism that was then exposed. A new interpretation was needed—one that would make sense of what was happening. In the early 1960s the search received impetus at the University of Wisconsin. There, in a journal called *Studies on the Left* and in the research of young faculty members and graduate students, a new past began to emerge. The quest for a new history was spearheaded by such scholars as William Appleman Williams, Eugene Genovese, Staughton Lynd, and Howard Zinn. The movement gathered momentum when the war in Indochina stimulated many to investigate the sources of perpetual conflict abroad, and historians all over the country began seeking explanations for our distorted priorities.

Some used a Marxian framework in their analysis of America's past. Beginning with the assumption, in the words of Eugene Genovese, "that the root of the great qualitative leaps in social development are to be sought in the rise, development, and confrontation of social classes," these historians taught us much about the sources of conflict inherent in the structure of American society. Conflict both at home and abroad did not appear for the first time in the 1960s; it was built into the nature of a class structure that treated workers as commodities in the name of national growth. Economic motivation in the guise of Manifest Destiny, efficient technology, and progress blocked the achievement of our ideals of equality and individualism.

The Marxian analysis stimulated many historians to seek answers to a multitude of related questions. The abuse of national resources, social injustice, the intensity of war and violence, the impact of racism, and the nature of the class structure all became subjects of investigation. These inquiries have led to further exploration of the psychological and sociological dimensions of our political and economic condition. Consequently, radical historians, motivated by concern with contemporary crisis, have directed their energies to the investigation of potential sources for social change.

Radicals begin with the fundamental precepts which rule their lives and guide their consciences. They regard certain values as basic to human life and do not believe that they are merely matters of opinion. The most important of these values places the survival, well-being, and creativity of the whole of the human community above all other concerns. The inability to achieve these values in a society whose ideology has proclaimed them to be fundamental requires explanation. Esther Kingston Mann has pointed out that "a radical historian writes with the assumption that those values have been repressed, ignored or distorted . . . by specific kinds of economic exploitation, specific instances of failure of governments to protect the interests of the majority of the community, and specific mechanisms which have discouraged the general expansion of individual and social creativity."

Despite fundamental changes in American historiography the debate that has engaged many historians since the beginning of the nineteenth century still continues. Can a scholar primarily concerned with the conditions of his own society, pejoratively called a presentist, also be a historian? Further, can one concerned with those conditions that relate to more than his own limited area of specialization really view the past with the objectivity required of a scholar? Because the contributions made by radical historians have grown out of contemporary issues, some mainstream historians have criticized their work. These traditional historians assert that the only real history is that which explores "objective" facts for their own sake. All the rest, they insist, is propaganda.

The notion that the historian is merely an instrument through which objective or "real" facts are supposed to pass untouched remains popular—and many scholars continue to grind their humanity into footnotes. Fifty years ago Carl Becker addressed himself to that syndrome in an essay entitled "What Are Historical Facts?" Becker wrote that facts, untouched, "do not say anything, do not impose any meaning." All meaning and significance, he maintained, is imposed by the historian: "The historian cannot eliminate the personal equation . . . no one can. . . . The universe speaks to us only in response to our purposes. The present influences our idea of the past, and our idea of the past influences the present."

The business of a historian is to reconstruct the lives and works of people in time—to join, as Marc Bloch wrote, "the study of the dead and of the living." Why bother to study the past at all if not for the light which it may shed on the crisis of the present? If all historians had listened to the admonitions of John Hopkins' philosopher Arthur O. Lovejoy when he wrote that the role of historians should not be confused with that of the social reformer and that the more a historian based his interests on problems of his own time "the worse historian he is likely to be," all historians would be engaged in the art of mental masturbation. Advising historians to maintain "impersonal standards" is as meaningless as advising medical doctors to treat all patients the same whether they happen to have cancer or a broken finger. A scholar actively pursuing the answers to the tragic events of the past cannot cut himself to pieces and preserve the political purity of the one piece labeled "historian" while all the other pieces are being consumed by moral outrage against a terrible reality.

Ecological disaster, international arrogance, and economic uncertainty—these are the conditions of life with which the United States faces the future. Political assassinations and official violence at home combined with the brutal war in Indochina and the campaign America's leadership seems to be waging against movements for peace and social justice have demoralized many citizens and undermined the government's credibility. Some historians believe they can no longer afford to celebrate the unbroken consensus that created the American empire or genuflect to the tinseled gods which gave us continual corporate growth.

Radical historians have begun to reassess our past and to rewrite our history books. They are concerned not merely with the ruling forces in our society but with the sources of its discontent. And they have begun to write of people and justice instead of domination and profit.

The following selections juxtapose the best of mainstream and radical history. The fundamental assumptions of the two are opposed to each other. Liberal and mainstream historians affirm the basic correctness of our institutions, although they are willing to reform them. They are, therefore, concerned with continuity. Radical historians seek alternatives to these institutions and focus on sources of social change. While rigid distinctions are not possible, the essays highlight some of the major areas of conflict between the two schools of historiography. In each case, excellence in scholarship and writing, which are essential for the future of humanistic study, have been among the criteria for inclusion in this volume.

1

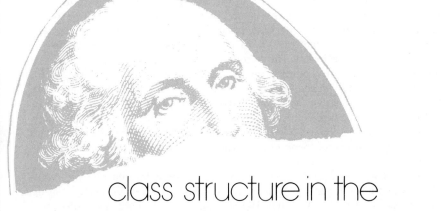

class structure in the
seventeeth and eighteenth centuries

Until recently, American historians, with all their differences, have argued that out of the colonial period grew at least a measure of democracy—of political equality and of economic opportunity. Many scholars now disagree. Building on the research of earlier generations of historians, they conclude that the puritans created an economic and social elite that never relinquished political leadership, and that class divisions in colonial society permanently inhibited both economic mobility and political freedom. The sum of their work is to deny that democracy was either a goal or a reality in colonial America. Their conclusions would have been impossible without the research of their predecessors.

Far from repudiating mainstream interpretations, radical historians often build upon them. Some mainstream historians, in their desire to see homogeneity and unity in our past, ignored deviations from the democratic norm; others, out of their desire to conserve social unity, attempted to understand threats against it. They therefore paid special attention to pluralist tendencies in religion and culture, revealing, paradoxically, some of the sources of tension and conflict in colonial society. Today most mainstream historians see the conflicts as exceptions in an otherwise unified direction, whereas radicals see the same conflicts as the determining factors in our development. For both, Puritanism's impact on economic and political life and the relationship of colonial class divisions to popular government have long been subjects of concern.

Late nineteenth and early twentieth century historians who first professionalized the study of history depicted the colonies in an evolutionary setting. Such scholars as Charles Andrews, Herbert Osgood, and George Louis Beer saw Puritanism as the cradle of democracy. In the years preceding the revolution, incipient democratic ideals struggled valiantly against British authority, until they erupted in the war for independence. Research has revealed much about the actions of colonial legislatures, uncovering, in consequence, groups that opposed the political elite and even some who rebelled against it. While rejecting the notion that democracy had evolved out of imperialist relations, later historians never doubted that a struggle for democracy had in fact occurred. Carl Becker, Vernon Parrington, James Truslow Adams, and others argued that its achievement rested on continuous conflict between classes in the colonial period. Democracy did not evolve out of a ready soil; it was a product of social conflict. Far from having nurtured democratic aspirations, the Puritans had created an elite leadership with rigid social forms. The eighteenth century witnessed a long struggle in which frontiersmen and small merchants tried to wrest control from both British and colonial aristocracy. To make their point, historians investigated incomes, land distribution, and economic structures.

In the period after World War II, new research increasingly challenged the evolutionary image of America's past. Those who wrote in the mainstream argued that neither conflict nor evolution described America's movement toward democracy; America had always had democratic political forms. One had only to look for them in our political past to find them in suffrage requirements, land holding, and social mobility. The Puritans once again emerged as democrats, seventeenth century style. Edmund Morgan pointed to the numbers of people who could vote, even where suffrage was restricted to church members. Charles Grant and Katherine Brown studied small communities, concluding that most adult white males possessed the vote. Arthur Schlesinger, in the article included here, found that the colonial aristocracy was open to men of wealth and talent. Daniel Boorstin, summing up the period, argued that an absence of speculative theology among the Puritans had paved the way for a colonial period in which effective and well-organized govern- ments ensured the "integrity and self-restraint" of leaders who prevented governments from being oppressive.

Many historians have now become convinced that democracy did not exist at all in early America. Arguing that colonial society always functioned for the benefit of its elite members, they deny that achieving democracy was ever the goal of colonial governments. The institutional framework of the society, they insist, reveals nothing of the lives people lived within it. The political forms of democracy cover up real and pervasive inequality. Robert Wall, in the article included here, presents the paradox of poor people who seem to have regularly voted for the wealthy. Other historians have questioned the nature of the political structure that gave power to so few despite widespread suffrage before the revolution.

Without rejecting the data uncovered by their predecessors, historians have begun to explore the behavior of people as opposed to the prescriptions of institutions. Perry Miller's studies revealing a complex orthodoxy in Mass- achusetts have prompted many to question the social sources of its demise. Did the tendency of American churches to fragment in the early eighteenth century reflect conflicts among economic interest groups? In his article, Aubrey Land finds that the wealthy had different sources of income than did the poor. And a deeper level of conflict emerges from Pauline Maier's essay which examines the behavior of those groups that refused to accept elite leadership.

In these analyses, the structure of society is less important than the self- perceptions of those then living. How did the colonial craftsman perceive his world? Could he see his own interests separately from those of his small sphere? The radical historian who would understand colonial America must examine the disjunctions between the individual and his society—the points at which people seem to have protested position and place—and ask what circumstances led a group of people to challenge accepted modes. We have a fairly precise picture of institutions. We now need to know how they affected people.

the aristocracy in colonial America

ARTHUR M. SCHLESINGER

In the following article, Arthur Schlesinger says, "The colonists unhesitatingly took for granted the concept of a graded society." All discussions of mobility occur within that framework. While radical historians argue that mobility was limited, Schlesinger insists that there was much movement into the upper class. Most radicals would agree with Schlesinger's contention that the aristocracy received the deference of those below, but they would focus on the sources of tensions between classes and attempt to understand the life styles of the vast majority of people who were not aristocrats and could not aspire to be.

For many years historical students have been so interested in discovering evidences of democracy in the colonial period that they have tended to distort the actual situation. This paper is an attempt to correct the balance.

The colonists unhesitatingly took for granted the concept of a graded society. It was the only kind they had known in Europe, and they had no thought of forgoing it in their new home. Indeed, they possessed a self-interested reason for retaining it. In this outpost of civilization it was man alone, not his ancestors, who counted. Even the humblest folk could hope to better their condition, for the equality of opportunity which they now had attained meant, as well, the opportunity to be unequal. The indentured servant, the apprentice, the common laborer, everyone in fact but the Negro bondsman, could expect to stand on his own feet and get on and up in the world.

Other factors, however, precluded a faithful duplicating of Europe's stratified order. As David Ramsay pointed out in his *History of the American Revolution* (1789), no remnants of the feudal age existed to thwart or hinder men's advancement.[1] The occasional nobleman who went to America deserted his accustomed "splendor and amusements" only for temporary exile, usually to cash in on a colonial proprietaryship or a royal governorship. Thomas Fairfax, settling in Virginia from England in 1747 at the age of fifty-four, was unique among the permanent comers in bearing so high a rank as baron, but he lived out the remaining thirty-four years of his life for the most part unobtrusively on his distant Shenandoah Valley estate.

Some settlers, however, notably in Virginia, were the untitled younger sons or kinsmen of peers, while to the northward many belonged to the English landed or mercantile gentry. By Old World standards, though, they were members of the upper middle class and at best could provide but the entering wedge for an aristocracy. They not only lacked noble rank but suffered from want of a royal

Arthur M. Schlesinger, "The Aristocracy in Colonial America," *Proceedings of the Massachusetts Historical Society*, LXXIV (1962), 3–21.

court to act as a stimulus and model. Nor could they rest their social edifice, as did the privileged caste at home, on a hereditary class of landless peasants and destitute workingmen. The enslaved blacks alone served the purpose, but they were to be found mainly in the South, where indeed the patrician order achieved its fullest development.

In the case of a few of the early colonies the English government sought by fiat to establish artificial class distinctions, but these efforts, occurring in the middle third of the seventeenth century, all came to grief. The London authorities, accustomed to titles of nobility at home, were blind to the very different conditions existing in the overseas wilderness. The people were sparse, strong-willed, and still scrambling for a living; the thought of a social strait jacket imposed from above outraged their mettlesome self-respect and, by the same sign, operated to deter prospective settlers.

One attempt was John Locke's blueprint of a quasi-feudal order in the Carolinas. Another took the form of the power granted Lord Baltimore as proprietor of Maryland to confer "whatever titles" he pleased. In the first instance the purpose was avowedly to "avoid erecting a numerous democracy"; the Maryland charter, on the other hand, put the case positively, asserting that short of such a provision "every access to honors and dignities may seem to be precluded, and utterly barred, to men well born."[2] Baltimore, however, for reasons unknown, never exercised the prerogative. Consequently, the plan of an American-based peerage, which collapsed after a brief trial in the Carolinas, did not even make a beginning in Maryland.

For the settlers to build a structured society on their own initiative and in their own interest was, however, quite another matter. This they proceeded to do in colony after colony as rapidly as time and circumstances permitted. In the case of Massachusetts, though, they did not have to wait. Not only did the founders themselves belong to Britain's rural and urban gentry but, as good Puritans, they considered their superior station divinely ordained. In the words of their first governor, John Winthrop, "God Almightie in his most holy and wise providence hath soe disposed of the Condicion of mankinde, as in all times some must be rich some poore, some highe and emminent in power and dignitie; others mean and in subieceion."[3] Accordingly, the men so favored immediately assumed the key positions in government and society, sharing the honors with the foremost clergymen.

They overreached themselves, however, when they sought to legalize class differences in dress. Despite the heavy penalties for disobedience, ordinary people in this new land did not understand that they were to be permanently ordinary. To no avail did the legislature in 1651 express "utter detestation" that men "of meane condition, education and callings should take uppon them the garbe of gentlemen by the wearing of gold or silver lace" and the like, and that "women of the same rank" should "wear silke or tiffany hoodes or scarfes."[4] Both there and in Connecticut, which had somewhat similar regulations, the resistance to them was so stubborn that they were presently allowed to fall into disuse.

In all other respects, however, the aristocracy retained its primacy, and as the years went on, families with fortunes newly made on land or sea won admittance to the circle. The traveler Joseph Bennett wrote in 1740 of Boston, "both the ladies and gentlemen dress and appear as gay, in common, as courtiers in England on a coronation or birthday."[5] And the author of *American Husbandry*, surveying the entire New England scene in 1775, reported that, though social demarcations were less conspicuous than abroad, "gentlemen's houses appear everywhere" and on the "many considerable land estates . . . the owners live much in the style of country gentlemen in England."[6]

In New York, while the colony was still New Netherland, the Dutch West India Company had introduced a system of patroonships—immense tracts along the Hudson which the possessors were to cultivate with tenants bound to them by a semifeudal relationship. But only a few of the grants were actually made before the British took over in 1664, and of these Rensselaerswyck, in what is now Albany County, was the only one to work out well. The English governors in their turn followed the Dutch example to the extent of awarding enormous estates to favored individuals; and on this basis a privileged class evolved which divided political and social pre-eminence in the province with the leading merchants and lawyers of New York City.

Although the historical background in Pennsylvania was different, the outcome there, too, was the same. Despite the lowly antecedents of most of the Quaker settlers and their devotion to "plain living," an aristocracy of great landholders and merchant princes likewise arose. John Smith, an old-time Friend looking back from the year 1764, sadly depicted the change as it had come over Philadelphia. During the first twenty years, he said, as the members began to accumulate means, they commenced "in some degree conforming to the fashions of the World," and after another score of years, when "many of the Society were grown rich," vanities like "fine costly Garments" and "fashionable furniture" became usual.[7] Indeed, the foremost families, not content with handsome urban residences, maintained in addition country estates as retreats from the intense heat of the Philadelphia summers.

But the Southern aristocracy attained the closest resemblance to the English landed gentry. There, in a predominantly rural economy, men on the make enjoyed the decisive advantage of an extensive servile class as well as of broad acres. There, also, to a degree unknown in the North, the Virginia patrician William Fitzhugh spoke for his class in avowing that his children had "better be never born than ill-bred."[8] Josiah Quincy, Jr., visiting South Carolina in 1773, wrote that "The inhabitants may well be divided into opulent and lordly planters, poor and spiritless peasants and vile slaves."[9] The Bostonian, however, overlooked the fact that, different from the other Southern provinces, the select circle in this particular one also included successful merchants, thanks to Charleston, the only important seaport south of Philadelphia.

Thomas Jefferson, analyzing from a more intimate knowledge the free population of Virginia, listed at the top "the great landholders"; next, "the descendants of the younger sons and daughters of the aristocrats, who inherited the pride of their ancestors, without their wealth"; thirdly, "the pretenders, men, who, from vanity or the impulse of growing wealth, or from that enterprise which is natural to talents, sought to detach themselves from the plebeian ranks"; next, "a solid and independent yeomanry, looking askance at those above, yet not venturing to jostle them"; and, finally, the "degraded" and "unprincipled" overseers, the smallest group.[10] The description would have pertained equally well to Maryland.

The Southern gentry, however, possessed an energy and resourcefulness uncharacteristic of its Old World prototype. To maintain its position the members had to be men of affairs—tireless and responsible directors of a system of agricultural labor alien to the homeland, which, moreover, was used for the raising of staple crops uncultivated there and grown on great and often scattered plantations. They could not, however much they wished, constitute in the same sense a leisure class.[11]

Two concepts of land inheritance derived from English law furnished potential support for an aristocratic order.[12] The principle of primogeniture ensured that the total family realty would descend automatically to the eldest son in default of a will. This arrangement prevailed not only throughout the South but also in New York and Rhode Island, and, in the modified form of a double share for the oldest boy, existed in all the remaining colonies but New Jersey. Entail, the other aspect of the system, enabled an owner to leave his estate intact to a specified heir or line of heirs. This practice had legal sanction everywhere. As a matter of fact, however, neither method was much used, for where land was so plentiful there did not exist the same need as in the mother country to guard against dissipating a matrimony. Moreover, these devices, even when employed, did not work the same hardship on the disinherited, who usually by their own means could acquire independent holdings and thereby actually enlarge the economic base of the upper class.

The English-appointed governor and his entourage in the provincial capital formed the apex of the social pyramid. These personages and their womenfolk emulated the pomp and circumstance of the royal court at home and furnished a pattern for the great landholders, mercantile princes, and the like who composed the native aristocracy. A beadroll of such families in the eighteenth century would include among others the Wentworths of New Hampshire, the Bowdoins, Quincys, Hutchinsons, Olivers, Faneuils, and Hancocks of Massachusetts, the Redwoods, Browns, and Wantons of Rhode Island, the Trumbulls and Ingersolls of Connecticut, the De Lanceys, Schuylers, Van Rensselaers, Livingstons, and Coldens of New York, the Logans, Allens, Morrises, Willings, Pembertons, and Shippens of Pennsylvania and, in the plantation colonies, the Dulanys and Carrolls of Maryland, the Byrds, Randolphs, Carters, Masons, Pages, Fitzhughs, Harrisons, and Lees of Virginia, and the Rutledges, Pinckneys, Draytons, Laurenses, and Izards of South Carolina.

Families like these buttressed their position by matrimonial alliances both within and across provincial boundaries.[13] To cite a few cases, the New Yorker John Franklin married Deborah Morris of Philadelphia, and her fellow townsman William Shippen wedded Alice Lee of the Old Dominion. The Allens of Philadelphia, the Redwoods of Newport, the New York De Lanceys, the Ervings of Boston, and the Izards of Charleston took mates in three or more colonies. The rare instances of gentlefolk marrying beneath their station scandalized their friends and kinsmen. To William Byrd II, for example, it was nothing short of a "tragical Story" when a wellborn Virginia girl in 1732 played "so senseless a Prank" as to marry her uncle's overseer, "a dirty Plebian."[14]

By custom and official usage members of the gentry enjoyed the privilege of attaching certain honorific tags to their names.[15] As in England, they alone could qualify as "Gentlemen," and they only had the right to the designations "Esquire" and "Master," although the latter term tended in ordinary speech to be pronounced "Mister." The common man, for his part, contentedly answered to "Goodman"—his day of being called "Mister" was yet to come. Equal consideration for class distinctions governed the allotment of pews in Congregational churches, where persons resisting their assignments were sometimes haled into court.[16] And at Yale until 1767 and Harvard until 1772 even the order of reciting in class and the place of students in academic processions bore a relation to the social standing of their parents.[17].

Not being to the manner born, most people aspiring to gentility had to learn from scratch how to act like their betters. Luckily manuals for the purpose lay at hand.[18] The great majority were English importations, but to meet the rising demand colonial printers, as the years went by, put out their own editions. These treatises followed originals appearing in France and Italy, where since the age of chivalry the standards of approved behavior had been set for the whole of Europe. Among the writings most often listed in American booksellers' announcements and the inventories of private libraries were Henry Peacham's *The Compleat Gentleman* (1622), Richard Brathwaite's *The English Gentleman* (1630), Richard Allestree's *The Whole Duty of Man* (1660), and, for feminine guidance, Lord Halifax's *The Lady's New Year's Gift: or, Advice to a Daughter* (1688), the anonymous *Ladies Library* (1714), the *Friendly Instructor* (1745) by an unknown, and William Kenrick's *The Whole Duty of Woman; or, a Guide to the Female Sex from the Age of Sixteen to Sixty* (1761). Even the commonsensical Benjamin Franklin wrote his wife from London in 1758 that he wanted their daughter Sally to "read over and over again the *Whole Duty of Man*, and the *Lady's Library*," and we know that George Washington as late as 1764 purchased an American reprint of the *Whole Duty of Man*.[19]

These handbooks held up integrity, courage, justice, courtesy, and piety as the hallmarks of the gentleman, with modesty, chastity, tenderness, godliness, and the duty of submission to one's husband as the essentials of a gentlewoman. Wifely docility not only befitted the innate inferiority of the sex but attested lasting penance for the first woman's disobedience. If her yokefellow proved unfaithful, wrote Lord Halifax, she should "affect ignorance" of it; if he were a sot, she should rejoice that the fault offset her own many frailties; if he were "Cholerick and Ill-humour'd," she should avoid any "unwary Word" and soothe him with smiles and flattery; if he lacked intelligence, she should take comfort in the thought that "a wife often made a better Figure, for her Husband's making no great one." The writers, when treating behavior in company, instructed the ladies what to wear, how to arrange a dinner, what diversions were proper, and how to converse (with the admonition: "Women seldom have Materials to furnish a long Discourse. . . .").[20]

Having discovered how to conduct themselves, the gentry further evidenced their status by the elegance of their attire. The pains they took to ape the latest court styles appear in their elaborate orders to English tailors and the loud complaints over the pattern or fit or color of the garments commissioned. George Washington, for one, cautioned his London agent, "Whatever goods you may send me, let them be fashionable, neat and good of their several kinds." According to the Englishman Daniel Neal in 1747, "there is no Fashion in London but in three or four Months is to be seen at Boston," and William Eddis after a few years in Annapolis wrote similarly in 1771 that he was "almost inclined to believe" that a new mode spread more rapidly among "polished and affluent" Americans than among "many opulent" Londoners.[21]

Subject to the season's vagaries in matters of detail, gentlemen wore cocked hats, white ruffled silk shirts, and embroidered broadcloth frock coats, with knee breeches of fine texture and gorgeous hues, silk hose fastened with ornamental garters, and pumps displaying gold or silver buckles.[22] Powdered wigs, an added adornment, began to lose favor about 1754, when George II discarded his, to be followed by the vogue of letting one's natural hair grow long and powdering it and queuing it behind or tying the tail in a small silk bag.

Gentlewomen on festive occasions tripped about on dainty high-heeled slippers in rustling gowns of imported brocade, bombazine, sarsenet, shalloon, damask, velvet, taffeta, and other expensive fabrics. They stiffened their bodices with whalebone stays and stretched their skirts over great hoops of the same material. They kept abreast of the latest English dress designs by means of clothed dolls sent over from London, and shortly before the Revolution they had the additional help of engraved pictures. Indicative of the irresistible sweep of style, the Yearly Meeting of Friends in 1726 at Philadelphia futilely decried the "immodest fashion of hooped petticoats" and such improprieties as "bare necks" and "shoes trimmed with gaudy colors."[23]

An object of special pride was milady's coiffure, a structure painstakingly erected on a concealed crepe roller or cushion. In preparation for a ball or party she would have her hair dressed the day before and perhaps sleep in a chair that night to keep it in condition. For going about outdoors the first families maintained their own equipages, stylish vehicles variously called chaises, calashes, chairs, and landaus, or, still more grandly, they traveled in coaches-and-four and berlins attended with liveried drivers and footmen.[24]

The apparel of the simple folk similarly evinced their status. The men, their hair short-cropped, typically wore caps, coarse linen shirts, leather coats and aprons, homespun stockings, and cowhide shoes with either long or short buckskin breeches, while the women's garments were of equal cheapness and durability. The French Revolution in its impact on America was in the years ahead to go far toward removing class differences in male attire, but portents of what awaited revealed themselves in unexpected ways in the events leading up to the rupture with Britain. Thus, to conceal their participation in the Stamp Act violence at Boston in August, 1765, "there were fifty gentlemen actors in this scene," wrote Governor Francis Bernard, "disguised with trousers and jackets on."[25] Their motive was doubtless to escape the possible legal consequences of their connivance, but it was probably just a desire for sheer creature comfort which caused the South Carolina Assembly in 1769 to permit the members to forgo wigs and knee breeches in order to transact committee business in caps and trousers—like "so many unhappy persons ready for execution," objected a newspaper commentator.[26]

For those on top of the heap the Anglican Church held a compelling attraction. Just as it was the allegiance of the upper class at home, so it was that of the Crown officials sent to America. The dignified ritualism of the Book of Common Prayer, with its setting of fine music, exerted an undoubted appeal, but the social prestige of membership probably formed the greater magnet. At any rate hundreds of Congregationalists, Presbyterians, Quakers, Lutherans, and others, as they moved upward in the world, forsook the faith of their fathers for the more stylish communion.[27].

Other evidences of snobbishness were even clearer. An English nobleman passing through the colonies never failed to stir the social waters.[28] Thus Lord Adam Gordon, one of the few members of Parliament ever to visit America, conquered all before him as he journeyed from Charleston to Boston in 1765; and Lord Charles Hope on a similar excursion in 1766 met with a like reception. Four years later Sir William Draper crowned his New York stay by wedding Susannah De Lancey.

Two crucial moments in life—marriage and death—afforded special opportunities for ostentation. Weddings were celebrated with banqueting, innumerable toasts, and like festivities sometimes extending over several days. A funeral obliged the bereaved family to provide the assemblage with such souvenirs of the occasion as mourning gloves, scarves, and gold rings as well as quantities of food and drink. At the burial of John Grove of Surrey County, Virginia, in 1673 the liquor consumed equaled the cost of a thousand pounds of tobacco.[29] Governor Jonathan Belcher of Massachusetts in 1736 distributed more than a thousand pairs of gloves in honor of his wife, but Peter Faneuil overtopped him two years later with three thousand at the services for his uncle Andrew.[30] In addition, the grief-stricken friends would don appropriate attire for a further period at their own expense.[31]

As this costly fashion seeped downward in society, it placed an excessive burden on families who, desiring to pay as great respect to their departed, could ill afford the outlay. To ease their plight the Yearly Meeting of Friends at Philadelphia in 1729 recommended to their co-religionists that "wine or other strong liquors" be furnished "but once."[32] The Massachusetts legislature went so far in a series of statutes between 1721 and 1741 as to prohibit under heavy fine the "very extravagant" expense of gloves, scarves, rings, rum, or wine.[33] But custom proved too stubborn; and no real change came about until the colonists, provoked by the Sugar Act of 1764 and its successors, saw a chance to strike back at Britain by disusing (among other things) the mourning materials they had hitherto imported.[34]

Now public meetings from New Hampshire to Georgia urged "the new mode" on all who loved their country. The Boston News-Letter, March 9, 1769, observed with special gratification that the rich Charlestonian Christopher Gadsden had worn simple homespun at his wife's obsequies and that "The whole expence of her funeral, of the manufacture of England, did not amount to more than £3. 10s our currency." At another South Carolina funeral the people in attendance spiritedly declined to accept the gifts which the family had provided.[35] The First Continental Congress in 1774 climaxed these efforts by subjecting to boycott all persons who distributed scarves or went "into any further mourning-dress, than a black crape or ribbon on the arm or hat, for gentlemen, and a black ribbon and necklace for ladies."[36] From this blow the practice never recovered.

One aspect of Old World patrician life, the code duello, the Americans did not achieve or even want to achieve. Perhaps because of their generally more humane disposition they instinctively recoiled from the settlement of disputes by personal combat. Though occasional duels took place during the century and a half, these typically involved royal officers on overseas assignment or recent comers not yet fully Americanized, unless perchance they partook of the shabby character of the encounter between the Charleston youth and a sea captain over what the South-Carolina Gazette, September 6, 1735, termed their "pretensions to the Favours of a certain sable Beauty."

The few affrays involving colonial aristocrats deeply shocked public sentiment and, if death resulted, provoked criminal prosecutions.[37] What was apparently the earliest such affair cost the life of Dr. John Livingston of New York in 1715 at the hands of Governor Dongan's nephew Thomas, whom the court two days afterward found guilty of manslaughter. In 1728 occurred a sword fight between two Boston young men in which Henry Phillips killed Benjamin Woodbridge over differences not then or since revealed. Before the grand jury could bring in an indictment for murder (which it did a month later, the victor fled to France with the help of Peter Faneuil, a kinsman by marriage. Some years following, in 1770, Dr. John Haly of Charleston fatally shot Peter De Lancey, the deputy postmaster, in a duel in the candlelit parlor of a tavern. Though he, too, like Dongan, was convicted of manslaughter, he avoided the consequences through the pardon of the governor. In 1775 came the last instance, also between two South Carolinians, but this one differed markedly from the earlier clashes in that Henry Laurens, while willing to accept the challenge of John Grimké, declined as a matter of principle to fire on him. Happily he escaped unscathed. No one could have foreseen as the colonial period ended that the discredited practice would under altered circumstances find wide favor in the next generation.

The continuous recruitment of the top stratum of the community from beneath reveals sharply the basic aspect of colonial society: its fluidity, the incessant movement of people upward. The American aristocracy, however undemocratic when once it took form, was undeniably democratic in the method of its forming. The only class struggle in that far day was the struggle to climb out of a lower class into a higher one, for, as Nathaniel Ames put it in one of his almanacs,

All Men are by Nature equal,
But differ greatly in the sequel.

The self-made man thus began his career in America, to become in time a national folk hero. In the absence of England's officially prescribed ranks it was, above all, the acquisition of wealth which elevated a family to the social heights. Extensive land grants and other perquisites from the government, obtained perhaps through favoritism or fraud, might expedite the process. Further help could, and often did come, from lucrative marriages. Newspapers, with no thought of impropriety, would describe a bride as "a most amiable young Lady with a handsome Fortune," sometimes stating the amount, though, of course, the unions not infrequently joined couples already well-to-do. But, for the most part, it was industry and ability applied imaginatively to beckoning opportunities that ensured the outcome.

As early as 1656 John Hammond, a Briton who had spent many years among the Virginia and Maryland settlers, wrote that "some from being wool-hoppers and of as mean and meaner imployment in England have there grown great merchants, and attained to the most eminent advancements the Country afforded."[38] And a century later, in 1765, the scholarly officeholder Cadwallader Colden similarly said of New York that "the most opulent families, in our own memory, have arisen from the lowest rank of the people."[39] If a writer in the *Pennsylvania Evening-Post*, March 14, 1776, is to be credited, half the property in the city of Philadelphia belonged to "men whose fathers or grandfathers wore LEATHER APRONS." Indeed, Colden believed that "The only principle of Life propagated among the young People is to get Money, and Men are only esteemed according to . . . the Money they are possessed of."[40] And even the pious *New-England Primer* taught:

He that ne'er learns his A, B, C,
For ever will a Blockhead be;
But he that learns these Letters fair
Shall have a Coach to take the Air.

Some examples of nobodies becoming somebodies will make the matter more concrete.[41] Thus Henry Shrimpton, a London brazier, so expanded his interests and activities after settling in Boston in 1639 that when dying twenty-seven years later he left an estate of nearly £12,000, and with this nest egg his son Samuel (who in filial gratitude displayed a brass kettle on his "very stately house") succeeded before his death in 1698 in making himself the town's richest citizen. The Belcher family of Massachusetts progressed in three generations from the vocation of innkeeping at Cambridge to mercantile greatness in Boston and then to the officeholding eminence of grandson Jonathan who served as royal governor of Massachusetts and New Hampshire from 1730 to 1741 and of New Jersey from 1747 to 1757.

In a like number of generations the Reverend John Hancock, an impecunious Lexington minister, apprenticed his son Thomas to a Boston bookseller; and Thomas, opening his own establishment in 1723 and later branching out into more profitable lines, amassed a fortune of £100,000 sterling, which at his demise in 1764 he willed to his nephew John, making him the Croesus of the patriot movement in Massachusetts. By the same token, Connecticut's Roger Sherman, another signer of the Declaration of Independence, started out as a shoemaker's apprentice and, after following the trade on his own for some years, turned to surveying, the law, and other fields which won him independent means.

In the Middle colonies Robert Livingston, son of a poor parson in Scotland and founder of the renowned New York clan, began his American career in 1673 at the age of twenty-one as town clerk in the frontier village of Albany and within another twenty-one years owned a princely domain of 160,000 acres. The great Manhattan merchant John Lamb, an associate of Livingston's descendants in Revolutionary days and general in the Continental army, was the American-born child of a Londoner who in 1724 had escaped hanging for burglary through commutation of his sentence to indentured service overseas.

Isaac Norris, the progenitor of the notable Pennsylvania family, arrived in Philadelphia from England in 1691 with a little more than £100 and in less than a quarter-century became the colony's principal landholder. George Taylor, coming as an indentured servant from Ireland in 1736, first worked at an iron furnace in Chester County, then, setting up in the trade with a partner, accumulated his ample means. He was another man of humble pedigree to sign the Declaration of Independence. The meteoric rise of Benjamin Franklin, the runaway apprentice from Boston, has become a legendary American success story.

Though the economic life of the Southern colonies differed markedly from that of the North, the outcome there too was the same. Thus the Irish-born Daniel Dulany, talented lawyer and political leader in early eighteenth-century Maryland, commenced his American years in 1703 as a penniless eighteen-year-old lad under indenture. In neighboring Virginia, John Carter, an English newcomer in 1649 of obscure antecedents, laid the material basis of one of that province's first families; his son Robert of Nomini Hall, known to his contemporaries as "King" Carter, owned some 300,000 acres, 700 slaves and over 2,000 horses and other livestock at the time of his decease in 1732. William Byrd, the forerunner of another Virginia dynasty, came from England in 1671 at the age of nineteen with the bequest of some land from an uncle, which he made the springboard for a great fortune in tobacco culture and trading before his death in 1704.

In South Carolina the Manigaults, Allstons, and Laurenses, among others, conformed to the familiar pattern. The first American Manigault, a French Huguenot emigré from London in 1695, originally tried farming, then made good at victualing and more remunerative ventures, and in 1729 he bequeathed an estate which his son Gabriel by the mid-eighteenth century built into the largest fortune in the province. By contrast, Jonathan Allston was "a gentleman of immense income, all of his own acquisition," according to Josiah Quincy, Jr., who visited his plantation in 1773. Henry Laurens, like the younger Manigault, owed the silver spoon in his mouth at birth to his father, in this case a Charleston saddler who had amassed riches in that and other undertakings.

But only a few Americans ever achieved the accolade of English noble rank, and this came about under circumstances so fortuitous as to make it the despair of other colonists. William Phips, who had risen from shepherd boy and shipwright's apprentice on the Maine frontier to prosper as a shipbuilder in Boston, was knighted in 1687 for raising in Haitian waters a Spanish galleon laden with £300,000 of treasure, of which the Crown awarded him £16,000 as well as his title. John Randolph, a distinguished Virginia lawyer and planter, obtained his knighthood in 1732 for his statesmanlike skill in negotiating certain differences between the London government and his colony. William Pepperrell, a business leader and landholder in Massachusetts and Maine, won the status of baronet in 1746 in return for commanding the victorious American forces against the French fortress of Louisbourg. A more dubious case was that of the well-to-do New Jersey officeholder William Alexander, who on the basis of tenuous evidence laid claim to being the sixth Earl of Stirling. Ignoring the rejection of his contention by a House of Lords committee in 1762, he continued to profess the title, and it was as Lord Stirling that he rendered valuable service to the American cause as a general in the War for Independence.

In a special category was the Cinderella-like story of Agnes Surriage. This comely, sixteen-year-old maiden, a barefoot servant in a Marblehead tavern in 1742, so captivated Charles Henry Frankland at first sight that the English-born revenue officer in Boston sent her to school at his own expense. Then he lived with her as his mistress in an elegant mansion he had built for her in Hopkinton. Even his inheritance of a baronetcy in no wise altered the relationship, but something that occurred while the couple were abroad in 1755 wrought the miracle, causing Sir Henry at long last to make Agnes his wife. According to tradition it was her daring rescue of him during the Lisbon earthquake. Boston society, hitherto scandalized, now forgot her past and as Lady Frankland received her with open arms. Warm-hearted by nature, she had by all accounts become through the years a person of cultivation and charm. Her unusual tale has fascinated numerous chroniclers, including Oliver Wendell Holmes, who recounted it in ballad form in *Songs in Many Keys* (1865).

Governor Francis Bernard of Massachusetts, seeing in the creation of an American peerage an opportunity to "give strength and stability" to supporters of Britain, urged the proposal on the Ministry in 1764 soon after the difficulties with the colonists arose. "Although *America*," he conceded, "is not now (and probably will not be for many years to come) ripe enough for an hereditary *Nobility*; yet it is now capable of a *Nobility* for life."[42] Indeed, in men like Thomas Hutchinson, Philip Livingston, Franklin, and Henry Laurens (to name no others) the colonies possessed personages who by Old World standards could qualify for even heritable rank. But whatever fate might have befallen the scheme if it had been put forward and adopted earlier, it could hardly have succeeded at so late a juncture. With the colonists already fearful of British designs on other counts, anybody who accepted an honorific dignity at this stage would have forfeited all public esteem. He would have marked himself indelibly as one who had sold out to the government. But the matter never came to a test, for the Ministry quietly shelved the suggestion.

By 1776 the colonial aristocracy had endured for more than a century and a half in the oldest regions, for over a century in others, and had sunk deep roots elsewhere. With the passage of time it had consolidated its position and constantly replenished its vitality with transfusions of new blood. Its members had not, moreover, used their station exclusively for self-aggrandizement and outward show but, as a class, had considered themselves trustees for the common good, identifying their welfare with that of the community at large. In the case of the Southern gentry the need to superintend the lives of hosts of slaves served to heighten this sense of stewardship, making them feel as fit to rule as were the guardians to whom Plato had entrusted his republic.

In all the colonies men of quality occupied responsible posts in every sphere of official activity; the executive department, the provincial and local lawmaking branches, the armed forces, the judiciary. True, the alternative would have been to allow ill-prepared and possibly rash underlings to seize the reins, but the deeper reason lay in the conviction that only the rich and wellborn possessed the required wisdom and capacity. In no less degree they provided the cultural leadership. They not only exemplified for all to see the refinements of living, but they set standards of tasteful architecture and well-kept grounds and through their patronage enabled portrait painters to pursue their calling. In like fashion they assembled the best private libraries and afforded their sons superior intellectual advantages. And from their largess came the principal benefactions to religion and education, to charity and projects of community improvement.

Nor did their role in any of these respects excite resentment among the mass of the population. Men in every walk of life not only accepted the concept of a layered society, but believed in its rightness. The clergy preached it; all classes practiced it. Whatever might be the shortcomings of the English aristocracy—and colonial editors repeated from the London press lurid accounts of its immoralities and profligacy—the American variety was no priviledged group living off the unearned increment of ancestral reputations. They, by and large, had mounted the heights through shrewdness and ability and had stayed there by the continued exercise of those faculties. The ordinary citizen deemed it only proper to accord them deference. Very rarely did their real or alleged abuses of authority provoke popular opposition, and such occasions seldom lasted long.

The quarrel with the mother country had nothing to do with the stratified character of British society, only with the objectionable policies of certain individuals in positions of power. Not even the fiery Tom Paine condemned it in his tract *Common Sense* when blasting the titular head of the system as "the royal brute."[43] Nor did the framers of the Declaration of Independence do so later that year. Though they proclaimed that all men are created equal, they merely rebuked their brethren at home for suffering George to act a "tyrant" toward his American subjects.

To be sure, in the events foreshadowing his final crisis the colonial gentry betrayed divided sympathies, notably in New York and Pennsylvania, some siding ardently with Britain or at least seeking to prevent an irreparable break.

But the well-informed Thomas McKean, himself a Signer, stated in retrospect that almost two-thirds of the country's "influential characters"—that is, the overwhelming majority—had favored the American cause.[44]

The heritage of a common history and culture bound the upper-class patriots to the homeland no less than it did the loyalist minority; but, unlike the latter, they had developed a passionate attachment to colonial self-government, a fierce jealousy of any encroachments on the authority which they had so long and capably wielded. Besides, the new taxation and trade legislation, falling heaviest on the well-to-do, supplied a clear economic motive which was intensified by the conviction that, if the present enactments went unchallenged, worse ones would follow. The phenomenal progess of the colonies during the many years that London had permitted them virtual autonomy thoroughly justified in their minds implacable resistance to the ministerial innovations.

To counteract the measures, however, they required the support of the humbler elements; but this they were accustomed to enjoy. Sometimes to their alarm these allies threatened the orderly course of opposition by gratuitously resorting to riot and violence, but the men of quality were invariably able to regain control. In recognition of their role the Continental Congress, when the war broke out, unanimously chose a Virginia aristocrat as commander in chief of the armed forces, and in due course a grateful Republic named him its first President. The revolt against upper-class dominance was to come in later times.

NOTES

1. David Ramsay, *The History of the American Revolution*, 2 vols. (Philadelphia, 1789), I, 46.

2. Herbert L. Osgood, *The American Colonies in the Seventeenth Century*, 3 vols. (New York, 1904–07), II, 208; Newton D. Mereness, *Maryland as a Proprietary Province* (New York, 1901), p. 515.

3. Max Savelle, *Seeds of Liberty* (New York, 1948), p. 231.

4. Alice M. Earle, *Customs and Fashions in Old New England* (New York, 1893), p. 317.

5. Joseph Bennett, "Boston in 1740," Massachusetts Historical Society, *Proceedings*, 1st Ser., V (1860–62), 125.

6. *American Husbandry*, ed. Harry J. Carman (New York, 1934), p. 46.

7. Frederick B. Tolles, *Meeting House and Counting House* (Chapel Hill, 1948), p. 123.

8. Mary N. Stanard, *Colonial Virginia* (Philadelphia, 1917), p. 271.

9. Josiah Quincy, Jr., "Journal," Massachusetts Historical Society, *Proceedings*, XLIX (1915–16), 454.

10. William Wirt, *Sketches of the Life and Character of Patrick Henry* (rev. edn., Philadelphia, 1841), p. 33.

11. For an elaboration of this point, see a letter of James Maury to Robert Jackson, July 17, 1762, in Albemarle County Historical Society, *Papers*, II (1941–42), 39–60.

12. Richard B. Morris, *Studies in the History of American Law* (New York, 1930), pp. 73–82.

13. Michael Kraus, *Intercolonial Aspects of American Culture on the Eve of the American Revolution* (New York, 1928), p. 44; Carl Bridenbaugh, *Cities in Revolt* (New York, 1955), pp. 346–347.

14. William Byrd, *Writings*, ed. J.S. Bassett (New York, 1901), p. 338.

15. Norman H. Dawes, "Titles as Symbols of Prestige in Seventeenth-Century New

England," *William and Mary Quarterly*, 3d Ser., VI (1949), 69-83, which also contains material on other colonies.

16. William B. Weeden, *Economic and Social History of New England, 1620-1789*, 2 vols. (Boston, 1890), I, 280, 417.

17. Clifford K. Shipton, "Ye Mystery of Ye Ages Solved, or, How Placing Worked at Colonial Harvard & Yale," *Harvard Alumni Bulletin*, LVII (1954-55), 258-259, 262-263.

18. Arthur M. Schlesinger, *Learning How to Behave: A Historical Study of American Etiquette Books* (New York, 1947), pp. 4-12.

19. Benjamin Franklin, *Writings*, ed. Albert H. Smyth, 10 vols. (New York, 1905-07, III; John C. Fitzpatrick, *George Washington Himself* (Indianapolis, 1933), pp. 149-150.

20. The parenthetical quotation is from William Darrell, *The Gentleman Instructed . . . To Which Is Added a Word to the Ladies* (8th edn., London, 1723), as cited by Julia C. Spruill, *Women's Life and Work in the Southern Colonies* (Chapel Hill, 1938), p. 219.

21. Paul L. Ford, *The True George Washington* (Philadelphia, 1896), p. 187; Daniel Neal, *History of New England*, 2 vols. (2d edn., London, 1747), II, 253; William Eddis, *Letters from America, Historical and Descriptive . . . 1769 to 1777* (London, 1792), p. 112.

22. The standard account of colonial apparel is Alice M. Earle, *Two Centuries of Costumes in America*, 2 vols. (New York, 1903), I, chaps. 1-14, II, chaps, 15-29.

23. Carl Bridenbaugh, *Cities in the Wilderness* (New York, 1955), p. 386. For similar action taken earlier, in 1695, see Tolles, *Meeting House and Counting House*, pp. 125-126.

24. Alice M. Earle, *Stage-coach and Tavern Days* (New York, 1900), pp. 256-258; Spruill, *Women's Life and Work in the Southern Colonies*, pp. 89-90. ·

25. Letter to Lord Halifax, in John G. Palfrey, *A Compendious History of New England*, 4 vols. (Boston, 1883), IV, 391.

26. *South-Carolina Gazette*, November 2, 1769.

27. Carl Bridenbaugh, *Mitre and Sceptre* (New York, 1962), pp. 213-214, and *Cities in Revolt*, pp. 336, 355; Tolles, *Meeting House and Counting House*, pp. 141-142.

28. Bridenbaugh, *Cities in Revolt*, pp. 344-346.

29. Philip A. Bruce, *Social Life of Virginia in the Seventeenth Century* (Richmond, 1907), p. 220.

30. Earle, *Customs and Fashions in Old New England*, p. 374.

31. Such attire, according to a Williamsburg shopkeeper's advertisement in the *Virginia Gazette*, March 1, 1737[/38], included "*Bombazeens, Crapes, and other Sorts of Mourning for Ladies; also Hatbands, and Gloves, for Gentlemen.*"

32. Rufus M. Jones, *The Quakers in the American Colonies* (London, 1911), p. 531.

33. *The Memorial History of Boston*, ed. Justin Winsor, 4 vols. (Boston, 1880-81), II, 474.

34. Arthur M. Schlesinger, *The Colonial Merchants and the American Revolution* (New York, 1918), *passim*.

35. *South-Carolina Gazette*, November 21, 1774.

36. Schlesinger, *Colonial Merchants*, p. 610.

37. Evarts B. Greene, "The Code of Honor in Colonial and Revolutionary Times," Colonial Society of Massachusetts, *Publications*, XXVI (1924-26), 367-376; Lucius M. Sargent, *Dealings with the Dead* (Boston, 1856), pp. 549-566.

38. John Hammond, "Leah and Rachel," p. 20, in *Tracts and Other Papers, Relating Principally to the . . . Colonies in North America*, ed. Peter Force, 4 vols. (Washington, 1836-46), III.

39. Letter to Lord Halifax, February 22, 1765, *Documents Relative to the Colonial History of the State of New York*, eds. Edmund B. O'Callaghan and Berthold Fernow, 15 vols. (Albany, 1856-87), VII, 705.

40. Esther Singleton, *Social New York under the Georges, 1714-1776* (New York, 1902), pp. 314-315.

41. The biographical data that follow are derived from the *Dictionary of American Biography*, eds. Allen Johnson and Dumas Malone, 21 vols. (New York, 1928-37) and from standard full-length lives of the persons concerned.

42. Francis Bernard, *Select Letters on the Trade and Government of America* (London, 1774), p. 83.

43. Thomas Paine, *Complete Writings*, ed. Philip S. Foner, 2 vols. (New York, 1945), I, 29.
44. Letter to John Adams, January, 1814, John Adams, *Works*, ed. Charles F. Adams, 10 vols. (Boston, 1850–56), X, 87.

a new look
at Cambridge

ROBERT EMMET WALL, JR.

One of the most persuasive arguments raised by mainstream historians who see democracy in colonial America has been to point to voting statistics that reveal that large percentages of white males in local communities held the franchise. In the following article, Robert Wall attempts to look beyond those figures. That the poor could vote, he argues, is less important than that they voted for the wealthy. Two questions emerge out of the article: What is the function of ideology in determining one's world view? How do social classes develop political identities? More concretely, one might ask why the poor vote for the well-off, or what the poor have in common with the wealthy.

Recently students of early Massachusetts history have concerned themselves with the question of the franchise. Scholars are attempting to determine what proportion of the adult male population was admitted to the rights of freemanship and, therefore, could vote. Older histories presumed that only a few of the first settlers voted in colony affairs since freemanship was limited to church members during a major part of the old charter period and since the bedrock of New England puritanism was the concept of limited church membership. Although new research has been limited to sample towns and has not yet established exactly what proportion of the population could vote, it is becoming clear that a greater proportion of people were freemen than had previously been suspected.[1]

There is no doubt that these discoveries concerning the franchise are of great importance to the study of early Massachusetts history. Having made these advances, however, scholars have not avoided the temptation to push conclusions too far. They have denied, or at least seriously doubted, the existence of a political elite. They have introduced evidence to show that not only did large numbers of men have the vote, but that public offices and political power were distributed widely among the population. Will the facts support these assertions?

The town of Cambridge, Massachusetts has in print its selectmen's, town, proprietors', and church records.[2] Because of the availability of these records to the scholar, Cambridge is one of the best towns for testing theories about seventeenth century Massachusetts politics.

The most important local officials in seventeenth century Cambridge were the selectmen. From 1634, when the records first mention them, until 1686, there were 139 different men who held the office of Cambridge selectman. Prior to

Robert Emmet Wall, Jr., "A New Look at Cambridge," *The Journal of American History*, LII (December 1965), 599–605.

1660 (or 1666) the town constables served ex officio as members of the board of selectmen with no recognizable distinction made between the two offices. After 1660 there seems to be some dispute concerning whether a distinction developed.[3] If there was a distinction and if constables were not numbered among the selectmen, then only 84 men held the post of Cambridge selectman from 1634 until 1686. The 139 selectmen-constables in Cambridge filled a total of 454 possible positions on the board of selectmen during this same period. If one excludes the constables after 1660, then the 84 selectmen filled a total of 391 possible positions.[4]

B. Katherine Brown in her work on Cambridge has stressed the fact that so large a number of men held this important office. Political officeholding seems to have been widespread and changeover in office frequent. On the other hand, one must not ignore another set of figures—those concerning frequent reelection to office of the same persons. A total of 13 men were elected selectmen 10 or more times between 1634 and 1686.[5] They represent 9.4 percent of the total of 139 and 15.5 percent of the alternate total of 84 selectmen. These same 13 men filled the post of selectman 231 times. In short, less than 10 percent of the selectmen filled 51 percent of the possible seats.[6]

Twenty-six men were elected from Cambridge as deputies to the General Court from 1634 until 1686, and the total possible number of seats in the General Court filled by Cambridge men was 155.[7] Those who served frequently as deputies (5 or more terms) were 11 in number—or less than half of the total.[8] These same 11 men served a total of 112 of the possible 155 terms in the General Court: less than one half of the deputies held about 72 percent of the possible seats.

Seven men of magisterial rank (governors, deputy governors, or assistants—members of the upper house of the General Court), elected by the freemen of the colony as a whole, lived at one time or another in the town of Cambridge. Of the 7 Cambridge magistrates, only 4—Roger Harlakenden, Herbert Pelham, Daniel Gookin, and Thomas Danforth—lived in Cambridge for a significant number of years. As magistrates, these men held enormous legislative, executive, and judicial powers within the whole of the colony, and without doubt their prestige in Cambridge must have been great.

Thus a total of 23 different men—the 11 deputies who sat 5 or more times, the 13 selectmen who sat 10 or more times, and the 4 magistrates (bearing in mind the 5 men common to 2 or more groups)—held a firm grip on officeholding in Cambridge. If one accepts 153 as the total number of different men holding the posts of selectman, deputy, and magistrate, then these 23 are but 15 percent of the total.[9] Despite this fact, they held between 64 and 70 percent of the total number of important elective offices. Reelection to office and repeated service—an important ingredient for political power—was limited to just a few Cambridge politicians.

One cannot rule out the possibility that voting for one individual became habit or that once a man attained power and political experience, he became the town's only logical candidate for election. Yet, can one reject the possibility that the town of Cambridge had a ruling elite? Why was one politician picked for reelection or advancement to a higher office while another politician was ignored? Were there any characteristics or qualifications which the most frequently reelected men had in common?

Until 1664 Massachusetts required that her voters and her officeholders be members of one of the recognized churches of the colony. It would follow, therefore, that one of the qualifications for achieving political power was church membership. In Cambridge 19 of the 23 most frequently reelected officeholders had joined the Cambridge church. The records of that body are not complete, and possibly the remaining 4 were also members.[10] It is clear that membership in the Cambridge church did not automatically guarantee power since even lowly servants were eligible for membership but it is also clear that membership was normally a necessary qualification for power.

In 1636 the General Court of Massachusetts Bay provided that "no person shall henceforth bee chosen to any office in the commonwealth but such as is a freeman."[11] Town officials were removed from this ban in 1647, but holders of colonywide offices had to be freemen. It is safe to conclude that freemanship and the suffrage which came with it was a necessary qualification for political power. The Massachusetts freemanship records are not entirely complete either, yet 19 of the 23 leading politicians of Cambridge had definitely joined the ranks of the freemen during the first charter period.[12]

Church membership and freemanship were qualifications required by law, but many met the legal qualifications for public office. There were other qualifications usually demanded of officeholders which never found their way into statute. One of these was wealth. There are surviving records of two large grants of land in Cambridge. They give some indication of the financial standing of those who were granted land since the amount of the grants depended on the amount of land already held. The grantees with the largest holdings prior to the grant received most of the new land. In the grant of 1652, the average amount of land granted to each of the leading politicans was 215 acres, while the average for each of the remaining citizens was 70 acres. In 1665 the leading politicians received an average of 51 acres and the rest received only 17 acres.[13]

In 1688 the town of Cambridge rated persons and estates in the town for the purposes of taxation on the basis of 1 penny per pound. The names of only 9 of the 23 most powerful officeholders can be found on the 1688 list. The rest had either left the town or were dead. The average rate for these 9 men was 7 shillings, while the average rate for the remaining list of 183 names was just over 3 shillings. The frequently elected officeholders listed in 1688 were obviously wealthier than the average citizen.[14]

Another measure of the relative wealth of the powerful officeholders and their constituents can be found in the probate records. At the time of death or shortly thereafter, men empowered by the courts would make an inventory of the deceased's possessions and estimate the worth of the various items. One can compare the figures for the frequently reelected politicians with the inventories of the remaining Cambridge men. The estate inventories of 9 of the 23 leading politicians were discovered. The average estate for these 9 was £761, while at the same time the average of the remaining Cambridge estates was £316.[15] The powerful politicians were more than twice as wealthy as their constituents.

Wealth alone could not bring political power in Cambridge. Each of the tests used above revealed that, on the average, the 23 repeatedly elected to office were wealthier than their constituents. At the same time the tests also indicated that there were several men who qualified as wealthy but held office either infrequently or not at all.[16]

A majority of the outstanding Cambridge politicians came from locally prestigious families in England or the colonies, or were related by marriage to those same families. Others were related to certain men who, because of their positions, lent prestige to cousins, sons-in-law, and the like. Thomas Danforth, perhaps the leading politician in Cambridge, was the son of Nicholas Danforth, a gentleman from Suffolk and a deputy to the Massachusetts General Court from Cambridge. Daniel Gookin was the son of an important Virginia planter and the son-in-law of Edward Tyng, a wealthy Boston merchant and a magistrate of the colony. Herbert Pelham was the grandson of Lord de la Ware. Roger Harlakenden was the second son of the leading family of Earls Colne in Essex. His family was wealthy enough to have their own chaplain—Thomas Shepard, later pastor of the church in Cambridge. The Cookes—George, Joseph I, and Joseph II—were neighbors of the Harlakendens in England and apparently of the same social class. George Cooke later served as a high ranking officer in the Parliamentary army. Samuel Shepard was the brother of the Cambridge pastor, while John Cooper was the nephew of Samuel Stone, the first teacher of the Cambridge church and later teacher of the Hartford church. Edward Oakes was the son-in-law of the great puritan theologian William Ames. These were the outstanding connections. Most of the other 13 had important although not outstanding family ties.[17] Proper family connections were an important if not essential ingredient in the establishment of a political career. Men like Edward Jackson and Edward Collins might serve 17 terms each in the General Court, but Thomas Danforth, Roger Harlakenden, and Herbert Pelham, with little or no experience, were elected to the upper house.

No one of these factors—church membership, freemanship, wealth, or family connections—was sufficient in itself to establish an important political career in Cambridge. But it was the possession of all of these along with natural ability which combined to transform a common citizen into one of the leaders of the community. If the ingredients were present in sufficient quantity, the community leader could become a truly powerful politician—a man to be reckoned with not only in Cambridge but in the whole of Massachusetts Bay.

Although large numbers of men in Cambridge held the different public offices, the vast majority of the total possible posts were held by only a few men. The men most frequently reelected had certain characteristics in common. They possessed a happy combination of natural talent, wealth, proper family, freemanship, and membership in the church. How then can any explanation of Cambridge politics which overlooks the role of these leaders be an adequate explanation? If Cambridge is at all typical, would an explanation of Massachusetts politics rejecting the possible existence of a political elite be penetrating and complete?

The discovery of the wide distribution of the franchise in Cambridge—if it can be shown to be true of the other Massachusetts towns—is of the utmost importance, for it will alter many prevailing ideas concerning Massachusetts Bay. But enthusiasm for this discovery must be tempered by the realization that Massachusetts Bay was governed by a political elite which drew its members from one social class.

NOTES

1. Two recent studies of importance are: B. Katherine Brown, "Puritan Democracy: A Case Study," *Mississippi Valley Historical Review*, L (Dec. 1963), 377–96, and Richard C. Simmons, "Freemanship in Early Massachusetts: Some Suggestions for a Case Study," *William and Mary Quarterly*, XIX (July 1962), 422–28.

2. See *The Proprietors' Records of Cambridge, Massachusetts* (Cambridge, 1896), hereafter cited as *Cambridge Proprietors' Records; The Records of the Town and Selectmen of Cambridge, Massachusetts, 1630–1703* (Cambridge, 1901), hereafter cited as *Cambridge Town Records*; and Stephen Sharples, ed., *Records of the Church of Christ at Cambridge in New England, 1632–1830* (Boston, 1906).

3. There is obvious disagreement here. Mrs. Brown states that the constables did not act as selectmen after 1660 while Lucius R. Paige states that there was no distinction between the two offices before 1666 and probably none after that date. The acceptance of either opinion will not greatly alter the figures presented in this account. Brown, "Puritan Democracy," 393, 394; Lucius R. Paige, *History of Cambridge, Massachusetts, 1630–1877, With a Genealogical Register* (Boston, 1877), 462 n., 463 n.

4. Paige, *History of Cambridge*, 462–64.

5. These men and respective number of terms were: John Bridge, 12; Edward Goffe, 16; Edward Winship, 14; John Stedman, 16; Thomas Oakes, 29; Thomas Danforth, 25; John Cooper, 34; John Fessenden, 13; Thomas Fox, 16; William Manning, 15; Francis Moore, 14; Daniel Gookin, 13; and Walter Hastings, 14. *Ibid.*, 463–64.

6. Or less than 16 percent filled 57 percent of the possible selectmen's positions.

7. Nineteen of the twenty-six were also selectmen holding a total of 142 of the possible number of seats. Of the seven who did not serve as selectmen, four migrated to Connecticut at a very early date and did not have much of an opportunity to serve in public office in Massachusetts Bay. In the early years of the colony (1634–1645) numerous sessions of the General Court were held in any given year and Cambridge sent representatives to most. Careful study of the colony records and the records of over fifty towns indicates that the normal procedure was to hold a new session of the General Court every May and that almost all the towns (including Cambridge) held elections for the May sessions. Each attendance, therefore, at a May session is considered an election to the General Court. Sessions held irregularly throughout the year create another problem. In all cases, if the deputy at the irregular session is the same one who represented Cambridge at the last May session he is considered to be serving on the basis of his May election unless the town records specifically mention a special election. If the deputy is not the man elected in May, he is considered newly elected to the Court whether the town records mention a special election or not. I have determined that from 1634 until 1686 there were 155 possible elective posts in the General Court filled by Cambridge men. This figure is an approximation. Yet it is as close to mathematical accuracy as the available evidence will allow and the margin of possible error is small enough not to affect markedly the final total. Robert Emmet Wall, Jr., "The Membership of the Massachusetts General Court, 1634–1686" (doctoral dissertation, Yale, 1965). For lists of deputies to the various sessions of the General Court see Nathaniel B. Shurtleff, ed., *Records of the Governor and Company of Massachusetts Bay* (5 vols., Boston, 1853), hereafter cited as *Mass. Col. Rec.* See also *Cambridge Town Records*.

8. These men and respective number of terms were: John Bridge, 6; Edward Collins, 17; George Cooke, 7; Joseph Cooke I, 12; Joseph Cooke II, 6; Edward Jackson, 17; Richard Jackson, 9; Edward Oakes, 17; Samuel Shepard, 7; Nathaniel Sparhawk, 6; and Edward Winship, 8. These figures disagree with those given by Paige, *History of Cambridge*, 460, 461. Paige asserts that each election to the General Court was for the period of one year. Although this was true in the latter part of the old charter period, it was not true in the first decade of Cambridge's history. In the early years new elections were often held with every call for a new session of the General Court (sometimes three or four times in a single year). Paige's figures, although accurate for the election of selectmen, are inadequate for the election of deputies. The figures used here were compiled from a careful comparison of the Cambridge records and the records of the General Court. It is nevertheless impossible to determine with absolute certainty when elections for the Court were held and these figures are best treated as close approximations. The named deputies to the General Court served at least the number of terms indicated.

9. If the total number of officeholders was 102, then 23 were less than 20 percent of the officeholders.

10. Colony law required that deputies and magistrates be freemen. The law also required that freemen be church members. Seven of the 23 men discussed in the work, however, never held these colonywide offices and were, therefore, after 1647 not under the same

regulations. Of these, seven were definitely members of the Cambridge church and five were definitely freemen.

11. *Mass. Col. Rec.*, I, 188.

12. There are lists of freemen and the dates of their admissions at the end of each volume of *Mass. Col. Rec.*

13. For land grants in 1665 see *Cambridge Proprietors' Records*, 145-48; for 1652 see *Cambridge Town Records*, 97, 98.

14. Paige, *History of Cambridge*, 440-44.

15. These inventories may be found in the Middlesex County Probate Records, mss and bound volumes kept in the Middlesex County Court House, Probate Division, Cambridge, Massachusetts. Others may be found in Charles Manwaring, *A Digest of Early Connec- ticut Probate Records, 1635-1700* (Hartford, 1904).

16. In 1688 the highest rate in Cambridge was that of Samuel Goffe, who never held important public office in the old charter period. He was, however, the son of Edward Goffe—one of the 23. The second highest Cambridge estate found in the probate records was that of President Leonard Hoar of Harvard who never held public office. In all likelihood this was because of his position at the college. Another high inventory was that of John Wolcott who held public office very infrequently.

17. For family connections see Paige, *History of Cambridge*; James Savage, *A Genealogical Dictionary of the First Settlers in New England* (4 vols., Boston, 1860); and genealogies of the particular families.

economic base and social structure: the northern Chesapeake in the eighteenth century

AUBREY C. LAND

Radical historians, concerned with questions of class, have routinely studied workers and the poor. Yet the actions of people at the bottom are influenced by a society led by people at the top. To be aware of the actions and consciousness of society's leaders is crucial to radical history. In the article reprinted here, Aubrey Land examines the sources of income for the wealthy in one community. Their entrepreneurial activities differ markedly from the agricultural pursuits of most of their contemporaries. Economic factors may provide an explanation for some of the sharp prerevolutionary divisions in our society.

The *Maryland Gazette* for 18 October 1749 carried an obituary of more than common interest:

On the Eleventh Instant Died, at his Seat on Wye River in Queen Anne's County, Richard Bennett, Esq. in the Eighty-third Year of his Age, generally lamented by all that knew him. As his great fortune enabled him to do much good, so (happily for many) his Inclination was equal to his Ability, to relieve the indigent and distressed, which he did very liberally, without regarding of what Party, Religion or Country, they were. As he was the greatest Trader in this Province, so great Numbers fell in his Debt, and a more merciful Creditor could not be, having never deprived the Widows or Orphans of his Debtors of a Support; and when what the Debtors left, was not sufficient for that purpose, frequently supply'd the deficiency. His long Experience and great Knowledge in Business, as well as his known Candor and generosity, occasion'd many to apply to him for Advice and Assistance, and none were ever disappointed of what was in his Power, and several by his means, extricated out of great Difficulties. . . .

A later issue adds some particulars:

On Wednesday last was solemnized the Funeral of Richard Bennett, Esq. of Wye River, in a very handsome and decent Manner, by the Direction of his sole executor, the Hon. Col. Edward Lloyd. Mr. Bennett, by his Will, has forgiven above one hundred and fifty of his poor Debtors, and has made Provision for the Maintenance of many of his Overseers, and other poor Dependents, and settled a Sum of Money to be paid annually to the Poor of a Parish in Virginia: and done many other Acts of Charity and Munificence. He was supposed to be the Richest Man on the Continent. . . .[1]

Aubrey C. Land, "Economic Base and Social Structure: The Northern Chesapeake in the Eighteenth Century," *Journal of Economic History*, XVV (December 1965), 639–654.

Bennett's obvious virtues as a Christian gentleman need no underscoring, but two comments of the eulogist should be noted: his great wealth and his calling as a "trader." Perhaps the enthusiastic editor went beyond the exact truth in estimating Bennett's fortune, though probably not much. The field certainly included a few other candidates for the richest man. A neighbor across the Bay, Charles Carroll, counted his total worth at something like a hundred thousand pounds sterling, including £ 30,000 loaned at 6 per cent interest. Robert Carter, south of the Potomac in Virginia, could reckon himself worth nearly as much. The second William Byrd had left an impressive heritage which his son of the same name had already begun to dissipate. Even by the standards of London these were wealthy men.

All three alternate possibilities for the title of richest man are better known than Bennett, because they have had biographers, or because they played important political roles, or both. They belong to what has been variously called the aristocracy, the ruling oligarchy, or the squirearchy. The pejorative connotations of all three terms incline me toward a label suggested by a profound student of early American social and cultural history, "the southern agrarian leaders."[2] We can understand them in a sense as leaders of an agrarian area. But when we inquire about the economic milieu in which they flourished or seek the mechanisms by which they acquired their dominant positions, we are faced with some difficulties.

The traditional historiography has leaned heavily on literary evidence, and when it does not ignore these questions often gives impressions that are positively misleading. As sources, personal letters, travel accounts, and memoirs have the great merit of being relatively easy to put into context and ideal to paraphrase. A few dozen up to a few thousand items of this kind can be quilted into interesting and convincing patterns. The procedure has the limitations of the sources. Even the most acute observer focuses on objects of high visibility. The high tor eclipses the molehill in the landscape until the king falls to his death because of the "little gentleman in black velvet."

In the eighteenth-century Chesapeake, the "great planters" were the element of high visibility. They held slaves, owned vast estates, and built magnificent houses that have survived as showpieces. Visitors came under the spell of these gracious livers and left charming accounts of their balls, their tables, and their luxury. Planters themselves contributed to the effect. They wrote letters and a few left diaries that have survived along with their great houses. Viewed through these sources they cut large figures and play the star roles in the arrangements that the people of the Chesapeake made for themselves in that period. These personages are accurately enough drawn, but they are a detail, though an important one, in the total production. Unfortunately the supporting cast and stage hands that made the production possible receive next to no attention, sometimes not even the courtesy of a billing. Just as *Hamlet* cannot be successfully staged without Hamlet, there can hardly be a play with Hamlet alone.

Not much literary evidence for the minor figures has come down; but another kind does exist and, even though bristling with difficulties and overawing in bulk, it can be compelled to yield some data for a fuller view. This body of material has been brought together in two depositories, the Maryland Hall of Records and the Virginia State Archives, and properly canvassed will fill in some gaps in our knowledge of Chesapeake affairs. It consists of inventories and accounts of the estates in personalty of all free men at the time of their death.[3]

The argument in this paper applies only to Maryland, for which a statistical analysis has been completed.[4] The Virginia counties that have been analyzed give me the clear impression that differences between the areas north and south of the Potomac are not very great in respect of the basic contention here. Both were a part of a single economic region which political boundaries could not split asunder and were treated as a unit in contemporary British commercial records.

To obtain from the voluminous Maryland records a sample that faithfully reflects conditions in the northern Chesapeake, some of the usual economies are not possible. Geographical sampling by selected counties is ruled out. The process of carving new counties out of large older counties went on continuously from 1690 to the Revolution. Consequently the county of one decade is not necessarily the same unit in a later decade. Accordingly, all counties of the province are included. Over the entire eighty-year period 1690–1770 for which the records are reasonably complete the alternate decades from 1690–1699 to 1750–1759 have been tabulated. If it can be assumed that these sizable samples reflect with reasonable accuracy the spectrum of planters' estates, then we have some basis for understanding an otherwise shadowy aspect of the Chesapeake economy.

The profile of estates in the decade January 1, 1690, to December 31, 1699, shows an unexpected imbalance. Three quarters of these estates (74.6 per cent, to be precise) are of the magnitude £ 100 sterling or less. In the next bracket, £ 100 to £ 200, the percentage drops to 12.1, and in succeeding hundred-pound brackets to 5.5 per cent, 2.7 per cent, 1.4 per cent, 1.3 per cent, 0.6 per cent, and 0.3 per cent. After a break in the distribution, a meager 1.5 per cent at the top are valued at £ 1,000 sterling or greater.

Beyond the obvious fact that the less affluent far outnumber the better off, this analysis tells us little. The estates, small or great, are all those of planters— a handful of physicians, mariners, and clergymen specifically excepted. "Planter," then, simply describes an occupation without indicating economic status of the individual. To get at what this distribution means in terms of worldly goods, standard of living, and possibly social status, it is necessary to look at particulars in the inventories themselves. Here impressions become vivid.

The planters at the bottom of the scale, those with estates of £ 100 or less, have a best a "country living": a saddle horse or two, half a dozen or fewer cows, a few swine to furnish fresh or salt meat for the table according to the season, a modest assortment of household utensils—sometimes nothing more than a cooking pot or skillet, a few tools, and agricultural implements. Many essentials of a household—for instance, plates and cups—are missing in fully half the inventories, an omission indicating that makeshifts such as wooden bowls and gourds took the place of these articles. The appraisers of estates overlooked no article, not even a cracked cup without a handle or a single glass bottle. In brief the standard of living might be described as rude sufficiency. The self-styled poet laureate of Maryland, Eben Cooke, call planters at this level "cockerouses."

The inventories also speak to the productivity of these small planters. In those inventories made during the autumn and winter after the tobacco had been cut the appraisers carefully estimated the size of the deceased's crop. Crop entries range from twelve hundred pounds, a trifle over two hogsheads, up to three thousand pounds, or about six hogsheads. This represented the producer's cash crop, almost his entire annual income, excepting possibly the occasional sale of a heifer, a pig, or a few bushels of corn to a neighbor or local trader. Reckoning the price of tobacco at ten shillings a hundred, these small producers could count their disposable incomes at a figure between £ 6 and £ 15 a year.[5]

Even taking into account the small planter's self-sufficiency in fresh vegetables from the kitchen garden, cereals from whatever field crops he grew besides tobacco, and meat from his own farm animals, an income of this size imposed iron limitations on him. Between investment and consumption he had no choice. Such necessities as thread, needles, powder and shot, coarse fabrics for clothing and featherbeds, and an occasional tool or a household utensil strained his credit at the country store until his crop was sold. For the small planter, provincial quitrents, church tithes, and taxes represented a real burden. He cast his ballot for a representative who could resist the blandishments of governors and hold public expenses to the barest minimum. In good part the pressures from men of his kind kept investment in the public sector to lowest dimensions, whether the object was a county courthouse, a lighthouse, or a governor's mansion. As a private person he could not invest from savings because he had none. With tobacco crops barely sufficient to cover his debt to the country merchant, a disastrous year could prostrate him. A lawsuit, the death of cattle in a winter freeze, or a fire in house or barn forced him to contract debts which had often not been paid at the time of his death and which ate up his entire personal estate, leaving his heirs without a penny. Not infrequently his administrator actually overpaid his estate in order to save trifling family heirlooms more precious than their valuation in the inventory. Investment in a slave or indentured servant to increase his productivity, though not completely out of the question, was very difficult.

The small planter clearly was not the beneficiary of the planting society of the Chesapeake. He bred his increase and added to the growing population that filled up vacant land from the shoreline to the mountains before the Revolution. In the language of the courts he qualified as a planter. Considering the circumstances of his life, it would stretch the usual meaning of the term to call him a yeoman, particularly if he fell in the lower half of his group.[6]

In the brackets above £ 100, different characteristics of the estates immediately strike the eye. Sumptuary standards of planters above this line were obviously higher. Kitchens had ampler stocks of utensils; and for dining, earthenware and china replaced the gourds and wooden makeshifts that apparently were the rule on tables of families in the lowest economic bracket. Ticking stuffed with flock gave way to bedsteads and bedding. Even more striking is the prevalence of bond labor, both indentured servants and slaves, in this higher stratum. The transition comes abruptly. In estates below £ 100, servants or slaves rarely appear and then only in those within a few pounds of the line. In the estates at £ 100 to £ 200, the inventories of eight out of ten estates list bond labor—a higher percentage, actually, than in any of the succeeding £ 100 brackets up to £ 500.

In fact, these estates falling between £ 100 and £ 500 form a relatively homogeneous group. Altogether they comprise 21.7 per cent of all estates. Though existence for the planter is less frugal, his worldly goods show few signs of real luxury. Not a single estate was debt free, though fewer than a tenth had debts amounting to more than half the value of the inventory. The number of slaves in single estates does not run high: from one to five in 90 per cent of the estates that had them at all. Yet even this small number represented between half and two thirds of the appraised valuation. Reflecting the additional hands for husbandry, tobacco crops ran higher roughly in proportion to the number of slaves or indentured servants. Crops ranged from twelve hundred pounds (planters with no bond labor) up to nearly twenty thousand pounds, or from a little over two up to forty hogsheads. Again using ten shillings per hundred for transforming tobacco values to sterling, we can put the incomes from tobacco production alone between £ 6 and £ 100 a year. Other sources of income for families with bond labor should not be ruled out. Doubtless off-season occupations such as riving staves or shingles, sawing plank, and making cereal crops occupied some productive time. Unfortunately only occasional data on this type of product appear, enough to call for acknowledgment but insufficient for measurement.

Nevertheless, with annual incomes of these dimensions from their tobacco crops, planters in this group had alternatives not open to the lowest income group. As respectable citizens with community obligations to act as overseers of roads, appraisers of estates, and similar duties, they might choose to lay by something to see their sons and daughters decently started in turn as planters or wives of planters. Or they might within the limitations of their estates live the good life, balancing consumption against income. Social pressure must have urged them in this direction, to a round of activities that included local politics and such country entertainments as dances, horseracing, and cockfights, occasionally punctuated with drinking brawls complete with eye-gougings and other practices not usually associated with the genteel life of the planter. Whatever the choice it is difficult to see how the planter in these circumstances could add appreciably to his estate in a short period of years, or even in a lifetime.

Still further up the scale, the estates appraised at sums above £ 500 form an even smaller percentage of the total. The five £ 100 brackets between £ 500 and £ 1,000 include altogether 2.2 per cent of all estates. At first glance this small group appears to be a plusher version of the preceding: somewhat more slaves, larger tobacco crops, more personal goods including some luxury items. These are planters of substance, much closer to the stereotype, as the character and contents of their inventories show. And in their activities they moved on a higher plane. One had represented his county for a term in the General Assembly and another had served on the county court as a justice of the peace. In the matter of indebtedness, however, some interesting differences appear. Just over half the inventories list debts owed to the estate among the major assets. In a few cases the portion of total assets in the form of debts owed the estate runs to half or more.

What I think we see here is an emerging business or entrepreneurial element, a small group of planters with sources of income other than planting alone. All were planters in the sense that they, or their bond labor, produced tobacco crops. But the appreciable number in the creditor category have other concerns. The nature of these concerns appears more clearly in the most affluent element, whose members can be studied individually as cases.

This element includes all persons with estates inventoried at more than £ 1,000 sterling. In the decade 1690–1699, they represent 1.6 per cent of the total. They were the "great planters" of the day.

The smallest estate in personalty, that of Nicholas Gassaway of Anne Arundel County, was inventoried at £ 1,017 14s. 11 1/2d. sterling; the largest, that of Henry Coursey of Talbot County, at £ 1,667 17s. 1 1/4d. Perhaps estates of this size would have cut a mean figure beside those of the sugar planters of the West Indies.[7] In the northern Chesapeake of the closing years of the seventeenth century, they loom high.

The composition of these largest estates varies a bit from what we might expect of the great planter's holdings. Slaves comprise less than a quarter of the assets and, in several, less than a fifth.[8] It should be remembered that this decade lies in the transition period when slaves were displacing indentured servants as field labor. Even so, the numbers seem unimpressive—often no greater than slave holdings in estates a third as large. By contrast, the number and the amount of assets in the form of debts owed the estate are striking. Altogether they comprised between a quarter and a half of the assets in individual estates.[9] In one of the largest estates, debts owed the deceased came to 78 per cent of the total assets.

The inventories themselves give some clues as to how these large planters had become creditors. Occasionally an industrious appraiser included information on how the debtor had incurred his obligation: for a pipe of wine, for a parcel of steers, for corn, for rent of a certain property, for goods. In short, the great planter had also become a "trader." Frequently a portion of the inventory is simply labeled "in the store" and the contents of that room or building listed under this heading. Then the origin of the debts becomes clear. Sometimes they ran well over a hundred major items and were carefully listed under captions "sperate debts" and "desperate debts."

Putting this cross section or sample against the general outlines of the Chesapeake economy, I suggest the hypothesis that the men of first fortune belonged functionally to a class whose success stemmed from entrepreneurial activities as much as, or even more than, from their direct operations as producers of tobacco. The Chesapeake closely resembles pioneer economies of other times and places. It was a region with a relatively low ratio of population to resources and an equally low ratio of capital to resources. External commerce was characterized by heavy staple exports and high capital imports. Internally this flow created a current of high capital investment, full employment, profit inflation, and rising property values.[10] The tobacco staple did not lend itself to bonanza agriculture, as did sugar in the West India islands where fortunes could be made in a decade. Consequently the Chesapeake planters did not go "back home" to dazzle the populace with their wealth. Their returns derived in the first instance from tobacco production, which afforded a competence, and secondly from enterprise, which gave greater rewards. As entrepreneurs, they gave the Chesapeake economy both organization and direction. They took the risks, made the decisions, and reaped the rewards or paid the penalties. And they worked unremittingly at these tasks, which could not be performed in their absence by the small planter or by overseers.

It is not easy to analyze the activities of this economic elite into neat categories. They were at once planters, political leaders, and businessmen. The first two roles tend to obscure the last. Their role in politics is a textbook commonplace. As planters they lived in the great tradition, some even ostentatiously. On this point testimony is abundant and unambiguous. Had they depended solely on the produce of their tobacco fields, they doubtless would have lived up to or beyond current income. And some did. But in fact many among them increased their fortunes substantially and a few spectacularly, while still maintaining their reputations as good livers. During the early years of the eighteenth century, when the tobacco trade was far from booming, some of the first families of the Chesapeake established themselves as permanent fixtures. Several had come to the first rank, or very near it, both in politics and wealth by 1700: the Taskers, the Catholic Carrolls, the Lloyds, and the Trumans. Others, less well known but eventually architects of equal or greater fortunes, were rising in the scale within another decade: the Bordleys, the Chews, the Garretts, the Dulanys, the Bennetts, and the Protestant Carrolls. The secret of their success was business enterprise, though almost to man they lived as planters separated from the kind of urban community in which their more conspicuously entrepreneurial counterparts to the north had their residences and places of business. An examination of the chief forms of enterprise discloses the mechanisms by which they came to the top of the heap.

One of the most profitable enterprises and one most commonly associated with the great planters of the Chesapeake, land speculation, appears early in the eighteenth century in both Virginia and Maryland. The Virginia Rent Roll of 1704, admitted as imperfect but the best that could be done at the time, shows half a dozen holdings that suggest speculative intent. After these tentative beginnings, speculators moved quite aggressively during the administration of Spotswood and his successors, when huge grants in the vacant back country became commonplace events for privileged insiders, with the governors themselves sharing the spoils of His Majesty's bounty. In the more carefully regulated land system of Maryland, agents of the Lords Baltimore made a few large grants to favored persons like Charles Carroll the Settler in the first two decades of the century. During these same decades other wary speculators took up occasional large grants. The Maryland system compelled speculators to be cautious, because it exacted some money for the patents and made evasion of quitrents nearly impossible. But by the 1730's, eager speculators had glimpsed a vision of the possible returns and kept the land office busy issuing warrants for unpatented areas. For a relatively modest outlay a small number of Marylanders obtained assets with which they experimented for years before discovering the last trick in turning them to account.

Speculators capitalized their assets in two chief ways, both enormously profitable. First, as landlords of the wild lands, they leased to tenants who paid rents and at the same time improved their leaseholds by clearing, planting orchards, and erecting houses, barns, and fences. Almost exclusively long-term leases, either for years (commonly twenty-one) or for lives, these instruments specified the improvements to be made. Tenants who could not save from current income thus under compulsion contributed their bit to capital formation to the ultimate benefit of the landlord. Literary sources give the impression that tenancy was not very widespread, but the records tell another story. Something over a third of the planters in the lowest £ 100 bracket in Maryland leased their land. Secondly, the large landholder sold off plantation-size parcels as settlement enveloped his holdings and brought values to the desired level. Not content to leave this movement to chance, many speculators hastened the process by encouraging immigration and by directing the movement of settlers toward their own properties. Jonathan Hagar in Maryland and William Byrd in Virginia are two among many who attempted to enhance the value of their properties in this way. It is difficult to determine profits even for single speculators except for short periods. Experience must have varied widely, and undoubtedly some speculators failed. But some of the successful ones made incredible gains in a relatively short span of years.

Even more ubiquitous than the planter-speculator was the planter-merchant.

The inventories and accounts contain much evidence on the organization of commerce in the tobacco counties of the Chesapeake. Hardly a parish lacked one or more country stores, often no more than a tiny hut or part of a building on the grounds of a planter who could supply, usually on credit, the basic needs of neighboring small producers—drygoods, hoes and other small implements, salt, sugar, spices, tea, and almost always liquor. Inventories show some small stores with a mere handful of those articles in constant demand. Others had elaborate stocks of women's hats, mirrors, mourning gloves, ribbons, patent medicines, and luxury goods. The names of several great families are associated with country stores, particularly in the earlier generations of the line. Frequently, storekeeping duties fell to a trusted servant or to a younger member of the family as a part of his training. Occasionally, an apprentice from one of the county families came to learn the mysteries of trade by measuring out fabrics or liquors and keeping the accounts.

As with land speculation, determining profits of merchants is next to impossible. Consumers complained bitterly of high markups, and a few storekeepers boasted of them. Even so, the country merchant's profits were not limited to sale of goods alone. He stood to gain on another transaction. He took his payment in tobacco, the crops of the two- to six-hogshead producers. The small planter participated directly in the consignment system of the early eighteenth century only to a limited extent. His petty wants and his small crop hardly justified the London merchant's time and trouble in maintaining him as a separate account. His nexus to the overseas market was the provincial merchant, who took tobacco at prices that allowed at least a small profit to himself on every hogshead.

Closely allied to merchandising, moneylending presents almost as great problems of analysis. The Chesapeake economy operated on an elaborate network of credit arrangements. Jefferson's famous remark that Virginia planters were a species of property attached to certain great British merchant houses may have been true of some planters, as it was of Jefferson himself. But the observation has created a mischievous view of credit relations between England and the tobacco colonies and does not describe the debt pattern within the area at all accurately.[11] A full account awaits the onslaught of an industrious graduate student armed with electronic tapes and computers. Meanwhile the accounts can tell us something. Country merchants had to be prepared to extend credit beyond that for goods purchased by their customers. They paid for some of their customers at least the church tithes, the tax levies, and the freedom dues of indentured servants who had served their terms. These petty book debts could be collected with interest in any county court. Loans to artisans—the shoemakers, tanners, and blacksmiths who multiplied in number toward mid century—were of a different order. For working capital, the artisan in need of £ 5 to £ 20 and upward turned to men of means, the "traders." Far from abating, the demand for capital increased as the century wore on.

Investment opportunities were never lacking for planters with ready money or with credit in England. As lenders, they squarely faced the conflict of the law and the profits. By law they could take interest at 6 per cent for money loans and 8 per cent for tobacco loans. One wonders why the Carrolls chose to loan their £ 30,000 sterling at 6 per cent, even on impeccable securities. Could the answer be in part that returns at this rate equaled those from further investment in planting? At any rate they did choose to lend, following the example of Bennett and a dozen or so others.

Far more profitable as an investment opportunity, manufacturing exercised an enduring fascination on imaginative men of the Chesapeake. During Virginia Company days, before the first settlement of Maryland, glass and iron had figured among the projects launched under Company stimulus. Although these had come to ruin in the massacre of 1622, Virginians never gave up hope of producing iron. Their success was limited; but in the upper reaches of the Bay a combination of easily worked ore, limitless forests for charcoal, oyster shell, and water transportation from the furnace site invited exploitation. British syndicates moved first to establish the Principio Works and later the Nottingham and Lancashire works. These remained in British hands until the Revolutionary confiscations. Last of the big four, the Baltimore Iron Works (1733) became the largest producer and the biggest money-maker. Five Maryland investors subscribed the initial capital of £ 3,500 sterling. The Baltimore enterprise was a triumph for native capital, though technicians and technology were both imported from Britain. After the first three years of operation the partners received handsome dividends but always plowed a substantial part of the profits back into the enterprise. By the early 1760's the share of each partner was valued at £ 6,000 sterling. The five partners were among the first fortunes in Maryland.

Beyond iron making, other forms of enterprise (mostly small-scale manufacturing or processing) attracted investment capital. In nearly all areas of the Chesapeake some shipbuilding, cooperage, and milling establishments provided essential local services or commodities. None of these required either the capital outlay or the organization of an ironworks. Consequently, as enterprises they were attractive to investors with modest capital but large ambitions. In the area of Balitmore, flour milling developed major proportions after mid century, as the upper counties of Maryland found grain more profitable than tobacco as a field crop.

An astonishing percentage of the personal fortunes of the northern Chesapeake had their roots in law practice. While not entrepreneurial in a technical sense, the rewards went to the enterprising. During the seventeenth century lawyers were neither numerous nor always in good odor. Private persons attended to their own legal business in the courts. By 1700, the fashion had changed as the courts insisted on greater formality in pleading and as the cumbersome machinery of the common law compelled the uninstructed to turn to the professional. Pleading "by his attorney" swiftly replaced appearances *in propria persona*. Still the legal profession remained trammeled. Laws strictly regulated fees attorneys could take and kept these at levels low enough that the ablest members of the Maryland bar went on strike in the 1720's. What lawyers lacked in size of fees they made up in number of cases. An attorney might, and frequently did, bring thirty or forty cases to trial in a three- or four-day session of a county court. Had these been litigation over land, an impression widely held by students who use the *Virginia Reports* and the *Maryland Reports*, attorneys might have spent their entire time in title searches, examining witnesses, and preparing their cases. The court proceedings at large, however, show fifty cases of debt collection for every case over land; and sometimes the ratio runs as high as a hundred to one. One traveler to the Chesapeake, remarking on the "litigious spirit," wryly concluded that this spectacle of everybody suing everybody else was a kind of sport peculiar to the area. In fact, the numbers of suits grew out of the very arrangements—a tissue of book debts, bills of exchange, and promissory notes—that kept the mechanism operating.

In this milieu the lawyer had an enviable position. From his practice he derived a steady income freed from direct dependence on returns from the annual tobacco fleet. In a phrase, he had ready money the year 'round. Furthermore, he had an intimate knowledge of the resources and dependability of the planters in the county— and, indeed, throughout the province if he also practiced at the bar of the superior courts. Consequently he could take advantage of opportunities on the spot, whether they were bargains in land, sales of goods or produce, or tenants seeking leases. He could besides avoid the costs of litigation that inevitably arose as he involved himself in land speculation, lending, or merchandising, as many did. As a rule the lawyers did well, and the most enterprising moved into the highest brackets of wealth. Perhaps the most spectacular example, Thomas Bordley, a younger son of a Yorkshire schoolmaster, came from an impecunious immigrant apprentice in a Maryland law office to distinction in the law, in politics, and in Maryland society within the span of a short lifetime. After his premature death in 1726 his executors brought to probate the largest estate in the history of the province to that time.

Quite commonly, lawyers added a minor dimension to their income from office holding. A fair percentage of Maryland offices were sinecures that could be executed by deputies for a fraction of the fees. Most carried modest stipends, but a few eagerly sought prizes paid handsomely. Baltimore's provincial secretary received £ 1,000 per annum.

This is not the place to argue the returns from planting, pure and simple. Many planters did well without other sources of income. But impressive fortunes went to those who, in addition, put their talents to work in some of the ways described above. A few engaged in all. The list is finite, for we are referring here to a small percentage of planters, those with estates above £ 1,000: in the decade 1690–1699 to 1.6 per cent, in 1710–1719 to 2.2 per cent, in 1730–1739 to 3.6 per cent, and in 1750–1759 to 3.9 per cent. When tabulated and examined for group characteristics, they resemble functionally a type that could easily come under that comprehensive eighteenth-century term, merchant. They look very unlike the planter of the moonlight-and-magnolias variety. It is a commentary on the prosperity of the northern Chesapeake that, as this favored category increased in percentage and in absolute numbers, so did the magnitude of its members' individual fortunes. The sample taken just before the turn of the century shows top fortunes between £ 1,000 and £ 2,000, with none above. The sample decade 1730–1739 includes an appreciable number over £ 2,000. The two largest were those of Samuel Chew (£ 9,937) and Amos Garrett (£ 11,508), both merchants. Even these did not match the fortunes left by Dr. Charles Carroll and Daniel Dulany the Elder in the decade 1750–1759, nor that of Benjamin Tasker in the next.

The poor were not excluded, individually or as a group, from the general prosperity of the Chesapeake. Four individuals—Thomas Macnemara, Thomas Bordley, Daniel Dulany, and Dr. Charles Carroll—moved up the scale from nothing to the top bracket of wealth, two of them from indentured servitude. These were extraordinary men, but their careers indicate the avenues open to their combination of talents for the law, land speculation, moneylending, merchandising, and manufacturing in which they engaged. Of course all were planters as well.

But for the mass, advance was by comparison glacial. The composition of the base on which such performances took place changed more slowly. In the fourth decade of the eighteenth century the percentage of planters in the lowest economic group, those with estates of £ 100 or less, had fallen to 54.7 per cent, in marked contrast to the 74.6 per cent of the decade 1690–1699. Between the same two sample decades the percentage in the next higher category of estates (£ 100 to £ 500) had increased to 35.7 per cent from 21.7 per cent.[12] If this means that the poor were getting richer, it also means for the great majority that they were doing so by short and slow steps. Together, these two lowest categories still made up 90.4 per cent of the planting families in 1730–1739, as compared with 96.3 per cent in the last decade of the seventeenth century. Nonetheless, the shift toward a higher standard of living within this huge mass of lesser planters is quite as important a commentary on the economic well-being of the Chesapeake as is the growth in numbers and magnitude of the great fortunes.

It is never easy to know just how much to claim for statistical evidence. Perhaps there is enough here to raise doubts about the descriptive accuracy of reports from Chesapeake planters themselves. These sound like a protracted wail of hard times, rising occasionally in crescendo to prophecies of impending ruin. Yet even during the early and least prosperous decades, the northern Chesapeake experienced some growth. During the second quarter of the century and on into the following decades the samples made for this study indicate a quickened rate. The results worked no magic change in the way of life or economic station for the small planter, the mass of Maryland. These were always the overwhelming percentage of the producers. As a social group they come in for little notice. Their lives lack the glitter and incident that has made the great planter the focus of all eyes. By the standards of the affluent society theirs was a drab, rather humdrum, existence bound to the annual rhythm of the field crop. The highest rewards were for those who could transcend the routine of producing tobacco and develop the gainful activities that kept the economy functioning.

NOTES

1. *Maryland Gazette*, October 18 and November 8, 1749.

2. Louis B. Wright, *The Cultural Life of the American Colonies, 1607–1763* (New York: Harper, 1957), pp. 1–22.

3. Women who had property in their own right were also included. Mainly widows and spinsters, they formed a tiny fraction of the total.

4. Detailed reference notes to source materials will not be given in this paper. The author expects to publish a monograph reporting fully on this research in 1966. The folio volumes of the Inventories and Accounts, from which the statistical material was taken, are in the Maryland Hall of Records, Annapolis. After Volume 39A, this series is divided, one for Inventories and another for Accounts.

5. Ten shillings per hundred appears in the inventories rather frequently during this decade as a formula for transforming tobacco into sterling value. It is not therefore completely arbitrary. No dependable tobacco-price series has yet appeared.

6. Students of Chesapeake history are indebted to the pioneer work of Thomas J. Wertenbaker for the note of realism he brought to discussion of economic and social classes in *The Planters of Colonial Virginia* (Princeton, N.J.: Princeton University Press, 1922).

7. Richard Pares, "Merchants and Planters," *Economic History Review*, Supplements, No. 4 (1960), p. 4.

8. The single exception was the estate of Edward Pye of St. Mary's County, appraised at £ 1150 13s. 6d. He had 42 slaves and 2 indentured servants (twice as many as the next

largest slave holder) valued at £ 783, or 67 per cent of his total estate (Inventories and Accounts, Vol. XV, folios 131–133).

9. Again with the exception of Pye.

10. W. A. Mackintosh, "Some Aspects of a Pioneer Economy," *Canadian Journal of Economics and Political Science*, II. No. 4 (Nov. 1936), 457–63.

11. To be sure, some planters had been caught in the toils of debt both to English merchants and to provincial capitalists. They were exposed to such disadvantages and liabilities when indebted to English houses that their efforts to extricate themselves were often almost frantic. But there were also many, as the inventories show, who had sterling balances with one or more English houses.

12. Jacob M. Price, "The Economic Growth of the Chesapeake and the European Market, 1697–1775," *Journal of Economic History*, XXIV (1964), 496–511, reports on impressive research that relates the growth of the Chesapeake to market structure. His analysis explains otherwise puzzling local variations within the Chesapeake, particularly in the last four decades of colonial dependency.

popular uprisings and civil authority in eighteenth-century America

PAULINE MAIER

If, as Robert Wall and Aubrey Land argue in the two preceding essays, a social elite existed in the colonies, how did the masses make themselves heard? Pauline Maier provides one answer: mobs act outside the political process to defend social mores that are not yet institutionalized. In their pioneer studies of mob action, British historians E. P. Thompson and Eric Hobsbawm indicate that mobs form in the interests of public justice where legal sanctions do not reflect public morality. In the following essay, Maier reveals the tension between existing sources of power and the demands of the powerless. She challenges the assumption that political paths to redress grievances were always available.

It is only natural that the riots and civil turbulence of the past decade and a half have awakened a new interest in the history of American mobs. It should be emphasized, however, that scholarly attention to the subject has roots independent of contemporary events and founded in long-developing historiographical trends. George Rudé's studies of pre-industrial crowds in France and England, E. J. Hobsbawm's discussion of "archaic" social movements, and recent works linking eighteenth-century American thought with English revolutionary tradition have all, in different ways, inspired a new concern among historians with colonial uprisings.[1] This discovery of the early American mob promises to have a significant effect upon historical interpretation. Particularly affected are the Revolutionary struggle and the early decades of the new nation, when events often turned upon well-known popular insurrections.

Eighteenth-century uprisings were in some important ways different than those of today—different in themselves, but even more in the political context within which they occurred. As a result they carried different connotations for the American Revolutionaries than they do today. Not all eighteenth-century mobs simply defied the law: some used extralegal means to implement official demands or to enforce laws not otherwise enforceable, others in effect extended the law in urgent situations beyond its technical limits. Since leading eighteenth-century Americans had known many occasions on which mobs took on the defense of the public welfare, which was, after all, the stated purpose of government, they were less likely to deny popular upheavals all legitimacy than are modern leaders. While not advocating popular uprisings, they could still grant such incidents an established and necessary role in free societies, one

Pauline Maier, "Popular Uprisings and Civil Authority in Eighteenth-Century America," *William and Mary Quarterly*, XXVII, 3rd Series (January 1970), 3-35.

that made them an integral and even respected element of the political order. These attitudes, and the tradition of colonial insurrections on which they drew, not only shaped political events of the Revolutionary era, but also lay behind many laws and civil procedures that were framed during the 1780's and 1790's, some of which still have a place in the American legal system.

I

Not all colonial uprisings were identical in character or significance. Some involved no more than disorderly vandalism or traditional brawls such as those that annually marked Pope's Day on November 5, particularly in New England. Occasional insurrections defied established laws and authorities in the name of isolated private interests alone—a set of Hartford County, Connecticut, land-owners arose in 1722, for example, after a court decision imperiled their particular land titles. Still others—which are of interest here—took on a broader purpose, and defended the interests of their community in general where established authorities failed to act.[2] This common characteristic linked otherwise diverse rural uprisings in New Jersey and the Carolinas. The insurrectionists' punishment of outlaws, their interposition to secure land titles or prevent abuses at the hands of legal officials followed a frustration with established institutions and a belief that justice and even security had to be imposed by the people directly.[3] The earlier Virginia tobacco insurrection also illustrates this common pattern well: Virginians began tearing up young tobacco plants in 1682 only after Governor Thomas Culpeper forced the quick adjournment of their assembly, which had been called to curtail tobacco planting during an economic crisis. The insurrections in Massachusetts a little over a century later represent a variation on this theme. The insurgents in Worcester, Berkshire, Hampshire, Middlesex, and Bristol counties—often linked together as members of "Shays's Rebellion"—forced the closing of civil courts, which threatened to send a major portion of the local population to debtors' prison, only until a new legislature could remedy their pressing needs.[4]

This role of the mob as extralegal arm of the community's interest emerged, too, in repeated uprisings that occurred within the more densely settled coastal areas. The history of Boston, where by the mideighteenth century "public order . . . prevailed to a greater degree than anywhere else in England or America," is full of such incidents. During the food shortage of 1710, after the governor rejected a petition from the Boston selectmen calling for a temporary embargo on the exportation of foodstuffs one heavily laden ship found its rudder cut away, and fifty men sought to haul another outward bound vessel back to shore. Under similar circumstances Boston mobs again intervened to keep foodstuffs in the colony in 1713 and 1729. When there was some doubt a few years later whether or not the selectmen had the authority to seize a barn lying in the path of a proposed street, a group of townsmen, their faces blackened, levelled the structure and the road went through. Houses of ill fame were attacked by Boston mobs in 1734, 1737, and 1771; and in the late 1760's the *New York Gazette* claimed that mobs in Providence and Newport had taken on responsibility for "disciplining" unfaithful husbands. Meanwhile in New London, Connecticut, another mob prevented a radical religious sect, the Rogerenes, from disturbing normal Sunday services, "a practice they . . . [had] followed more or less for many years past; and which all the laws made in that government, and executed in the most judicious manner could not put a stop to."[5]

Threats of epidemic inspired particularly dramatic instances of this community oriented role of the mob. One revealing episode occurred in Massachusetts in 1773–1774. A smallpox hospital had been built on Essex Island near Marblehead "much against the will of the multitude" according to John Adams. "The patients were careless, some of them wantonly so; and others were suspected of designing to spread the smallpox in the town, which was full of people who had not passed through the distemper." In January 1774 patients from the hospital who tried to enter the town from unauthorized landing places were forcefully prevented from doing so; a hospital boat was burned; and four men suspected of stealing infected clothes from the hospital were tarred and feathered, then carted from Marblehead to Salem in a long cortege. The Marblehead town meeting finally won the proprietors' agreement to shut down the hospital; but after some twenty-two new cases of smallpox broke out in the town within a few days "apprehension became general," and some "Ruffians" in disguise hastened the hospital's demise by burning the nearly evacuated building. A military watch of forty men was needed for several nights to keep the peace in Marblehead.[6]

A similar episode occurred in Norfolk, Virginia, when a group of wealthy residents decided to have their families inoculated for smallpox. Fears arose that the lesser disease brought on by the inoculations would spread and necessitate a general inoculation, which would cost "more money than is circulating in Norfolk" and ruin trade and commerce such that "the whole colony would feel the effects." Local magistrates said they could not interfere because "the law was silent in the matter." Public and private meetings then sought to negotiate the issue. Despite a hard-won agreement, however, the pro-inoculation faction persisted in its original plan. Then finally a mob drove the newly inoculated women and children on a five-mile forced march in darkness and rain to the common Pest House, a three-year old institution designed to isolate seamen and others, particularly Negroes, infected with smallpox.[7]

These local incidents indicate a willingness among many Americans to act outside the bounds of law, but they cannot be described as anti-authoritarian in any general sense. Sometimes in fact—as in the Boston bawdy house riot of 1734, or the Norfolk smallpox incident—local magistrates openly countenanced or participated in the mob's activities. Far from opposing established institutions, many supporters of Shays's Rebellion honored their leaders "by no less decisive marks of popular favor than elections to local offices of trust and authority."[8] It was above all the existence of such elections that forced local magistrates to reflect community feelings and so prevented their becoming the targets of insurrections. Certainly in New England, where the town meeting ruled, and to some extent in New York, where aldermen and councilmen were annually elected, this was true; yet even in Philadelphia, with its lethargic closed corporation, or Charleston, which lacked municipal institutions, authority was normally exerted by residents who had an immediate sense of local sentiment. Provincial governments were also for the most part kept alert to local feelings by their elected assemblies. Sometimes, of course, uprisings turned against domestic American institutions—as in Pennsylvania in 1764, when the "Paxton Boys" complained that the colony's Quaker assembly had failed to provide adequately for their defense against the Indians. But uprisings over local issues proved extrainstitutional in character more often than they were anti-institutional; they served the community where no law existed, or intervened beyond what magistrates thought they could do officially to cope with a local problem.

The case was different when imperial authority was involved. There legal authority emanated from a capital an ocean away, where the colonists had no integral voice in the formation of policy, where governmental decisions were based largely upon the reports of "king's men" and sought above all to promote the king's interests. When London's legal authority and local interest conflicted, efforts to implement the edicts of royal officials were often answered by uprisings, and it was not unusual in these cases for local magistrates to participate or openly sympathize with the insurgents. The colonial response to the White Pines Acts of 1722 and 1729 is one example. Enforcement of the acts was difficult in general because "the various elements of colonial society . . . seemed inclined to violate the pine laws—legislatures, lumbermen, and merchants were against them, and even the royal governors were divided." At Exeter, New Hampshire, in 1734 about thirty men prevented royal officials from putting the king's broad arrow on some seized boards; efforts to enforce the acts in Connecticut during the 1750's ended after a deputy of the surveyor-general was thrown in a pond and nearly drowned; five years later logs seized in Massachusetts and New Hampshire were either "rescued" or destroyed.[9] Two other imperial issues that provoked local American uprisings long before 1765 and continued to do so during the Revolutionary period were impressment and customs enforcement.

As early as 1743 the colonists' violent opposition to impressment was said to indicate a "Contempt of Government." Some captains had been mobbed, the Admiralty complained, "others emprisoned, and afterwards held to exorbitant Bail, and are now under Prosecutions carried on by Combination, and by joint Subscription towards the expense." Colonial governors, despite their offers, furnished captains with little real aid either to procure seamen or "even to protect them from the Rage and Insults of the People." Two days of severe rioting answered Commodore Charles Knowles's efforts to sweep Boston harbor for able-bodied men in November 1747. Again in 1764 when Rear Admiral Lord Alexander Colville sent out orders to "procure" men in principal harbors between Casco Bay and Cape Henlopen, mobs met the ships at every turn. When the *St. John* sent out a boat to seize a recently impressed deserter from a Newport wharf, a mob protected him, captured the boat's officer, and hurled stones at the crew; later fifty Newporters joined the colony's gunner at Fort George in opening fire on the king's ship itself. Under threat to her master the *Chaleur* was forced to release four fishermen seized off Long Island, and when that ship's captain went ashore at New York a mob seized his boat and burned it in the Fields. In the spring of 1765 after the *Maidstone* capped a six-month siege of Newport harbor by seizing "all the Men" out of a brigantine from Africa, a mob of about five hundred men similarly seized a ship's officer and burned one of her boats on the Common. Impressment also met mass resistance at Norfolk in 1767 and was a major cause of the famous *Liberty* riot at Boston in 1768.[10]

Like the impressment uprisings, which in most instances sought to protect or rescue men from the "press," customs incidents were aimed at impeding the customs service in enforcing British laws. Tactics varied, and although incidents occurred long before 1764—in 1719, for example, Caleb Heathcote reported a "riotous and tumultuous" rescue of seized claret by Newporters—their frequency, like those of the impressment "riots," apparently increased after the Sugar Act was passed and customs enforcement efforts were tightened. The 1764 rescue of the *Rhoda* in Rhode Island preceded a theft in Dighton, Massachusetts, of the cargo from a newly seized vessel, the *Polly*, by a mob of some forty men with blackened faces. In 1766 again a mob stoned a customs official's home in Falmouth (Portland), Maine, while "Persons unknown and disguised" stole sugar and rum that had been impounded that morning. The intimidation of customs officials and of the particularly despised customs informers also enjoyed a long history. In 1701 the South Carolina attorney general publicly attacked an informer "and struck him several times, crying out, this is the Informer, this is he that will ruin the country." Similar assaults occurred decades later, in New Haven in 1766 and 1769, and New London in 1769, and were then often distinguished by their brutality. In 1771 a Providence tidesman, Jesse Saville, was seized, stripped, bound hand and foot, tarred and feathered, had dirt thrown in his face, then was beaten and "almost strangled." Even more thorough assaults upon two other Rhode Island tidesmen followed in July 1770 and upon Collector Charles Dudley in April 1771. Finally, customs vessels came under attack: the *St. John* was shelled at Newport in 1764 where the customs ship *Liberty* was sunk in 1769—both episodes that served as prelude to the destruction of the *Gaspée* outside Providence in 1772.[11]

Such incidents were not confined to New England. Philadelphia witnessed some of the most savage attacks, and even the surveyor of Sassafras and Bohemia in Maryland—an office long a sinecure, since no ships entered or cleared in Sassafras or Bohemia—met with violence when he tried to execute his office in March 1775. After seizing two wagons of goods being carried overland from Maryland toward Duck Creek, Delaware, the officer was overpowered by a "licentious mob" that kept shouting "Liberty and Duck Creek forever" as it went through the hours-long rituals of tarring and feathering him and threatening his life. And at Norfolk, Virginia, in the spring 1766 an accused customs informer was tarred and feathered, pelted with stones and rotten eggs, and finally thrown in the sea where he nearly drowned. Even Georgia saw customs violence before independence, and one of the rare deaths resulting from a colonial riot occurred there in 1775.[12]

White Pines, impressment, and customs uprisings have attracted historians' attention because they opposed British authority and so seemed to presage the Revolution. In fact, however, they had much in common with many exclusively local uprisings. In each of the incidents violence was directed not so much against the "rich and powerful"[13] as against men who—as it was said after the Norfolk smallpox incident—"in every part of their conduct .. acted very inconsistently as good neighbors or citizens." The effort remained one of safeguarding not the interests of isolated groups alone, but the community's safety and welfare. The White Pines Acts need not have provoked this opposition had they applied only to trees of potential use to the Navy, and had they been framed and executed with concern for colonial rights. But instead the acts reserved to the Crown all white pine trees including those "utterly unfit for masts, yards, or bowsprits," and prevented colonists from using them for building materials or lumber exportation even in regions where white pine constituted the principal forest growth. As a result the acts "operated so much against the convenience and even necessities of the inhabitants," Surveyor John Wentworth explained, that "it became almost a general interest of the country" to frustrate the acts' execution. Impressment offered a more immediate effect, since the "press" could quickly cripple whole towns. Merchants and masters were affected as immediately as seamen: the targeted port, as Massachusetts' Governor William Shirley explained in 1747, was drained of mariners by both impressment itself and the flight of navigation to safer provinces, driving the wages for any remaining seamen upward. When the press was of long duration, moreover, or when it took place during a normally busy season, it could mean serious shortages of good or firewood for winter, and a general attrition of the commercial life that sustained all strata of society in trading towns. Commerce seemed even more directly attacked by British trade regulations, particularly by the proliferation of customs procedures in the mid-1760's that seemed to be in no American's interest, and by the Sugar Act with its virtual prohibition of the trade with the foreign West Indies that sustained the economies of colonies like Rhode Island. As a result even when only a limited contingent of sailors participated in a customs incident officials could suspect—as did the deputy collector at Philadelphia in 1770—that the mass of citizens "in their Hearts" approved of it.[14]

Because the various uprisings discussed here grew out of concerns essential to wide sections of the community, the "rioters" were not necessarily confined to the seamen, servants, Negroes, and boys generally described as the staple components of the colonial mob. The uprising of Exeter, New Hampshire, townsmen against the king's surveyor of the woods in 1754 was organized by a member of the prominent Gillman family who was a mill owner and a militia officer. Members of the upper classes participated in Norfolk's smallpox uprising, and Cornelius Calvert, who was later attacked in a related incident, protested that leading members of the community, doctors and magistrates, had posted securities for the good behavior of the "Villains" convicted of mobbing him. Captain Jeremiah Morgan complained about the virtually universal participation of Norfolkers in an impressment incident of 1767, and "all the principal Gentlemen in Town" were supposedly present when a customs informer was tarred and feathered there in 1766. Merchant Benedict Arnold admitted leading a New Haven mob against an informer in 1766; New London merchants Joseph Packwood and Nathaniel Shaw commanded the mob that first accosted Captain William Reid the night the *Liberty* was destroyed at Newport in 1769, just as John Brown, a leading Providence merchant, led that against the *Gaspée*. Charles Dudley reported in April 1771 that the men who beat him in Newport "did not come from the . . . lowest class of Men," but were "stiled Merchants and the Masters of their Vessels"; and again in 1775 Robert Stratford Byrne said many of his Maryland and Pennsylvania attackers were "from Appearance . . . Men of Property." It is interesting, too, that during Shays's Rebellion—so often considered a class uprising—"men who were of good property and owed not a shilling" were said to be "involved in the train of desperado's to suppress the courts."[15]

Opposition to impressment and customs enforcement in itself was not, moreover, the only cause of the so-called impressment or customs "riots." The complete narratives of these incidents indicate again not only that the crowd acted to support local interests, but that it sometimes enforced the will of local magistrates by extralegal means. Although British officials blamed the *St. John* incident upon that ship's customs and impressment activities, colonists insisted that the confrontation began when some sailors stole a few pigs and chickens from a local miller and the ship's crew refused to surrender the thieves to Newport officials. Two members of the Rhode Island council then ordered the gunner of Fort George to detain the schooner until the accused seamen were delivered to the sheriff, and "many People went over the Fort to assist the Gunner in the Discharge of his Duty." Only after this uprising did the ship's officers surrender the accused men.[16] Similarly, the 1747 Knowles impressment riot in Boston and the 1765 *Maidstone* impressment riot in Newport broke out after governors' request for the release of impressed seamen had gone unanswered, and only after the outbreaks of violence were the governors' requests honored. The crowd that first assembled on the night the *Liberty* was destroyed in Newport also began by demanding the allegedly drunken sailors who that afternoon had abused and shot at a colonial captain, Joseph Packwood, so they could be bound over to local magistrates for prosecution.[17]

In circumstances such as these, the "mob" often appeared only after the legal channels of redress had proven inadequate. The main thrust of the colonists' resistance to the White Pines Acts had always been made in their courts and legislatures. Violence broke out only in local situations where no alternative was available. Even the burning of the *Gaspée* in June 1772 was a last resort. Three months before the incident a group of prominent Providence citizens complained about the ship's wanton severity with all vessels along the coast and the colony's governor pressed their case with the fleet's admiral. The admiral, however, supported the *Gaspée*'s commander, Lieutenant William Dudingston; and thereafter, the *Providence Gazette* reported, Dudingston became "more haughty, insolent and intolerable, . . . personally ill treating every master and merchant of the vessels he boarded, stealing sheep, hogs, poultry, etc. from farmers round the bay, and cutting down their fruit and other trees for firewood." Redress from London was possible but time-consuming, and in the meantime Rhode Island was approaching what its governor called "the deepest calamity" as supplies of food and fuel were curtailed and prices, especially in Newport, rose steeply. It was significant that merchant John Brown finally led the Providence "mob" that seized the moment in June when the *Gaspée* ran aground near Warwick, for it was he who had spearheaded the effort in March 1772 to win redress through the normal channels of government.[18]

II

There was little that was distinctively American about the colonial insurrections. The uprisings over grain exportations during times of dearth, the attacks on brothels, press gangs, royal forest officials, and customsmen, all had their counterparts in seventeenth- and eighteenth-century England. Even the Americans' hatred of the customs establishment mirrored the Englishman's traditional loathing of excisemen. Like the customsmen in the colonies, they seemed to descend into localities armed with extraordinary prerogative powers. Often, too, English excisemen were "thugs and brutes who beat up their victims without compunction or stole or wrecked their property" and against whose extravagances little redress was possible through the law.[19] Charges of an identical character were made in the colonies against customsmen and naval officials as well, particularly after 1763 when officers of the Royal Navy were commissioned as deputy members of the customs service,[20] and a history of such accusations lay behind many of the best-known waterfront insurrections. The Americans' complaints took on particular significance only because in the colonies those officials embodied the authority of a "foreign" power. Their arrogance and arbitrariness helped effect "an estrangement of the Affections of the People from the Authority under which they act," and eventually added an emotional element of anger against the Crown to a revolutionary conflict otherwise carried on in the language of law and right.[21]

The focused character of colonial uprisings also resembled those in England and even France where, Rudé has pointed out, crowds were remarkably single-minded and discriminating.[22] Targets were characteristically related to grievances: the Knowles rioters sought only the release of the impressed men; they set free a captured officer when assured he had nothing to do with the press, and refrained from burning a boat near Province House for fear the fire would spread. The Norfolk rioters, driven by fear of smallpox, forcefully isolated the inoculated persons where they would be least dangerous. Even the customs rioters vented their brutality on customs officers and informers alone, and the Shaysite "mobs" dispersed after closing the courts which promised most immediately to effect their ruin. So domesticated and controlled was the Boston mob that it refused to riot on Saturday and Sunday nights, which were considered holy by New Englanders.[23]

When colonists compared their mobs with those in the Mother Country they were struck only with the greater degree of restraint among Americans. "These People bear no Resemblance to an English Mobs," John Jay wrote of the Shaysites in December 1786, "they are more temperate, cool and regular in their Conduct—they have hitherto abstained from Plunder, nor have they that I know of committed any outrages but such as the accomplishment of their Purpose made necessary." Similar comparisons were often repeated during the Revolutionary conflict, and were at least partially grounded in fact. When Londoners set out to "pull down" houses of ill fame in 1688, for example, the affair spread, prisons were opened, and disorder ended only when troops were called out. But when eighteenth-century Bostonians set out on the same task, there is no record that their destruction extended beyond the bordellos themselves. Even the violence of the customs riots—which contrast in that regard from other American incidents—can sometimes be explained by the presence of volatile foreign seamen. The attack on the son of customsman John Hatton, who was nearly killed in a Philadelphia riot, occurred, for example, when the city was crowded by over a thousand seamen. His attackers were apparently Irish crew members of a vessel he and his father had tried to seize off Cape May, and they were "set on," the Philadelphia collector speculated, by an Irish merchant in Philadelphia to whom the vessel was consigned. One of the most lethal riots in the history of colonial America, in which rioters killed five people, occurred in a small town near Norfolk, Virginia, and was significantly perpetrated entirely by British seamen who resisted the local inhabitants' efforts to reinstitute peace.[24] During and immediately after the Revolutionary War some incidents occurred in which deaths are recorded; but contemporaries felt these were historical aberrations, caused by the "brutalizing" effect of the war itself. "Our citizens, from a habit of putting . . . [the British] to death, have reconciled their minds to the killing of each other," South Carolina Judge Aedanus Burke explained.[25]

To a large extent the pervasive restraint and virtual absence of bloodshed in American incidents can best be understood in terms of social and military circumstance. There was no large amorphous city in America comparable to London, where England's worst incidents occurred. More important, the casualties even in eighteenth-century British riots were rarely the work of rioters. No deaths were inflicted by the Wilkes, Anti-Irish, or "No Popery" mobs, and only single fatalities resulted from other upheavals such as the Porteous riots of 1736. "It was authority rather than the crowd that was conspicuous for its violence to life and limb": all 285 casualties of the Gordon riots, for example, were rioters.[26] Since a regular army was less at the ready for use against colonial mobs, casualty figures for American uprisings were naturally much reduced.

To some extent the general tendency toward a discriminating purposefulness was shared by mobs throughout western Europe, but within the British Empire the focused character of popular uprisings and also their persistence can be explained in part by the character of law enforcement procedures. There were no professional police forces in the eighteenth century. Instead the power of government depended traditionally upon institutions like the "hue and cry," by which the community in general rose to apprehend felons. In its original medieval form the "hue and cry" was a form of summary justice that resembled modern lynch law. More commonly by the eighteenth century magistrates turned to the *posse commitatus*, literally the "power of the country," and in practice all able-bodied men a sheriff might call upon to assist him. Where greater and more organized support was needed, magistrates could call out the militia.[27] Both the *posse* and the militia drew upon local men, including many of the same persons who made up the mob. This was particularly clear where these traditional mechanisms failed to function effectively. At Boston in September 1766 when customsmen contemplated breaking into the house of merchant Daniel Malcom to search for contraband goods, Sheriff Stephen Greenleaf threatened to call for support from members of the very crowd suspected of an intent to riot; and when someone suggested during the Stamp Act riots that the militia be raised Greenleaf was told it had already risen. This situation meant that mobs could naturally assume the manner of a lawful institution, acting by habit with relative restraint and responsibility. On the other hand, the militia institutionalized the practice of forcible popular coercion and so made the formation of extralegal mobs more natural that J. R. Western has called the militia "a relic of the bad old days," and hailed its passing as "a step towards . . . bringing civilization and humanity into our [English] political life."[28]

These law enforcement mechanisms left magistrates virtually helpless whenever a large segment of the population was immediately involved in the disorder, or when the community had a strong sympathy for the rioters. The Boston militia's failure to act in the Stamp Act riots, which was repeated in nearly all the North American colonies, recapitulated a similar refusal during the Knowles riot of 1747.[29] If the mob's sympathizers were confined to a single locality, the governor could try to call out the militias of surrounding areas, as Massachusetts Governor William Shirley began to do in 1747, and as, to some extent, Governor Francis Bernard attempted after the rescue of the *Polly* in 1765.[30] In the case of sudden uprisings, however, these peace-keeping mechanisms were at best partially effective since they required time to assemble strength, which often made the effort wholly pointless.

When the disorder continued and the militia either failed to appear or proved insufficient, there was, of course, the army, which was used periodically in the eighteenth century against rioters in England and Scotland. Even in America peacetime garrisons tended to be placed where they might serve to maintain law and order. But since all Englishmen shared a fear of standing armies the deployment of troops had always to be a sensitive and carefully limited recourse. Military and civil spheres of authority were rigidly separated, as was clear to Lord Jeffrey Amherst, who refused to use soldiers against antimilitary rioters during the Seven Years' War because that function was "entirely foreign to their command and belongs of right to none but the civil power." In fact troops could be used against British subjects, as in the suppression of civil disorder, only upon the request of local magistrates. This institutional inhibition carried, if anything, more weight in the colonies. There royal governors had quickly lost their right to declare martial law without the consent of the provincial councils that were, again, usually filled with local men.[31]

For all practical purposes, then, when a large political unit such as an entire town or colony condoned an act of mass force, problems were raised "almost insoluble without rending the whole fabric of English law." Nor was the situation confined to the colonies. After describing England's institutions for keeping the peace under the later Stuarts, Max Beloff suggested that no technique for maintaining order was found until nineteenth-century reformers took on the task of reshaping urban government. Certainly by the 1770's no acceptable solution had been found—neither by any colonists, nor "anyone in London, Paris, or Rome, either," as Carl Bridenbaugh has put it. To even farsighted contemporaries like John Adams the weakness of authority was a fact of the social order that necessarily conditioned the way rulers could act. "It is vain to expect or hope to carry on government against the universal bent and genius of the people," he wrote, "we may whimper and whine as much as we will, but nature made it impossible when she made man."[32]

The mechanisms of enforcing public order were rendered even more fragile since the difference between legal and illegal applications of mass force was distinct in theory, but sometimes indistinguishable in practice. The English common law prohibited riot, defined as an uprising of three or more persons who performed what Blackstone called an "unlawful act of violence" for a private purpose. If the act was never carried out or attempted the offense became unlawful assembly; if some effort was made toward its execution, rout; and if the purpose of the uprising was public rather than private—tearing down whore houses, for example, or destroying all enclosures rather than just those personally affecting the insurgents—the offense became treason since it constituted a usurpation of the king's function, a "levying war against the King." The precise legal offense lay not so much in the purpose of the uprising as in its use of force and violence "wherein the Law does not allow the Use of such Force." Such unlawful assumptions of force were carefully distinguished by commentators upon the common law from other occasions on which the law authorized a use of force. It was, for example, legal for force to be used by a sheriff, constable, "or perhaps even . . . a private Person" who assembled "a competent Number of People, in Order with Force to suppress Rebels, or Enemies, or Rioters"; for a justice of the peace to raise the *posse* when opposed in detaining lands, or for Crown officers to raise "a Power as may effectually enable them to over-power any . . . Resistance" in the execution of the king's writs.[33]

In certain situations these distinctions offered at best a very uncertain guide as to who did or did not exert force lawfully. Should a *posse* employ more force than was necessary to overcome overt resistance, for example, its members acted illegally and were indictable for riot. And where established officials supported both sides in a confrontation, or where the legality of an act that officials were attempting to enforce was itself disputed, the decision as to who were or were not rioters seemed to depend upon the observer's point of view. Impressment is a good example. The colonists claimed that impressment was unlawful in North America under an act of 1708, while British authorities and some—but not all—spokesmen for the government held that the law had lapsed in 1713. The question was settled only in 1775, when Parliament finally repealed the "Sixth of Anne." Moreover, supposing impressment could indeed be carried on, were press warrants from provincial authorities still necessary? Royal instructions of 1697 had given royal governors the "sole power of impressing seamen in any of our plantations in America or in sight of them." Admittedly that clause was dropped in 1708, and a subsequent parliamentary act of 1746, which required the full consent of the governor and council before impressment could be carried on within their province, applied only to the West Indies. Nonetheless it seems that in 1764 the Lords of the Admiralty thought the requirement held throughout North America.[34] With the legality of impressment efforts so uncertain, especially when opposed by local authorities, it was possible to see the press gangs as "rioters" for trying en masse to perpetrate an unlawful act of violence. In that case the local townsmen who opposed them might be considered lawful defenders of the public welfare, acting much as they would in a posse. In 1770 John Adams cited opposition to press gangs who acted without warrants as an example of the lawful use of force; and when the sloop of war Hornet swept into Norfolk, Virginia, in September 1767 with a "bloody riotous plan . . . to impress seamen, without consulting the Mayor, or any other magistrate," the offense was charged to the pressmen. Roused by the watchman, who called out "a riot by man of war's men," the inhabitants rose to back the magistrates, and not only secured the release of the impressed men but also imprisoned ten members of the press gang. The ship's captain, on the other hand, condemned the townsmen as "Rioters." Ambiguity was present, too, in Newport's St. John clash, which involved both impressment and criminal action on the part of royal seamen and culminated with Newporters firing on the king's ship. The Privy Council in England promptly classified the incident as a riot, but the Rhode Island governor's report boldly maintained that "the people meant nothing but to assist [the magistrates] in apprehending the Offenders" on the vessel, and even suggested that "their Conduct be honored with his Majesty's royal Approbation."[35]

The enforcement of the White Pines Acts was similarly open to legal dispute. The acts seemed to violate both the Massachusetts and Connecticut charters; the meaning of provisions exempting trees growing within townships (act of 1722) and those which were "the property of private persons" (act of 1729) was contested, and royal officials tended to work on the basis of interpretations of the laws that Bernhard Knollenberg has called farfetched and, in one case, "utterly untenable." The Exeter, New Hampshire, "riot" of 1734, for example, answered an attempt of the surveyor to seize boards on the argument that the authorization to seize logs from allegedly illegally felled white pine trees in the act of 1722 included an authorization to seize processed lumber. As a result, Knollenberg concluded, although the surveyors' reports "give the impression that the New Englanders were an utterly lawless lot, . . . in many if not most cases they were standing for what they believed, with reason, were their legal and equitable rights in tree growing on their own lands."[36]

Occasions open to such conflicting interpretations were rare. Most often even those who sympathized with the mobs' motives condemned its use of force as illegal and unjustifiable. That ambiguous cases did arise, however, indicates that legitimacy and illegitimacy, posses and rioters, represented but poles of the same spectrum. And where a mob took upon itself the defense of the community, it benefited from a certain popular legitimacy even when the strict legality of its action was in doubt, particularly among a people taught that the legitimacy of law itself depended upon its defense of the public welfare.

Whatever quasi-legal status mobs were accorded by local communities was reinforced, moreover, by formal political thought. "Riots and rebellions" were often calmly accepted as a constant and even necessary element of free government. This acceptance depended, however, upon certain essential assumptions about popular uprisings. With words that could be drawn amost verbatim from John Locke or any other English author of similar convictions, colonial writers posited a continuing moderation and purposefulness on the part of the mob. "Tho' innocent Persons may sometimes suffer in popular Tumults," observed a 1768 writer in the New York Journal, "yet the general Resentment of the People is principally directed according to Justice, and the greatest Delinquent feels it most." Moreover, upheavals constituted only occasional interruptions in well-governed societies. "Good Laws and good Rulers will always be obey'd and respected"; "the Experience of all Ages proves, that Mankind are much more likely to submit to bad Laws and wicked Rulers, than to resist good ones." "Mobs and Tumults," it was often said, "never happen but thro' Oppression and a scandalous Abuse of Power."[37]

In the hands of Locke such remarks constituted relatively inert statements of fact. Colonial writers, however, often turned these pronouncements on their heads such that observed instances of popular disorder became prima facie indictments of authority. In 1747, for example, New Jersey land rioters argued that "from their Numbers, Violences, and unlawful Actions" it was to be "inferred that . . . they are wronged and oppressed, or else they would never rebell agt. the Laws." Always, a New York writer said in 1770, when "the People of any Government" become "turbulent and uneasy," it was above all "a certain Sign of Maladministration." Even when disorders were not directly levelled against government they provided "strong proofs that something is much amiss in the state" as William Samuel Johnson put it; that—in Samuel Adams's words—the "wheels of good government" were "somewhat clogged." Americans who used this argument against Britain in the 1760's continued to depend upon it two decades later when they reacted to Shays's Rebellion by seeking out the public "Disease" in their own independent governments that was indicated by the "Spirit of Licentiousness" in Massachusetts.[38]

Popular turbulence seemed to follow so naturally from inadequacies of government that uprisings were often described with similes from the physical world. In 1770 John Adams said that there was "Church-quakes and state-quakes in the moral and political world, as well as earthquakes, storms and tempests in the physical." Two years earlier a writer in the New York Journal likened popular tumults to "Thunder Gusts" which "commonly do more Good than Harm." Thomas Jefferson continued the imagery in the 1780's, particularly with his famous statement that he liked "a little rebellion now and then" for it was "like a storm in the atmosphere." It was, moreover, because of the "imperfection of all things in this world," including government, that Adams found it "vain to seek a government in all points free from a possibility of civil wars, tumults and seditions." That was "a blessing denied to this life and preserved to complete the felicity of the next."[39]

If popular uprisings occurred "in all governments at all times," they were nonetheless most able to break out in free governments. Tyrants imposed order and submission upon their subjects by force, thus dividing society, as Jefferson said, into wolves and sheep. Only under free governments were the people "nervous," spirited, jealous of their rights, ready to react against unjust provocations; and this being the case, popular disorders could be interpreted as "Symptoms of a strong and healthy Constitution" even while they indicated some lesser shortcoming in administration. It would be futile, Josiah Quincy, Jr., said in 1770, to expect "that pacific, timid, obsequious, and servile temper, so predominant in more despotic governments" from those who lived under free British institutions. From "our happy constitution," he claimed, there resulted as "very natural Effects" an "impatience of injuries, and a strong resentment of insults."[40]

This popular impatience constituted an essential force in the maintenance of free institutions. "What country can preserve it's [sic] liberties if their rulers are not warned from time to time that their people preserve the spirit of resistance?" Jefferson asked in 1787. Occasional insurrections were thus "an evil . . . productive of good": even those founded on popular error tended to hold rulers "to the true principles of their institution" and generally provided "a medecine necessary for the sound health of government." This meant that an aroused people had a role not only in extreme situations, where revolution was requisite, but in the normal course of free government. For that reason members of the House of Lords could seriously argue—as A. J. P. Taylor has pointed out— that "rioting is an essential part of our constitution"; and for that reason, too, even Massachusetts's conservative Lieutenant Governor Thomas Hutchinson could remark in 1768 that "mobs a sort of them at least are constitutional."[41]

III

It was, finally, the interaction of this constitutional role of the mob with the written law that makes the story of eighteenth-century popular uprisings complexity itself.[42] If mobs were appreciated because they provided a check on power, it was always understood that, insofar as upheavals threatened "running to such excesses, as will overturn the whole system of government," "strong discouragements" had to be provided against them. For eighteenth-century Americans, like the English writers they admired, liberty demanded the rule of law. In extreme situations where the rulers had clearly chosen arbitrary power over the limits of law, men like John Adams could prefer the risk of anarchy to continued submission because "anarchy can never last long, and tyranny may be perpetual," but only when "there was any hope that the fair order of liberty and a free constitution would arise out of it." This desire to maintain the orderly rule of law led legislatures in England and the colonies to pass antiriot statutes and to make strong efforts—in the words of a 1753 Massachusetts law—to discountenance "a mobbish temper and spirit in . . . the inhabitants" that would oppose "all government and order."[43]

The problem of limiting mass violence was dealt with most intensely over a sustained period by the American Revolutionary leadership, which has perhaps suffered most from historians' earlier inattention to the history of colonial uprisings. So long as it could be maintained—as it was only fifteen years ago—that political mobs were "rare or unknown in America" before the 1760's, the Revolutionaries were implicitly credited with their creation. American patriots, Charles McLean Andrews wrote, were often "lawless men who were nothing more than agitators and demagogues" and who attracted a following from the riffraff of colonial society. It now seems clear that the mob drew on all elements of the population. More important, the Revolutionary leaders had no need to create mob support. Instead they were forced to work with a "permanent entity," a traditional crowd that exerted itself before, after, and even during the Revolutionary struggle over issues unrelated to the conflict with Britain, and that, as Hobsbawm has noted, characteristically aided the Revolutionary cause in the opening phases of conflict but was hard to discipline thereafter.[44]

In focusing popular exuberance the American leaders could work with long-established tendencies in the mob toward purposefulness and responsibility. In doing so they could, moreover, draw heavily upon the guidelines for direct action that had been defined by English radical writers since the seventeenth century. Extralegal action was justified only when all established avenues to redress had failed. It could not answer casual errors or private failings on the part of the magistrates, but had to await fundamental public abuses so egregious that the "whole people" turned against their rulers. Even then, it was held, opposition had to be measured so that no more force was exerted than was necessary for the public good. Following these principles colonial leaders sought by careful organization to avoid the excesses that first greeted the Stamp Act. Hutchinson's query after a crowd in Connecticut had forced the resignation of stampman Jared Ingersoll—whether "such a public regular assembly can be called a mob"—could with equal appropriateness have been repeated during the tea resistance, or in 1774 when Massachusetts *mandamus* councillors were forced to resign.[45]

From the first appearance of an organized resistance movement in 1765, moreover, efforts were made to support the legal magistrates such that, as John Adams said in 1774, government would have "as much vigor then as ever" except where its authority was specifically under dispute. This concern for the maintenance of order and the general framework of law explains why the American Revolution was largely free from the "universal tumults and all the irregularities and violence of mobbish factions [that] naturally arise when legal authority ceases." It explains, too, why old revolutionaries like Samuel Adams or Christopher Gadsden disapproved of those popular conventions and commit-tees that persisted after regular independent state governments were estab-lished in the 1770's. "Decency and Respect [are] due to Constitutional Author-ity," Samuel Adams said in 1784, "and those Men, who under any Pretence or by any Means whatever, would lessen the Weight of Government lawfully exercised must be Enemies to our happy Revolution and the Common Lib-erty."[46]

In normal circumstances the "strong discouragements" to dangerous disorder were provided by established legislatures. The measures enacted by them to deal with insurrections were shaped by the eighteenth-century understanding of civil uprisings. Since turbulence indicated above all some shortcoming in government, it was never to be met by increasing the authorities' power of suppression. The "weakness of authority" that was a function of its dependence upon popular support appeared to contemporary Americans as a continuing virtue of British institutions, as one reason why rulers could not simply dictate to their subjects and why Britain had for so long been hailed as one of the freest nations in Europe. It was "far less dangerous to the Freedom of a State" to allow "the laws to be trampled upon, by the licence among the rabble . . . than to dispence with their force by an act of power." Insurrections were to be answered by reform, by attacking the "Disease"—to use John Jay's term of 1786—that lay behind them rather than by suppressing its "Symptoms." And ultimately, as William Samuel Johnson observed in 1768, "the only effectual way to prevent them is to govern with wisdom, justice, and moderation."[47]

In immediate crises, however, legislatures in both England and America resorted to special legislation that supplemented the common law prohibition of riot. The English Riot Act of 1714 was passed when disorder threatened to disrupt the accession of George I; a Connecticut act of 1722 followed a rash of incidents over land title in Hartford County; the Massachusetts act of 1751 answered "several tumultuous assemblies" over the currency issue and another of 1786 was enacted at the time of Shays's Rebellion. The New Jersey legislature passed an act in 1747 during that colony's protracted land riots; Pennsylvania's Riot Act of 1764 was inspired by the Paxton Boys; North Carolina's of 1771 by the Regulators; New York's of 1774 by the "land wars" in Charlotte and Albany [counties].[48] Always the acts specified that the magistrates were to depend upon the *posse* in enforcing their provisions, and in North Carolina on the militia as well. They differed over the number of people who had to remain "unlawfully, riotously, and tumultuously assembled together, to the Disturbance of the Publick Peace" for one hour after the reading of a prescribed riot proclamation before becoming judicable under the act. Some colonies specified lesser punishments than the death penalty provided for in the English act, but the American statutes were not in general more "liberal" than the British. Two of them so violated elementary judicial rights that they were subsequently condemned—North Carolina's by Britain, and New York's act of 1774 by a later, Revolutionary state legislature.[49]

In one important respect, however, the English Riot Act was reformed. Each colonial riot law, except that of Connecticut, was enacted for only one to three years, whereas the British law was perpetual. By this provision colonial legislators avoided the shortcoming which, it was said, was "more likely to introduce *arbitrary Power* than even an *Army* itself," because a perpetual riot act meant that "in all future time" by "reading a Proclamation" the Crown had the power "of hanging up their Subjects wholesale, or of picking out Those, to whom they have the greatest Dislike." If the death penalty was removed, the danger was less. When, therefore, riot acts without limit of time were finally enacted—as Connecticut had done in 1722, Massachusetts in 1786, New Jersey in 1797—the punishments were considerably milder, providing, for example, for imprisonment not exceeding six months in Connecticut, one year in Massachusetts, and three years in New Jersey.[50]

Riot legislation, it is true, was not the only recourse against insurgents, who throughout the eighteenth century could also be prosecuted for treason. The colonial and state riot acts suggest, nonetheless, that American legislators recognized the participants in civil insurrections as guilty of a crime peculiarly complicated because it had social benefits as well as damages. To some degree, it appears, they shared the idea expressed well by Jefferson in 1787: that "honest republican governors" should be "so mild in their punishments of rebellions, as not to discourage them too much."[51] Even in countering riots the legislators seemed as intent upon preventing any perversion of the forces of law and order by established authorities as with chastising the insurgents. Reform of the English Riot Act thus paralleled the abolition of constituent treasons—a traditional recourse against enemies of the Crown—in American state treason acts of the Revolutionary period and finally in Article III of the Federal Constitution.[52] From the same preoccupation, too, sprang the limitations placed upon the regular army provided for in the Constitution in part to assure the continuation of republican government guaranteed to the states by Article IV, Section iv. Just as the riot acts were for so long limited in duration, appropriations for the army were never to extend beyond two years (Article I, Section vii, 12); and the army could be used within a state against domestic violence only after application by the legislature or governor, if the legislature could not be convened (Article IV, Section iv).

A continuing desire to control authority through popular action also underlay the declaration in the Second Amendment that "a well regulated Militia being necessary to the security of a free State," citizens were assured the "right . . . to keep and bear Arms." The militia was meant above all "to prevent the establishment of a standing army, the bane of liberty"; and the right to bear arms—taken in part from the English Bill of Rights of 1689—was considered a standing threat to would-be tyrants. It embodied "a public allowance, under due restrictions, of the *natural right of resistance and self preservation*, when the sanctions of society and laws are found *insufficient* to restrain the *violence of oppression*." And on the basis of their eighteenth-century experience, Americans could consider that right to be "perfectly harmless. . . . If the government be equitable; if it be reasonable in its exactions; if proper attention be paid to the education of children in knowledge, and religion," Timothy Dwight declared, "few men will be disposed to use arms, unless for their amusement, and for the defence of themselves and their country."[53]

The need felt to continue the eighteenth-century militia as a counterweight to government along with the efforts to outlaw rioting and to provide for the use of a standing army against domestic insurrections under carefully defined circumstances together illustrate the complex attitude toward peacekeeping that prevailed among the nation's founders. The rule of law had to be maintained, yet complete order was neither expected nor even desired when it could be purchased, it seemed, only at the cost of forcefully suppressing the spirit of a free people. The constant possibility of insurrection—as institutionalized in the militia—was to remain an element of the United States Constitution, just as it had played an essential role in Great Britain's.

This readiness to accept some degree of tumultuousness depended to a large degree upon the lawmakers' own experience with insurrections in the eighteenth century, when "disorder" was seldom anarchic and "rioters" often acted to defend law and justice rather than to oppose them. In the years after independence this toleration declined, in part because mass action took on new dimensions. Nineteenth-century mobs often resembled in outward form those of the previous century, but a new violence was added. Moreover, the literal assumption of popular rule in the years after Lexington taught many thoughtful Revolutionary partisans what was for them an unexpected lesson—that the people were "as capable of despotism as any prince," that "public liberty was no guarantee after all of private liberty."[54] With home rule secured, attention focused more exclusively upon minority rights, which mob action had always to some extent imperiled. And the danger that uprisings carried for individual freedom became ever more egregious as mobs shed their former restraint and burned Catholic convents, attacked nativist speakers, lynched Mormons, or destroyed the presses and threatened the lives of abolitionists.

Ultimately, however, changing attitudes toward popular uprisings turned upon fundamental transformations in the political perspective of Americans after 1776. Throughout the eighteenth century political institutions had been viewed as in a constant evolution: the colonies' relationship with Britain and with each other, even the balance of power within the governments of various colonies, remained unsettled. Under such circumstances the imputations of governmental shortcoming that uprisings carried could easily be accepted and absorbed. But after Independence, when the form and conduct of the Americans' governments were under their exclusive control, and when those governments represented, moreover, an experiment in republicanism on which depended their own happiness and "that of generations unborn," Americans became less ready to endure domestic turbulence or accept its disturbing implications. Some continued to argue that "distrust and dissatisfaction" on the part of the multitude were "always the consequence of tyranny or corruption." Others, however, began to see domestic turbulence not as indictments but as insults to government that were likely to discredit American republicanism in the eyes of European observers. "Mobs are a reproach to Free Governments," where all grievances could be legally redressed through the courts or the ballot box, it was argued in 1783. They originated there "not in Oppression, but in Licentiousness," an "ungovernable spirit" among the people. Under republican governments even that distrust of power colonists had found so necessary for liberty, and which uprisings seemed to manifest, could appear outmoded. "There is some consistency in being jealous of power in the hands of those who assume it by birth . . . and over whom we have no controul . . . as was the case with the Crown of England over America," another writer suggested. "But to be jealous of those whom we chuse, the instant we have chosen them" was absurd: perhaps in the transition from monarchy to republic Americans had "bastardized" their ideas by placing jealousy where confidence was more appropriate.[55] In short, the assumptions behind the Americans' earlier toleration of the mob were corroded in republican America. Old and new attitudes coexisted in the 1780's and even later. But the appropriateness of popular uprisings in the United States became increasingly in doubt after the Federal Constitution came to be seen as the final product of long-term institutional experimentation, "a momentous contribution to the history of politics" that rendered even that most glorious exertion of popular force, revolution itself, an obsolete resort for Americans.[56]

Yet this change must not be viewed exclusively as a product of America's distinctive Revolutionary achievement. J. H. Plumb has pointed out that a century earlier, when England passed beyond her revolutionary era and progressed toward political "stability," radical ideology with its talk of resistance and revolution was gradually left behind. A commitment to peace and permanence emerged from decades of fundamental change. In America as in England this stability demanded that operative sovereignty, including the right finally to decide what was and was not in the community's interest, and which laws were and were not constitutional, be entrusted to established governmental institutions. The result was to minimize the role of the people at large, who had been the ultimate arbiters of those questions in English and American Revolutionary thought. Even law enforcement was to become the task primarily of professional agencies. As a result in time all popular upheavals alike became menacing efforts to "pluck up law and justice by the roots," and riot itself gradually became defined as a purposeless act of anarchy, "a blind and misguided ourburst of popular fury," of "undirected violence with no articulated goals."[57]

NOTES

1. See the following by George Rudé: *The Crowd in the French Revolution* (Oxford, 1959); "The London 'Mob' of the Eighteenth Century," *The Historical Journal*, II (1959), 1–18; *Wilkes and Liberty: A Social Study of 1763 to 1774* (Oxford, 1962); *The Crowd in History: A Study of Popular Disturbances in France and England, 1730–1848* (New York, 1964). See also E. J. Hobsbawm, *Primitive Rebels: Studies in Archaic Forms of Social Movement in the 19th and 20th Centuries* (New York, 1959), esp. "The City Mob," 108–125. For recent discussions of the colonial mob see: Bernard Bailyn, *Pamphlets of the American Revolution* (Cambridge, Mass., 1965), I, 581–584; Jesse Lemisch, "Jack Tar in the Street: Merchant Seamen in the Politics of Revolutionary America," *William and Mary Quarterly*, 3d Ser., XXV (1968), 371–407; Gordon S. Wood, "A Note on Mobs in the American Revolution," *Wm. and Mary Qtly.*, 3d Ser., XXIII (1966), 635–642, and more recently Wood's *Creation of the American Republic, 1776–1787* (Chapel Hill, 1969), *passim*, but esp. 319–328. Wood offers an excellent analysis of the place of mobs and extralegal assemblies in the development of American constitutionalism. Hugh D. Graham and Ted R. Gurr, *Violence in America: Historical and Comparative Perspectives* (New York, 1969) primarily discusses uprisings of the 19th and 20th centuries, but see the chapters by Richard M. Brown, "Historical Patterns of Violence in America," 45–84, and "The American Vigilante Tradition," 154–226.

2. Carl Bridenbaugh, *Cities in the Wilderness: The First Century of Urban Life in America, 1625–1742* (New York, 1964), 70–71, 223–224, 382–384; and Carl Bridenbaugh, *Cities in Revolt: Urban Life in America, 1743–1776* (New York, 1964), 113–118; Charles J. Hoadly, ed., *The Public Records of the Colony of Connecticut. . .* (Hartford, 1872), VI, 332–333, 341–348.

3. See particularly Richard M. Brown, *The South Carolina Regulators* (Cambridge, Mass., 1963). There is no published study of the New Jersey land riots, which lasted over a decade and were due above all to the protracted inability of the royal government to settle land disputes stemming from conflicting proprietary grants made in the late 17th century. See, however, "A State of Facts concerning the Riots and Insurrections in New Jersey, and the Remedies Attempted to Restore the Peace of the Province," William A. Whitehead *et al.*, eds., *Archives of the State of New Jersey* (Newark, 1883), VII, 207–226. On other rural insurrections see Irving Mark, *Agrarian Conflicts in Colonial New York, 1711–1775* (New York, 1940), Chap. IV, V; Staughton Lynd, "The Tenant Rising at Livingston Manor," *New York Historical Society Quarterly*, XLVIII (1964), 163–177; Matt Bushnell Jones, *Vermont in the Making, 1750–1777* (Cambridge, Mass., 1939), Chap. XII, XIII; John R. Dunbar, ed., *The Paxton Papers* (The Hague, 1957), esp. 3–51.

4. Richard L. Morton, *Colonial Virginia* (Chapel Hill, 1960), I, 303–304; Jonathan Smith, "The Depression of 1785 and Daniel Shays' Rebellion," *Wm. and Mary Qtly.*, 3d Ser., V (1948), 86–87, 91.

5. Bridenbaugh, *Cities in Revolt*, 114; Bridenbaugh, *Cities in the Wilderness*, 196, 383, 388–389; Edmund S. and Helen M. Morgan, *The Stamp Act Crisis*, rev. ed. (New York, 1963), 159; Anne Rowe Cunningham, ed., *Letters and Diary of John Rowe, Boston Merchant, 1759–1762, 1764–1779* (Boston, 1903), 218. On the marriage riots see *New York Gazette* (New York City), July 11, 1765—and note that when the reporter speaks of persons "concern'd in such unlawful Enterprises" he clearly is referring to the husbands, not their "Disciplinarians." On the Rogerenes see item in *Connecticut Gazette* (New Haven), Apr. 5, 1766, reprinted in Lawrence H. Gipson, *Jared Ingersoll* (New Haven, 1920), 195, n. 1.

6. John Adams, "Novanglus," in Charles F. Adams, ed., *The Works of John Adams* (Boston, 1850–1856), IV, 76–77; Salem news of Jan. 25 and Feb. 1, 1774, in *Providence Gazette* (Rhode Island), Feb. 5, and Feb. 12, 1774.

7. Letter from "Friend to the Borough and county of Norfolk," in Purdie and Dixon's

Virginia Gazette Postscript (Williamsburg), Sept. 8, 1768, which gives the fullest account. This letter answered an earlier letter from Norfolk, Aug. 6, 1768, available in Rind's *Va. Gaz. Supplement* (Wmsbg.), Aug. 25, 1768. See also letter of Cornelius Calvert in Purdie and Dixon's *Va. Gaz.* (Wmsbg.), Jan. 9, 1772. Divisions over the inoculation seemed to follow more general political lines. See Patrick Henderson, "Smallpox and Patriotism, The Norfolk Riots, 1768-1769," *Virginia Magazine of History and Biography*, LXXIII (1965), 413-424.

8. James Madison to Thomas Jefferson, Mar. 19, 1787, in Julian P. Boyd, ed., *The Papers of Thomas Jefferson* (Princeton, 1950-), XI, 223.

9. Bernhard Knollenberg, *Origin of the American Revolution: 1759-1766* (New York, 1965), 126, 129. See also Robert G. Albion, *Forests and Sea Power* (Cambridge, Mass., 1926), 262-263, 265. Joseph J. Malone, *Pine Trees and Politics* (Seattle, 1964), includes less detail on the forceful resistance to the acts.

10. Admiralty to Gov. George Thomas, Sept. 26, 1743, in Samuel Hazard *et al.*, eds., *Pennsylvania Archives* (Philadelphia, 1852-1949), I, 639. For accounts of the Knowles riot see Gov. William Shirley to Josiah Willard, Nov. 19, 1747, Shirley's Proclamation of Nov. 21, 1747, and his letter to the Board of Trade, Dec. 1, 1747, in Charles H. Lincoln, ed., *Correspondence of William Shirley* . . . *1731-1760* (New York, 1912), I, 406-419; see also Thomas Hutchinson, *History of the Province of Massachusetts Bay*, ed. Lawrence S. Mayo (Cambridge, Mass., 1936), II, 330-333; and *Reports of the Record Commissioners of Boston* (Boston, 1885), XIV, 127-130. David Lovejoy, *Rhode Island Politics and the American Revolution, 1760-1776* (Providence, 1958), 36-39, and on the *Maidstone* in particular see "O. G." in *Newport Mercury* (Rhode Island), June 10, 1765. Bridenbaugh, *Cities in Revolt*, 309-311; documents on the St. John episode in *Records of the Colony of Rhode Island and Providence Plantations* (Providence, 1856-1865), VI, 427-430. George G. Wolkins, "The Seizure of John Hancock's Sloop 'Liberty,' " *Massachusetts Historical Society, Proceedings* (1921-1923), LV, 239-284. See also Lemisch, "Jack Tar," *Wm. and Mary Qtly.*, 3d Ser., XXV (1968), 391-393; and Neil R. Stout, "Manning the Royal Navy in North America, 1763-1775," *American Neptune*, XXIII (1963), 179-181.

11. Heathcote letter from Newport, Sept. 7, 1719, *Records of the Colony of Rhode Island*, IV, 259-260; Lovejoy, *Rhode Island Politics*, 35-39. There is an excellent summary of the *Polly* incident in Morgan, Stamp Act Crisis, 59, 64-67; and see also *Providence Gaz.* (R. I.), Apr. 27, 1765. On the Falmouth incident see the letter from the collector and comptroller of Falmouth, Aug. 19, 1766, Treasury Group 1, Class 453, Piece 182, Public Records Office. Hereafter cited as T. 1/453, 182. See also the account in Appendix I of Josiah Quincy, Jr., *Reports of the Cases Argued and Adjudged in the Superior Court of Judicature of the Province of Massachusetts Bay, between 1761 and 1772* (Boston, 1865), 446-447. W. Noel Sainsbury *et al.*, eds., *Calender of State Papers, Colonial Series, America and the West Indies* (London, 1910), *1701*, no. 1042, xi, a. A summary of one of the New Haven informer attacks is in Willard M. Wallace, *Traitorous Hero: The Life and Fortunes of Benedict Arnold* (New York, 1954), 20-23. Arnold's statement on the affair which he led is in Malcolm Decker, *Benedict Arnold, Son of the Havens* (Tarrytown, N. Y., 1932), 27-29. Gipson, in *Jared Ingersoll*, 277-278, relates the later incidents. For the New London informer attacks see documents of July 1769 in T. 1/471. On the Saville affair see Saville to collector and comptroller of customs in Newport, May 18, 1769, T. 1/471, and *New York Journal* (New York City), July 6, 1769. On later Rhode Island incidents see Dudley and John Nicoll to governor of Rhode Island, Aug. 1, 1770, T. 1/471. Dudley to commissioners of customs at Boston, Newport, Apr. 11, 1771, T. 1/482. On the destruction of the *Liberty* see documents in T. 1/471, esp. comptroller and collector to the governor, July 21, 1769.

12. On Philadelphia violence see William Sheppard to commissioners of customs, Apr. 21, 1769, T. 1/471; Deputy Collector at Philadelphia John Swift to commissioners of customs at Boston, Oct. 13, 1769, *ibid.*; and on a particularly brutal attack on the son of customsman John Hatton, see Deputy Collector John Swift to Boston customs commissioners, Nov. 15, 1770, and related documents in T. 1/476. See also Alfred S. Martin, "The King's Customs: Philadelphia, 1763-1774," *Wm. and Mary Qtly.*, 3d Ser., V (1948), 201-216. Documents on the Maryland episode are in T. 1/513, including the following: Richard Reeve to Grey Cooper, Apr. 19, 1775; extracts from a Council meeting, Mar. 16, 1775; deposition of Robert Stratford Byrne, surveyor of His Majesty's Customs at Sassafras and Bohemia, and Byrne to customs commissioners, Mar. 17, 1775. On the Virginia incident see William Smith to Jeremiah Morgan, Apr. 3, 1766, Colonial Office Group, Class 5, Piece 1331, 80, Public Record Office. Hereafter cited as C. O. 5/1331, 80. W. W. Abbot, *The Royal Governors of Georgia*,

1754-1775 (Chapel Hill, 1959), 174-175. These customs riots remained generally separate from the more central intercolonial opposition to Britain that emerged in 1765. Isolated individuals like John Brown of Providence and Maximilian Calvert of Norfolk were involved in both the organized intercolonial Sons of Liberty and in leading mobs against customs functionaries or informers. These roles, however, for the most part were unconnected, that is, there was no radical program of customs obstruction *per se*. Outbreaks were above all local responses to random provocations and, at least before the Townshend duties, usually devoid of explicit ideological justifications.

13. Hobsbawm, *Primitive Rebels*, III. For a different effort to see class division as relevant in 18th century uprisings, see Lemisch, "Jack Tar," *Wm. and Mary Qtly.*, 3d Ser., XXV (1968), 387.

14. "Friends to the borough and county of Norfolk," Purdie and Dixon's *Va. Gaz. Postscrpt.* (Wmsbg.), Sept. 8, 1768. Wentworth quoted in Knollenberg, *Origin of American Revolution*, 124-125. Lemisch, "Jack Tar," *Wm. and Mary Qtly.*, 3d Ser., XXV (1968), 383-385. Shirley to Duke of Newcastle, Dec. 31, 1747, in Lincoln, ed., *Shirley Correspondence*, I, 420-423. Dora Mae Clark, "The Impressment of Seamen in the American Colonies," *Essays in Colonial History Presented to Charles McLean Andrews* (New Haven, 1931), 199-200; John Swift to Boston customs commissioners, Nov. 15, 1770, T. 1/476.

15. Malone, *White Pines*, 112. "Friends to the borough and county of Norfolk," Purdie and Dixon's *Va. Gaz. Postscrpt.* (Wmsbg.), Sept. 8, 1768; Calvert letter, *ibid.*, Jan. 9, 1772. Capt. Jeremiah Morgan, quoted in Lemisch, "Jack Tar," *Wm. and Mary Qtly.*, 3d Ser., XXV (1968), 391; and William Smith to Morgan, Apr. 3, 1776, C. O. 5/1331, 80. Decker, *Benedict Arnold*, 27-29; deposition of Capt. William Reid on the *Liberty* affair, July 21, 1769, T. 1/471; Ephraim Bowen's narrative on the *Gaspée* affair, *Records of the Colony of Rhode Island*, VII, 68-73; Charles Dudley to Boston customs commissioners, Apr. 11, 1771, T. 1/482, and deposition by Byrne, T. 1/513. Edward Carrington to Jefferson, June 9, 1787, Boyd, ed., *Jefferson Papers*, XI, 408; and see also Smith, "Depression of 1785," *Wm. and Mary Qtly.*, 3d Ser., V (1948), 88—of the 21 men indicted for treason in Worcester during the court's April term 1787, 15 were "gentlemen" and only 6 "yeomen."

16. Gov. Samuel Ward's report to the Treasury lords, Oct. 23, 1765, Ward Manuscripts, Box 1, fol. 58, Rhode Island Historical Society, Providence. See also deposition of Daniel Vaughn of Newport—Vaughn was the gunner at Fort George—July 8, 1764, Chalmers Papers, Rhode Island, fol. 41, New York Public Library, New York City. For British official accounts of the affair see Lieut. Hill's version in James Munro, ed., *Acts of the Privy Council of England, Colonial Series* (London, 1912), VI, 374-376, and the report of John Robinson and John Nicoll to the customs commissioners, Aug. 30, 1765, Privy Council Group, Class I, Piece 51, Bundle 1 (53a), Public Record Office. Hill, whose report was drawn up soon after the incident, does not contradict Ward's narrative, but seems oblivious of any warrant-granting process on shore; Robinson and Nicoll—whose report was drawn up over a year later, and in the midst of the Stamp Act turmoil—claimed that a recent customs seizure had precipitated the attack upon the *St. John*.

17. On the Knowles and *Maidstone* incidents see above, n. 10. On the *Liberty* affair see documents in T. 1/471, esp. the deposition of Capt. William Reid, July 21, 1769, and that of John Carr, the second mate, who indicates that the mob soon forgot its scheme of delivering the crew members to the magistrates.

18. Malone, *White Pines*, 8-9, and *passim*. *Records of the Colony of Rhode Island*, VII, 60, 62-63, 174-175, including the deposition of Dep. Gov. Darius Sessions, June 12, 1772, and Adm. Montagu to Gov. Wanton, Apr. 8, 1772. Also, Wanton to Hillsborough, June 16, 1772, and Ephraim Bowen's narrative, *ibid.*, 63-73, 90-92. *Providence Gaz.* (R. I.), Jan. 9, 1773.

19. Max Beloff, *Public Order and Popular Disturbances, 1660-1714* (London, 1938), *passim*; Albion, *Forests and Sea Power*, 263; J. H. Plumb, *England in the Eighteenth Century* (Baltimore, 1961, [orig. publ., Oxford, 1950]), 66.

20. See, for example, "A Pumkin" in the *New London Gazette* (Connecticut), May 14, 18, 1773; "O. G." in *Newport Merc.* (R. I.), June 10, 1765; *New London Gaz.* (Conn.), Sept 22, 1769; complaints of Marylander David Bevan, reprinted in Rind's *Va. Gaz.* (Wmsbg.), July 27, 1769, and *New London Gaz.* (Conn.), July 21, 1769. Stout, "Manning the Royal Navy," *American Neptune*, XXIII (1963), 174. For a similar accusation against a surveyor-general of the king's woods, see Albion, *Forests and Sea Power*, 262.

21. Joseph Reed to the president of Congress, Oct. 21, 1779, in Hazard *et al.*, eds., *Pennsylvania Archives*, VII, 762. Five years earlier Reed has tried to impress upon Lord

Dartmouth the importance of constraining Crown agents in the colonies if any reconcilia-tion were to be made between Britain and the colonies. See his letter to Earl of Dartmouth, Apr. 4, 1774, in William B. Reed, *Life and Correspondence of Joseph Reed* (Philadelphia, 1847), I, 56–57. For a similar plea, again from a man close to the American Revolutionary leadership, see Stephen Sayre to Lord Dartmouth, Dec. 13, 1766, Dartmouth Papers, D 1778/2/258, William Salt Library, Stafford, England.

22. Rudé, *Crowd in History*, 60, 253–254. The restraint exercised by the 18th century mobs has often been commented upon. See, for example, Wood, "A Note on Mobs," *Wm. and Mary Qtly.*, 3d Ser., XXIII (1966), 636–637.

23. Joseph Harrison's testimony in Wolkins, "Seizure of Hancock's Sloop 'Liberty,' " Mass. Hist. Soc., *Proceedings*, LV, 254.

24. Jay to Jefferson, Dec. 14, 1786, Boyd, ed., *Jefferson Papers*, X, 597. Beloff, *Public Order*, 30. John Swift to Boston customs commissioners, Nov. 15, 1770, Gov. William Franklin's Proclamation, Nov. 17, 1770, and John Hatton to Boston customs commissioners, Nov. 20, 1770, T. 1/476. The last mentioned riot occurred in November 1762. A cartel ship from Havanna had stopped for repairs in October. On Nov. 21 a rumor spread that the Spaniards were murdering the inhabitants, which drew seamen from His Majesty's ship, *Arundel*, also in the harbor, into town, where the seamen drove the Spaniards into a house, set fire to it, and apparently intended to blow it up. A dignitary of the Spanish colonial service, who had been a passenger on the cartel ship, was beaten and some money and valuables were stolen from him. Local men tried to quell the riot without success. It was eventually put down by militiamen from Norfolk. See "A Narrative of a Riot in Virginia in November 1762," T. 1/476.

25. Burke and others to the same effect, quoted in Jerome J. Nadelhaft, The Revolutionary Era in South Carolina, 1775–1788 (unpubl. Ph.D. diss., University of Wisconsin, 1965), 151–152. See also account of the "Fort Wilson" riot of October 1779 in J. Thomas Scharf and Thompson Westcott, *History of Philadelphia, 1609-1884* (Philadelphia, 1884), I, 401–403.

26. Rudé, *Crowd in History*, 255–257.

27. On the "hue and cry" see Frederick Pollock and Frederic W. Maitland, *The History of English Law before the Time of Edward I* (Cambridge, Eng., 1968 [orig. publ., Cambridge, Eng., 1895]), II, 578–580, and William Blackstone, *Commentaries on the Laws of England* (Philadelphia, 1771), IV, 290–291. John Shy, *Toward Lexington: The Role of the British Army in the Coming of the American Revolution* (Princeton, 1965), 40. The English militia underwent a period of decay after 1670 but was revived in 1757. See J. R. Western, *The English Militia in the Eighteenth Century* (London, 1965).

28. Greenleaf's deposition, T. 1/446; *Providence Gaz.* (R. I.), Aug. 24, 1765. Western, *English Militia*, 74.

29 Gov. William Shirley explained the militia's failure to appear during the opening stages of the Knowles riot by citing the militiamen's opposition to impressment and consequent sympathy for the rioters. See his letter to the Lords of Trade, Dec. 1, 1747, in Lincoln, ed., *Shirley Correspondence*, I, 417–418. The English militia was also unreliable. It worked well against invasions and unpopular rebellions, but was less likely to support the government when official orders "clashed with the desires of the citizens" or when ordered to protect unpopular minorities. Sir Robert Walpole believed "that if called on to suppress smuggling, protect the turnpikes, or enforce the gin act, the militia would take the wrong side." Western, *English Militia*, 72–73.

30. Shirley to Josiah Willard, Nov. 19, 1747, Lincoln, ed., *Shirley Correspondence*, I, 407; Bernard's orders in *Providence Gaz.* (R. I.), Apr. 27, 1765.

31. Shy, *Toward Lexington*, 39–40, 44, 47, 74. Amherst, quoted in J. C. Long, *Lord Jeffrey Amherst* (New York, 1933), 124.

32. Shy, *Toward Lexington*, 44; Beloff, *Public Order*, 157–158; Bridenbaugh, *Cities in Revolt*, 297; C. F. Adams, ed., *Works of Adams*, IV, 74–75, V, 209.

33. The definition of the common law of riot most commonly cited—for example, by John Adams in the Massacre trials—was from William Hawkins, *A Treatise of the Pleas of the Crown* (London, 1716), I, 155–159. See also, Blackstone, *Commentaries*, IV, 146–147, and Edward Coke, *The Third Part of the Institutes of the Laws of England* (London, 1797), 176.

34. Clark, "Impressment of Seamen," *Essays in Honor of Andrews*, 198–224; Stout, "Manning the Royal Navy," *American Neptune*, XXIII (1963), 178–179; and Leonard W.

Labaree, ed., *Royal Instructions to British Colonial Governors, 1670-1776* (New York, 1935), I, 442-443.

35. L. Kinvin Wroth and Hiller B. Zobel, eds., *Legal Papers of John Adams* (Cambridge, Mass., 1965), III, 253. Account of the Norfolk incident by George Abyvon, Sept. 5, 1767, in Purdie and Dixon's *Va. Gaz.* (Wmsbg.), Oct. 1, 1767. Capt. Morgan quoted in Lemisch, "Jack Tar," *Wm. and Mary Qtly.*, 3d Ser., XXV (1968), 391. Munro, ed., *Acts of the Privy Council, Colonial Series*, VI, 374; Gov. Samuel Ward to Treasury lords, Oct. 23, 1765, Ward MSS, Box 1, fol. 58.

36. Knollenberg, *Origin of the Revolution*, 122-130; Albion, *Forests and Sea Power*, 255-258.

37. *N. Y. Jour.* (N. Y. C.), Aug. 18, 1768 (the writer was allegedly drawing together arguments that had recently appeared in the British press); and *N. Y. Jour. Supplement* (N. Y. C.), Jan. 4, 1770. Note also that Jefferson accepted Shays's rebellion as a sign of health in American institutions only after he had been assured by men like Jay that the insurgents had acted purposefully and moderately, and after he had concluded that the uprising represented no continuous threat to established government. "An insurrection in one of the 13. states in the course of 11. years that they have subsisted amounts to one in any particular state in 143 years, say a century and a half," he calculated. "This would not be near as many as has happened in every other government that has ever existed," and clearly posed no threat to the constitutional order as a whole. To David Hartley, July 2, 1787, Boyd, ed., *Jefferson Papers*, XI, 526.

38. John Locke, *The Second Treatise of Government*, paragraphs 223-225. "A State of Facts Concerning the Riots . . . in New Jersey," *New Jersey Archives*, VII, 217, *N. Y. Jour. Supp.* (N. Y. C.), Jan. 4, 1770. Johnson to Wm. Pitkin, Apr. 29, 1768, Massachusetts Historical Society, *Collections*, 5th Ser., IX (1885), 275. Adams as "Determinus" in *Boston Gazette*, Aug. 8, 1768; and Harry A. Cushing, ed., *The Writings of Samuel Adams* (New York, 1904-1908), I, 237. Jay to Jefferson, Oct. 27, 1786, Boyd, ed., *Jefferson Papers*, X, 488.

39. Wroth and Zobel, eds., *Adams Legal Papers*, III, 249-250; *N. Y. Jour. Supp.* (N. Y. C.), Aug. 18, 1768; Jefferson to Abigail Adams, Feb. 22, 1787, Boyd, ed., *Jefferson Papers*, XI, 174. C. F. Adams, ed., *Works of Adams*, IV, 77, 80 (quoting Algernon Sydney).

40. Jefferson to Edward Carrington, Jan. 16, 1787, Boyd, ed., *Jefferson Papers*, XI, 49, and Rev. James Madison to Jefferson, Mar. 28, 1787, *ibid.*, 252. Wroth and Zobel, eds., *Adams Legal Papers*, III, 250. Quincy's address to the jury in the soldiers' trial after the Boston Massacre in Josiah Quincy, *Memoir of the Life of Josiah Quincy, Junior, of Massachusetts Bay, 1744-1775*, ed. Eliza Susan Quincy, 3d ed. (Boston, 1875), 46. See also Massachusetts Assembly's similar statement in its address to Gov. Hutchinson, Apr. 24, 1770, Hutchinson, *History of Massachusetts Bay*, ed. Mayo, III, 365-366. This 18th century devotion to political "jealousy" resembles the doctrine of "vigilance" that was defended by 19th century vigilante groups. See Graham and Gurr, *Violence in America*, 179-183.

41. Jefferson to William Stephen Smith, Nov. 13, 1787, Boyd, ed., *Jefferson Papers*, XII, 356, Jefferson to Carrington, Jan. 16, 1787, *ibid.*, XI, 49, Jefferson to James Madison, Jan. 30, 1787, *ibid.*, 92-93. Taylor's remarks in "History of Violence," *The Listener*, CXXIX (1968), 701. ("Members of the House of Lords . . . said . . . if the people really don't like something, then they wreck our carriages and tear off our wigs and throw stones through the windows of our town-houses. And this is an essential thing to have if you are going to have a free country.") Hutchinson to [John or Robert] Grant, July 27, 1768, Massachusetts Archives, XXVI, 317, State House, Boston. See also the related story about John Selden, the famous 17th century lawyer, told to the House of Commons in Jan. 1775 by Lord Camden and recorded by Josiah Quincy, Jr., in the "Journal of Josiah Quincy, Jun., During his Voyage and Residence in England from September 28th, 1774, to March 3d, 1775," Massachusetts Historical Society, *Proceedings*, L (1916-1917), 462-463. Selden was asked what lawbook contained the laws for resisting tyranny. He replied he did not know, "but I'll tell [you] what is most certain, that it has always been the custom of England— and the Custom of England is the *Law* of the *Land*."

42. On the developing distinction Americans drew between what was legal and constitutional see Wood, *Creation of the American Republic*, 261-268.

43. *N. Y. Jour. Supp.* (N. Y. C.), Jan. 4, 1770; Wroth and Zobel, eds., *Adams Legal Papers*, III, 250, and C. F. Adams, ed., *Works of Adams*, VI, 151. Adams's views were altered in 1815, *ibid.*, X, 181. It is noteworthy that the Boston town meeting condemned the Knowles rioters not simply for their method of opposing impressment but because they insulted the

governor and the legislature, and the Massachusetts Assembly acted against the uprising only after Gov. Shirley had left Boston and events seemed to be "tending to the destruction of all government and order." Hutchinson, *History of Massachusetts Bay*, ed. Mayo, II, 332–333. *Acts and Resolves of the Province of Massachusetts Bay*, III, 647. (Chap. 18 of the Province laws, 1752–1753, "An Act for Further Preventing all Riotous, Tumultuous and Disorderly Assemblies or Companies or Persons. . . . ") This act, which was inspired particularly by Pope's Day violence, was renewed after the Boston Massacre in 1770 even though the legislature refused to renew its main Riot Act of 1751. *Ibid.*, IV, 87.

44. Arthur M. Schlesinger, "Political Mobs and the American Revolution, 1765–1776," *Proceedings of the American Philosophical Society*, XCIX (1955), 246; Charles M. Andrews, *The Colonial Backround of the American Revolution*, rev. ed. (New Haven, 1939), 176; Charles M. Andrews, "The Boston Merchants and the Non-Importation Movement," Colonial Society of Massachusetts, *Transactions*, XIX (1916–1917), 241; Hobsbawm, *Primitive Rebels*, III, 123–124.

45. Hutchinson to Thomas Pownall, [Sept. or Oct. 1765], Mass. Archives, XXVI, 157. Pauline Maier, From Resistance to Revolution: American Radicals and the Development of Intercolonial Opposition to Britain, 1765–1776 (unpubl. Ph.D. diss., Harvard University, 1968), I, 37–45, 72–215.

46. C. F. Adams, ed., *Works of Adams*, IV, 51; Rev. Samuel Langdon's election sermon to third Massachusetts Provincial Congress, May 31, 1775, quoted in Richard Frothingham, *Life and Times of Joseph Warren* (Boston, 1865), 499; Samuel Adams to Noah Webster, Apr. 30, 1784, Cushing, ed., *Writings of Samuel Adams*, IV, 305–306. On Gadsden see Richard Walsh, *Charleston's Sons of Liberty* (Columbia, 1959), 87.

47. N. Y. Jour. Supp. (N. Y. C.), Jan. 4, 1770; Jay to Jefferson, Oct. 27, 1786, Boyd, ed., *Jefferson Papers*, X, 488; Johnson to William Pitkin, July 23, 1768, Massachusetts Historical Society, *Collections*, 5th Ser., IX, 294–295.

48. *The Statutes at Large* [of Great Britain] (London, 1786), V, 4–6; Hoadly, ed., *Public Records of Connecticut*, VI, 346–348 for the law, and see also 332–333, 341–348; *Acts and Resolves of Massachusetts Bay*, III, 544–546, for the Riot Act of 1751, and see also Hutchinson, *History of Massachusetts Bay*, ed. Mayo, III, 6–7; and *Acts and Laws of the Commonwealth of Massachusetts* (Boston, 1893), 87–88, for Act of 1786; "A State of Facts Concerning the Riots . . . in New Jersey," *N. J. Archives*, VII, 211–212, 221–222; *The Statutes at Large of Pennsylvania* . . . (n.p., 1899), VI, 325–328; William A. Saunders, ed., *The Colonial Records of North Carolina* (Raleigh, 1890), VIII, 481–486; *Laws of the Colony of New York in the Years 1774 and 1775* (Albany, 1888), 38–43.

49. See additional instruction to Gov. Josiah Martin, Saunders, ed., *Colonial Records of North Carolina*, VIII, 515–516; and *Laws of the State of New York* (Albany, 1886), I, 20.

50. *The Craftsman*, VI (London, 1731), 263–264. Connecticut and Massachusetts laws cited in n. 45; and *Laws of the State of New Jersey* (Trenton, 1821), 279–281.

51. Jefferson to Madison, Jan. 30, 1787, Boyd, ed., *Jefferson Papers*, XI, 93.

52. See Bradley Chapin, "Colonial and Revolutionary Origins of the American Law of Treason," *Wm. and Mary Qtly.*, 3d Ser., XVII (1960), 3–21.

53. Elbridge Gerry in Congressional debates, quoted in Irving Brant, *The Bill of Rights, Its Origin and Meaning* (Indianapolis, 1965), 486; Samuel Adams, quoting Blackstone, as "E. A." in *Boston Gaz.*, Feb. 27, 1769, and Cushing, ed., *Writings of Samuel Adams*, I, 317. Timothy Dwight, quoted in Daniel J. Boorstin, *The Americans: The Colonial Experience* (New York, 1958), 353.

54. Wood, *Creation of the American Republic*, 410.

55. Judge Aedanus Burke's Charge to the Grand Jury at Charleston, June 9, 1783 in *South-Carolina Gazette and General Advertiser* (Charleston), June 10, 1783; "A Patriot," *ibid.*, July 15, 1783; and "Another Patriot," *ibid.*, July 29, 1783; and on the relevance of jealousy of power, see a letter to Virginia in *ibid.*, Aug. 9, 1783, "Democratic Gentle-Touch," *Gazette of the State of South Carolina* (Charleston), May 13, 1784.

56. Wood, *Creation of the American Republic*, 612–614.

57. J. H. Plumb, *The Origins of Political Stability, England 1675–1725* (Boston, 1967), xv, 187; John Adams on the leaders of Shays's Rebellion in a letter to Benjamin Hitchborn, Jan. 27, 1787, in C. F. Adams, ed., *Works of Adams*, IX, 551; modern definitions of riot in "Riot Control and the Use of Federal Troops," *Harvard Law Review*, LXXXI (1968), 643.

bibliography

Prerevolutionary America has held less fascination for radicals than have most other periods in the American past. The best analyses of the nature of Puritanism from a Marxist perspective are, therefore, still Christopher Hill's studies of England. *Society and Puritanism* (Schocken Books, 1964) and *Puritanism and Revolution* (Schocken Books, 1958) provide both background for insight into the American experience. Perry Miller's major works set the stage within which American religious historians operate. The two volumes of *The New England Mind: The Seventeenth Century* (Macmillan, 1939), and *From Colony to Province* (Harvard University Press, 1953), and a group of essays collected into *Errand into the Wilderness* (Harper & Row, 1956), present the substance of his thought. Alan Heimert, who has succeeded Miller as the dean of Puritan studies, has a provocative essay, "Puritanism, the Wilderness and the Frontier," *New England Quarterly*, 26 (Spring 1953), 361-382. On the Great Awakening, see Richard Bushman, "Jonathon Edwards and the Puritan Consciousness," *Journal for the Scientific Study of Religion*, 5 (1966), 383-396. Richard H. Niebuhr, *The Social Sources of Denominationalism* (Holt, 1929) is still unsurpassed as a study of fragmenting tendencies in early American religion. William G. McLaughlin, "Pietism and the American Character," *American Quarterly*, 17 (1965), 163-185, discusses the search for perfect moral order and freedom in American history. The same author's "The American Revolution as a Religious Revival: The Millennium in One Country," *New England Quarterly*, 40 (1967), 99-110, asserts the importance of Calvinism in revolutionary politics.

The conflict over social structure and politics is most aptly represented by James Henretta's widely reprinted "Economic Development and Social Structure in Colonial Boston," *William and Mary Quarterly*, 3rd Ser., 3, 22 (1965), 75-92. James T. Lemon and Gary B. Nash reveal much about the methods of new quantitative studies in the "Distribution of Wealth in Eighteenth Century America: A Century of Change in Chester County Pennsylvania, 1693-1802," *Journal of Social History*, 2nd Ser., 1 (Fall 1968), 1-24. Irving Mark, *Agrarian Conflicts in Colonial New York, 1771-1775* (Columbia University Press, 1940) provides crucial information on a much discussed but little researched area. The best study of one conflict that spilled into the open is Richard Maxwell Brown, *The South Carolina Regulators* (Belknap Press, 1963). Insight into the class structure comes from Bernard Bailyn and Lotte Bailyn *Massachusetts Shipping, 1697-1714: A Statistical Study* (Harvard University Press, 1959). To understand how the circumstances of life may have affected political behavior, more studies like that of John Demos, *A Little Commonwealth: Family Life in Plymouth Colony* (Oxford University Press, 1970), are needed.

the revolution reconsidered as a social movement

Most historians agree that there was nothing particularly revolutionary about America's revolution. Yet the debate about what happened between 1763 and 1790 is surely one of the most absorbing of our past. All would agree that we fought a war for independence from Britain and that out of the war, new political institutions emerged that validated some of the exciting political theory of the Enlightenment. But controversy still rages over whether the revolutionary period was motivated by or produced any substantial changes in social structure. Did democracy exist in prerevolutionary America? Did the revolution witness a movement toward an egalitarian society? These are the questions examined by the articles in this chapter.

Nineteenth century historians dealt with such questions in a political context. George Bancroft, comparing the pre- and postrevolutionary periods, exulted in more representative state assemblies, in restrictions on slavery, and in lowered property qualifications for voters. The revolution, he argued, was the cul-mination of a long struggle for liberty. Later, historians of the Imperial school, who blamed the inconsistent, often harsh policies of Britain for colonial revolt, tended to confirm this view. Separation from Britain provided the colonists not only with new economic impetus but also with new aspirations.

But some historians at the turn of the century regarded the revolution as more than merely a struggle against Britain. Colonists themselves vied with each other for power. Progressive historians pointed to the existence of two orders of society—an elite who held government offices before the revolution and a group of small merchants and disgruntled back-country men who tried to wrest power from the elite as their price for supporting independence. Carl Becker's *History of Political Parties in the Province of New York* (University of Wisconsin Press, 1960 [1909]) described the struggle over "who should rule at home" in one state. Arthur Schlesinger, Sr.'s *The Colonial Merchants and the American Revolution* (Facsimile Library, 1939 [1918]) depicted merchants as leaders of opposition to Britain, who, frightened by the demands of the lower orders, drew back temporarily, only to find that they had gone too far. According to Merrill Jensen's *Articles of Confederation* (University of Wiscon-sin Press, 1940), the elite lost control of the revolution to regain it only after a disastrous Confederation period revealed the necessity for order.

At the core of Progressive interpretations was the assumption that rev-olutionary society was sharply divided along narrowly defined economic lines. Charles Beard's important book, *An Economic Interpretation of the Constitution* (Macmillan, 1913), described a convention of the financial elite who created a system of government that would foster their own economic well-being. Destroying this argument took little effort. If one could demonstrate that complex class divisions existed, the revolution could be presumed to rest on a consensus drawn together not by economic interest but by common discontent with Britain. A host of scholars addressed themselves to this task. Robert Brown, Forrest McDonald, and E. James Ferguson attacked Beard's statistical analysis. Benjamin Wright pointed to the remarkable continuity of political institutions before and after the Revolution. Louis Hartz and Daniel Boorstin attributed a unity of aims to all the revolutionaries. When the passions had cooled, serious studies of social structure and of ideology revealed on the one hand a relatively fluid, but certainly class-divided society, and on the other a remarkable agreement in principle, if not yet in practice, as to the basis of a new society.

But these answers were not entirely satisfying. If a more fluid social situation existed in the American colonies than elsewhere, it was nevertheless clear that, as radical historian Jesse Lemisch and others have pointed out, not all Americans were property holders. Indeed, studies of social structure, like that by Jackson Turner Main, reveal that some 30 percent of Boston's population appear to have been poor. A crucial issue was raised by Staughton Lynd who observed that while workingmen were considered the most militant of revolutionaries, they had nevertheless supported a reactionary constitution that favored property holders. If individuals could not be lumped into rigid economic categories, radicals argued, neither could such categories be completely rejected. The problem assumes critical importance in the light of recent quantitative assessments like that of Allan Kulikoff. Not only does Kulikoff demonstrate the existence of a stratified society, but he denies that the well-off took care of the poor.

If there were economic divisions in our society, why was there no class consciousness among workers? How did deferential attitudes limit workers' actions? If ideas can move men to act, then the colonists, as mainstream historian Bernard Bailyn has argued, may have fought to defend not their immediate economic interests, but their conception of liberty. Property, argued the eighteenth century political theorist, was essential to freedom. A nation, like an individual, had a uniform interest in maximizing its property. If there were short-run economic gains to be had by one class, all would nevertheless benefit in the long run. Exploring the relationships of lower-class people to ideology and economy would perhaps reveal that democracy was not at issue. Rather, convinced that their interests lay in strengthening America's economic position, the working classes were far more nationalistic than class oriented.

Radical historians who operate within this framework do not ask if the revolution was democratic. They investigate classes to determine the nature of consciousness within them. They are concerned with consciousness because they want to understand the sources of a social movement that was not, but that might have been, a revolution.

the nature of class in revolutionary America

JACKSON TURNER MAIN

In the concluding chapter of his book, *The Social Structure of Revolutionary America*, Jackson Turner Main confronts head-on the issue of whether or not class existed in colonial America. His conclusions support conventional myths about fluid class lines and extraordinary mobility. While they answer some questions, they leave others unanswered: Is income the most effective way of defining class? What is the nature of class consciousness among the 30 percent that Main believes to be below the middle class?

The student of revolutionary society must ask two questions: whether or not classes existed, and whether the social structure was democratic or undemocratic. If the word "class" requires the presence of class consciousness, if it can be used only when men are aware of a hierarchical structure and of their own rank within it, then this study indicates that America during the period 1763–1788 was relatively classless. Certainly it was both classless and democratic by comparison with the America of 1900 or with England in 1776. Moreover, rural New England, and the frontier and subsistence farming areas generally, furnish impressive evidence of a nearly equal division of wealth and a relative absence of classes.

If on the other hand the existence of classes does not depend upon class consciousness but implies nothing more than a rank order within which an individual can move up or down without any insurmountable difficulty, then revolutionary America can and indeed must be described in terms of classes. The society of the towns and of most commercial farm areas, the great distinctions between rich and poor, and the concentration of property, are decisive evidence of the presence of an economic class structure. Furthermore, a social hierarchy based upon a consciousness of class distinctions, a prestige order, can be identified, although it cannot be so precisely defined.

Although revolutionary America is seen to have contained classes, the question of democracy remains unsettled. On the one hand the societies in which class distinctions were prominent were aristocratic rather than equalitarian. In some commercial farm regions and in the major cities, a wealthy, fairly stable upper class had appeared, most of whose members had inherited their position, and who owned over half of the property; while a large lower class, often servile, also had developed. The opportunity to rise was restricted,

"Conclusion" (The Nature of Class in Revolutionary America), from Jackson Turner Main, *The Social Structure of Revolutionary America* (copyright © 1965 by Princeton University Press; Princeton Paperback, 1969), 270–284. Reprinted by permission of Princeton University Press.

or even denied altogether. In contrast the new country contained other sections in which most people were small property holders, wealth was equally distributed, and the poor man usually prospered. Revolutionary society was certainly not classless, yet neither was it entirely aristocratic. It contained the essential elements for an aristocracy while at the same time possessing the potential for a social and economic democracy.

There was, of course, a "permanent proletariat" consisting of those who always remained at the bottom. Slaves formed the largest part of this class. They totalled 23 percent of the whole population in 1760 and a little less than that thirty years later. Four-fifths of these were in the South, concentrated especially near the coast. A few sections of the country, then, contained a Negro labor force comprising considerably over half of the population, whereas most of the country had only a small such element, and vast areas none at all. Where slaves were scarce, white indentured servants or wage-workers were used instead. Less numerous than the Negroes, the white laborers usually formed only about one-fifth of the whites, though the proportion was doubled in certain areas. The exact number who remained in the lowest status is uncertain, but certainly fewer than half, possibly only one-fourth of them failed to become small property holders. Therefore out of twenty whites only one or two remained permanently poor. The evidence suggests that by the time of the Revolution even indentured servants had a chance of success nearly equal to that of the free workers. If this is true, then immigrants and native-born alike had reason to be confident about their future, and the few whites who failed were defeated not because of any external circumstance but because they lacked some essential quality. Thus the whole permanent proletariat, white and black, totalled less than 30 percent of the population.

At any point in time, revolutionary society contained a lower class comprising between one-third and two-fifths of the men. If defined by occupation, it included Negro slaves, white servants, and landless laborers employed by property owners such as farmers, artisans, and merchants. If defined by income, the lower class characteristically had almost none, except that they were given food, clothing, and shelter; free workers, however, did receive a money wage which enabled them to save. If defined by property, the men of this economic rank almost always had estates of less than £ 50, and usually they had none.

The free workers, with their money and opportunities for advancement, belonged to an intermediate category. They were partially independent, owned some property and perhaps some skill, were poor but not impoverished, and often were moving up into the middle class. Many farmers were no better off. There were, for example, numerous landowners in western Massachusetts and southern Delaware, the annual value of whose land was assessed at under £ 5; and according to the probate records (a more accurate indication of wealth) something like one-eighth of the yeomen had personal estates of less than £ 50. Many tenants were also poor, while perhaps 30 percent of the skilled artisans, especially many weavers, cordwainers, housewrights, coopers, and tailors, left very small estates. These men probably did earn enough to support their families adequately most of the time. Many of them moved from place to place, generally westward, perhaps improving their position, perhaps always balanced precariously upon the boundary between poverty and success. In England such men, together with the true lower class, constituted a latent threat to the existing order, and were kept under control by an educational system which (if it existed at all) taught them morality, by a religion which enjoined them to accept their lot submissively, and by force. In America, many members of this marginal class were young men with prospects. Discipline was rarely needed except by the slaves; even the uprisings of tenants and the flight of servants were not so much protests against their condition as a testimony to the opportunities which they knew existed.

The middle class in America consisted of small property holders who were usually self-employed. Its members are distinguished, at the lower end of the scale, from servants and slaves or others who had little or no property, and from the wage workers who depended entirely upon their daily labor; while at the other end they merge without any sharp definition into the upper class of men with large estates. Whereas the lower class lived at or barely above the subsistence level, the "middling sort" lived in comfort. The less fortunate among them usually owned at least £ 200 worth of real and personal property and netted perhaps £ 10 in excess of the minimum cost of living. The majority held property worth £ 400 to £ 500 and earned the £ 75 to £ 100 (or its equivalent) which supported their families in decency. The class included probably 70 percent of the whites and may be subdivided into the lower middle or marginal segment discussed above (roughly 20 percent, a middle middle (40 percent), and an upper middle (10 percent).

This largest and most important segment of revolutionary society was made up of several occupational groups. Small farmers were the most numerous element, comprising 40 percent of the whites and one-third of the whole population. If farmers who were substantial but not large landowners are added, the proportion rises to very nearly half of the whites and two-fifths of all the people. These farmers furnished most of their own necessities and earned at least £ 16 in cash (or credits) which permitted them to pay their debts and taxes, buy a few luxury articles, and save a little. Very few could hope to enlarge their farms without borrowing, but since they generally held 100 or 200 acres their prosperity depended more upon improving their methods and developing their land than upon adding acreage. Most of them could not provide for surplus sons, but the frontier or the towns took care of these. The more fortunate, who had good land in commercial farming areas, cleared much more than £ 16 and presented an agreeable picture of the ideal American, the prosperous farmer.

Second in number among the middling sort were the "artisans and mechanics" or "craftsmen." These were of two types. Some of them were not entrepreneurs but skilled workers who hired themselves out by the day, week, or year. Receiving from £ 40 to £ 50 annually, they could save a good deal of money so long as they remained single, but the married man just broke even; indeed if he had to rent a house and buy all of his food, £ 50 scarcely met expenses. Fortunately most of these artisans raised much of their own food and were thereby able to live in reasonable comfort and even acquire some property. Apparently almost half of them significantly improved their economic position.

The great majority of artisans in the rural areas, and probably a majority everywhere, were independent entrepreneurs who ordinarily kept a workshop in or near their houses. These were equivalent to farmers in that they were self-employed, but they usually ranked somewhat below the yeomen both in wealth and prestige. Their income and chance of increasing it depended upon their particular craft. The majority never rose above the middle rank, for the trades of cooper, cordwainer, blacksmith, tailor, weaver, or carpenter seldom provided a large return. On the other hand they also required little equipment and were in great demand, so that the apprentice could quite easily become a master. A few types of enterprise were by their nature more expensive to undertake and more profitable for the enterpriser. Distillers, ropemakers, goldsmiths, and the like were capitalists whose economic position compared favorably with that of prosperous farmers and many professional men.

Professional men as a whole also belonged to the middle class, earning considerably more than most farmers and artisans but not enough to raise them decisively into the economic elite. Two segments of the professional group were exceptional. Lawyers ordinarily received large incomes and formed part of the "better sort," while teachers often had so little property that they ranked economically even below skilled workers, though they may have had greater prestige. The other professionals, among whom ministers and doctors were the most numerous, typically earned £ 100 to £ 200, a sum which allowed some luxuries and enabled them to accumulate £ 500 worth of property. This property in turn added to their income and further raised their standard of living. They therefore could spare the cash to educate their children for the professions or for trade: indeed it seems possible that the clergy at least was to a large extent a self-recruiting group, partly because most Americans could not send their children to school whereas the ministers could and did. In the middle class too belonged the overseers, innkeepers, ships' captains, retailers, clerks, and most government officials.

The upper class was composed of large property owners. By European standards there was, of course, no upper class at all, since there was no hereditary aristocracy. There were in certain areas families who had retained wealth and position for several generations, and who were then and have been since called "aristocrats"; but the word, if it is to be used at all, must be defined to fit the American scene. Probably it is better simply to structure revolutionary society on its own terms. Entrance into the upper class followed at once upon selection to certain public offices, and most often upon acquiring a certain amount of property. Any definition is certainly arbitrary, but a reasonable one is the ownership of £ 2,000, which made one well-to-do, or of £ 5,000, which meant wealth. The southern planter who owned 500 acres and 20 slaves possessed at least the former sum, which was, incidentally, the amount required for membership in the South Carolina Senate. Probably 10 percent of the landowners, the same proportion of ministers and doctors, most lawyers, a few artisans, and not far from half of the merchants qualified as well-to-do or wealthy—the total being roughly 10 percent of the whites. These men had incomes which were almost by definition in excess of £ 500,[1] and they controlled about 45 percent of the country's wealth.[2] It is important to remember that this was not a closed class. Another tenth of the men owned estates of £ 1,000 or so, and movement from one rank to another was frequent. Although the very wealthiest Virginia planters formed a fairly tight social group, it is probable that entrance into the lesser planter society was much easier. The urban elite even before the Revolution contained many men who began life with little property.

Such was the class structure of the United States viewed as a whole. There were, however, several quite different sub-societies based upon geographical and historical factors. Each colony had in 1763 certain peculiarities, and the contrast between North Carolina and Virginia, adjacent though they were, was as striking as that between the Old Dominion and New Hampshire. Moreover every colony contained three or four distinct social structures. Fortunately these sub-societies reappear everywhere so that the country can still be treated as a whole.

Most colonies still had a frontier area. Pioneer societies were of two types. In some cases land speculators obtained large tracts which they then rented, sold, or occasionally farmed. Ordinarily the speculator was not a resident, so that no upper class was present, but real property was more than usually concentrated in the hands of large proprietors, while the lower class of landless men was more numerous than on most frontiers. The typical frontier class structure, however, was "democratic": most men belonged to the middle class, property was equally distributed, and the poor man found it easy to become a farmer.

Subsistence—or more accurately subsistence-plus—farms existed wherever the farmers could raise or market little produce in excess of their immediate needs. Poor soil, inadequate transportation, lack of capital, or a shortage of labor, were inhibiting factors. Since agriculture was not particularly profitable under these circumstances, few wealthy men lived in such areas. The lower class also was small, for few men could afford servants or slaves, while the hired hand quickly obtained a farm of his own or left for better soils. The great majority of the men were small farmers who, together with a few artisans and professional men, formed a very large middle class. Property was equally distributed; the subsistence farm society, like that of the frontier, was democratic.

In areas where agriculture was profitable, commercial farming developed. The result might be only a general increase in the prosperity of small farmers, but typically some landowners became rich, controlled an increasing amount of the property, and bought or hired an expanding labor force. Class distinctions quickly appeared. The society (at least in the North) also became more diversified because the large farmers tended to specialize in staple crops and to buy whatever else they needed, while their higher incomes allowed them to purchase luxuries. More artisans were present, more traders, and more professional men. The southern "plantation" social structure did not ordinarily contain such a large non-farm element (unless some slaves are counted as artisans), but exceeded the northern commercial farm sections in the size of the upper and lower classes, the concentration of property, and the general wealth. While the commercial farm area was first undergoing development, men were able quickly and easily to increase their property and prestige. Once that process had been completed, opportunities for those without capital diminished and class lines tended to harden.

By contrast, urban societies everywhere offered opportunity to men of all ranks. The cities contained many wage earners and some slaves, so that the lower class was even larger than in commercial farm regions except for those parts of the South in which slaves were especially numerous. With the same exception the towns contained the highest proportion of wealthy men, who had an unusually large share of the city's property. Despite the economic inequal-ities which characterized urban society, the middle class was seldom less than half of the whole population, the general standard of living was high, and economic opportunities in a great variety of occupations afforded the poor man a chance to acquire property.

Just as the unequal distribution of property proves the existence of economic classes, so also the different styles of living testify to the inequality of income. The revolutionary family which had to pay cash for everything needed at least £ 50 annually. The lower class and even some skilled workers received less than this. Had they depended entirely upon a cash income, they must have lived below the subsistence level, but fortunately several factors intervened to save almost all of these people from actual want. The majority—slaves and indentured servants—were supported by their masters. Others owned a little land on which they produced much of their food. Still others were single men without dependents who needed much less money and in fact could save a little. By the time they married they usually had acquired a farm or a skill which raised them into the middle class. Therefore the members of the lower class were guaranteed at least an adequate livelihood.

The middle class generally enjoyed a comfortable living. Small farmers did without much money but raised almost all of their food, made some of their clothing, and supplied other household needs, so that they usually showed a net cash profit. Professional men, substantial farmers and artisans, and other members of what was by colonial standards an upper middle class, generally exceeded the £ 100 or thereabouts which their style of living required. The upper class too was fortunate. Merchants, lawyers, and planters very seldom earned enough to live like European aristocrats, but in the new world £ 400 or so would enable anyone who produced his own food to live like a gentleman.

Crucially important to the early American was his ability to improve his economic and social position. Comparisons with other societies are dangerous when there are no comparable facts, but the evidence points decisively toward a much higher degree of mobility in revolutionary America than had been usual elsewhere. Several circumstances contributed to this result. One was of course the absence for most Americans of legal or social impediments. All whites were permitted to acquire property, and as they did so they progressed up the social scale, acceptance even at the highest levels coming almost at once. Another factor was the general economic expansion combined with a rapid growth in the population. There was always more room at the top. Important too were the vast quantities of unoccupied land, some of it excellent, available at a low price with several years to pay. This land contained untouched natural resources, notably lumber. Finally, the American could move easily from place to place. Had he been in some manner constrained within his home neighbor- hood, his prospects would have been considerably diminished, for economic opportunities in the older farm areas, while greater than in Europe, were much less than in the newer regions; but he was always able to move to the town or to the frontier.

This geographical mobility did not usually involve long-distance migration. The occupation of western Pennsylvania, Kentucky, and Tennessee naturally required a considerable journey, but during the years 1763–1788 most of the movement was local, the distance travelled short. The young man moved a few score miles at most, to a town or country lying roughly westward as transportation facilities dictated. The occupation of a frontier, as far as the present study reveals the situation, was carried out by those living adjacent to it. The westward course seldom was reversed: few men returned to the east. Probably the process was largely a rural phenomenon, for city folk did not have the farmer's skills, and ordinarily stayed in the towns. There may have been some movement of artisans to the country where they continued to practice their trades, but opportunities in the towns (at least in the North) were good enough so that a "safety valve" was seldom needed.

The man who started without property had the best chance of advancement if he went west. Indeed four out of five pioneers obtained land, usually within a few years after their arrival. Immigrants, even indentured servants, had nearly as good a chance for success as native-born whites; the failures occurred among the unskilled regardless of their origin. Those frontier areas subject to large-scale speculation sometimes offered less opportunity to the prospective land-owners—much of the land in New York and northern Virginia was rented to tenants rather than sold—but ordinarily the man with some skill was almost certain of entering the middle class.

If he lived in an older community the certainty was gone but the probability of advancement was still fairly high. About one out of three landless laborers in such areas obtained land without moving out of the county. More than half of the artisans advanced economically and even indentured servants had some success. Obviously the fact that the good land had long since been occupied was the principal limiting factor, and had all of the people stayed put, those at the bottom might have been fated to remain there. Fortunately the constant movement out of the country created openings locally, and if one failed to seize the change, there was always another one farther west.

But though someone of ability might look forward with confidence to entering the rural middle class, he could seldom achieve higher rank. If the situation in Virginia is at all typical, an established rural upper class admitted very few new members. Those who made good came not from among the small farmers but from the businessmen and lawyers. Admittedly conclusions based upon one colony ought not to be pushed too far, but it seems that in the South it was rare for any parvenu to achieve eminence among the landholders (by revolutionary times) unless he did so through buying land on a frontier which rapidly became commercial. Probably the same was true in the North.

Urban society was much more open than that of the commercial farm areas. Although the unskilled workers (including mariners) seldom acquired much property, the chance of becoming an independent artisan was excellent in those occupations which demanded little venture capital. Success in the larger enterprises and in commerce was more difficult. Nevertheless even the wealthy merchant class of colonial New York was composed partly of self-made men: whereas not over one in ten wealthy Virginians were *nouveaux riches*, about one in three members of the Chamber of Commerce were of humble origin. The proportion of self-made men was even higher after the war, but this probably was an abnormal situation due to the forcible displacement of Loyalist merchants by enterprising rebels.

Just as the revolutionary American could increase his wealth, he could also advance in prestige. The "social class" or "status" order which the colonists brought with them from Europe was based upon a hereditary system of ranks, symbolized or identified by the discriminatory use of titles. This hierarchical society (which even in England was not inflexible) gradually disappeared in America partly because no European aristocracy was present to perpetuate it, but largely because of the actual condition of social equality and the remark-able ease with which the colonial could improve his position. Therefore the old order was eventually replaced by one which developed out of the new economic circumstances. The indigenous class structure was based upon property rather than inherited status.[3] When a new prestige order was created, it corresponded closely with economic classes. It seems reasonable to suppose that, since titles were losing their symbolic significance, the Americans found a substitute in their style of life, by which they distinguished themselves visibly from their inferiors.

The outcome made social advancement relatively easy. Perhaps the principal method was simply by making money, for there were no social barriers which property could not surmount, and there existed a general admiration for the man who acquired an estate. A high regard for material possessions permitted anyone to achieve status approximately in proportion to his income. Another way of winning esteem was to obtain a high political office. The degree of democracy during the revolutionary era is disputed, but no one denies that preferment included Americans from more walks of life than was the case with contemporary European officialdom; while the Revolution itself unquestionably opened the doors to a greater number of artisans and farmers. The position of justice of the peace did not mean quite so much as in England but it was still an important and prestigeful office which could be reached, at least in the North, by men of small property. Education, though available principally to the upper class, occasionally elevated the man of merit, while during the war some soldiers of lowly birth won high rank and universal regard.

This social mobility was of course limited just as was economic mobility. Titles still had some significance. The great majority of "esquires" were large property holders, while "gentlemen" owned about twice the average wealth. Still, only a minority of the upper class merited the "esquire," while in the North most of the "gentlemen" and one-third of the "esquires" were of humble birth, and "Mr." meant practically nothing at all anywhere. Despite the frequent public eulogies addressed to farmers, they had no monopoly of these symbols of prestige, for such titles were granted to merchants, professional men, and even to artisans.

Although Americans seemed to express an excessive regard for farmers and were publicly critical of lawyers and traders, they had a generally accurate view of their own society. They preferred to think of it as one of equality and proudly pointed to such features as the large middle class, the absence of beggars, the comfortable circumstances of most people, and the limitless opportunities for those who worked hard and saved their money. Still, few had any illusion that perfection had been achieved. The existence of slaves and poor whites, of rich merchants and planters, and of what seemed to many an increasing concentration of wealth, prevented any complacency and aroused anxious criticism of the inequalities which marred the vision of the Good Society. Our modern division of American society into three classes corresponds closely to their contemporary analysis, and they likewise recognized the economic basis of class. European travellers similarly saw that the American social structure, while far less aristocratic and more fluid than that of the Old World, had obvious economic and social inequalities.

NOTES

1. Not all of this £ 500 had to be in cash, of course. Most well-to-do farmers probably cleared far less than this, but supplied much of their own food, fuel, and shelter.

2. Anyone who uses this figure for comparing the distribution of wealth then and now should be informed that the slaves are not here included as part of the population. If they are added, the figure becomes a little higher because the population is larger by nearly one-fourth, so that more individuals would be included among the top tenth of property holders. Their share of the wealth would become about 50 percent overall. The following table shows the approximate situation. Figures in parentheses are obtained when slaves are included.

Share of Wealth of the Richest 10%

	North	South
Frontier	33%	40% (40+)
Subsistence farm	35	40 (45)
Commercial farm	45–60	55 (65)
City	55–60	60+ (65)
General	45	50 (55)

3. See Sigmund Diamond, *The Creation of Society in the New World* (Chicago, 1963); Bernard Bailyn, "Politics and Social Structure in Virginia," in James Morton Smith, ed., *Seventeenth-Century America: Essays in Colonial History* (Chapel Hill, 1959), 90–115.

what made our revolution?

JESSE LEMISCH

Criticizing mainstream history often involves radicals taking potshots at particularly vulnerable interpretations of the past without criticizing their assumptions. In his review of Bernard Bailyn's *The Origins of American Politics*, Jesse Lemisch challenges Bailyn's assumptions to reveal the scope of radical discontent with much of traditional history. Bailyn had argued in his important book that ideas about freedom and liberty were transformed in the revolutionary period and resulted in new ideals toward which Americans could aspire. Lemisch responds by asking: Which Americans were affected by these new ideas? To view our past from the perspective of its elite members is, he argues, to play the game by the rules of the elite in the revolutionary period. On the other hand, Lemisch ignores the fact that such an interpretation of history was made possible by the apparent deference of so much of society toward its leading citizens.

Bernard Bailyn sees the American Revolution as an event in the history of ideas. He shows how the disparity between American political realities and the English experience from which certain political ideas derived, finally led to the revolution. Much of what he says is novel and persuasive. But it misleads us about the nature of the American Revolution, and it also is representative of certain glaring blind spots of recent American historiography.

Social conditions in 18th-century England seem a natural starting-point for an exploration of the revolutionary ideology which emerged there. Bailyn quotes J. H. Plumb, who describes a savage and violent society of slums, starvation, epidemic, "rick burnings, machine-smashing, hunger-riots"; the poor "herded" into jails and workhouses which "resembled concentration camps"; ten-year-olds hanged for petty thefts. But this is the last we are to hear of the poor. Bailyn shifts from this Hogarthian reality to the world of Gainsborough so abruptly that the brief appearance of the poor becomes inexplicable; everything which follows seems to deny their existence: "England was rich, and getting richer." (Bailyn omits Plumb's suggestion that things were getting worse for the poor.) But once he has let the poor out of the bag, they remain with the reader, who has a right to be puzzled by "eighteenth-century Britons' sense of their multifarious accomplishments . . . and their distinctiveness in the achievement of liberty." How can Bailyn speak of an era of "harmony and political stability" in the face of widespread riot and protest? How could the English pride themselves on having "eliminated . . . arbitrary power" from government when, to take one instance, the press gang was omnipresent, abusive of human liberty, and—according to learned jurists—legal?

Although Bailyn repeatedly describes the self-congratulatory mood as simply "English," it turns out that these beliefs were "universally shared by all

Jesse Lemisch, "What Made Our Revolution?" *The New Republic*, Vol. 158, no. 21 (May 25, 1968), 25–28. Reprinted by permission of *The New Republic,* © 1968, Harrison-Blaine of New Jersey, Inc.

informed Englishmen" (emphasis added). How universal is that? Not very, Bailyn suggests a few footnotes later: "the uninformed and credulous of all classes . . . were the majority." He views British society from the vantage point of a minority, an "informed" elite. Not the entire elite; Bailyn's focus is on Walpole's opposition: Bolingbroke on the "far right" and, on the "far left," a group of "left-wing" writers and "coffeehouse radicals" of whom the "most effective" were John Trenchard and Thomas Gordon. Left and right merge on "fundamental points," and somehow, with a mathematics which the contemporary left might well envy, it all adds up to an ideology which Bailyn describes variously as "radical," "democratic" and "popular."

The opposition as a whole was in fact part of the mainstream on "major points of doctrine." Bailyn's radicals saw their task as the preservation of a proper balance within government, lest magistrates become "plunderers and murderers." But magistrates *were* plunderers and murderers. Edward Thompson has described the politics of a slightly later period as a game in which the king was the croupier; the opposition seems to have wanted simply to have the croupier play by the rules, not to end the game.

Trenchard and Gordon thought a commonwealth or republic the ideal government, but they rejected it in practice, since it could be brought about only through "bloodshed and upheaval" (of which, Bailyn seems to have forgotten, there was a great deal in England, much of it official). The *Dictionary of National Biography* tersely describes Trenchard as "a Whig with popular sympathies, but by no means a republican, as his opponents wished to consider him." Elsewhere, Bailyn belatedly but temporarily notes that his radicals did not seek "to recast the social order" or to deal with "problems of economic inequality and the injustices of stratified societies."

When Bailyn says that the views of the English opposition were determinative of American views, we want to know, *which* Americans? By Americans, he means "informed" ones, especially certain pamphleteers whose work he collected and analyzed in his *Pamphlets of the American Revolution*. It should come as no surprise that Bailyn's study of such sources "confirmed [his] rather old-fashioned view that the American Revolution was above all else an ideological-constitutional struggle" and convinced him that "in no obvious sense was the American Revolution undertaken as a social revolution." These conclusions arose directly out of his choice of sources, not necessarily out of reality. Did he expect to find an attack on elitism in the thought of the colonial elite? What assumptions led him to suppose that study of the pamphlets gave him an "interior" view of the "Revolutionary movement"? In what sense are the "informed" closer to reality than the "uninformed"? Whose definition of the Revolution shall we accept, John Adams' or that of the men who fought in it? Why not *both*?

Bailyn describes political practices in the colonial legislatures. Where there was harmony in England, there was strife in America: strife between and among executive and legislature. Legally the executive had more power in America than in England. But the "private" constitution through which the executive maintained control in England—e.g., patronage and an easily manipulated electoral system—scarcely existed here. Thus American politics was a matter of "swollen claims and shrunken powers." Colonials applied the view of politics acquired from the English opposition: the mixed constitution was the ideal, and the colonial executives seemed to threaten a proper balance. That threat seemed deliberate and conspiratorial and, in the 1760's and 1770's, overt.

Americans went to war to maintain the Glorious Revolution, to oppose arbitrary power.

Bailyn has made a major contribution in making sense of the legislatures' fears; it seems very clear that they did indeed see the actions of the governors through lenses acquired from Trenchard and Gordon. But is it correct to see the struggle of the legislatures as one in which they are "radical," stand for "popular interests," "popular forces" and "an over-great democracy"? Bailyn's account of the conflicts of colonial politics is to an extraordinary extent a story of economic interests competing to divide the treasure of America: rarely has a scholar arguing for an "ideological" interpretation presented so much evidence to delight economic determinists. Conflicts occur among "ambitious merchant farmers," "merchants and landowners," a governor who came to America "to recoup his dwindling fortune." Traders struggle with traders and are supported by a syndicate of London export merchants; a governor is supported by merchants whose interest in military contracting he favors: he is accused of "profiteering." Colonial politics presents "an almost unchartable chaos of competing groups." Although economic groups sought political expression, there were no "classes," only "stratified 'dignities.' " (Bailyn earlier found a similar diversity among 17th-century New England merchants—who "formed not a singular social entity, but a spectrum; not a clearly defined bloc"—and in 17th-century Virginia, although in the latter case he was able to detect what he called a "ruling class.")

The conduct of the legislators among themselves, or even in conflict with the governors, really tells us next to nothing about democracy. The only way in which we can even approach valid judgments on such matters as class and democracy is to examine the smaller group as it relates to the larger; in the case of colonial America, we must look to those outside of and below the legislature.

Another way of putting the issue is to ask: were there, with regard to the populace at large, matters on which the contentious legislators agreed and thus did not *have* to argue? As in England, both administration and opposition accepted the necessity of the tripartite constitutional balance. They did not argue about the social structure because they did not wish to change it; their silence on this matter makes them more partisan than neutral. They all agreed that effective power should not be given to the people; dispute as they might over who was to get what share in America, the legislators and the governors agreed that that was a matter to be decided *for* the people, not *by* them.

The consensus was not total: Bailyn has not in fact explored here what he calls "the full range of advanced ideas." The existence of Tom Paine and a few other political thinkers—who do not appear in this book—indicates that it was possible to conceive *more* advanced ideas. There was an alternative body of political thought, majoritarian and democratic, rejecting checks and balances, which were seen, correctly, as a means of shackling the popular will. The quality of mainstream "democratic" consensus is better defined by its response to these deviant doctrines than by its quarrels with the governors. John Adams "dreaded the Effect so popular a pamphlet" as Paine's *Common Sense* might have, with its proposals which he thought "so democratical, without any restraint or even an attempt at any Equilibrium or Counterpoise, that it must produce confusion and every Evil work."

When we view the colonial legislatures from below, it is immediately evident that the underlying ingredient of the consensus which held the elite together was anti-populism. Did Trenchard and Gordon's American followers believe in freedom of speech and press? For themselves, yes, but certainly not for those outside the legislature. What Bailyn seems uncritically to accept as libertarian-ism has been more accurately described by Leonard Levy as a "legacy of suppression," much of it done by the legislatures.

Although he seems to accept the dubious idea that government in 18th-century England did not "act on society," Bailyn sees the colonial legislatures as being led, "willy-nilly . . . to exercise creative powers." A large part of that creativity was economic. "Out of the necessity of the situation," writes Bailyn, there devolved upon colonial legislatures the power of distributing land. "Social institutions too had to be created, or legalized." But the content of colonial legislation reveals a forthright expression of class interest; its execution shows a pattern of class justice. If the colonial governors found themselves largely powerless against the economic onslaught of the legislatures, what of the people? Why do we acknowledge a conflict of economic interest in the former instance and ignore it in the latter?

For Bailyn, political representation in the colonies was either "remarkably equitable" or well on its way there, because it was "dynamic, growing": "freehold tenure was almost universal among the white population." (That universality is almost immediately halved when he says that "fifty to seventy-five percent of the adult male white population was entitled to vote.") His argument for universality is based in part on acceptance of the work of Robert Brown. Since 1955, when Brown advanced this idea, there has been over a decade of critical scholarship, some of it attacking Brown's statistical methods and suggesting that the truth might be the opposite of what he contended, but for Bailyn, it is as if this decade never existed. Not only have historians challenged the universality of suffrage in the colonies; they have carried the debate to a higher level, pointing out that voting may have nothing to do with political power.

Bailyn's contention that representation in the colonies was equitable reduces to the argument that apportionment kept pace with geography. This seems a narrow measure of equitability. If every new town was represented, we still want to know something of the dynamics of control in small towns: *which* townspeople were represented? who gets elected when balloting is open? A town meeting may be one of the most easily controlled institutions in a democracy.

There is another sense in which representation in the colonies was anything but equitable, dynamic or "well adjusted to the growth . . . of population." In this book Bailyn focuses on the "openness" of the colonial economy. In his other work he has shown that the long-term trend in colonial society was towards increasing social stratification; "mobility was slowing down." Others have revealed that this was happening on all levels. The open economy was closing down: seamen earned a decreasing share of the rising productivity of shipping; the propertiless multiplied. Thus when we consider representation in terms not of geography but of class we find that the trend is the reverse of dynamic. One wants to reexamine the meaning of America as a land of opportunity in the light of declining opportunity. One wants to consider the meaning of the slogan "no taxation without representation" for those who had nothing to be taxed.

Bailyn has successfully depicted the ideology of the American ruling class. Yet this gives us hardly an inkling of what the Revolution meant to three million Americans. That revolution was led by men who defined their own privilege as synonymous with "liberty"; Bailyn accepts them on their own terms and ignores what they chose to ignore.

In an ironic sense, he has described the origins of American politics. For some time now our historians have been telling us that our politics has been one of consensus: although there have been disagreements among Americans, there has been agreement about fundamentals. In fact there have been real divisions in American life, together with pain, suffering, atrocity and genocide. Our politics has not reflected this; politics has achieved consensus by the simple device of being a politics of exclusion. Daniel Bell blundered onto this when he defined democratic politics as "bargaining between *legitimate* groups and the search for consensus" (emphasis added). Thus those academic boosters who have revelled in the non-ideological nature of American politics and the lack of substantial differences within it have been defining what is essentially a one-party politics. To find the other party we must move outside the political structure, beyond the "mainstream."

The habit of identifying elitist politics with reality has deeply misled us and has in large part brought us to our present crisis. Despite all his concern for "ideology," Bailyn has laid a belated foundation stone for the end of ideology by identifying as "democratic," quarrels among the powerful at which the powerless were expected at best to be spectators. Similar ways of thinking have led us to see poverty as affluence, and "pluralism" where there has in fact been only argument among those groups powerful enough to define themselves as "legitimate."

As reality begins to break through, we emerge from our own self-congratulatory Augustan age. There is very little time left in which to learn radically new ways of thought. Before we undertake more studies of "informed" people, we must ask ourselves, who is better informed about the realities of life in America today. Everett Dirksen, or a ghetto resident? It is time that intellectuals become less parochial, stopped patting their colleagues on the back, and strive for a more objective perspective. In our history as in our public life we must move beyond elitism.

listening to the "inarticulate": William Widger's dream and the loyalties of American revolutionary seamen in British prisons

JESSE LEMISCH

Jesse Lemisch supported his attacks on elitist history with his own studies of the so-called inarticulate. The article that follows is a methodological tour de force. It demonstrates not only what kinds of sources can lead us into the minds of those without power, but also, how asking questions of those who are not normally found in history books forces us to reassess long-established ideas.

"Of kings and gentlemen," wrote W.E.B. Du Bois, "we have the record ad nause[a]m and in stupid detail. . . ."[1] But of "the common run of human beings," he went on, "and particularly of the half or wholly submerged working group, the world has saved all too little of authentic record and tried to forget or ignore even the little saved." "Who built the seven towers of Thebes?" echoed Bertolt Brecht, "The books are filled with names of kings."[2] Such appeals for what might be called a history of the inarticulate have come not only from the left, nor have they necessarily been populist in intent. A century ago, looking at history with somewhat different sympathies, Frederick Law Olmsted, a self-proclaimed "honest growler," spoke as much to the question of validity as to that of humanity:

Men of literary taste . . . are always apt to overlook the working-classes, and to confine the records they make of their own times, in a great degree, to the habits and fortunes of their own associates, or to those of people of superior rank to themselves, of whose sayings and doings their vanity, as well as their curiosity, leads them to most carefully inform themselves. The dumb masses have often been so lost in this shadow of egotism, that, in later days, it has been impossible to discern the very real influence their character and condition has had on the fortune and fate of nations.[3]

Should the character and condition of the "dumb masses" play a minor role in historiography? Must they? The answer to the first question, at least, seems clear: the most conservative standards of evidence and proof require that

Jesse Lemisch, "Listening to the 'Inarticulate': William Widger's Dream and the Loyalties of American Revolutionary Seamen in British Prisons." © 1971 by Peter N. Stearns. Reprinted from the *Journal of Social History*, Vol. IV, no. 4, pp. 333–356, by permission of the editor.

historiography include a history of the inarticulate. No generalization has much meaning until we have actually examined the constituent parts of the entity about which we are generalizing. No contention about the people on the bottom of society—neither that they are rebellious nor docile, neither that they defer to an authority whose legitimacy they accept nor that they curse an authority which they deem illegitimate, neither that they are noble nor that they are base—no such contention even approaches being proved until we have in fact attempted a history of the inarticulate. Consensus, in order to demonstrate its validity, must confront the conservative rocks of evidence and sail safely through them, as must any generalization which claims to describe a society on the basis of research on only a part of that society.[4]

Can we write a history of the inarticulate? It was, in part, to answer that question that I undertook my study of merchant seamen in early America. That study began in dissatisfaction with the role assigned to this group in the secondary literature of the American Revolution.[5] In that literature, seamen appear with great frequency, battling over impressment and rioting in the streets of colonial cities. But although the accounts suggest that seamen acted consistently against British authority, when historians narrate such events it seems to me that they generally evade their central task—explanation.[6] In the absence of other explanations, it frequently appears that Jack Tar rioted because he is and always has been boisterous and irresponsible, the willing victim of alcoholic fantasies, seeking merely to blow off steam. Or at best the seamen rioted because they were manipulated by certain ill-defined groups.

Even accepting a large role for the accidental and the irrational in human affairs, it seems to me that the job of the historian as social scientist is to limit as much as possible the area within which explanation must rely upon such factors. Manipulation exists and irrationality exists, and the historian must acknowledge them when he finds them. But the historian who would make his discipline a more rigorous one should have as his *working assumption* that human actions are generally purposeful and are related to some system of values as well as needs; given that assumption, it is inadequate for him to "explain" the recurrent conduct of large groups of men who seem to act consistently in accord with certain values by making those groups simply the puppets of their social superiors or the victims of alcohol.

In order to explain the seamen's conduct, I found that I would have to ask of them some of the same kinds of questions which intellectual historians generally ask of an elite: questions concerning loyalties and beliefs, all examined within a context which assumed that Jack Tar, like Thomas Jefferson, had ideas and perhaps something which might be called an ideology. On the track of these ideas, I found that actions which might in themselves appear inexplicable made more sense when causality was explored: the historian decides in advance that Jack Tar is a rebel without cause when he neglects to look for cause. The rioting of the pre-Revolutionary decades, for instance, makes more sense when seen against the background of an ancient and bloody tradition of violent resistance to British authority; impressment, commented a Pennsylvania Revolutionary leader, had produced "an estrangement of the Affections of the People from the Authority" of the British, which had led in turn, "by an easy Progression . . . to open Opposition . . . and Bloodshed."[7]

I found inadequacies in the approach to the Revolution—primarily from the top down—generally taken by historians. *Of course*, British officials—insensitive

as they were to grievances of the victims of the policies which they administe-
red—could find no better explanation than manipulation for the conduct of
these men. *Of course*, Admiralty records distorted the realities of impressment,
leading those who based their research on such sources to see impressment in
the context of a manning problem rather than in the context of deprivation of
personal liberty.

The struggle to get inside Jack Tar's head suggested the notion of what might
be called an "experimental history." One way of evaluating the contention that
a crowd is manipulated is to ask, what would the crowd do in the absence of
those alleged to be its manipulators? The social psychologist might devise such
a condition, but the historian has no choice but to accept the data provided by
the past. As it happens, in the New York Stamp Act riots of 1765, precisely
such a condition existed: witnesses who are in conflict on other matters agree
that at one point whatever leaders the crowd had had lost control.[8] At this
point, eschewing plunder, the crowd (including some four to five hundred
seamen) marched some distance in a new direction and in orderly fashion to
attack the logical political target. What is of interest to us here is not that in
this particular instance a crowd demonstrably had political thoughts of its own
but rather that if one attempts to devise conditions under which one might
evaluate the thought and conduct of crowds, one may find a historical situation
which approximates these conditions.[9]

The notion of an "experimental history" seems crucial for a history of the
inarticulate. Given the absence of a laboratory and the impossibility of
controlling conditions experimentally, one must sensitize oneself to seek such
conditions in the existing data. In effect, the historian of the inarticulate must
train himself to think as if he were an experimental social psychologist; he
must try to devise experiments for testing various contentions; then he must
look to history and do his best to find a "natural experiment"—a situation in
which such an experiment was in fact acted out.[10]

One night in 1781—which is some sixty thousand nights ago—American
seaman William Widger, who was nobody,[11] dreamt this dream as sentries
marched around his Revolutionary War prison:

Last night I Dreamed I was in Marblehead and See [saw] Sylvester Stevens[.][12] after
discourseing with him about his Giting home I said to him tis Damd hard now I have Got
so near home and Cant git their. . . . he asked me What the Matter was[;] I sayes Why
you See I am this Side of the weay and the Souldiers Standing Sentrey over by Mr.
Roundays house. . . . I Left him and Went a Little further & met Georg Tucker down by
the eand of Bowden's Lain wheir he Stouped and Shock hands with me and Said he Was
Glad to See me[;] he Said my Wife was Just Deliver'd a Boy. . . . I Started at that and
Said it was a dam'd Lye it was imposable for I had been Gone tow [two] years and leatter
[later] and it was inposable. . . . I Left him in a Great pashan and I was Going Down
towards Nickes cove I met my Mother and Stopt and talked with hur[.] She asked me
wheir [whether] I was not a Going home to see my wife[.] I told hur no I was dam'd if
ever I desired to See hir a Gain[.] She Said the Child was a honest begotten Child and it
was Got before I went to See and it was mine[.] I Said it was inposable for the Child to be
Mine for I had been Gone Mour then two years and it was Inpousable[.] I told hur I was a
dam'd foule to Coum home but I Could go back in the Brig I came in. . . . She pursuaded
upon me to go home but . . . I was in Such a pashan I Swore I would Never See hur a
Gain. . . . She intreated me to go home but I swore I would not and it was no use to ask
me[;] but before I was don talking With hur a bout it I awaked.

What did you, who are somebody, dream last night—or a thousand nights ago? This is not an argument for dream analysis. It simply says that even the most fragile and evanescent sort of historical evidence can be retrieved if we will only look for it. The naval prisons of the American Revolution are an especially rewarding place to look for evidence for the history of the inarticulate. A rich concentration of sources from conflicting points of view enables us to look into the mind of the common seaman; here, we can begin to say meaningful things about what significance the Revolution had for at least some of the inarticulate.

During the Revolution, captured American seamen found themselves impris-oned up and down the Atlantic coast and offshore,[13] and at various places in the British Isles.[14] The three major prisons for captured seamen were a fleet around the prison ship Jersey at New York and, in England, Mill and Forton prisons on land at Plymouth and Portsmouth. During the war these three prison complexes held upwards of ten thousand and perhaps as many as twenty or thirty thousand captured American seamen.[15]

These prisons, in many ways different, had this in common: here thousands of American common seamen were imprisoned, most of them under atrocious conditions, segregated from their officers, and with little hope of release but much opportunity to defect. They were confronted with the necessity to make decisions which they themselves perceived as tests of their loyalty to one another and to the new nation. Those decisions were expressed in specific acts which can be measured quantitatively. These preconditions, then, make our laboratory: here we find solid data concerning the conduct of common seamen; in addition, the sources enable us to move beyond conduct into consciousness. William Widger's dream suggests how deeply into consciousness—some would say beyond—we can dig. In the prisons we can observe the society which the men construct on their own, how they govern themselves, their culture, their values, their ethos, and their ideology.

A situation in certain ways similar, that of Americans in prisoner-of-war camps in North Korea in the early 1950's, seemed not only to military men, but also to psychiatrists, psychologists, sociologists, and journalists, a basis for a sometimes critical re-examination of the American as civilian.[16] Conduct in prison, they said, could be explained in terms of "diverse aspects of our culture,"[17] and thus that conduct in turn illuminated American culture, character, and values. (Dr. Spock himself reconsidered permissiveness.)[18] Although it is tempting to draw conclusions about comparative strengths of national loyalties in the eighteenth and twentieth centuries from an exam-ination of the two sets of prisoners, that is not what is intended here. (In any case, conditions were too dissimilar for facile comparisons of the two groups.) Korea is introduced here solely as a methodological analogue, that is, a recent instance in which scholars in various disciplines felt that an examination of a war-prisoner situation could reveal something of the culture and values of the men. Like Korea, the British prisons of the American Revolution offer a ready-made laboratory for the examination of the degree and quality of national and group loyalty. In the British prisons we can study the estrangement of American popular affection from British authority and the process by which Americans came to see a new authority as legitimate.

Jersey and the other prison ships at New York were places of crowding, filth, disease, and death.[19] Contemporaries estimated that close to 12,000 died there during the war.[20] Interestingly—and not unpredictably—the historian who relied only on Jersey's logs and other official sources would be left almost totally unaware of the realities which led Henry Steele Commager and Richard B. Morris to describe the prison ships as the Revolution's Andersonville.[21]

A few prisoners had the misfortune to spend time both in Jersey and in one of the old buildings used as prisons at Plymouth and Portsmouth in England; they invariably concluded that Jersey was worse.[22] Part of the difference between Jersey and the English prisons is simply the difference between imprisonment ashore and imprisonment in a ship. Another major element of difference offers sharp testimony to the cruelty of civil war. In occupied New York, the prisoners' fellow Americans could hardly bring themselves to acknowledge their presence and their troubles;[23] in England, however, people at all levels of society poured out charity, aid, and comfort, some of it open, some of it underground. "Why, Lard, neighbour," observed a surprised Sunday gawker at Forton, the Americans "be white paple; they taulk jest as us do, by my troth."[24] Englishmen filled the prisoners' charity boxes, raised several thousand pounds for them in meetings throughout England, supported them on the floor of Parliament, and finally helped them to escape and concealed them.[25]

Although never so bad as Jersey, the English prisons, too, had their share of bad food,[26] overcrowding, and bad health,[27] brutal guards, and harsh punishment.[28] To the prisoners, the agent who ran the prison was "the old crab," "arbitary cruel & inhuman," "as full of Spite as an Infernal fiend could bee," "divested of every humane feeling."[29] When a friendly peer visiting Mill Prison was told that the agent was a "dirty fellow," he replied: "Government keeps dirty fellows, to do their dirty Work."[30] But although the Commissioners of Sick and Hurt Seamen did not succeed in securing prisoners from "every evil of captivity, but captivity itself," the story of Mill and Forton is less a story of physical deprivation than is Jersey.[31] This provides us with a valuable comparison, enabling us more nearly to test the quality of the men's response to captivity itself rather than simply to physical deprivation.

There is no ambiguity about the meaning of Jersey: by any standard it is undoubtedly a tale of atrocity. Despite Samuel Eliot Morison's exhortation that we not "stir up" the "unpleasant subject of the treatment of American naval prisoners,"[32] there would seem to be important reasons to do so. If history contains horrors, the attempt to forget them is likely to lead to the necessity to relive them. But in noting that the American Revolution was, among other things, a cruel war, we do so not only out of motives of humanity, but because we want to know the truth of the matter. Was the American Revolution different from others—say, the French Revolution? Certainly it was. Was the American Revolution peculiar in that it was primarily legalistic and not so bloody? The facts of life and death in the prison ships do not jibe with that picture; America, too, was born in bloodshed. In any case, we will never have an accurate answer so long as we study the legalisms and avoid the bloodshed.

But our aim goes beyond the telling of atrocities: our interest is in the thought and conduct of the men. In order to understand that thought and conduct, we must consider the ways in which prisoners could regain their freedom. For much of the war, exchange a prisoners of war seemed hopeless. First of all, they were not prisoners of war; they were rebels, candidates for hanging,[33] detained under a suspension of *habeas corpus*.[34] If informal exchanges took place, formal cartels were repeatedly delayed. We cannot explore here the intricacies of exchange policies on both sides and the tortuous discussions of the matter. It should be noted that if legal status was an obstacle to exchange on the British side, American governments were also sometimes dilatory and uninterested. In

America, Washington instructed the commissary-general of prisoners "absolutely to reject every overture for exchanging" captured privateersmen, who were civilians and therefore not "proper subjects of military capture."[35] Washington took little interest in the exchange of naval prisoners in general,[36] and the civilians in the prison ships at New York were at the bottom of the heap, their fate essentially in the hands of their friends, relatives, home towns. Washington's policy stressed instead palliation of conditions in the ships, and the logic of the policy was stated most bluntly by Secretary of War Benjamin Lincoln: ". . . to reconcile them as much as possible to the miseries of a loathsome confinement until they can be exchanged—and to prevent them— from an idea that they are neglected, engaging in the service of Britain. . . ."[37]

In France, Franklin devoted more energy to trying to arrange exchanges. The British—and sometimes the French—presented obstacles.[38] The British told the prisoners that the Americans were responsible for delays.[39] In common with some officials in America, Franklin thought that the British deliberately delayed exchanges in order to influence the prisoners to go into the British navy, and there is evidence from the prisoners that, regardless of the cause, delays were often so used by recruiting officers.[40] "Where to lay the blame I'm at a loss," wrote one prisoner from Mill.[41] "If Job himself was here," wrote another, "his patience would be worn out."[42] Hopes for exchange fluctuated, many became cynical, and finally concluded, "them hopes are gone. . . ," "Out of all hopes."[43]

"There is nothing but death or entering into the British service before me," wrote a prisoner from Jersey.[44] The narrow limits of the choices available to capture seamen forced them to consider the alternative.[45] There was no confusion in the prisoners' minds about the meaning of enlistment: it constituted a clear act of disloyalty, what we call "defection"—as did they. "What an honour to walk his majestey['s] Quarter deck," roared a recent captive who refused.[46] To prisoners, to join meant, in their words, to be "seduced," to "desert their country's cause."[47] They called those who refused to defect the "brave Americans," "true sons of America."[48] A seaman delivering a speech to his fellow prisoners in Jersey congratulated them for their refusal to be bribed into deserting "the banners of our country."[49] Defectors were coerced, "hooted at and abused,"[50] and prisoners solemnly swore to remain loyal to their country.[51]

Service in the British navy meant "fighting against the liberties of their country" to Americans in Paris and back home.[52] For our purposes it is more significant, and historiographically useful, that the prisoners *themselves* saw it that way. The act of enlistment may mean different things to those who are actually faced with the choice and to those who only consider it from afar. And even among the prisoners, defection had many individual causes and consequences, some of them in conflict. Regardless of the diverse and individual significances of defection, we can say that the men in prisons had a set of beliefs, an ethos concerning defection. In that ethos, refusal to defect was seen as loyalty to the Revolution, defection as disloyalty. The adherence of the prisoners to this belief establishes one of the major preconditions for our natural experiment studying the seamen's loyalties under pressure.

The laboratory is by no means perfect. Many enlisted, or were impressed, between the time of their capture and their arrival at prison.[53] Once in prison, some enlisted because various coercions seemed to them strong enough to remove the voluntary quality of the decision, and some doubtless enlisted because they genuinely believed that that course would increase their opportunities for escape.[54] But most of the factors which make the prisons a less than ideal laboratory tend to mislead us in a conservative direction; that is, we know that defection was, if anything, a maximal measure of disloyalty; a few may have defected despite a high degree of loyalty to the American cause. Finally, an important positive feature of the prisons as laboratory is that the men were quartered separately from their captains; the officers demanded separation, protested to the British when they felt that separation was inadequate and tried to arrange it themselves.[55] In most cases our sources allow us to distinguish between seamen and captains and to be reasonably certain that we are describing the activities of common seamen.

Thus with no apparent way out, the men were offered a choice. If the conditions under which the choice was made are not so clean as they would be were we constructing an experimental situation to study the choice, interpretations of the Korean prisoner-of-war experience suggest that this is nonetheless a fruitful site for the study of the loyalties of the inarticulate in the American Revolution.

To an extraordinary degree, captured American seamen remained Americans. In the prisons our measure of loyalty can approach precision. For Jersey, a generous estimate indicates that, with death more likely than exchange, for every one hundred men who arrived in the ship, only eight chose to defect.[56] Similarly, in Mill and Forton, the overall defection rate was between seven and eight percent,[57] and of the defectors it is possible that fifty percent were what the prisoners called "Old Countrymen,"[58] born in the British Isles. Thus, while birthplace clearly did make a difference, the similarity of conduct under the immensely different conditions of Mill and Forton on the one hand and Jersey on the other suggests that the degree of physical deprivation was not relevant: the men's conduct seems to have been rooted more in who they were, and what their loyalties were, than in the material circumstances of their imprisonment.

Men escaped more often than they defected—perhaps three or four times as often: almost eight hundred escaped from Mill and Forton.[59] What did escape mean to the prisoners? It was a serious matter, involving great and sometimes mortal risks both for those going out and those remaining inside. Those attempting escape from Jersey might be shot in the act[60] or flogged in punishment.[61] In the English prisons, failure meant forty days on half allowance in the Black Hole and a plunge to the bottom of the exchange list.[62] Getting out of Jersey still meant a perilous swim to the shore and the possibility of recapture once ashore.[63] In England, where a large reward was offered for escaped Americans, men whom the prisoners called "five pounders"—"peasants, who were always lurking about" and who "would sell their fathers"—beat the bushes with dogs and clubs;[64] some of them had probably been tipped off by guards with whom they were in collusion.[65]

If most prisoners displayed a great deal of courage and ingenuity in their escape attempts, some were merely in collusion with guards, turnkeys, or civilians, splitting the five pound reward, sometimes after a night and day of sex and liquor in a civilian's home on the outside.[66] Joyrides such as these suggest some of the complexities involved in generalizing about what escape meant to prisoners.[67] We can note, however, that for the majority who were serious about it, escape meant a rejection of the most available alternative way of leaving prison: defection. Just as defection implied disloyalty, escape implied loyalty; we have evaluated the loyalties of twentieth-century prisoners in this way,[68] just as Washington did when he commended escaped seamen as he would have praised brave and loyal soldiers.[69] "We committed treason through his [Majesty's] earth," was the way one captive described his escape.[70] A seaman laughed as prisoners made it past "the grand Lobster guard";[71] others mocked defection by using the pretense of enlisting as a mask for organized escape.[72] "Kiss my arse!" signaled an escapee, once out of Jersey's firing range.[73] "Do you know that it is a great crime to break one of His Majesty's locks?" asked a prison commander;[74] "I told him that I did not regard His Majesty nor his locks. What I was after was my liberty."

Underlying escape was organization and cooperation. Not only those escaping but also many of those staying behind were direct participants in escape attempts. There were tools to be gotten and concealed, locks to be picked, bars to be broken, holes to be cut or dug, dirt to be hidden.[75] Plans for the escape had to be agreed upon, contingency plans had to be made in case detection took place, signals had to be devised, and arrangements made for rendezvous. The decision had to be made that the time had come to put the plan into execution. During the escape itself, guards had to be deceived or overwhelmed, prisoners had to be assisted out through holes or broken ports. The one hundred and nine men who escaped from Mill one night in December 1778 after a month's digging had previously drawn lots to decide the order of egress, and two men checked them off a list as they entered the hole.[76] None of these decisions and plans made themselves; a historical record which presents us with *faits accomplis*, decisions made and carried out, should invite us to look beyond, into the process leading to these decisions, and to recognize that these actions could not have been taken without serious thought, much discussion, and mutual trust.

The cooperation behind escapes is one facet of the larger story of prisoner organization and self-government. What follows, although only a sampling of the material available, is intended to suggest that exploration of the specifics of the prisoners' self-government and even their culture is feasible.[77] First of all, just as prison officials posted a list of regulations to let the prisoners know, as the officials put it, "what behaviour is expected on their Part,"[78] there was a parallel but in many senses more inclusive structure erected by the prisoners themselves, who, as one put it, "adventured to form themselves into a republic, framed a constitution and enacted wholesome laws, with suitable penalties."[79] Early in the war, prisoners created "a code of By-Laws . . . , for their own regulation and government. . . ."[80] These codes, or "Articles," had a quite literal existence; written copies existed, and they were posted and read aloud periodically.[81] These rules, and the behavior which *they* sanctioned, competed with the official rules for the prisoners' respect.

Legislation by prisoners ranged from health to morality to political conduct. There were rules requiring "personal cleanliness . . . , as far as . . . practicable" and forbidding smoking, "blackguarding," drunkenness, and theft.[82] "Due observance of the Sabbath . . ." was honored in the breach.[83] Consider this, and consider prisoners petitioning for a clergyman,[84] and the shame of one at being overheard praying "like a minister,"[85] and consider another, complaining, "It is a great grievance to be . . . debarred from hearing the gospel preached on the Lord's day. . . ."[86] In such evidence as this, and more like it, there hangs a tale, not yet told, of the real meanings of religion in early America. (And other untold tales, of Franklinian virtues among the inarticulate, are to be found in men fretting over their shipmates' "blaspheming their Maker continually,"[87] and others, keeping accounts of whittled ladles sold to visitors at a shilling apiece,[88] and others, struggling toward literacy through diligent study, leaving prison captains-to-be.)[89]

Survival requires that any group living together make rules on such matters as hygiene. But just as prison or legislation in more political areas—to be examined shortly—expresses an active rather than a passive response to their situation, so some of their rules for moral conduct indicate that their culture is not fully explicable simply in terms of the minimal necessities for group survival. "No giant like man should be allowed to tyranize over, or abuse another who was no way his equal in strength."[90] "No prisoner, when liberated, could remove his chest."[91] Many distributed other property before escape or exchange[92] or, afterwards, tried to will money left in the prison agent's hands to other prisoners.[93] Loyalties to town and crew flourished,[94] and communal institutions established by the captors—such as the mess—were imbued by the captives with a deeper meaning than the British intended.[95]

"A secret, . . . revealed to the guard, was death."[96] Committees were formed to deal with informers; trials were held, sentences handed down, punishments carried out.[97] In Jersey, a prohibition of defection may have been written into the by-laws.[98] An antidefection agreement carrying harsh penalties was posted in Forton,[99] and in Mill over one hundred signed this paper:

> We, whose names are hereunto subscribed, do, of our own free and voluntary consent, agree firmly with each other, and hereby solemnly swear, that we are fully determined to stand, and so remain as long as we live, true and loyal to our Congress, our country, our wives, children and friends, and never to petition to enter on board any of His Britannic Majesty's ships or vessels, or into any of his services whatsoever.[100]

Those prisoners who sought to defect did so only "very slyly."[101] Even Old Countrymen, complained a British admiral, "dare not make known their Intentions," lest they be exposed, like the defecting Americans, "to the Resentment of the other Prisoners, who threaten the lives of those who offer to serve in the Navy. . . ."[102]

It is clear that some prisoners stayed only under compulsion, disobeying many of the prisoner-made rules described above, and undergoing harsh punishments at the hands of other prisoners. What stands out in the prisons is not that there was disunity but that, in this hostile environment, there was sufficient unity to maintain effective self-government. There were various forms of organization: there were votes and lotteries, and other arrangements, to assure the equitable distribution of food and clothing; there were committees for trial and punishment and committees of correspondence which drew up, read aloud, and circulated for signatures petitions and remonstrances, addressed to Franklin, to Washington, to the House of Lords, to "Friends and Fellow Countrymen in America." Hundreds signed these documents, protesting prison conditions, seeking to publicize their situation on the outside and to bring about exchange or amelioration. Beneath the guns and bayonets of the British the prisoners maintained a legal structure which in many ways directly contradicted the official structure.[103]

When Captain Thomas Dring sat down in 1824 to recall his experiences as a twenty-three year old imprisoned in Jersey in 1782, he found it "an astonishing fact" that the prisoners had obeyed the by-laws so long and so well.[104] The prisoners were "so numerous" and, thought the old captain—by now a leading citizen of Providence—they were "of that class . . . who are not easily controlled, and usually not the most ardent supporters of good order." And yet, men so prone to disorder as Dring supposed them to be had paid what he called "a willing submission" to the rules. They mutually supported their own good order and reserved for themselves the right to decide when British authority deserved obedience and when they would reject it as unjust and therefore unworthy of obedience: ". . . if any man misbehaves and deserves punishment, we will deliver him up, or punish him ourselves, rather than he should go unpunished; but rather than see a man chastised unjustly, we will do our utmost, for his rescue."[105] In this way they attempted to overrule British authority, through demonstration and direct action, based always on what Edward Thompson has called "some legitimising notion of right."[106] They had withdrawn their loyalties from the British and had given legitimacy to their own prison government, a government deriving its just powers from the consent of the governed.

If the government of the prisoners was legitimate, that was not only because it was the prisoners' own but also because it was *American*. They were quite articulate in their nationalism. We have already seen how they viewed the decision concerning defection in the context of national loyalty. In addition, from the very beginning, they expressed contempt for what they perceived as the merely pretended legalisms by which the British attempted to define them as rebels, pirates, and traitors. "D[am]n his Majesty & his pardon too . . . what murder or treason have we done Prey [?]"[107] They damned the King and tried and punished those who damned the Continental Congress.[108] They delivered fiery patriotic speeches and held contemptuous dialogues with their captors.[109] They sang defiant and exultant songs, of the Stamp Act and the Boston Tea Party, and Bunker Hill, along with songs of lamentation by English widows and generals on the harshness of the war in America, longing for peace. Their songs wished "bad luck to the King and Queen/ And all the Royal family. . . ,"

Success unto America likewise to Washington
Here is a health unto America that scorns to be control'd.[110]

There were frequent patriotic demonstrations and celebrations of American victories: American flags and thirteen cheers for the French King's birthday; cheers to commemorate the defeat of Burgoyne; huzzas for the French, for the Spanish, and for the Dutch; for the capture of Cornwallis, American flags in hatbands, a parade around the prison yard, and, at night, an illumination: ". . . generale Respect agreable to the present ability of the prison."[111] And, on the Fourth of July: stars and stripes, cheers and songs, and, for some, bayonets and death. On their cockades they wrote, "INDEPENDENCE" and "LIBERTY OR DEATH." Seeing what was on their heads, but never really knowing what was on their minds, the prison keeper doubled the guard.[112]

Unquestionably, the seamen were nationalists. That is not, however, a mark of distinctiveness. Indeed, their nationalism might be seen as a measure of the extent to which they shared in the consensus and did not conceive of their interests as distinctive;[113] they rallied strongly to the support of a government which was not theirs.[114]

To say, simply, that the seamen were nationalists says nothing about the *content* of their nationalism—what it was they thought they were being loyal to when they were loyal to "America," the values which they fastened to their nationalism and expressed through it.

The prisoners articulated a collectivist ethical code. Their government was egalitarian, and in their culture and conduct they showed a high degree of awareness of themselves as a group and loyalty to that group. There is a distinctive flavor about this egalitarianism and collectivism, seeming to set the seamen's values apart from the individualism and hierachism[115] of the leaders of the Revolution. But does this constitute politics? The line between politics and what has been called "pre-politics"[116] is uneven and unclear, and no law of nature nor of man dictates that the one become the other, that potentiality become actuality. Although ethical code and group conduct would seem to have both implications and potentialities for politics, they are probably closer to "pre-politics" than to politics. What of constitution-making, laws, trials, petitions, committees, votes, and the rest of the structure of self-government in the prisons? This seems more nearly to be politics, especially when we note that the seamen self-consciously connected them with the ideals of the larger struggle; they governed themselves in accord with abstract notions of liberty, justice, and right, and they associated these notions with the birth of a new and better nation. Their nationalism clearly had political dimensions.

If the seamen had politics, that does not mean that they had class politics in the prisons. "Class happens," writes Edward Thompson, "when some men, as a result of common experiences . . . , feel and articulate the identity of their interests as between themselves, and as against other men whose interests are different from . . . theirs."[117] This describes what happened in the prisons, but with the vital qualification that it happened in the *nationalist* sense.[118] If *class* happened, it would be more likely to occur after the war, when independence *per se* was no longer the predominant issue and the seamen were able to test against the new realities the ideals for which they had fought.

The decision of the inarticulate to give their loyalties to one side or another in war has been a matter of fundamental importance in history, a decision with enormous political meaning. In the Revolution, men like William Widger chose the American side. William Widger was somebody; he had individuality, dignity, and values of his own. He expressed those values, in part, in his nationalism, and he and his fellow prisoners held to their nationalism with a strength which cannot be explained by manipulation. The nationalism of the seamen was as authentic as the nationalism of a Jefferson, an Adams, or a Franklin; in this sense, the Revolution happened from the bottom up as well as from the top down.

We know what William Widger dreamt sixty thousand nights ago.[119] If we can find William Widger's dream in the published *Historical Collections* of the Essex Institute; if we can find, in Yale's Franklin Collection, rich and poignant letters from seamen which even convey, through their spelling, something of the sound of the spoken language;[120] if Philip Freneau, the man who came to be called "The Poet of the American Revolution," shared some of the experiences of "The British Prison Ship" and wrote of them;[121] if the seamen themselves left us ample materials which invite us to examine their politics, their loyalties, and their culture; if sources such as these and others exist, from which it is possible to construct laboratories in which the inarticulate can be heard—then is it not time that we put "inarticulate" in quotation marks and begin to see the term more as a judgment on the failure of historians than as a description of historiographical reality?[122]

NOTES

1. For this and the following, see Du Bois' preface to Herbert Aptheker, ed., *A Documentary History of the Negro People in the United States* (New York, 1951), p. v.

2. *Selected Poems*, trans. H. R. Hays (New York, 1947), pp. 108–109.

3. *A Journey in the Seaboard Slave States, with Remarks on Their Economy* (New York, 1861), pp. 214–215, quoted in Stephan Thernstom, *Poverty and Progress: Social Mobility in a Nineteenth-Century City* (Cambridge, Mass., 1964), p. 1. For Olmsted's self-description, see p. ix of *Journey*.

4. For further remarks on inaccuracies in the historiography of early America due to elitism, see my "The American Revolution Seen From the Bottom Up," in Barton J. Bernstein, ed., *Towards A New Past: Dissenting Essays in American History* (New York, 1968), pp. 3–45. Cf. Michael Rogin, "Progressivism and the California Electorate," *Journal of American History*, LV (Sept. 1968), 298: "conclusions that progressivism was not a movement of 'the people' can hardly be sustained until the behavior of the people is actually examined."
Similar comments may be made concerning the use of the concept of ideological hegemony. Deriving the term from Antonio Gramsci, a Marxist theoretician who was especially concerned with the role of intellectuals in twentieth-century Italian politics, Eugene D. Genovese defines ideological hegemony as "the seemingly spontaneous loyalty that a ruling class evokes from the masses through its cultural position and its ability to promote its own world view as the general will" ("Marxian Interpretations of the Slave South," in Bernstein, ed., *Towards a New Past*, p. 123). Genovese correctly contends that an understanding of "class struggle . . . presupposes a specific historical analysis of the constituent classes" (p. 98), but he draws conclusions about the hegemony of the slaveholders with very little examination of "the masses," who, he contends, accepted that hegemony (pp. 90–125; see also his *The Political Economy of Slavery: Studies in the Economy and Society of the Slave South* [New York, 1965]). Genovese's work has produced rich results for our understanding of the slaveholders, but it tells us less about the "loyalty" or otherwise of the nonslaveholders; one does not need to contend that the latter were in open, or even furtive, rebellion to note that there remain enormous complexities which prevent a definition of "to rule" as synonymous with "to evoke loyalty." The existence of hegemonic mechanisms does not demonstrate the existence of hegemony. This important area needs fuller exploration. (See also my "New Left Elitism," *Radical America*, I [Sept.–Oct. 1967], 43–53; and my "Communication," *American Historical Review* [in press].)

5. For a partial summary of this research, see my "Jack Tar in the Streets: Merchant Seamen in the Politics of Revolutionary America," *William and Mary Quarterly*, 3d Ser., XXV (July 1968), 371–407. Except where otherwise noted, this is the source for the following statements about seamen and historiography.

6. For some notable exceptions, see Carl Bridenbaugh, *Cities in Revolt: Urban Life in America, 1743–1776* (New York, 1955), pp. 114–117, 305–312; Richard B. Morris, *Government and Labor in Early America* (New York, 1946), pp. 188–193, 225–278; and Oliver M. Dickerson, *The Navigation Acts and the American Revolution* (Philadelphia, 1951), pp. 218–219.

7. Joseph Reed, President of Pa., quoted in my "Jack Tar in the Streets," p. 395.

8. See my unpubl. diss. (Yale, 1962), "Jack Tar vs. John Bull: The Role of New York's Seamen in Precipitating the Revolution," pp. 88–91.

9. Cf. Merle Curti's criticism of historians for their reluctance "to try to adapt experimental logic to situations where actual experimentation is impossible" (rev. of C. Vann Woodward, ed., *The Comparative Approach to American History* [New York, 1968] in *Journal of American History*, LV [Sept. 1968], 373). Historians are of course limited to what psychologists call "natural experiments"; their predictions are made *a posteriori*, and

the experiment cannot be rerun under other conditions to determine whether the variable focused upon is in fact the decisive one.

10. Such training might fruitfully begin with study of the imaginative and rigorous experiments on obedience and defiance devised by Stanley Milgram. See his "Behavioral Study of Obedience," *Journal of Abnormal and Social Psychology*, LXVII (1963), 371–378; "Issues in the Study of Obedience: A Reply to Baumrind," *American Psychologist*, XIX (Nov. 1964), 848–852; "Some Conditions of Obedience and Disobedience to Authority," *Human Relations*, XVIII (1965), 57–76; and "Liberating Effects of Group Pressure," *Journal of Personality and Social Psychology*, I (Feb. 1965), 127–134. Milgram's experiments were called to my attention by Prof. Naomi Weisstein of the Dept. of Psychology, Loyola Univ., Chicago. Weisstein briefly discusses Milgram's work and other experiments with broad implications for the writing of history (especially work by R. Rosenthal and by S. Schachter and J. E. Singer) in "Kinder, Kuche, Kirche as Scientific Law: Psychology Constructs the Female," a paper presented at the meeting of The American Studies Association, Univ. of California, Davis, Oct. 1968 (revised version forthcoming in *Psychology Today*).

11. Widger (1748–1823) was a Marblehead privateersman captured in the brig *Phoenix*, Feb. 12, 1779, and committed to Mill Prison, May 10, 1779. After the war Widger became master of the brig *Increase*. For his dream, see "Diary of William Widger of Marblehead, Kept at Mill Prison, England, 1781," *Essex Institute Historical Collections* (Salem, Mass.), LXXII–LXXIV (1937–38), 347 (hereafter cited as *EIHC*). Concerning Widger, see "Diary," *ibid.*, LXXXIII, 311–312; *Boston Gazette, and the Country Journal*, July 1, 1782; Benjamin J. Lindsey, *Old Marblehead Sea Captains and the Ships in Which They Sailed* (Marblehead, 1915), p. 131; Thurlow S. Widger, "The Widger Family" (n.d.; typescript at Essex Institute), pp. 4, 9–13. I am indebted to Dorothy M. Potter, Librarian at the Essex Institute, for helping in securing biographical information about Widger.

12. One of Widger's shipmates; Stevens escaped from Mill Prison (*Boston Gazette, and the Country Journal*, July 1, 1782).

13. For New York, see the numerous citations in the following pages.

For Norfolk, see "Biographical Memoir of Commodore [Richard] Dale," *The Port Folio*, VIII, ser. 3 (June 1814), 500.

For Rhode Island: John K. Alexander, ed., "Jonathan Carpenter and the American Revolution: The Journal of an American Naval Prisoner of War and Vermont Indian Fighter," *Vermont History*, XXXVI (Spring 1968), 78–79; Charles Collins to Benjamin Franklin, July 8, 1779, in Franklin Papers (American Philosophical Society), XV, 26; "Diary of George Thompson of Newburyport, Kept at Forton Prison, England, 1777–1781," *EIHC*, LXXVI (July 1940), 222.

Quebec: "Reminiscences of the Revolution: Prison Letters and Sea Journal of Caleb Foot," *EIHC*, XXVI (March 1889), 105–108.

Halifax: Commissioners of Sick and Hurt Seamen (hereafter abbreviated as CSHS) to Admiralty, Feb. 25, 1777, Jan. 5, 1778, Sept. 17, 1779, Public Record Office, Admiralty 98/11/86, 153–154, 12/176–179; Admiralty to CSHS, Aug. 1, 1777, Jan. 14, 1778, Sept. 8, 1779, March 15, 1782, National Maritime Museum, Greenwich, Adm/M/404, 405; [Boston] *Independent Chronicle and the Universal Advertiser*, Feb. 5, 1778; John Blatchford, *Narrative of the Life & Captivity . . .* (New London, 1778), pp. 3–6.

St. John's: *Salem* [Mass.] *Gazette*, Oct. 17, 1782.

West Indies: Admiralty to CSHS, July 3, Dec. 7, 1780, Sept. 15, 1781, Sept. 3, 1782, Adm/M/404, 405; Account of George Ralls, Nov. 7, 1778, New-York Historical Society; Secretary of State to Admiralty, Dec. 5, 1781, Adm/1/4146.

14. For Mill and Forton Prisons, see numerous citations in the following pages. Smaller numbers of Americans were kept, usually temporarily, at such places as Kinsale, Kilkenny, and the Cove of Cork in Ireland, at Edinburgh, at Liverpool, Deal, at the Nore, off Chatham, at Bristol, Pembroke, Shrewsbury, Falmouth, Weymouth, and Yarmouth. Mention of these is scattered throughout the correpondence between the Admiralty and the CSHS (Admiralty to CSHS, 1777–83, National Maritime Museum, Greenwich, Adm/M/404–405; CSHS to Admiralty, 1777–83, Public Record Office, London, Adm 98/11–14). A fuller description of these prisons and more specific citations will appear in my full-length study, "Jack Tar in the Darbies: American Seamen in British Prisons during the Revolution," to be completed shortly.

15. For almost complete figures for Mill (1296 American prisoners) and Forton (1200) see John Howard, *The State of the Prisons in England and Wales . . .* (4th ed.; London, 1792), pp. 185, 187. Jersey's logs list a total of 7773 (Adm 51/493 and Adm 51/4228). But more than twenty ships held captured seamen at New York during the war, and although Jersey was the major prison ship, others, such as *Good Hope*, held more than three hundred at one time (*New Hampshire Gazette*, Feb. 9, 1779), and Jersey did not receive her first prisoners until June, 1779. Thus it is likely that the total for New York will be more than doubled when figures are found for the other prison ships. In addition, the figure for Jersey alone is low because there are two gaps in the logs (Nov. 21, 1777–Aug. 2, 1778, and Dec. 25, 1780–Feb. 14 1781) one of them during the period of Jersey's service as a prison ship, and because, as will be seen below, those who kept Jersey's logs were far from faithful record keepers.

Mill and Forton were set up early in 1777 explicitly for Americans captured at sea: Admiralty to CSHS, March 13, April 19, 1777, Adm/M/404; Commissioners' Memoran-dum, March 14, 1777, Adm 98/11/87-88; CSHS to Admiralty, Dec. 15, 1777, Adm 98/11/149; Commissioners' Minute, April 22, 1777, Adm 99/49. The New York prison ships primarily held soldiers after the Battle of Long Island, e.g., Jabez Fitch, *A Narrative of the Treatment with which the American Prisoners Were Used, Who Were Taken by the British and Hessian Troops on Long Island . . .* [publ. as *Prison Ship Martyr, Captain Jabez Fitch: His Diary in Facsimile*] (New York, 1903). But by the end of 1777 and for the rest of the war the prison ships were reserved for seamen, while soldiers and their officers were kept on land: Albert G. Greene, ed., *Recollections of the Jersey Prison-Ship: Taken and Prepared for Publication from the Original Manuscript of the late Captain Thomas Dring, of Providence, R.I., One of the Prisoners* (New York, 1961 [1st ed.: Providence, 1829]), p. 50; Danske Dandridge, ed., *American Prisoners of the Revolution* (Charlottesville, 1911), p. 405; [New York] *Royal Gazette*, Jan. 15, 1779.

16. The content of that re-examination varied greatly; for conflicting interpretations, together with summaries of the views of others, see Eugene Kinkead, *In Every War But One* (New York, 1959) and Albert D. Biderman, *March to Calumny: The Story of American POW's in the Korean War* (New York, 1963).

17. The phrase appears in Kinkead, p. 18. According to Biderman, "Kinkead's book is misleading with regard to the strengths as well as the weaknesses that may be characteristically American" (p. 45). Biderman sees among the prisoners in Korea "a noteworthy display of group organization and discipline (although not always the traditional Army variety of organization or one that can easily be perceived by the more traditionalistic Army officers. . . .)"; he finds the roots of certain kinds of prisoner resistance in characteristics and "generalized dispositions" which are "peculiarly" or "distinctively" American (pp. 43–45 and *passim*).

18. "Are We Bringing Up Our Children Too 'Soft' For the Stern Realities They Must Face?" *Ladies' Home Journal*, Sept. 1960, 20–25, discussed in Betty Friedan, *The Feminine Mystique* (New York, 1963), pp. 373–374. Both Spock and Friedan accepted Kinkead uncritically.

19. Ample documentation for this contention may be found in the various sources cited in this article. For reasons of space, I am here giving only brief attention to physical conditions in the prisons and prison ships, while focusing instead on the conduct of the men.

20. The figure usually offered is 11,644; although it was generally offered for Jersey alone, it was probably intended as a total for all the twenty or so prison ships at New York, of which Jersey was the best known. See *Connecticut Gazette*, April 25, 1783; *Pennsylvania Packet*, April 29, 1783; *New York Packet, and the General Advertiser* [Fishkill], May 8, 1783; David Ramsay, *The History of the American Revolution* (Philadelphia, 1789), II, 285; Dring, pp. 4-5; Thomas Andros, *The Old Jersey Captive; or, A Narrative of the Captivity of Thomas Andros, (Now Pastor of the Church in Berkley,) on Board the Old Jersey Prison Ship at New York, 1781* (Boston, 1833), p. 8. (For a lower estimate, see Henry Steele Commager and Richard B. Morris, eds., *The Spirit of 'Seventy-Six: The Story of the American Revolution as Told by Participants* [2 vols; New York, 1958], II, 854.)

Since we do not know how the figure was derived, we must distrust it. But British prison officials who were in New York after the war had ample opportunity to deny it and never did (James Lenox Banks, *David Sproat and Naval Prisoners in the War of the Revolution* [New York, 1909], p. 107 [cf. p. 22], Charles I. Bushnell, ed., *The Adventures of Christopher*

Hawkins . . . first Printed from the original Manuscript. Written by Himself [New York, 1864], p. 263). Conservative projections on the basis of known daily death rates derived from sources cited in this article produce a total over 11,000. (Almost one third of one captured crew was dead within seven weeks—Henry Onderdonk, Jr., *Revolutionary Incidents of Suffolk and Kings Counties with an Account of the Battle of Long Island, and the British Prisons and Prison-Ships at New-York* [New York, 1849], p. 240.) There may be support for a large projection in the most substantial sort of evidence: actual remains, uncovered over the years; see I. N. P. Stokes, *The Iconography of Manhattan Island, 1498–1909* (New York, 1895–1928), V, 1398, 1493; Henry R. Stiles, ed., *Account of the Interment of the Remains of American Patriots who Perished on Board the Prison Ships during the American Revolution* (New York, 1865), p. 10; and Prison Ship Martyrs' Monument Assoc., *Secretary's Report of the Obsequies of the Prison Ship Martyrs at Plymouth Church, Brooklyn, New York, June 16, 1900* (New York, 1901), p. 17; cf. Dring, pp. 60, 146.

21. II, 854. One captain stopped recording deaths in Jersey's log after six weeks, and the others never started; see entries for Feb. 20, March 4, April 3, 5, 1781, Adm 51/4228, and see logs *ibid., passim,* and Adm 51/493. The only disease mentioned anywhere in the logs is smallpox, and that is mentioned only once (June 5, 1782). See also my "Jack Tar in the Streets," p. 402n. (Conversely, relying solely on accounts by prisoners would also be misleading; for some criticism of these sources, see nn.24, 45 below.)

22. E.g., "Journal of William Russell," in Ralph D. Paine, ed., *The Ships and Sailors of Old Salem: The Record of a Brilliant Era of American Achievement* (New York, 1909), p. 169. The Continental Congress agreed; see Worthington Chauncey Ford, ed., *Journals of the Continental Congress, 1774–1789* (Washington, 1904–37), XXII, 245–246. See also Dring, pp. 79–80.

Both Mill and Forton had held French and Spanish prisoners during the Seven Years War, although neither had been designed for that purpose (Admiralty to CSHS, March 13 and April 19, 1777, Adm/M/404; CSHS to Admiralty, Nov. 22, 1780, Adm 98/13/137). Forton had been built as a hospital for sick and wounded seamen at the beginning of the century and was still referred to in Admiralty correspondence early in the war as "Forton Hospital" (John S. Barnes, ed., *Fanning's Narrative: Being the Memoirs of Nathaniel Fanning, an Officer of the Revolutionary Navy* [New York, 1912], p. 9; Admiralty to CSHS, March 13, 1777, Adm/M/404). At least one of the buildings at Mill dated back to Queen Anne's time (Andrew Sherburne, *Memoirs of Andrew Sherburne: A Pensioner of the Navy of the Revolution* [2nd ed.; Providence, 1831], p. 84).

23. For some possible minor exceptions, see Dring, pp. 74–78, and Onderdonk, p. 248.

24. Fanning, p. 11. Although in this instance contemporary evidence almost precisely confirms Fanning's report (cf. Charles Herbert, *A Relic of the Revolution* [Boston, 1847], pp. 19–20), most reminiscences of dialogue must of course be taken with a grain of salt. (Fanning seems to have written the section of his *Narrative* dealing with his imprisonment before and/or during 1801, although he "compiled" and "copied" it from his "old journal" [pp. i, 123n., 124].) While most of the sources on which this article is based are contemporary, a few are later reminiscences. The latter must be used with caution—just as we would use the memoirs of a Benjamin Franklin, or a Henry Adams, or old former slaves. In each case we should, as Edward P. Thompson advises, hold sanctimoniousness up to "a Satanic light and read backwards"; our sources must be "critically fumigated" (*The Making of the English Working Class* [New York, 1964], p. 58, 493). At the same time, we must be certain that we are not—as so often seems to be the case—applying critical standards which vary by race or class, so that the reminiscences of an aged Franklin seem acceptable as sources, while the reminiscences of aged former slaves are dismissed. (Consider also the tendency of historians of slavery to accept plantation records while largely ignoring the rich materials contained in the Federal Writers' Project's Slave Narrative Collection.) Such sources as the latter are complex and difficult to use; rather than ignoring them, we would do better to develop methodologies for distinguishing what is genuine in them from what is later superimposition. For such an attempt, see Jesse Lemisch, J. Gordon Melton, and John R. Cory, "A Methodology of Gospel Scholarship Applied to the History of the 'Inarticulate' " (in preparation).

25. Olive Anderson, "The Treatment of Prisoners of War in Britain during the American War of Independence," *Bulletin of the Institute of Historical Research,* XXVIII (1955), 81; John K. Alexander, "Forton Prison during the American Revolution: A Case Study of British Prisoner of War Policy and the American Response to that Policy," *EIHC,* CIII (Oct. 1967), 378–379; Herbert, p. 85–89; Petition of two hundred prisoners to the Lords in

Parliament, June, 1781, Adm/M/405; Admiralty to CSHS, Dec. 11, 1777, Adm/M/404; "Journal of Samuel Cutler," *New-England Historical and Genealogical Register*, XXXII (Jan.-Oct., 1878), 187; *Annual Register for 1778* (London, 1779), pp. 78-79. The Americans were somewhat more effective in getting help to their countrymen in England than to those imprisoned in America; see, e.g., CSHS to Admiralty, Jan. 2, 1778, Adm 98/11/152. For English help to American escapees, see n.65 below.

26. Widger, "Diary," LXXIII, pp. 316, 320; Herbert, pp. 60, 75, 140; Ralls Account, New-York Historical Society; Cutler, p. 396; "Humanitas" to Admiralty, Aug. 29, 1777, encl. in Admiralty to CSHS, Sept. 3, 1777, Adm/M/404; "A Yankee Privateersman in Prison in England, 1777-79 [Journal of Timothy Connor]," *New-England Historical and Genealogical Register*, XXX-XXXIII (1876-79), XXX, 352. (Connor's authorship is uncertain; see William R. Cutter to Librarian of State Dept., Jan. 31, 1893, with the original manuscript in the Library of Congress, Manuscript Div., U.S. Navy, Accession 748.)

27. CSHS to Admiralty, July 23, 1779, Feb. 11, 1783, Adm 98/12/106-107, 14/301; Carpenter, p. 83.

28. Widger, "Diary," LXXIII, 335; Thompson, "Diary," p. 227; Connor, XXXII, 165.

29. Fanning, p. 10; Ralls Account, New-York Historical Society; Widger, "Diary," LXXIV, 37; *Pennsylvania Journal*, Sept. 22, 1781.

30. Russell, p. 164. One historian who failed to find anything "recriminatory or vindictive" in the correspondence between the Admiralty and the CSHS offered this as evidence of "tolerance and good sense" in official attitudes toward the prisoners (Eunice H. Turner, "American Prisoners of War in Great Britain, 1777-1783," *Mariners' Mirror*, XLV [Aug. 1959], 200). This proves nothing of the sort and suggests the reverse: consensus among administrators should be an ominous sign for those who study the administrated. Olive Anderson—who defends prisoner policy in England as "strikingly enlightened" and dismisses harsher versions as originated by "propagandists" and perpetuated by "race-tradition"—nonetheless moves away from Turner's formalism and closer to the truth of actual decision-making when she notes that the Admiralty "rarely had enough time, knowledge or interest to take an independent line. Normally therefore they merely authorized or implemented the commissioners' proposals. . ." (pp. 65, 82, 83).

31. The Commissioners, Sept. 1779, quoted in Anderson, 72 According to figures derived from official sources, 4.57 percent of the prisoners in Mill and Forton died (Howard, pp. 185, 187, 191). Such figures seem to be confirmed by an American source (*Boston Gazette, and the Country Journal*, June 24, July 1, 8, 1782) whose 3.5 percent figure for deaths in Mill alone almost precisely duplicates the British source. I am indebted to John K. Alexander, a graduate student at the Univ. of Chicago, for the latter figure and for other valuable assistance in many areas, especially in connection with my research on the English prisons. (For figures for Forton, see Alexander, "Forton Prison," pp. 380, 280n.)

32. *John Paul Jones: A Sailor's Biography* (Boston, 1959), pp. 165-166. (Morison did not want to provide "fuel for American Anglophobes. . . .")

33. Until March 25, 1782 (22 Geo. III, c. 10). See, e.g., Benjamin Franklin to John Adams, April 21, 1782, Adams Mss. Trust, Mass. Historical Society.

34. 17 Geo. III, c. 9 ("North's Act").

35. Washington to John Beatty, Aug. 19, 1779, John C. Fitzpatrick, ed., *The Writings of George Washington from the Original Manuscript Sources, 1745-1799* (Washington, 1931-44), XVI, 131.

36. Washington to Major General William Heath, June 29, 1780, *Writings*, XIX, 93; Washington to Mrs. Theodosia Prevost, May 19, 1779, *Writings*, XV, 105; Washington to Board of War, June 16, 1780, *Writings*, XIX, 17.

37. Banks, pp. 99-100.

38. See, e.g., American Commissioners to Stormont, April 3, 1777, *London Chronicle*, Nov. 6, 1777; Benjamin Franklin to Wuibert, Lund, McKellar and other prisoners at Forton, Oct. 20, 1778, Library of Congress (copy); Benjamin Franklin to David Hartley, Jan. 25, 1779, Library of Congress (transcript); Alexander, "Forton Prison," p. 385.

39. This produced some poignant letters from prisoners to Franklin, e.g., Jacob Smith to Benjamin Franklin, Jan. 24, 1783, Franklin Papers, XXVII, 47, APS; two hundred eighty American Prisoners at Forton to Benjamin Franklin, Feb. 3, 7, 1780, Historical Society of Pa.; Samuel Harris to Benjamin Franklin, June 12, 1781, Bache Collection, APS.

40. Franklin to David Hartley, March 21, 1779, Library of Congress (letterbook copy);

Franklin to S[amuel] Huntington, March 4, 1780, National Archives; Connor, XXXII, 281; *New-York Gazette; and the Weekly Mercury*, Feb. 12, 1781; Banks, pp. 79, 88–89; Dandridge, ed., *American Prisoners*, p. 403.

41. Russell, p. 134.

42. Herbert, p. 219.

43. Herbert, pp. 78, 135, 164; Connor, XXXI, 20, 213, 286, XXXII, 280, 283; Thomas Smith, "Letter," *EIHC*, XLI (April 1905), 227.

44. Onderdonk, p. 238.

45. Some had no choice in the matter. Impressment of captured seamen in the early stages of the war brought complaint from Jefferson in the Declaration of Independence (Carl L. Becker, *The Declaration of Independence: A Study in the History of Political Ideas* [New York, 1958], p. 190). For other information concerning impressment, both before and after captives' arrival in prison, see, e.g., Admiralty to Vice-Admiral Graves, Sept. 9, 1775, Adm 2/550; Graves to Admiralty, Nov. 10, 20, 1775, Adm 1/485; John Fisher to Admiralty, Dec. 5, 1781, Adm 1/4146; *New-Jersey Gazette*, May 9, 1781; Hawkins, pp. 31–32; and George Little *et al.* to Benjamin Franklin, Aug. 25, 1781, Franklin Papers, LX, 16, APS; Ebenezer Fox, *The Adventures of Ebenezer Fox in the Revolutionary War* (Boston, 1847), pp. 93–94. At another point (p. 136), Fox, whose reminiscences are cast in the form of somewhat sanctimonious grandfather stories, acknowledges drawing upon Ramsay, William Gordon's *History of the Rise, Progress, and Establishment of the Independence of the United States of America* (London, 1788), and Charles Botta's *History of the War of Independence of the United States of America*, trans. George Alexander Otis (New Haven, 1840–41). He does not acknowledge that sections dealing with *Jersey*, he often borrows and adapts from Dring (cf., e.g., Fox, pp. 100 ff., and Dring, pp. 23 ff.; Fox, p. 114, Dring, p. 38). Although his memory of certain events which occurred while he was in *Jersey* is thus strongly assisted by Dring, most of what Fox says is clearly his own.

There is also plagiarism in some of the diaries and journals of the English prisons. See Alexander's " 'American Privateersmen in the Mill Prison during 1777–1782': An Evaluation," *EIHC*, CII (Oct. 1966), pp. 322–326; cf. Howard Lewis Applegate, "American Privateersmen in the Mill Prison during 1777–1782," *EIHC*, XCVII (Oct. 1961), 303–320; Alexander, "Forton Prison," p. 366n., and "Jonathan Haskins' Mill Prison 'Diary': Can it Be Accepted at Face Value?" *New England Quarterly*, XL (Dec. 1967), 561–564. In each such case, it is only the identity of the author, not the authenticity of the information provided, which is in question. Wherever I have found plagiarism, I have attempted to use the more reliable of the two sources.

46. Robert Wilden Nesser, ed., *Letters and Papers Relating to the Cruises of Gustavus Conyngham, a Captain of the Continental Navy, 1777–1779* (New York, 1915), p. 161.

47. Andros, p. 18; Dring, p. 71; Russell, p. 127.

48. Herbert, pp. 156, 177.

49. Dring, p. 93.

50. Henry B. Dawson, ed., *Recollections of the Jersey Prison-Ship: From the Original Manuscripts of Captain Thomas Dring* (Morrisania, N.Y., 1865), p. 187. See also, e.g., Sir Thomas Pye to Admiralty, May 30, 1781, in Admiralty to CSHS, June 5, 1781, Adm/M/405.

51. Herbert, p. 202.

52. American Commissioners to Lord North, Dec. 12, 1777, Library of Congress; Russell, 94–95. See also Franklin's remarks at the Constitutional Convention, quoted in my "Jack Tar in the Streets," p. 404.

53. For one instance in which 25 out of a crew of 100 entered in the ship which captured them, see Connor, XXXI, 284, and Alexander, "Forton Prison," p. 368. (For some indication of the coercive circumstances under which this took place, see Fanning, pp. 2–4.) It should be noted that capturing vessels, including this one, were also the scene of resistance and escape attempts on the way in (see Fanning, pp. 2–5). For some other instances of resistance, escape and refusal to defect between capture and imprisonment, see Carpenter, p. 79; CSHS to Admiralty, Dec. 29, 1780, Adm 98/13/166; Marion S. Coan, ed., "A Revolutionary Prison Diary: The Journal of Dr. Jonathan Haskins," *New England Quarterly*, XVII (June–Oct. 1944), 295; Cutler, p. 187; Hawkins, p. 63; and Fox, pp. 93–94. For what appears to be the commitment of almost an entire 120-man crew to Mill Prison some five months after capture and after much pressure to defect and shunting about

from ship to ship, see Herbert, pp. 17–44, 258; *Boston Gazette, and the Country Journal,* June 24, 1782; and Haskins, p. 295. At present, no meaningful quantitative statements on the relative frequency of defection as opposed to escape *before* imprisonment can be made. For quantitative statements on these matters *after* imprisonment, see below.

54. Fox, pp. 146–147, 149, 167 ff., 209; Blatchford, p. 22; Anderson, p. 71.

55. For the separate quartering of men and officers in both prison ships and prisons ashore, see, e.g., Cutler, pp. 395, 396; Herbert, p. 92; CSHS to Admiralty, Jan. 14, 30, 1778, Adm 98/11/154–55, 164–165; Fanning, pp. 14, 15; Russell, p. 171; Dring, pp. xiv–xv, 25, 39–40. Insofar as the British were responsible for the separation, there is some indication that they did it because they felt that quartering officers and men together operated to inhibit defection by the men (*New-York Gazette; and the Weekly Mercury,* Feb. 12, 1781). See also, Conyngham, p. 171. For American officers' demands and arrangements for separation, see Dring, p. 25, and CSHS to Admiralty, Jan. 30, 1778, Adm 98/11/164–166. For a related complaint by Congress, see *Journals,* XX, 622.

56. *Jersey's* logs (Adm 51/493 and 51/4228) record no one entering before May 17, 1781. This presumably reflects a failure to keep records on the matter rather than an absence of defection. After that date, the tally is regular and probably reliable. Between May 17, 1781, and April 7, 1783, the log describes 487 men as "entered," "volunteered," or "enlisted" (a few in services other than the navy). The figure may be generous, since some of these were doubtless impressed. During the same period, 5995 men are listed as arriving.

57. See my "Jack Tar in the Streets," p. 403n., where British and American sources are in close agreement. Cf. Alexander, "Forton Prison," p. 384, where an American prisoner in Forton offers information indicating a defection rate in *Forton alone* of 5.7 percent (in the period June 14, 1777–July 2, 1779).

58. Anderson (p. 72n.) says that "a high proportion" of the defectors were "old countrymen." For some descriptions of defections by "old countrymen," see Connor, XXXI, 288, and Herbert, pp. 63, 107, 155 (where one group of 30 defectors is described as "chiefly old countrymen"). Of 64 defectors in Herbert, 243–257, 32 were from England, Scotland, or Ireland. See also n.103 below.

59. In Mill and Forton, over-all escape figures are between 17.4 percent (derived from *Boston Gazette,* May 24–July 8, 1782) and 30.0 percent (derived from Adm 98/11–14; Howard, pp. 185, 187). The disparity may be partially explained by the fact that British figures are based simply on reports of escapees—many of whom were later retaken, and of whom many tried again—while the American figures are totals of escapees *not retaken.* Thus the higher figure is an approximate measure of the prisoners' *intent,* the lower figure a measure of their *success.* In Forton alone, Adm 98/11–14 gives a figure of 44.7 percent, while an American prisoner gives a figure of 27.0 percent (for 1777–79) (Connor, XXXIII, 36–39).

Jersey's log is almost totally silent on the matter of escapees, mentioning only two attempts (March 7, 1781, and Feb. 3, 1782, Adm 51/493 and 51/4228). Numerous references to escapees in other sources cited in this paper indicate that the captains simply did not record escapees. On the other hand, the log does list frequent repairs of ports broken open by prisoners presumably escaping or planning to do so. For repair of ports, see logs, Oct. 9, 1780, Oct. 11, 1781, May 15, 16, June 5, 12–14, Oct. 31, and Nov. 11, 1782. Several of these entries explicitly describe the repairs as necessary in order to prevent escapes. For prisoners' descriptions of such destruction as a necessary preliminary to escape, see, e.g., Hawkins, p. 78; Onderdonk, p. 236. Fox (p. 131) describes the apparent escape of 200 men in a three-month period (cf. Hawkins, p. 72) during which time the log lists a maximum of 68 defections (log of *Jersey,* March–May, 1782). This suggests a ratio of escape to defection of approximately 3 to 1. None of the figures offered above include escapes between the time of capture and arrival in prison.

60. For *Jersey,* see, e.g., Andros, p. 23; Hawkins, p. 74; Dring, pp. 110–112. Even those trying to flee a shipboard fire could expect to be shot (*New-York Gazette; and the Weekly Mercury,* Feb. 12, 1781). In Mill and Forton, at least in the early part of the war, the guards did not have orders to fire at escaping prisoners (Alexander, " 'American Privateersmen,' " pp. 336–337, and "Forton Prison," p. 381). There is indication that these orders were later revised, or that there was a difference between orders and actual execution (Herbert, p. 150; Widger, "Diary," LXXIV, 152; Russell, p. 159).

61. *New-York Gazette; and the Weekly Mercury,* Feb. 12, 1781.

62. Herbert, p. 54; Thompson, "Diary," p. 238; CSHS to Admiralty, June 26, 1778, Jan. 5,

1779, Oct. 31, 1781, Adm 98/11/206, 398-400, 13/493-495; Benjamin Golden to Benjamin Franklin, Dec. 2, 1781, Franklin Papers, XXIII, 94, APS; Ralls Account, New York Historical Society.

63. See, e.g., Hawkins, pp. 73-75, 82-87; log of *Jersey*, March 7, 1781, Adm 51/4228; Onderdonk, pp. 236-237; [N.Y.] *Royal Gazette*, Dec. 8, 1781.

64. Connor, XXX, 347, XXXI, 19, XXXII, 165; Fanning, p. 10; Haskins, p. 299.

65. CSHS to Admiralty, Oct. 27, 1779, Nov. 14, 1780, Adm 98/12/240-241, 13/133-134; Admiralty to CSHS, April 29, 1782, Adm/M/405. Prisoners also received a great deal of help from a kind of underground railway in which British clergymen played a major role: Thompson, "Diary," pp. 232-233, 241-242; John Thornton to American Commissioners. Memorandum, Jan. 5-8, 1778, Harvard College Library; Philip Hancock to American Commissioners, Aug. 2, 1778, Franklin Papers, L(i), 45, APS; G. Williams to Benjamin Franklin, Oct. 2, 1778, Franklin Papers, XII, 5; Cutler, p. 397.

66. Luke Matthewman, "Narrative," *Magazine of American History*, II (March 1878), p. 182; Admiralty to CSHS, Oct. 17, 1781, Adm/M/405; Justices of Peace of Fareham to Admiralty, Sept. 29, 1779, in Admiralty to CSHS, Oct. 15, 1779, Adm/M/404, Major General Smith to Secretary at War, Feb. 14, 1782, in Admiralty to CSHS, March 2, 1782, Adm/M/405; CSHS to Admiralty, Nov. 22, 1780, April 12, 1782, Adm 98/13/139, 14/141.

67. But we can say that conclusive escapes were *in addition* to such totals as the 27 percent for *successful* escapes (see n.59 above), since those in collusion with guards were returned to prison.

68. In Korea, "not one of our men escaped from a permanent enemy prison camp and successfully made his way back to our lines" (Kinkead, pp. 16-17. For a strong qualifica-tion of this statement and disagreement about its implications, see Biderman, pp. 84-90 and *passim*.) One of the results of the Korean experience was the promulgation by President Eisenhower in 1955 of a new Code of Conduct for the Armed Forces. Article III included a pledge that, if captured, "I will make every effort to escape and aid others to escape" (Biderman, p. 279).

69. Dring, p. 180.

70. Conyngham, p. 194.

71. Carpenter, p. 83.

72. Fox, pp. 124-125.

73. Fox, pp. 129-130.

74. For this and the following see Foot, p. 107.

75. For some of the cooperative actions described here and below, see Hawkins, pp. 78-83, Dring, pp. 109-110; Fox, pp. 116, 119-120, 124; Onderdonk, p. 236; Matthewman, p. 182; Herbert, p. 52; and CSHS to Admiralty, July 24, 1781, Adm 98/13/413-414.

76. CSHS to Admiralty, Jan. 5, 1779, Adm 98/11/398-401, 411-412: Herbert, pp. 203-207.

77. My "Jack Tar in the Darbies" will give fuller attention to these matters. For some model studies dealing with the politics and culture of lower-class groups in different environments, see e.g., Thompson, *Making of the English Working Class*, and several excellent studies by Herbert G. Gutman (e.g., "The Worker's Search for Power: Labor in the Gilded Age," in H. Wayne Morgan, ed., *The Gilded Age: A Reappraisal* [Syracuse, 1963], pp. 38-68, and "Protestantism and the American Labor Movement: The Christian Spirit in the Gilded Age," *American Historical Review*, LXXII [Oct. 1966], 74-101). The stance and methodology of Black historiography are also rich with models and implica-tions for the rewriting of white history "from the bottom up." See, e.g., communications by Anna Mary Wells, Vincent Harding, and Mike Thelwell, *N.Y. Rev. of Books*, Nov. 7, 1968; and John Henrik Clarke, ed., *William Styron's Nat Turner: Ten Black Writers Respond* (Boston, 1968).

78. For the rules, see Thompson, "Diary," pp. 238-240. CSHS to Admiralty, Jan. 28, 1778, Adm 98/11/162, notes that the rules were first posted Nov. 30, 1777. Cf. Herbert, p. 82, and Howard, pp. 473-474.

79. Sherburne, p. 83.

80. Dring, p. 84. Cf. Herbert, pp. 145-146; Sherburne, p. 85. There is no evidence of such a written code at Forton, although there is ample evidence of organized self-government, e.g., CSHS to Admiralty, Jan. 27, 1779, Adm 98/11/442-444.

81. Dring, p. 86, 91-94; Herbert, pp. 145-146, 148; Sherburne, p. 85.

82. Dring, p. 85; Herbert, pp. 68, 145; Widger, "Diary," LXXIV, 144; Russell, p. 155; Sherburne, p. 83.

83. Dring, pp. 85, 89; Andros, pp. 18–19, and n.86 below.

84. Widger, "Diary," LXXIV, 142.

85. Sherburne, p. 99.

86. Herbert, p. 78.

87. Haskins, p. 425.

88. Cutler, pp. 187, 306; Herbert, pp. 45–46.

89. Fanning, pp. 15, 15n.; Sherburne, p. 83–84. Some of the Franklinian virtues suggest an individualistic strain amidst what seems a predominantly collectivist ethos. Disobedience by prisoners to prisoner-made rules and norms constitutes another significant area of deviation (see n.103 below).

90. Andros, p. 18.

91. Dring, p. 129.

92. Dring, p. 129; Hawkins, p. 81.

93. CSHS to Admiralty, May 6, 1779, Adm 98/12/9–10.

94. E.g., Sherburne, p. 82–83; Herbert, p. 161.

95. Thompson, "Diary," p. 240; Dring, pp. 33–34, 81–82; Fox, pp. 115–120; Herbert, p. 67; Sherburne, pp. 85–86.

96. Andros, p. 17.

97. Thompson, "Diary," pp. 225, 226; Andros, pp. 17–18; Herbert, p. 116; Hawkins, pp. 69–71; CSHS to Admiralty, Jan. 27, 1779, Nov. 12, 1781, Adm 98/11/442–444, 13/503–505.

98. See Andros, pp. 17–18, where prisoners' refusal to defect is described in the context of an enumeration and discussion of the prisoners' rules; also, see Dring, pp. 91–94, where a shipboard orator, using the rules as the "text of . . . his discourse," praised his fellow prisoners for not defecting.

99. Thompson, "Diary," p. 225.

100. Herbert (p. 202) contends that more supported the document than signed it.

101. Herbert, p. 183.

102. Sir Thos. Pye to Admiralty, May 30, 1781, in Admiralty to CSHS, June 5, 1781, Adm/M/405.

103. Defection and informing were of course major forms of disobedience to prisoner government. In the English prisons, in regard to defection as well as other matters, we often find that the division is between Americans and Old Countrymen: "The Americans unanimously hang together, and endeavor to keep peace in prison, but if the [Old Countrymen] were stronger than . . . [the Americans] we should have a hell upon earth" (Herbert, p. 119). For committees, trials, and punishments for theft, see Widger, "Diary," LXXIV, 144; Sherburne, pp. 83, 85; Herbert, pp. 68, 145–146; and Dring, pp. 85–86. For forms of distribution of food and clothing, see, in addition to the mess, Herbert, pp. 166 (voting), and Russell, p. 157 (lottery). For petitions and remonstrances, see Committee of Prisoners in *Jersey* to "Friends and Fellow Countrymen in America," [N.Y.] *Royal Gazette*, June 12, 1782; Petition signed by 100 prisoners in *Jersey*, Aug. 15, 1782, Banks, p. 101; 280 American Prisoners in Forton Prison to Benjamin Franklin, Feb. 7, 1780, Historical Society of Pa.; Herbert, p. 62 (petition read aloud in prison yard); CSHS to Admiralty, Sept. 8, 1777, Adm 98/11/132; To the House of Lords from "upwards of two hundred American Prisoners . . . in Mill Prison . . . in behalf of themselves and others, their countrymen and Fellow Captives," June, 1781, encl. in Admiralty to CSHS, June 23, 1781, Adm/M/405; and CSHS to Admiralty, Oct. 4, 1782, Adm 98/14/254.

104. For this and the following, See Dring, pp. iii–iv, 84–85.

105. Herbert, p. 184; see also pp. 78, 174.

106. P. 68. For such action, see, e.g., Widger, "Diary," LXXIII, 335, LXXIV, 41; J. How to Major General Mocher, Feb. 23, 1782, in Admiralty to CSHS, March 16, 1782, Adm/M/405; Russell, p. 162; Connor, XXX, 352, XXXI, 213 ("Our provisions not being good we condemmed them. . . ."); Dring, ed. Dawson, p. 179; CSHS to Admiralty, Oct. 28, 1782, Adm 98/14/262.

107. Carpenter, pp. 83–84. See also Mary Barney, ed., *A Biographical Memoir of the Late*

Commodore Joshua Barney: From Autobiographical Notes and Journals (Boston, 1832), p. 88; Herbert, pp. 34, 44; and Haskins, p. 433. The challenge to the legitimacy of the prisoners' commitment was in many senses a just one; see CSHS to Admiralty, May 17, 1780, Adm 98/12/456 for an attempt by the Commissioners to have some Americans sent to Mill "although we are aware they possibly cannot be legally committed to Prison for want of Evidence. . . ." And of course North's Act, under which they were committed, came under fire for its suspension of *habeas corpus* (*Annual Register for 1777* [London, 1778], pp. 53–66; *The Works of the Right Honorable Edmund Burke* [rev. ed.; Boston, 1866], II, 193).

108. Haskins, p. 305.

109. Dring, pp. 89–95; Carpenter, p. 84.

110. Prisoners' songs are a rich source for the patriotic as well as other aspects of the seamen's lives. See, e.g., Hawkins, pp. 63–64; Carpenter, p. 86. The songs quoted above are part of a manuscript from Forton Prison in the Library of Congress, containing more than fifty songs. Most songs are given a specific date (in 1778); there is a journal entry and several notations such as "Success to the Honourable Continental Congress. . . ." George Carey of the Dept. of English, Univ. of Maryland, is at work on a monograph on these "Songs of Jack Tar in the Darbies." I am grateful to him for the use of his transcript and a xerox of the songs and for some useful advice.

111. Connor, XXXII, 72; Herbert, p. 175; Russell, p. 131; Widger, "Diary," LXXIV, 43–44, 156–157; Sherburne, pp. 88–89; Benjamin Golden to Benjamin Franklin, Dec. 2, 1781, Franklin Papers, XXIII, 94, APS.

112. Herbert, p. 141–142; Russell, p. 129; Widger, "Diary," LXXIV, 30; Dring, pp. 97–105.

113. Ironically, one way in which the seamen moved in the direction of a distinctive definition of their own interests was on those few occasions when they tempered their nationalism with rage over what they saw as their country's desertion of them and threatened in turn to desert their country unless Washington and others made stronger efforts to exchange them. See [N.Y.] *Royal Gazette*, June 12, 1782, and n.44 above.

114. See, e.g., my "Jack Tar in the Streets," pp. 378–380, 387–388, 404.

115. Although the term itself is rarely applied to the political thought and conduct of the Revolution's leaders, it seems to fit the descriptions offered by recent analysts: see, e.g., studies by Roy N. Lokken, J. R. Pole, and Richard Buel, Jr., cited in my "American Revolution Seen from the Bottom Up," pp. 34–35.

116. "*Pre-political* people . . . have not yet found, or [have] only begun to find, a specific language in which to express their aspirations about the world" (E. J. Hobsbawm, *Primitive Rebels: Studies in Archaic Forms of Social Movement in the 19th and 20th Centuries* [New York, 1965], p. 2; see *passim* for a working out of the definition in more specific terms).

117. P. 9.

118. I am indebted to Christopher Z. Hobson for insights into the relations between class and nationalist consciousness; see his unpubl. M.A. thesis (Univ. of Chicago, 1969), "Economic Discontent, Ghana 1951–66: A Study in the Class Dynamics of Third-World Nationalist Movements," especially chap. V. See also Staughton Lynd, *Class Conflict, Slavery, and the United States Constitution: Ten Essays* (Indianapolis, 1967), pp. 13–14.

119. For some other dreams and fever fantasies, see Russell, pp. 152–153, and Sherburne, pp. 93–94, 99–100.

120. In addition to letters cited above from Americans in English prisons, many Americans—some of whom had been captured by the French as English—wrote Franklin from French prisons, begging his assistance, e.g., Jonathan Atkin to Benjamin Franklin, Nov. 10, 1778, Franklin Papers, LX, 3, APS; William Gardner to Benjamin Franklin, March 21, 1779, Franklin Papers, XIII, 215; and James Mathews to Benjamin Franklin, Oct. 19, 1782, Historical Society of Pa. All of the correspondence to and from Franklin cited in this article was originally examined in photocopy form at the Franklin Collection at Yale (citations are given to original repositories). I am grateful to Leonard W. Labaree and to Helen C. Boatfield in connection with these items and for innumerable other kindnesses over many years.

121. Fred Lewis Pattee, ed., *The Poems of Philip Freneau, Poet of the American Revolution* (3 vols.; Princeton, 1902–07), II, 18–39, and Freneau's *Some Account of the Capture of the Ship "Aurora"* (New York, 1899).

122. Not considered in this paper are certain ideological barriers to writing a history of the "inarticulate." Prominent among these is pluralism, aptly described by Michael Paul Rogin (*The Intellectuals and McCarthy: The Radical Specter* [Cambridge, 1967], p. 282), as "not . . . the product of science but . . . a liberal American venture into conservative political theory." Pluralism is an explicitly elitist doctrine; it praises the distribution of power among elites, and in so doing it justifies the exclusion from political power of the "illegitimate." Thus Daniel Bell writes, "Democratic politics means bargaining between *legitimate* groups and the search for consensus" ("Passion and Politics in America," *Encounter*, VI [Jan. 1956], p. 61; emphasis added). Just as pluralism as political philosophy justified the exclusion of the "illegitimate," pluralism as historiography justified the exclusion of the past "illegitimate," which is to say the "inarticulate." Thus we have seen the past too uncritically through the eyes of such men as Olmsted's "Men of literary taste" and too little through eyes defined by pluralists as illegitimate. (See my rev. of Bernard Bailyn, *The Origins of American Politics* [New York, 1968], in *New Republic*, May 25, 1968, pp. 25–28, and also my study in progress, "Anti-Communism as a Goal of Recent American Historiography.")

the progress of inequality in revolutionary Boston

ALLAN KULIKOFF*

William Widger's dream demonstrated one way of assessing the attitudes of the poor, although it does not tell us how many poor there were. Allan Kulikoff illustrates how quantitative techniques can summon up the realities of the past. He reveals not only that the poor existed in large numbers but that the elite demonstrated little responsibility toward them. Moreover, class differences, judged by such economic circumstances as income and property, increased after the Revolution. In the light of the growing inequality presented here, how can one explain the continuing deference shown by the poor to their social superiors?

O n February 2, 1785, the *Massachusetts Centinel* in Boston complained that "We daily see men speculating, with impunity, on the most essential articles of life, and grinding the faces of the poor and laborious as if there was no God," yet five months later to the day, Sam Adams wrote to his cousin John, "You would be surprizd to see the Equipage, the Furniture and expensive Living of too many, the Pride and Vanity of Dress which pervades thro every Class, confounding every Distinction between the Poor and the Rich."[1] As these quotations suggest, opinion divided sharply in post-Revolutionary Boston on the direction of major social change, and impressionistic evidence can be found to sustain a broad range of interpretation. Relying on this material, historians have perpetuated the contemporary diversity of opinion. Scholars of the Progressive era, like J. Franklin Jameson, tend to agree with Adams that the Revolution had a leveling effect, while more recent studies have found some change as whigs replaced tories and a new propertied class emerged, but less democratization than had been supposed.[2]

This essay attempts to discover the magnitude of change in Boston from 1771 to 1790 by testing controllable, quantitative materials to answer the following questions: How did the town's occupational structure change? Did the distribution of wealth become more or less equal? How closely related were wealth and status? Did political power become more democratically shared? By how much did population increase? What social and economic patterns of

From Allan Kulikoff, "The Progress of Inequality in Revolutionary Boston," *William and Mary Quarterly*, XXVIII, 3rd Series, (July 1971), 375–393, 400–411.

*Mr. Kulikoff is a graduate student at Brandeis University. He would like to thank Stuart Blumin, M. I. T.; John Demos, Marvin Meyers, and members of the graduate seminar, Brandeis University; Kenneth Lockridge, University of Michigan; and Paul Kleppner and Alfred Young, Northern Illinois University, for their advice and criticism. David Fischer, Brandeis University, who directed the paper, made numerous helpful criticisms.

residence could be found? What changes occurred in the rate of geographic and economic mobility?

Before the Revolution, Boston had been an intensely unequal society. Wealthy men of high status dominated government and social life. The top 10 per cent of the taxpayers in 1771 owned nearly two-thirds of the wealth and held most of the important town offices. While demanding respect from the poor, many of the wealthy lived in the center of town, segregated from the impoverished. Poorer men possessed no significant political power, but held numerous minor town offices. And largely because many poor men and women were migrating from nearby towns, the poor in Boston were becoming more numerous.[3] These trends continued and accelerated during the war and the Confederation period. Not a less stratified, but an even more unequal society developed in Boston after the Revolution.

Late eighteenth-century Boston was a typical "consumer city" in Max Weber's phrase. It was a town of under 20,000 inhabitants in which "the purchasing power of its larger consumers rests on the retail for profit of foreign products on the local market . . . the foreign sale for profit of local products or goods obtained by native producers . . . or the purchase of foreign products and their sale . . . outside."[4]

The economy of Boston still rests squarely on foreign trade. Close to a quarter of her workers—merchants, mariners, captains, chandlers, and wharfingers— earned their livelihood from commerce. Another 15 per cent were directly concerned with trade. Retailers sold and distributed foreign goods; coopers made barrels bound for the sea; laborers supplied the manpower necessary to unload ships; and distillers used foreign sugar in their product.

Unlike Weber's "producer city," Boston was not an exporter of the goods she produced.[5] Most of those not engaged in commerce produced goods and services for the local market. No industrial group included large numbers of workers. About 7 per cent worked with cloth, 5 per cent with leather, and 5 per cent with metals. Construction workers were under a tenth of all those employed. The small proportion of innkeepers (3 per cent) and men in the food trades (7 per cent) showed that Boston was not a major food market; nor had a large bureaucracy developed, since only 3 per cent of the labor force was employed in government—and many of these worked only part-time.

Large enterprises were uncommon: the median number of workers in ninety-six artisan crafts was only three, and the mean number thirteen. The typical middling artisan employed his sons and several other workers. These young apprentices and journeymen lived with the families of master craftsmen, not alone in rented rooms.[6]

There was an excess population in the working ages, composed mostly of women and including many widows, who were outside the occupational structure. Between 1765 and 1800, the proportion of people in the productive ages above fifteen years increased by 17 per cent, thereby providing workers for any factories that might open. There were 19 per cent more women than men of working age in 1765, and 14 per cent more in 1800. About a tenth of these women were widows, and three-quarters of them supported dependents.[7]

Two small factories were operating in 1790, but they were not part of a general industrialization, and only one of them utilized this surplus laboring population. At a "duck cloth manufactory" employing four hundred workers in 1792, there were only seventeen male employees two years before. A few of the

TABLE I. Boston's Occupational Structure, 1790[a]

Occupational Group	Number in Group	Number of Trades in Group	Percentage of Work Force
Government Officials	67	4	2.6
Professionals[b]	105	8	4.1
Merchants-Traders	224	3	8.7
Retailers	184	7	7.1
Sea Captains	114	1	4.4
Other Business[c]	66	6	2.6
Clerks and Scribes	66	2	2.6
Building Crafts	245	7	9.3
Cloth Trades	182	8	7.1
Leather Crafts	113	5	5.1
Food Trades	175	11	6.8
Marine Crafts	219	13	8.5
Metal Crafts	132	11	5.1
Woodworkers	106	7	4.1
Other Artisans	105	35	4.1
Transportation	80	6	3.2
Service	103	4	4.0
Mariners	117	4	4.5
Unskilled	188	4	7.4
Total Artisans	1,271	96	49.1
Total Other	1,314	49	50.9
Total Employed	2,585	145	100.0
Servants (white)	63		
Unemployed and Retired[d]	106		
Total	2,754		

Notes: [a]Boston Tax Taking and Rate Books, 1790, City Hall, Boston, Mass. Hereafter cited as Tax and Rate Books, 1790. These records were checked with the Boston city directories for 1789 and 1796, *Report of the Record Commissioners of the City of Boston* (Boston, 1876-1909), X, 171-296. Hereafter cited as *Record Commissioners' Report.* A total accounting of each trade is found in the original article.
[b]Includes 20 untaxed clergymen counted in Thomas Pemberton, "A Topographical and Historical Description of Boston, 1794," Massachusetts Historical Society, *Collections,* 1st Ser., III (1794), 256-264.
[c]Includes groups such as wharfingers, chandlers, brokers, and auctioneers.
[d]Includes 23 gentlemen, 27 poor, 28 sick and poor, and 28 little or no business.

others were young girls; the rest were women. The factory had been established to promote American manufactures and at the same time to aid the poor. According to the *Massachusetts Centinel* in 1788, it and a small glass works "promise soon to be completed and to give employment to a great number of persons, especially females who now eat the bread of idleness, whereby they may gain an honest livelihood." By 1800, the duckcloth factory was out of business.[8]

About three-quarters of the one thousand workers in the other large enterprise, a cotton and wool card factory, were children. About a fifth of all the children in Boston from eight to sixteen years of age were probably employed there. The owners chose to hire them rather than women, since children could easily run the machinery and were paid less.[9]

At least until 1820, Boston's occupational structure remained close to the "consumer city" model. Less than one-tenth of 1 per cent of men listed in the 1820 directory were manufacturers, and the proportion of merchants, retailers, and building tradesmen remained almost the same. Domestic commerce was becoming more important as foreign trade declined. A reduction in the percentage of mariners, captains, and marine tradesmen from 17.4 per cent in 1790 to 10.6 per cent in 1820 illustrates the trend. Meanwhile, the town had become more important as a food market, with the proportion of men in the food trades climbing from 6.8 per cent to 10.7 per cent.[10]

Most of Boston's taxable wealth—real estate, stock in trade, and income from trade[11]—rested in fewer and fewer hands as time passed. Boston followed a pattern similar to both American towns and rural areas. Although in the seventeenth century wealth in American towns was typically less concentrated than in sixteenth-century English towns, where the poorer half of the population owned less than a tenth of the wealth and the richest tenth owned between half and seven-tenths, the English pattern soon reappeared in America and intensified.[12]

From 1687 to 1790, Boston's wealth became very concentrated. A glance at the Lorenz curves shows that the amount of change between 1687 and 1771 was similar to that between 1771 and 1790. Statistically, changes in the distribution of wealth measured by increases in the Schutz coefficient (see Table II B) were greater between 1771 and 1790 (.0735) than during the preceding 87 years (.0647). However, the proportion of wealth held by the richest tenth of the taxpayers had almost reached its peak by 1771 and 29 per cent were without taxable property both before and after the Revolution. The wealth of the lower middle group, where assessments ranged from £25 to £100, was cut in half. Three-quarters of this decline was gained by the upper middle group, assessed between £100 and £500.

The sale of forty-six loyalist estates in Suffolk County to ninety-six men, two-thirds of whom already owned land in the county, had little effect on the overall distribution. The sale may have permitted a few poorer men to enter the upper middle group, but the small gain in wealth between 1771 and 1790 made by the top tenth suggests that a wealthy group of patriots replaced an equally wealthy group of tories.[13]

Were the relatively poor becoming poorer? Brissot de Warville discovered full employment in Boston in 1788 and "saw none of those livid, ragged wretches that one sees in Europe, who, soliciting our compassion at the foot of the altar, seem to bear witness . . . against our inhumanity."[14] Brissot's European standard of comparison allowed him to underestimate the extent of poverty in Boston. At this time, a fifth to a third of those living in English and French towns were beggars, paupers, and others who could not make a living for themselves. Another third were the near poor of the English towns and the *sans-culottes* and *menu peuple* in French towns—persons who could become destitute in times of crisis.[15]

The poor and near poor were growing more numerous in Boston. The percentage of poor can be roughly estimated at 7 per cent of the population in

TABLE II. A. Distribution of Taxable Wealth in Boston, 1790[a]

Assessment in Pounds	Number in Category	Percentage of Taxpayers in Category	Wealth in Category in Pounds	Percentage of Wealth in Category
0	892	29.8	0	0.0
25	388	12.9	9,700	1.0
26–50	240	8.0	11,162	1.2
51–75	148	4.9	11,012	1.2
76–100	167	5.6	16,662	1.8
101–150	186	6.2	24,938	2.7
151–200	147	4.9	27,887	3.0
201–300	186	6.2	49,113	5.3
301–400	128	4.3	46,713	5.0
401–500	116	3.9	54,300	5.9
501–700	124	4.1	75,775	8.3
701–999	71	2.4	58,775	6.1
1000–1,999	122	4.1	159,875	17.2
2000–4,999	58	1.9	165,250	17.8
5000+	22	0.8	217,775	23.5
Totals	2,995	100.0	928,937	100.0

TABLE II. B. Distribution of Wealth in Boston, 1687 to 1830[a]

Percentage of Taxpayers	Percentage of Wealth Held			
	1687	1771	1790	1830
Bottom 30	2.48	0.10	0.03	0.00
Low-Mid 30	11.29	9.43	4.80	7.92
Upper-Mid 30	39.63	27.01	30.47	26.94
Top 10	46.60	63.46	64.70	65.14
Total	100.00	100.00	100.00	100.00
Top 1%	9.51	25.98	27.14	26.15
Schutz Coefficient	.4896	.5541	.6276	.6370

Notes: [a] Tax and Rate Books, 1970. Group at 0 paid only poll tax: £25 was the first assessment. Untaxed widows found on the census are not included.
[b] See Table II A for 1790 figures; 1687 and 1771 figures are from Henretta, "Economic Development and Social Structure," *Wm. and Mary Qtly.*, 3d Ser., XXII (1965), 80, 82, with those paying only poll tax added; 1830 figures were estimated from imprecise, grouped data in Shattuck, *Report*, 95. The Schutz coefficient of inequality measures income concentration—0 equals total equality, 1 total inequality. Robert B. Schutz, "On the Measurement of Income Inequality," *American Economic Review*, XLI (1951), 107–122; Blumin, "Mobility and Change," in Thernstrom and Sennett, eds., *Nineteenth Century Cities*, 204.

1771 and 10 per cent in 1790. The change is illustrated by the slow increase in the numbers of destitute, old, and sick men and women, and dependent children in the poorhouse at a time of relatively little population increase . . . : 146 in 1742, never over 180 before the Revolution, and 250 in August 1790, with 300 to 400 expected the following winter.[16] Because personal property was not taxed, it is difficult to determine the percentage of near poor, but an estimate can be made.[17] Composed of widows, blacks, seamen, laborers, and poorer artisans who might dip below the minimum level of subsistence when unemployment increased, this group probably ranged from 30 to 40 per cent in 1771 and from 37 to 47 per cent in 1790.

Unemployed, old, or sick, most of the poor and their families lived outside the poorhouse. Alexander Lord, a poor laborer, had "gone broke, wife as broke"; they had a son under sixteen to share their misery. Jacob Bull, an old shoemaker, and his wife were both ill, but two other women lived in their household. And Samuel Goddard, "shoemaker, no business, poor and supported by charity," could provide his family of five with few comforts.[18] Only the very old, the totally destitute, and the terminally ill entered the poorhouse, for the social conditions there steadily declined. In 1790, the poorhouse was filthy, dark, crowded, and odoriferous. "Persons of every description and disease are lodged under the same roof and in some instances in the same or Contiguous Apartments, by which means the sick are disturbed, by the Noise of the healthy, and the infirm rendered liable to the Vices and diseases of the diseased, and profligate."[19]

The lives of the near poor were only somewhat better than those of the poor. While the number of people per dwelling declined from 9.53 in 1742 to 7.58 in 1790 . . . , many of the near poor lived in grossly inferior housing. The tax assessors found 90 families living in single rooms. Sixty-five of the same families were also counted by the census taker; three-quarters of this group had families of fewer than five members. Joseph Blayner, carpenter, lived with his wife and two children in a kitchen chamber while John Cartwright, cooper, his eight children, wife, and a boarder, crowded into the back of a house. Elijah Tolams, a "very poor carpenter," lived in one room with his three children, and Ebenezer Pilsbury, shoemaker, slept and worked with his six children in only two rooms.

There was a close relationship between wealth and status. Although status was not legally defined as in England, and the reputations of various trades were unstable,[20] the order of precedence in a parade honoring President Washington in 1789 gives some indication of the prestige of various groups. The military, town and state officers, professional men, merchants and traders, and sea captains led the parade. They were followed by forty-six different artisan crafts, "alphabetically disposed, in order to give general satisfaction." No mechanical art was deemed better than the next. Sailors brought up the rear, and laborers were not included in the line of march.[21]

As Table III shows, the eleven wealthiest occupations included professional men of high status, merchants, retailers, along with several artisan trades. Most of those in the economic elite—men assessed over £1,000—were in these groups. Sea captains, with a mean wealth of £240, were lower on the list than their status might indicate. Most others whose wealth fell between £100 and £260 were artisans. Immediately below a mean of £100 were the building trades, schoolmasters, and shipwrights. Other sea artisans, and such traditionally poorer trades as tailor, shoemaker, and barber, fell between £40 and £75.

Bringing up the rear were the industrial trades of ropemaker and duckcloth maker, and mariners and laborers.

An analysis of variance showed a highly significant relationship between occupation and wealth, but the magnitude of this relationship was small. Only about 19.4 per cent of the variations in the wealth of all the individuals included in Table III was accounted for by differences between occupations. The rest of the variation was within each occupation.[22] In most trades, a few men had wealth far above the group mean; a number of hatters, printers, and bakers, for example, owned large establishments. As a result, in all but three trades below chaisemaker on the table, the median wealth was fifty pounds or less. Most fishermen, sailors, and laborers had no taxable wealth at all.

Those who possessed the highest status, reputation, and wealth expected visible differences of "Equipage, Furniture, . . . and Dress" between themselves and the rest of society. They socialized mostly with each other and separated themselves from the masses by forming exclusive organizations. One of these, a dinner club that encouraged members to relax and enjoy good conversation, was open to only sixteen men, each admitted by a unanimous vote. Another, the Massachusetts Historical Society, was incorporated in 1794 by ministers, doctors, lawyers, and a scientist to diffuse historical learning. This group limited its membership to thirty.[23]

Wealthy artisans were granted substantial respect. In the parade honoring President Washington, each trade was led by a member whose wealth averaged 225 per cent more than the mean wealth of his group: the leader of the tailors, Samuel Ballard, was assessed £500; goldsmith Benjamin Bert, £400; shoemaker Samuel Bangs, £500; and carpenter William Crafts, £400. Nathaniel Balch, who was assessed £925, not only led his fellow hatters in the parade, but his shop was described as "the principle lounge even of the finest people in the town. Governor Hancock himself would happen into this popular resort, ready for a joke or a political discussion with Balch."[24]

While poorer groups were expected to defer to the elite, they in turn were accorded little respect. Not only did poorer artisans have less status than those who were richer, the elite tolerated insults and attacks on black men and old black women by lower-class whites. Prince Hall, leader of the black masonic lodge, nevertheless urged Boston's Negroes to ignore their white attackers and trust "men born and bred in Boston," because we "had rather suffer wrong than to do wrong, to the disturbance of the community and the disgrace of our reputation."[25]

Did the elite demonstrate any sense of social responsibility toward the poor? Noblesse oblige was practically nonexistent. The Massachusetts Humane Society, founded mainly to save people from drowning, chose to build three small huts on islands where shipwrecks were common, rather than aid the poor sailors who populated Boston's North End.[26] Men often complained to the assessors that they were poor, sick, lame, or had "little or no business." The only relief granted them was tax abatement; seventy men found on both the 1790 census and 1790 tax lists paid no taxes.

However, benevolence to widows was considered a community responsibility. A husband's death, commented one minister, "deprives a weak and helpless woman . . . of the sole instrument of her support, the guide of her children's youth, and their only earthly dependance."[27] Any charity granted by town or church went to them. The overseers of the poor distributed minimal aid from bequests. In 1787, for example, they gave money to sixty-six different widows,

TABLE III. Mean Assessed Wealth of Selected Occupations in Boston, 1790[a]

Rank	Occupation	Mean Assessment in Pounds	Number of Persons in Category
1	Merchant	1,707	206
2	Lawyer	846	21
3	Doctor	795	26
4	Apothecary	657	17
5	Distiller	642	47
6	Broker	622	16
7	Retailer	601	133
8	Taverner	522	26
9	Grocer	472	33
10	Chandler	347	17
11	Wharfinger	335	24
12	Tobacconist	260	17
13	Boarder-keeper	258	24
14	Printer	247	17
15	Sea Captain	240	114
16	Hatter	233	29
17	Clerk	232	28
18	Chaisemaker	188	16
19	Baker	170	64
20	Goldsmith	166	23
21	Painter	154	34
22	Cabinetmaker	131	15
23	Cooper	130	70
24	Founder	120	15
25	Sailmaker	112	30
26	Mason	95	44
27	Carpenter	92	140
28	Schoolmaster	89	16
29	Truckman	84	50
30	Blacksmith	83	59
31	Shipwright	78	65
32	Scribe	77	38
33	Barber	65	42
34	Blockmaker	63	16
35	Tailor	61	100
36	Caulker	53	14
37	Sea Cooper	46	16
38	Shoemaker	45	78
39	Mate	41	20
40	Ropemaker[b]	35	37
41	Duckcloth maker	25	16
42	Fisherman	15	37
43	Sailor	9	58
44	Laborer	6	157

Notes: [a]Computed from Tax and Rate Books, 1790.
[b]Excludes 5 ropewalk owners with a mean wealth of £760.

most receiving nine or twelve shillings, and only fifteen women were helped more than once. The First Church, perhaps typical, collected donations for the poor quarterly and on the Sunday before Thanksgiving. Several dozen women received a pittance of two or three shillings each month from this money.[28]

Who held political office in Boston after the Revolution? In pre-Revolutionary Boston, wealthy men of high social status monopolized important positions. Minor offices went to those of less wealth and status and gave their holders a sense of belonging in the community. After the Revolution, recent research indicates, the Massachusetts legislature included more moderately wealthy men than before the war.[29] Did Boston officeholding become more widely distributed?

TABLE IV. Assessed Wealth of Boston Officeholders, 1790[a]

Office	Mean Wealth	Median Wealth	Number in Group
State Legislators	4,044	1,750	9
Overseers of Poor	3,398	1,610	12
Fire Wards	2,850	1,350	15
School Committee	1,633	1,000	9
Clerks of Market	954	875	12
Selectmen	642	500	9
Cullers of Hoops and Staves	208	175	21
Assessors, Collectors	207	200	9
Fire Companies	125	50	138
Constables	115	75	12
Surveyors of Boards	78	50	15

Note: [a]Tax and Rate Books, 1790; *Record Commissioners' Report,* XXXI, 217–224; X, 207–211. Information for a few officers could not be determined. These included 14 members of the fire companies, 4 cullers of hoops, 3 surveyors of boards, and 3 untaxed ministers who were members of the school committee. Four legislators are missing from the table: 3 were Suffolk County senators, probably residents of other parts of the county, and the other was a representative whose name was too common to identify. All other officers are included.

Table IV shows, the economic elite still dominated the most important town offices. All the state legislators from Boston were assessed over a thousand pounds and were among the wealthiest 6.8 per cent of the population. Four were merchants, two were wealthy gentlemen, one was a doctor, one a lawyer, and one a hardware store owner. Only a quarter of the firewards, who protected valuable property in case of fire, dipped below a thousand pounds; most of them were merchants, wharfingers, and wealthy shipwrights. The school committee, a newly created agency of the government, included three clergymen, three lawyers, three doctors, and two businessmen.

Probably the two most important town offices were the selectmen and the overseers of the poor. In 1790, only one of the overseers was assessed below a thousand pounds. From 1785 to 1795, eight merchants, three hardware store owners, one auctioneer, two distillers, one apothecary, one ropewalk owner, and a wealthy baker served as overseers. During the same period, selectmen included five merchants, two lawyers, the county treasurer, a captain, a retailer, an apothecary, a wharfinger, and a wealthy hatter. Five others were probably retired businessmen, whose low assessments reduced the selectmen's mean wealth.[30]

Remarkably little turnover occurred in these two time-consuming, nonpaying positions. From 1760 to 1770, the average selectman served between three and four years; there was a small rise in tenure between 1785 and 1795. Overseers served even longer terms. In the decade 1760 to 1770, the average overseer served four or five years; after the war tenures increased to from six to eight years. At annual elections, both before and after the Revolution, typically only one or two selectmen or overseers were replaced. Bostonians served longer and replaced their officials less frequently than did the citizens of many other Massachusetts towns before the Revolution.[31]

The middling artisans, assessed between £100 and £500, were a group far larger than the economic elite, yet after the war they still held only a small percentage of major offices. Assessors and tax collectors, full-time paid officials who determined and collected taxes, were the only powerful officers of middle-class wealth. Other positions gave artisans some recognition of their special talents, but no political power. Carpenters, joiners, and cabinetmakers dominated the position of surveyor of boards; shoemakers were sealers of leather, and coopers were cullers of hoops and staves. Marine artisans formed a majority in the fire companies, the only agencies dominated by the poor and near poor. These jobs, dirty and unpaid, gave the economic elite an opportunity to share civic participation while keeping political power in its own hands.

The elite was suspicious of any attempt to organize the laboring force politically, however deferential the organizers initially were. Artisans of middle wealth, whose share of the town's taxable property had increased since 1771, founded the Mechanics Association in 1795. Only two members of the group had belonged to the economic elite in 1790, at which time the assessments of 63 per cent of those who became members fell between £100 and £500. In 1796 the group petitioned the General Court for incorporation because "the disconnected state of the mechanics of the town of Boston . . . retarded the mechanic arts of the state" whose "situation as a manufacturing country promised the greatest extension." Twenty leading merchants were personally urged to support the petition, "to patronize an institution formed for the reciprocal benefits of the merchant and mechanic." But despite the Association's broadly conceived purpose, the legislature feared the group's potential political power and three times refused to grant incorporation. The Association finally succeeded in obtaining a charter in 1806.[32]

The poorer sort commanded no political resource other than ineffective deferential appeals to the wealthy. The accumulated grievances of poor mechanics were partially relieved by harassing the black population; only the middling artisans were able to organize successfully. Pressure from below on the elite was nonexistent after the Revolution, and criminal activity was rare. Between 1787 and 1790, nine men were hanged, all for robbery, while twenty-six were punished for other crimes.[33]

Boston's population steadily increased from 1630 to 1740 as the townsmen settled the entire Shawmut Peninsula, but after 1740 people migrated from eastern New England in large numbers, so that from 1742 to 1790 Boston's population grew only 8.4 per cent, a gain of 1.68 per cent per decade. . . . During the same period, the American population overall expanded at the Malthusian rate of 34.7 per cent per decade. Migration patterns bypassed eastern New England; people generally traveled up the Connecticut Valley into western Massachusetts, New Hampshire, and Maine. The results may be seen in the differential population growth of areas of Massachusetts between 1765 and 1790: Massachusetts's total population increased 54.1 per cent; Boston's (based on the smaller population of 1765) 16.2 per cent; the surrounding towns of Brookline, Cambridge, Charlestown, Chelsea, and Roxbury, 18.3 per cent; and the eastern Massachusetts counties of Suffolk, Essex, Plymouth, and Middlesex, 28.5 per cent.[34] Boston's population fell after 1742 but recovered by 1771 until the British occupied the city in 1776, when people left en masse for the countryside and only slowly returned. The exodus postponed major population growth until after recovery from the effects of the war. Between 1790 and 1820 the town's population increased at the rate of 31.3 per cent per decade.[35]

Boston's social geography was similar to other pre-industrial towns. In those towns, wealthy merchants, lawyers and retailers lived on or near the main business streets. Residents of middling wealth generally lived next to them. On the outskirts, farthest from the economic center of town, and in its most crowded sections, resided poorer artisans and laborers. . . . Social groups in Boston were physically divided from each other. . . . Boston's propertyless residents—nearly 40 percent of the population—were the most segregated group (as measured by an index of dissimilarity) and mostly lived in economic ghettos at either end of town. Wealthier, and thus smaller, economic groups were less concentrated and spread more evenly across the city.*

In late eighteenth-century Boston, individuals were becoming increasingly more mobile, moving from place to place and from one economic position to another, while society itself was becoming more stratified. Almost all newcomers to Boston were "warned out," officially informed that the town would not care for them if they ever needed charity.[36] Since there is no indication that warnings out were limited to the poor, they are rough measures of migration into Boston. While the scrutiny of the overseers may have increased over the period, the pattern found in Table V is too strong to be discounted. The number of migrants remained small until 1775, then in terms both of numbers and rates, rapidly increased. After 1765, at least a tenth of Boston's residents had been in town five years or less.[37]

What would explain this dramatic change in the intensity of migration? Migrants in most modern societies tend to travel short distances, going from remote villages to nearby towns and from towns to more distant cities. They stop and settle at the first place where a job is offered, and travel farther only if the opportunity disappears.[38] These generalizations apply to post-Revolutionary Boston. Almost three-quarters of the migrants entering Boston in 1791 came from Massachusetts, and a third traveled ten miles or less. In point of origin, the other quarter principally divided between foreign lands and more distant American cities like New York and Philadelphia.

The migrants formed three distinct streams. Twenty-three per cent arrived

*The index of dissimilarity, which measures the average deviation within wards of the percentage of each group from its mean percentage in the total population, runs from 0 (perfect integration) to 100 (total segregation). The index for those without assessed wealth was 56.8; assessed L1-75, 26.4; L76-275, 16.7; L276-999, 41.7; and 1000+ 28.5. For construction of the index see, Karl E. and Alma F. Taeuber, *Negroes in Cities: Residential Segregation and Neighborhood Change* (Chicago, 1965), 37–41.

TABLE V. Warnings Out in Boston, 1745 to 1792[a]

Year	Number Warned	Number Warned/1000 Population
1745-1749	363	23.1
1750-1754	528	33.6
1755-1759	1,160	74.2
1760-1764	765	49.3
1765-1769	2,499	151.1
1770-1773	1,587	95.9
1791-1792	2,405	133.9

Note: [a] Warnings Out in Boston, 1745-1792, Records of the Overseers of the Poor of Boston, Mass., Mass. Hist. Soc. From 1745 to 1773, children and wives were listed with husbands; the 1791-1792 lists often include many entries under a single family name, but the relationships are not indicated. The 1791-1792 number/1000 population is comparable with the others; at that time a resident could be warned until he resided in the town four years. Robert W. Kelso, *The History of Public Poor Relief in Massachusetts, 1620-1920* (Boston, 1922), 59. This table represents minimum migration into Boston.

from foreign ports. The other two groups, totaling 71.2 per cent of all migrants, traveled from Massachusetts towns. Most of them, 39.8 per cent of the total, migrated from nearby coastal areas such as Charlestown, Plymouth, Cape Cod, Ipswich, Salem, and Newburyport. This seaport-to-seaport stream probably brought numerous marine artisans and mariners into Boston. If the mobility of this group was as great in the 1760s, it may help to explain the number and volatility of the crowds in pre-Revolutionary Boston.[39] The final group, constituting 31.4 per cent of all migrants, came from neighboring agricultural areas that were experiencing population pressure on land. In these areas during the late eighteenth century, poverty and geographical mobility increased as the average size of landholdings fell.[40] Forced off the land and unaccustomed to urban life, these men at least temporarily joined and augmented the number of poor and near poor.

Though Boston drew many people from smaller ports, declining agricultural areas, and foreign lands, her own opportunities were limited. By 1790, 45 per cent of the taxpayers in town in 1780 had disappeared from tax lists. Some had died; the rest left town. The figure is higher than that found in stable, rural communities where land is plentiful, but is low compared to nineteenth-century American cities or frontier areas.[41] Those who moved out of Boston were the poorest and least successful members of the community. As Table VII shows, only 42 per cent of those without real estate (rents) in 1780 remained in town in 1790. In Newburyport between 1850 and 1880, 41 per cent of the laborers persisted during each decade, a rate almost identical to that of the unpropertied in Boston seventy years earlier.[42] As the amount of rent reported increased, the rate of persistence rose; only one-quarter of the upper 10 per cent of those listed in 1780 had moved or died by 1790. Even if the death rates of the poor were higher, and their slippage from one list to another greater, this table suggests that a larger proportion of the poor than the rich were mobile.

Inward and outward mobility suggests a small, but significant, floating population of men and women at the bottom of society who moved from seaport to seaport and town to town in search of work. Many of the 278 men

TABLE VI. Birth Places of Those Warned Out of Boston, 1791[a]

Foreign	237	Other States	62	Massachusetts	740
England	84	Philadelphia	28	Within 10 miles of Boston	341
Ireland	52	New York City	19	Southeast of Boston	181
Scotland	31	Carolina	4	North of Boston	143
Africa	29	Maryland	3	West of Boston	75
Germany	16	New Hampshire	3		
France	14	Albany	3		
Nova Scotia	3	Hartford	2		
West Indies	8				

Total: 1,039

Note: [a] Warnings Out in Boston, Overseers of the Poor Records, Mass. Hist. Soc.

TABLE VII. Geographic Mobility in Boston, 1780 to 1790[a]

Rent in Pounds in 1780	Number Reported in 1780	Number Missing in 1790	Persistence Rate
0	546	318	42
1–20	448	215	52
21–40	360	169	53
41–60	217	83	62
61–80	219	83	62
100–199	226	78	66
200+	209	54	74
Total	2,225	1,000	56

Note: [a] Assessors' Books, 1780, compared with Tax and Rate Books, 1790. The persistence rate is the percentage of the number reported in 1780 found on the 1790 list.

who were assessed for only the poll tax in 1790, but who disappeared before the census was taken, were probably among them.[43] The nature of this floating population was very similar to that in nineteenth-century Newburyport.[44] Impoverished, unemployable men dominated the wanderers in both places. The fifteen men whipped for various offenses in Boston in September 1790 were transients who had not been listed by the assessors a few months earlier.[45] Other migrants from Boston landed in the poorhouses of neighboring towns, triggering angry correspondence between their overseers and those of Boston.[46]

Uprooted, unwanted, unhealthy migrants could call no town their home. The potent identity given an individual by his community was not theirs. Thomas Seymore, an old man living off poor relief in Abington in 1805, was born and attended school in Boston, and later moved to Barnstable, Sandwich, Weymouth, and Abington, but never "gained a settlement" by paying taxes for five successive years. In his whole life, he never found a home. Similarly, Braintree demanded in 1804 that Boston "remove Stephen Randal belonging to your town." Since his arrival there in 1802, he had received relief from the town. "He has been wandering about from place to place. . . . Some part of the time chargeable. About four weeks ago he froze himself very bad in the feet and is att the Expense of two Dollars and 50 cents per week, Besides a Dollar attendance, there is no prospect of his being better very soon."[47]

After the Revolution, the old laws used to deal with migrants fell apart. Even though the state accepted responsibility for transients without legal residence anywhere in the commonwealth, the time limit for towns to present migrants with warnings out was extended from two years to three, four, and ultimately five years between 1790 and 1793. In 1794, when the state became responsible for all migrants, warnings out were finally eliminated. Instead, legal residency required payment of taxes on an assessed estate of sixty pounds for five successive years. A former apprentice who practiced his trade for five years or anyone over twenty-one years of age who lived in town for ten years and paid taxes for five became a resident. The law discouraged transients, but encouraged artisans with capital to remain.[48]

But did "expensive Living . . . [pervade] thro every Class, confounding every Distinction between the Poor and the Rich," as Samuel Adams insisted? Enough examples could be found to keep him worried. Thomas Lewis was a shoemaker assessed for £40 rent in 1780 and a wharfinger taxed on £700 in 1790; Josiah Elliot was an agent for a merchant in 1780 and owned no real estate, but in 1790 he operated a hardware store and was assessed for property worth £450; Robert Davis was a leather dresser with £30 rent in 1780, and a merchant assessed £600 in 1790.

Adams failed to see more modest gains. "Mechanics of sober character, and skilled in their trades, of almost every kind, may find employment, and wages equal to their support," wrote the Boston Immigrant Society.[49] The society was partially right. When the Mechanics Association, open only to master crafts-men, was founded in 1795, a fifth of its original members were not on the 1790 tax list; they had either been apprentices in 1790 or had entered town since that time.

A comparison of 1780 and 1790 tax lists shows that occupational mobility was very moderate and that opportunity may well have been declining. Since only those who remained in town for ten years are considered, the results are biased toward success. Only 28 per cent changed jobs, while merely 14 per cent made even minor changes in status. Changes from one artisan job to another and changes among merchants, grocers, retailers, and captains were typical—and rather trivial. Other changes resulted in new status; and about the same number rose as declined. Seventeen artisans became small shopkeepers, wharfingers, and merchants, and four advanced to professional status, while thirteen declined to laborer status. Twenty-eight tradesmen and professionals declined to artisan status, and one became a laborer.

Some new men from outlying areas probably migrated to Boston, bought tory estates, and joined the elite classes immediately after the Revolution,[50] but opportunity soon diminished and the situation became critical. As population grew, more men competed for fewer jobs; many, according to Samuel Breck, became unemployed, "so much so that several gentlemen who associated for the purpose of building three ships had solely in view the occupation of the carpenters and tradespeople."[51] Breck may not have greatly exaggerated. The percentage of laborers and other unskilled men more than doubled: between 2 and 3 per cent were in the group in 1780; the number had grown to 7.4 per cent in 1790.[52] Within the groups staying in town for the ten years, opportunities seem to have been slightly closing at the top and opening at the bottom. While ten merchants and traders became government functionaries (all but one in a full-time position), the total number of tradesmen declined by 11 per cent. On the other hand, the number of men in the marine-laborer category declined 12 per cent.[53]

Upward mobility among sons of artisans was somewhat greater. Jackson Main discovered that the fathers of about a quarter of the merchants sampled from the 1789 directory had been artisans such as brewers, coopers, hatters, carpenters, and tailors. Since each of these trades included a few wealthy members whose sons should have risen in the normal course of events, and Main discovered none from his sample among the wealthiest merchants, his findings, like mine, point to very modest upward mobility.[54]

While a small minority changed their status, almost two-thirds of the group changed their relative economic position in the community. Table IX shows that 30 per cent lost and 31 per cent gained wealth. However, these figures are deceptive; probably most of those who moved during the decade feared economic decline. When geographic mobility is considered, more men lost than gained wealth. In each of the three middle categories of Table IX, the number who fell slightly approximated the number who gained slightly. Unpropertied men who left town were probably those who could not gain a foothold in Boston, for 71 per cent of those who remained became property owners. Most made minor gains; the twenty-eight men who entered the top categories were mostly merchants who had not yet bought property in Boston in 1780. The very top category—as Sam Adams asserted—was in a state of flux; less than half the

TABLE VIII. Occupational Mobility in Boston, 1780 to 1790[a]

Occupation in 1790	Occupation in 1780				Total in 1790
	Professional	Tradesman	Artisan	Marine-Laborer	
Professional	42	15	4	0	61
Tradesman[b]	0	162	17	0	179
Artisan	5	23	311	9	348
Marine-Laborer	0	1	13	24	38
Total in 1780	47	201	345	33	626

Note: [a]Assessors' Books, 1780; Tax and Rate Books, 1790. Table VIII represents only about half the people who remained in Boston during the decade. Wards 5, 6, and 10 do not have occupations listed for 1780, and Negroes and widows were rarely listed. The columns are 1780, the rows 1790 (e.g., 61 professionals in 1790, 47 in 1780, 311 artisans remained artisans over the decade, 23 tradesmen became artisans). Lateral changes within the groups, which included no change in status, involved 4 professionals, 37 tradesmen, 42 artisans, 4 marine-laborers. Total changes of status: 87. Total lateral changes: 87. Total changes: 174.
[b] Retailers, merchants, businessmen.

men in that group in 1780 managed to remain there in 1790, but men from the next lower category rushed to fill their places.

What all these changes meant to most workers was buying—or losing—a small piece of real estate, finding a new, somewhat different job, or receiving a small profit from one's trade. Joseph Snelling, an unpropertied joiner in 1780, gained £25 of real estate by 1790; John Scutter, a propertyless fisherman in 1780, was a journeyman goldsmith with £25 of real estate in 1790. Tailor Samuel Beales owned £12 10s. of real estate in 1780; by 1790, he owned property assessed at £125 and had six children and four apprentices or journeymen in his house. Small losses were equally common. John Douglass, a cooper with real estate worth £12 10s. in 1780, was a combmaker without taxable property in 1790. Samuel Clark, tailor, lost real estate worth £20 over the decade, and Richard Salter, a merchant with a rent of £180 in 1780, was a small shopkeeper with property worth only £25 in 1790.

What pattern explains these small changes? Men in some trades—merchants, professional men, builders, coopers—tended to gain wealth, while others—bakers, shoemakers, tailors—tended to lose it. Whole classes, however, neither rose nor fell; some individuals in most groups became prosperous and some poor.[55] As Table X illustrates, over 70 per cent of Boston's workers assumed different occupations or economic conditions over the decade. While there is a significant (and expected) tendency for some to rise or fall both in wealth and occupation, 74 per cent of those changing in one variable did not change the other.

Though occupational mobility had little relationship to economic mobility, age in most occupational groups was probably related to wealth.[56] A young man might begin working with little money, gain wealth, and perhaps change occupations as he grew older, lose wealth when he became an old man, and

TABLE IX. Property Mobility in Boston, 1780 to 1790[a]

1790 Income Groups	1780 Income Groups					Total in 1790
	High 1	2	3	4	Low 5	
High 1	55	39	15	3	7	119
2	43	85	63	7	21	219
3	12	46	107	59	39	263
4	4	17	51	87	55	214
Low 5	7	14	32	71	51	175
Total in 1780	121	201	268	227	173	990

Note: [a] Assessors' Books, 1780; Tax and Rate Books, 1790. Some persons could not be ranked. Columns are 1780, rows 1790. The income groups were determined by comparing 1780 rents (hypothetically 1/6 of the real estate assessment) with total assessments in 1790. In the table, 1 is the highest and 5 the lowest group. The real figures for each group in 1780 and 1790 respectively are: 1, £200+ and £1000+; 2, £75–£199 and £276–£999; 3, £30–£74 and £76–£275; 4, £1–£29 and £1–£75; 5, £0 for both years.

TABLE X. Occupational and Property Mobility in Boston, 1780 to 1790[a]

	Occupation Up	Occupation Same	Occupation Down	Total
Wealth Up	32	164	14	210
Wealth Same	26	186	33	245
Wealth Down	12	84	52	148
Total	70	434	99	603

Note: [a] Assessors' Books, 1780; Tax and Rate Books, 1790. Occupations in Table X are ranked as in Table III, and ranks for other occupations have been interpolated to determine direction of mobility. The occupational mobility figures are not identical to those of Table VIII because of the differences in the categories of Table III; the method used here allowed inclusion of cases of lateral mobility mentioned in n. a to Table VIII. Some cases have been lost, and several cases of men employed in 1780 and unemployed in 1790 added. Ratios of downward/downward and upward mobility in Tables VIII-X show that Table X may be biased toward upward property mobility (51.1% downward/downward and upward mobility in Table IX and only 41.3% downward in Table X). Since Table IX has the larger number of cases, it should be more accurate. But with its more exact methodology, Table X points to a bias toward upward occupational mobility in Table VIII (48.2% downward mobility in Table VIII, 58% in Table X). Chi Square was significant at less than .01.

leave his widow with few worldly goods. Some impressionistic evidence supports this thesis. John Hooton followed his father's trade of oarmaker in 1780 and lived at home, but by 1790 he was a wharfinger taxed for £275. In 1780 Benjamin Jervis was a propertyless journeyman working for merchant Pascol Smith; by 1790 Jervis had set up as a merchant himself and was assessed £450. Aged Joseph Morton, propertyless in 1790, had been a taverner with a rent of £200 in 1780; John Maud, an old tailor, had a £30 rent in 1780 but was propertyless in 1790.

The social condition of the town's widows also supports this thesis. In 1790, only 76 of Boston's 575 widows owned any taxable property. Widows of very successful men managed to hold on to some property: of the widows taxed, 17 were assessed under £125, 23 from £125 to £200, 21 from £201 to £500, 10 from £500 to £1,000, and 5 over £1,000. Probably some husbands lost wealth before they died; widows quickly lost the rest. Their decline in wealth and status was steeper than almost any experienced by their husbands; the resulting loneliness and unhappiness appear in the assessor's marginal comments. Widow Gray was a "dogmatic lady," and Widow Turrell was a "talking woman." A number of widows followed callings that allowed contact with the public. Twenty-eight of them combated poverty and isolation by operating boarding houses; five others owned taverns; three managed millinery shops; and eight owned other types of retail establishments.

Inequality rapidly advanced in Boston during the Revolutionary period. Wealth was less evenly distributed than before the war, and the proportion of wealth held by the poor and middling classes declined. The growth of poverty was a major problem. As continued migration increased the numbers of poor, a surplus female population of working age was only temporarily helped by the duckcloth factory. Many citizens were able to gain economic security, but unsuccessful families lived in crowded housing or wandered from place to place in search of employment.

Rich and poor were divided by wealth, ascribed status, and segregated living patterns. Individuals could rarely breach a status barrier in fewer than two generations. While social mobility may have been relatively easy for a few immediately after the Revolution, these extraordinary opportunities tended to disappear as population returned to its pre-Revolutionary size. Since political power was monopolized by the wealthy, the poor could only deferentially appeal for aid. The economic elite socialized only among themselves, never showed visitors the semi-ghetto of the North End, and rode through the South End without seeing the poor. But increased segregation could eventually undermine deference by eliminating opportunities for the lowly to defer to their superiors.

A class system based primarily on economic divisions slowly developed. Occupation and wealth determined a man's position in the community; the few titles that survived became functional descriptions of groups, not indicators of a special status. Tax records show that "gentleman" ceased to be a social distinction, but was instead a term reserved for retired tradesmen; "esquire" was a title generally limited to lawyers and public officials. Increased wealth alone could bring higher status to tradesmen and artisans—a fact probably behind Samuel Adams's complaints.

At the same time Boston was becoming more stratified, a new political philosophy emerged. Whig theory divided society and government into three orders, democracy, aristocracy, and monarchy, and demanded that each be perpetually a check and balance on the others. After the Revolution this theory slowly gave way to a model that put the people above the entire government. They held "constituent power," enabling them to call conventions to write constitutions restraining the powers of government. Sovereignty was transferred from the king (or a branch of the legislature) to the people, and political equality was enshrined in the country's legal documents.[57]

Yet the city of Boston, increasingly democratic in theory, and increasingly stratified and divided economically and socially, managed to avoid major civil disturbances after the Revolution. Not only did social and political trends seem to run in opposite directions, but the groups of near poor who manned preindustrial crowds in Europe—apprentices, journeymen, and artisans—lived in greater profusion in Boston than in contemporary European towns.[58] What social forces kept these groups quiet after the Revolution?

Definitive answers to this question await further research, but at least some speculation is in order. Before the Revolution, crowd action was considered a legitimate means for producing social change and protecting the community. When the monarchial order seemed to deny the people their liberties, the people took to the streets. The resulting disturbances were not class conflicts, for pre-Revolutionary crowds in America were supported by the upper classes and peopled by the near poor.[59]

After the Revolution, the ideological props for violence slowly disintegrated. If the people were sovereign, if they held "constituent power," crowd action was a revolt against the people, not a conflict to restrain one branch of government. This change did not eliminate violence, but it altered its nature.[60] Crowds would no longer be the weapons of one order, composed of elements from many economic classes, to be directed against another, but would be revolutionary instruments of class conflict.

Post-Revolutionary Boston, however, provided several structural restraints against this development. The possibility of moderate economic success and the safety valve of short-distance migrations probably limited the chance for confrontation. Unless economic disaster strikes a large number of men (and there is no evidence of this in Boston at this time), group conflict can be generated only when two organized interests compete for the same goods or power.[61] But Boston's only organized society of workers—whose members were of firm middle-class standing—willingly deferred to their social superiors.

NOTES

1. *Massachusetts Centinel* (Boston), Feb. 2, 1785; Samuel Adams to John Adams, July 2, 1785, *The Writings of Samuel Adams*, ed. Harry Alonzo Cushing, IV (New York, 1908), 315-316.

2. J. Franklin Jameson, *The American Revolution Considered as a Social Movement* (Princeton, 1926); Richard D. Brown, "The Confiscation and Disposition of Loyalists' Estates in Suffolk County, Massachusetts," *William and Mary Quarterly*, 3d Ser., XXI (1964), 534-550, surveys the relevant historiography.

3. James A. Henretta, "Economic Development and Social Structure in Colonial Boston," *Wm. and Mary Qtly.*, 3d Ser., XXII (1965), 75-92.

4. Max Weber, *The City*, trans. and ed. Don Martindale and Gertrud Neuwirth (New York, 1958), 69.

5. *Ibid.* Philadelphia closely resembled a "producer city." See James T. Lemon, "Urbanization and the Development of Eighteenth-Century Southeastern Pennsylvania and Adjacent Delaware," *Wm. and Mary Qtly.*, 3d Ser., XXIV (1967), 504-510.

6. Tax and Rate Books, 1790, compared with *Heads of Familes At the First Census, 1790. Massachusetts* (Washington, 1906), 188-195; and "Names of the Inhabitants of the Town of Boston in 1790," *Record Commissioners' Report*, XXII, 443-511. Numerous dependent males over 16 years of age are found in the census, but not in the tax lists. Almost all of them were in homes of artisans of middling wealth. This suggests that many of them were transient journeymen and apprentices and not older sons hidden from the assessor. Tax and census records are the source for any uncited comments.

7. Lemuel Shattuck, *Report to the Committee of the City Council Appointed to Obtain the Census of Boston for the Year 1845*, . . . (Boston, 1846), 4, 45. A sample of every sixth column of the Washington edition of the census was checked for widows; three-quarters had dependents. Joseph J. Spengler, "Demographic Factors and Early Modern Economic Development," *Daedalus*, XCVII (1968), 440-443, defines productive ages as from 15 to 65 years. Data in Shattuck does not allow such fine distinctions, but the percentage of people over 65 is probably too small to materially change the following statistics:

Age Ratios	Percentage over 15 yrs. old			Sex Ratios	Number of Men/100 Women		
	1765	1790	1800		1765	1790	1800
Total	44.30	. . .	61.93	All ages	95.48	82.07	90.27
Male	41.71	56.13	60.42	Over 15	81.42	. . .	86.14
Female	47.26	. . .	63.31				

8. *Mass. Centinel* (Boston), Sept. 6, 1788, quoted in William R. Bagnall, *The Textile Industries of the United States*, . . . (Cambridge, Mass., 1893), 112-116; Pemberton,

"Description of Boston," Mass. Hist. Soc., *Collections*, 1st Ser., III (1794), 252-253, 279; Samuel Breck to Henry Knox, Sept. 12, 1790, Knox Papers, Mass. Hist. Soc., Boston.

9. Nathaniel Cutting, "Extracts from a Journal of a Gentleman visiting Boston in 1792," Sept. 6, 1792, Mass. Hist. Soc., *Proceedings*, 1st Ser., XII (1871-1873), 61-62.

10. See Table I; David Reed, Membership in the Massachusetts Peace Society, 1816-1820 (unpubl. seminar paper, Brandeis University, 1968), 60-63.

11. *The Acts and Resolves, Public and Private, of the Province of Massachusetts Bay*, V (Boston, 1886), 1163, 1165.

12. W. G. Hoskins, *Provincial England* (London, 1963), 90-91; J. F. Pound, "The Social and Trade Structure of Norwich 1525-1575," *Past and Present*, No. 34 (July 1966), 50-53; Donald Warner Koch, "Income Distribution and Political Structure in Seventeenth-Century Salem, Massachusetts," *Essex Institute Historical Collections*, CV (1969), 54, 59; James T. Lemon and Gary B. Nash, "The Distribution of Wealth in Eighteenth Century America: A Century of Changes in Chester County, Pennsylvania, 1693-1802," *Journal of Social History*, II (1968-1969), 9-12; Stuart Blumin, "Mobility and Change in Antebellum Philadelphia," in Stephan Thernstrom and Richard Sennett, eds., *Nineteenth-Century Cities: Essays in the New Urban History* (New Haven, 1969), 204-206; Robert E. Gallman, "Trends in the Size Distribution of Wealth in the Nineteenth Century," in Lee Soltow, ed., *Six Papers on the Size Distribution of Wealth and Income* (New York, 1969), 22-23; Merle Curti, *The Making of an American Community: A Case Study of Democracy in a Frontier County* (Stanford, Calif., 1959), 78.

13. Brown, "Confiscation of Loyalists' Estates," *Wm. and Mary Qtly.*, 3d Ser., XXI (1964), 546-549.

14. Jacques Pierre Brissot de Warville, *New Travels in the United States of America, 1788*, trans. Mara Soceanu Vamos and Durand Echeverria, ed. Durand Echeverria (Cambridge, Mass., 1964), 87, 98-100.

15. In this paper, "poor" refers to the destitute, "near poor" to those living at or near the minimum level of subsistence. For Europe see Hoskins, *Provincial England*, 90-93; Hoskins, *Industry, Trade and People in Exeter, 1688-1800, . . .* (Manchester, Eng., 1935), 119; Pound, "Structure of Norwich," *Past and Present*, No. 34 (July 1966), 50-51; George Rudé, "La population ouvrière de Paris de 1789 à 1791," *Annales Historiques de la Révolution Française*, XXXIX (1967), 21-27; Jeffry Kaplow, "Sur la population flottante de Paris, à la fin de l'Ancien Régime," *ibid.*, 7-8; Pierre Deyon, *Amiens, Capitale Provinciale. Etude sur la Société Urbaine au 17° Siècle* (Paris, 1967), 349-357. I am indebted to Gerald Soliday, Brandeis University, for the French materials.

16. See Table VI; *Record Commissioners' Report*, XXXI, 239.

17. Since the total amount of property remains unknown, any "poverty line" chosen from Table II would be arbitrary. Instead, estimates of poor have been calculated by adding poorhouse and unemployed figures from Table I and of near poor by adding the number of widows from the census to the number of persons without taxable property and of those in the lowest category of taxpayers. A fifth of the propertyless and 15% of the lowest category have been subtracted from the near poor figure to account for upward mobility. The figures, especially for 1771, are very rough, but the direction of change they indicate is accurate, and the estimates are minimal figures of the extent of poverty.

18. "Gone broke, wife as broke," and all similar short comments are marginalia from the Tax and Rate Books, 1790.

19. *Record Commissioners' Report*, XXXI, 239.

20. Jackson Turner Main, *The Social Structure of Revolutionary America* (Princeton, 1965), *passim*, esp. 200-211.

21. Committee to Arrange a Procession, *Procession* (Boston, 1789).

22. An F test was significant at less than the .01 level. This means there is less than a 1% chance that the differences shown in Table III are random. The test is a comparison of two quantities: 1. the sum of the squared variations of each case in each occupation subtracted from the group mean; and 2. the sum of the squared variations of each group subtracted from the grand mean. Eta^2, calculated from the same data, tests the strength or degree of relationship. In this case, Eta^2 was .194, which means that about 19.4% of the difference between the means in Table III is accounted for by the differences between occupational groups. See Herbert M. Blalock, Jr., *Social Statistics* (New York, 1960), 242-252, 255-257. Stuart Blumin's calculations of ETA^2 on Philadelphia data from 1860 were almost

identical (.17). "The Historical Study of Vertical Mobility," *Historical Methods Newsletter*, I, No. 4 (Sept. 1968), 8-10.

23. Brissot de Warville, *New Travels*, 90; *Handbook of the Massachusetts Historical Society* (Boston, 1949), 1-3. On the continuation of deference see Josiah P. Quincy, "Social Life in Boston: From the Adoption of the Federal Constitution to the Granting of the City Charter," in Justin Winsor, ed., *The Memorial History of Boston, Including Suffolk County, Massachusetts, 1630-1880*, IV (1886), 2, 4; David Hackett Fischer, *The Revolution of American Conservatism: The Federalist Party in the Era of Jeffersonian Democracy* (New York, 1965), xiv-xv, 4-10.

24. *Independent Chronicle* (Boston), Oct. 28, 1789 (I am indebted to Alfred Young for the source); Samuel Breck, *Recollections of Samuel Breck with Passages from His Note-Books (1771-1862)* (London, 1877), 108.

25. Prince Hall, *A Charge Delivered to the African Lodge . . .* (Boston, 1797), 10-11; and Hall, *A Charge Delivered to the Brethren of the African Lodge . . .* (Boston, 1792). About half the blacks were servants and therefore had little choice but to be respectful.

26. M. A. DeWolfe Howe, *The Humane Society of the Commonwealth of Massachusetts: An Historical Review, 1785-1916* (Boston, 1918), Chaps. 1-2; *The Institution of the Humane Society of the Commonwealth of Massachusetts . . .* (Boston, 1788).

27. Peter Thacher, *A Sermon, Preached in Boston, . . .* (Boston, 1795), 13.

28. *Record Commissioners' Report*, XXVII, 11-12, 15, 20, 25-26, 31, 33, 37, 40; First Church Poor and Sacramental Fund, First Church, Boston.

29. Henretta, "Economic Development and Social Structure," *Wm. and Mary Qtly.*, 3d Ser., XXII (1965), 84, 89; Jackson Turner Main, "Government by the People: The American Revolution and the Democratization of the Legislatures," *Wm. and Mary Qtly.*, 3d Ser., XXIII (1966), 404; and Main, *The Upper House in Revolutionary America, 1763-1788* (Madison, Wis., 1967), 162-174.

30. The profile of officers was drawn from sources cited in Table IV; Boston city directories, 1789 and 1796, *Record Commissioners' Report*, X, 171-296; XXXI, 53, 59-60, 65, 97, 102, 133-134, 147, 160-161, 185, 200, 217, 224, 232, 243-245, 253, 276-277, 283, 319, 349-350, 384, 391; "Assessors' 'Taking Books' of the Town of Boston, 1780," *Bostonian Society Publications*, 1st Ser., IX (1912), 9-59. Hereafter cited as Assessors' Books, 1780.

31. See n. 30; Robert Francis Seybold, *The Town Officials of Colonial Boston, 1634-1775* (Cambridge, Mass., 1939), 289-305. For other Massachusetts towns before the Revolution, see Michael Zuckerman, *Peaceable Kingdoms: New England Towns in the Eighteenth Century* (New York, 1970), 274-276. Boston turnover and service rates were as follows:

Years	Number of Offices	Number of Officeholders	Years of Service		Rate of Turnover/Year	
			mean	median	mean	median
Selectmen						
1760–70	7	19	4.0	3.0	1.7	1.5
1785–95	9	23	4.3	4.0	2.2	1.0
Overseers of the Poor						
1760–70	12	28	4.7	4.0	1.6	1.0
1785–95	12	23	6.3	8.0	1.2	0.5

32. Joseph H. Buckingham, *Annals of the Massachusetts Charitable Mechanics Society* (Boston, 1853), 6-10, 12-14, 57-58, 80, 94-97.

33. Edward H. Savage, *Police Records and Recollections; or, Boston by Daylight and Gaslight . . .* (Boston, 1873), 40-42. Savage lists only punishments, not unsolved crimes.

34. J. Potter, "The Growth of Population in America, 1700-1860," in D. V. Glass and D. E. C. Eversley, eds., *Population in History: Essays in Historical Demography* (London, 1965),

636-641; Evarts B. Greene and Virginia D. Harrington, *American Population Before the Federal Census of 1790* (New York, 1932), 21-24, 46; Herman R. Friis, *A Series of Population Maps of the Colonies and the United States, 1625-1790*, American Geographical Society Mimeographed Publication, No. 3 (New York, 1940), 16 and maps 10a, 10b, 12a, 12b.

35. Leo F. Schnore and Peter R. Knights, "Residence and Social Structure: Boston in the Ante-Bellum Period," in Thernstrom and Sennett, eds., *Nineteenth-Century Cities*, 250.

36. Josiah Henry Benton, *Warning Out in New England* (Boston, 1911), 55-62; *Record Commissioners' Report*, XXV, 28, 34, 166, 212, 242.

37. Rates for 1765-1790 were almost as great as in early modern London, but less than those in antebellum Boston. E. A. Wrigley, "A Simple Model of London's Importance in Changing English Society and Economy 1650-1750," *Past and Present*, No. 37 (July 1967), 45-49; Peter R. Knights, "Population Turnover, Persistence and Residential Mobility in Boston, 1830-1860," in Thernstrom and Sennett, eds., *Nineteenth-Century Cities* 258-274.

38. E. G. Ravenstein, "The Laws of Migration," *Journal of the Royal Statistical Society*, XLVIII (1885), 167-227, esp. 198-199; Ravenstein, "The Laws of Migration: Second Paper," *ibid.*, LII (1889), 241-305; Samuel A. Stoffer, "Intervening Opportunities: A Theory Relating Mobility and Distance," *American Sociological Review*, V (1940), 845-867; George Blackburn and Sherman L. Ricards, Jr., "A Demographic History of the West: Manistee County, Michigan, 1860," *Journal of American History*, LVII (1970), 616-617.

39. Pauline Maier, "Popular Uprisings and Civil Authority in Eighteenth-Century America," *Wm. and Mary Qtly.*, 3d Ser., XXVII (1970), 3-35.

40. Kenneth Lockridge, "Land, Population and the Evolution of New England Society 1630-1790," *Past and Present*, No. 39 (Apr. 1968), 62-80; Philip J. Greven, *Four Generations: Population, Land, and Family in Colonial Andover, Massachusetts* (Ithaca, N. Y., 1970), 212-214; Charles S. Grant, *Democracy in the Connecticut Frontier Town of Kent* (New York, 1961), 94-103; Bruce E. Steiner, "New England Anglicanism: A Genteel Faith?" *Wm. and Mary Qtly.*, 3d Ser., XXVII (1970), 122-135.

41. Other rates, all expressed in terms of per cent per decade: 51% in 17th-century English towns; 22% in Dedham, Mass., 1670-1700; 56% in Boston, 1830-1860; 73% in Trempealeau Co., Wis., 1860-1880. Peter Laslett and John Harrison, "Clayworth and Cogenhoe," in H. E. Bell and R. L. Ollard, eds., *Historical Essays 1600-1750, Presented to David Ogg* (London, 1963), 173-177; Kenneth Lockridge, "The Population of Dedham, Massachusetts, 1636-1736," *Economic History Review*, 2d Ser., XIX (1966), 322-324; Knights, "Population Turnover," in Thernstrom and Sennett, eds., *Nineteenth-Century Cities*, 262; Curti, *American Community*, 68.

42. Stephan Thernstrom, *Poverty and Progress: Social Mobility in a Nineteenth Century City* (Cambridge, Mass., 1964), 85.

43. The census was taken between Aug. 2 and 22 (*Record Commissioners' Report* edition of census); when assessments were made is unknown, but assessors were elected in March and some widows of men who were taxed appear in the census.

44. Thernstrom, *Poverty and Progress*, 84-89.

45. *Boston Gazette* (Mass.), Sept. 20, 1790.

46. Overseers of the Poor of Boston, Mass., Miscellaneous Papers, 1735-1855, Mass. Hist. Soc. Most letters are from the period 1800-1805; for similar examples in the 1760s see *Record Commissioners' Report*, XX, 201-202, 281-289.

47. Overseers of the Poor, Misc. Papers, 1735-1855, Mass. Hist. Soc.

48. Kelso, *Public Poor Relief*, 55-61.

49. Immigrant Society in Boston, *Information for Immigrants to the New-England States* (Boston, 1795).

50. Brown, "Confiscation of Loyalists' Estates," *Wm. and Mary Qtly.*, 3d Ser., XXI (1964), 546-549; Oscar and Mary F. Handlin, "Radicals and Conservatives in Massachusetts after Independence," *New England Quarterly*, XVII (1944), 352-355.

51. Breck, *Recollections*, 178.

52. Laborers constitute 6.1% of the people whose occupations in 1780 are known. However, the three wards from which there is no occupational data housed only 11% of the laborers in 1790. The figure of 6.1% is therefore far too high. A number of others in other wards have no occupations listed, and some of them may have been laborers. For a conservative

estimate of the proportion of laborers, I added 30% to the number listed (38), and divided that number (50) by 2,225, the total number of males on the 1780 list. The result was 2.3%.

53. These percentages, based on a small number of cases, must be taken as indicative only of the direction of change, not of the extent of change. It is probable that some of the difference is random. However, the figures may be minimums; Table VIII probably underestimates the extent of downward mobility. See note to Table X.

54. Main, *Social Structure*, 191-192.

55. The problem is discussed in Blumin, "Historical Study of Mobility," *Hist. Meth. Newsletter*, I, No. 4 (Sept. 1968), 1-13.

56. Age and mobility were related to 19th-century Canada. Michael Katz, "The Social Structure of Hamilton, Ontario," in Thernstrom and Sennett, eds., *Nineteenth-Century Cities*, 209-244.

57. Robert R. Palmer, *The Age of the Democratic Revolution: A Political History of Europe and America, 1760-1800* (Princeton, 1959), I, Chap. 8; Gordon S. Wood, *The Creation of the American Republic, 1776-1787* (Chapel Hill, 1969), Chaps. 8-9.

58. George Rude, *The Crowd in History: A Study of Popular Disturbances in France and England, 1730-1848* (New York, 1964), *passim*, but esp. Chap. 13; Ralf Dahrendorf, *Class and Class Conflict in Industrial Society* (Stanford, Calif., 1959), 216-218.

59. Maier, "Popular Uprisings," *Wm. and Mary Qtly.*, 3d Ser., XXVII (1970), 3-30.

60. *Ibid.*, 30-33.

61. Dahrendorf, *Class and Class Conflict*, Chaps. 5-6.

bibliography

Jesse Lemisch and Staughton Lynd have made the greatest contributions to the field of radical revolutionary history. Lynd's substantive work has been collected in a book of essays, *Class Conflict, Slavery, and the United States Constitution* (Bobbs-Merrill, 1967). Lemisch's essays are more widely dispersed, but many have been reprinted. "Jack Tar in the Streets: Merchant Seamen in the Politics of Revolutionary America" originally appeared in *William and Mary Quarterly*, 3rd Ser., 21 (July 1968), 371-407. "The American Revolution Seen from the Bottom Up," in Barton Bernstein, ed., *Towards a New Past: Dissenting Essays in American History* (Pantheon, 1968), suggests ways to "approach the history of the inarticulate," and "to outline what such a history might look like." Lemisch's most recent essay, written in collaboration with John K. Alexander, "The White Oaks, Jack Tar, and the Concept of the 'Inarticulate,' *William and Mary Quarterly*, 3rd Ser., 29 (January 1972) reassesses the use of the term "inarticulate."

William Appleman Williams in *The Contours of American History* (Quadrangle, 1966) saw the revolution as an attempt by a growing entrepreneurial class to shed onerous mercantile restrictions imposed for the benefit of a distant mother country. This view, widely accepted by radical historians, is opposed by Bernard Bailyn. In *The Pamphlets of the American Revolution* (Harvard University Press, 1965) and the *Ideological Origins of the American Revolution* (Harvard University Press, 1967), Bailyn argues that challenges to a hierarchical social structure as well as to governments based on God's sanctions became the basis for a society in which human aspirations were limitless. Bailyn's interpretation of the revolution as the foundation for eliminating arbitrary authority reintroduced ideas into a debate that had long centered on economics. Gordon Wood, *The Creation of the American Republic* (University of North Carolina Press, 1970), extends Bailyn's argument. Caroline Robbins, *The Eighteenth Century Commonwealthman: Studies in the Transmission, Development and Circumstance of English Liberal Thought from the Restoration of Charles II until the War with the Thirteen Colonies* (Harvard University Press, 1969), provides essential background for those ideas. Alfred Young studies incipient Jeffersonians in *The Democratic Republicans of New York: The Origins, 1763-1797* (University of North Carolina Press, 1967), while William H. Nelson, *The American Tory* (Clarendon Press, 1961), explores the opposition. Useful historiographical information can be found in Bernard Friedman, "The Shaping of the Radical Consciousness in Provincial New York," *Journal of American History*, 56 (March 1970), 781-801.

the emerging economy: workers and Indians

In *The Rising American Empire*, Richard W. Van Alstyne exploded for all time the notion held by so many traditional historians that America's expansion in its formative years was qualitatively different from the aggressive imperialism associated with the expansion of other white Western nations. In March 1783, George Washington referred to the United States as a "rising empire" and Van Alstyne considered the phrase a precise description of what Washington and his contemporaries had in mind: "an *imperium*—a dominion, state or sovereignty that would expand in population and territory, and increase in strength and power."

For many American revolutionaries the example of the Roman Empire was apt. William Henry Drayton, a leading planter and chief justice of South Carolina, declared in 1776 that

the days of Roman greatness lasted only thirty-three years, but . . .
the Almighty . . . has made choice of the present generation to erect the American Empire. . . .
And thus has suddenly arisen in the World, a new Empire, stiled the United States of America. An Empire that as soon as started into existence, attracts the attention of the Rest of the Universe; and bids fair, by the blessing of God, to be the most glorious of any upon Record.

William Appleman Williams in the *Contours of American History*, noted that Jedidiah Morse, a Congregational minister and author of *American Geography*, also believed that with the ratification of the Constitution America embarked on the road to what was destined to become "the largest empire that ever existed." Thomas Jefferson, who acquired the Louisiana Territory to hasten the process, specifically rejected the idea that a republic could only survive "in a small territory." Conditions in the United States proved, he insisted, that the opposite was true and he, along with James Madison and even John Adams, committed the new country to a perpetual policy of territorial expansion combined with a government-supported mercantile economy to ensure contin-ued growth and prosperity.

According to Van Alstyne, Benjamin Franklin had championed an American empire for forty years before the revolution and used the terms "national" and "imperial" interchangeably. Despite Daniel Boorstin's contention in *The Americans: The Colonial Experience* that Franklin did not oppose a just Indian policy, Benjamin Franklin believed Indians blocked the progress of American settlement and concluded that "rum should be regarded as an agent of Providence 'to extirpate these savages in order to make room for the cultivation of the earth.' "

The nature of emerging America was shaped by the unfolding of its imperial design, the attitudes Americans held about business and material plenty, the function and position of workers, and the relationship between the government and the economic structure. The policies adopted toward the natives of this land, called the Indians by their conquerors, were determined by the vision the founders of the United States had of America's destiny.

The following essays explore those issues and indicate some of the reasons that historians disagree about them. William Appleman Williams and Alfred Young, two of the foremost radical historians in the United States, analyze different aspects of America's early economy from critical perspectives. Mainstream historian Daniel Boorstin, on the other hand, explores yet another factor in the development of America's economy, but with no hint of critical analysis. Similarly, Francis Paul Prucha's assessment of Andrew Jackson's

Indian policies represents that increasingly diminishing group of historians who celebrate white conquest of Indian territory and regard America's extermination policies toward the Indians as incidental to that conquest. Prucha's book, for example, *The Role of the United States Army in the Development of the Northwest, 1815–1860*, relates the activities of the Army "to the peaceful processes of territorial expansion and social development." Blanche Wiesen Cook's essay takes the opposite point of view and highlights the impact of American expansionism on the Indians.

the age of mercantilism: an interpretation of the American political economy, 1763 to 1828

WILLIAM APPLEMAN WILLIAMS

William Appleman Williams has inspired much of the new thinking about America's past; and the following article is among the most provocative and illuminating of his essays.

To satisfy the demands of continual expansion, government support of the national economy was required. Economic nationalism, or mercantilism, consisted of government investments in and tax protection for domestic manufacturing, land development policies, nationally protected markets, and expansion abroad. Ultimately, the Monroe Doctrine represented one side of a mature American mercantilism. The other side was represented by the fact that by 1826 "the government was the largest single economic entrepreneur in the country." Mercantilism, however, implied a corporate commonwealth; and America's commitment to the rights of individual ownership promoted a conflict in American economic history between "the common good" and the laissez-faire ideology that triumphed between the Jacksonian period and World War I. The reinterpretation of America's newly defined empire required the reassessment of our economy in its historical perspective.

Based upon the suggestion by Curtis P. Nettels that one of the consequences of British mercantilism was the creation "of a new mercantilist state on this side of the Atlantic," and upon recent re-evaluations of mercantilism by William D. Grampp, Gunnar Myrdal, Jacob Viner, Charles Wilson, and others, this essay advances the hypothesis that the central characteristic of American history from 1763 to 1828 was in fact the development and maturation of an American mercantilism.[1] Let it be emphasized that the interpretation is offered as a hypothesis and no more—as an idea to be examined and tested, then accepted, modified, or rejected on the basis of its relevance and validity. There is no intention, furthermore, even to imply that the approach as here stated offers final answers to all the vexing problems connected with understanding early American society. It is merely proposed that a re-examination of the era from this angle may lead to new insights, and hence contribute to a broader interpretation of the period.[2]

At the outset, for example, the use of the concept of mercantilism restores to its properly central place the fact that Americans thought of themselves as an empire at the very beginning of their national existence—as part of their assertive self-consciousness which culminated in the American Revolution. Though it may seem surprising, especially when contrasted with the image of isolationism which has been accepted so long, in reality this early predominance of a pattern of empire thought is neither very strange nor very difficult to explain. Having matured in an age of empires as part of an empire, the colonists naturally saw themselves in the same light once they joined issue with the mother country.

Revolutionary leaders were confident of their ability "not only to take territory by the sword, but to hold and govern it under a colonial status."[3] Long before the break with England, for example, Benjamin Franklin was a leader of those who entertained a "burning interest in westward expansion." At the threshold of the revolution he visualized an American Empire including Canada, the Spanish Floridas, the West Indies, and perhaps even Ireland.[4] George Washington, John Adams, John Livingston, and Thomas Lee were among those who shared such conceptions of an American Empire.[5] By the end of the war, such men as Silas Deane looked forward to the time when "Great Britain, America and Russia united will command not barely Europe, but the whole world united."[6] And in 1789, after remarking that "it is well known that empire has been travelling from east to west," Congregational minister and geographer Jedidiah Morse concluded that "probably her last and broadest seat will be America . . . the largest empire that ever existed."[7]

While the vigor, even cockiness, of such statements may be explained by the consciousness of having whipped the champion, the underlying emphasis on expansion and empire was an integral part of the general outlook of mercantilism, a conception of the world shared by most of the revolutionary generation. Though they revolted against British mercantilism, there is considerable evidence to suggest that early American leaders did not, as so often is assumed, rebel against the idea and practice of mercantilism itself. In stressing the role of natural-rights philosophy in the thinking of the leaders of the revolution, the traditional view of the American Revolution has slighted this key point.

An acceptance of natural law is not incompatible with mercantilism, as is indicated by John Locke's vigorous espousal of both systems. Much of the talk in America about natural rights, moreover, concerned what Thomas Paine called the "natural right" to one's own empire.[8] And though they were willing to use Adam Smith's polemic in behalf of laissez faire as a weapon against British mercantilism (and against their domestic opponents), most Americans adhered firmly in their own practice to the principle that the state had to intervene in economic affairs. America's romance with Smith's laissez faire came later and was of relatively short duration. Hence it would appear that a better understanding of early American history depends in considerable measure upon a grasp of the nature and practice of American mercantilism as it developed between 1763 and 1825.

Traditionally thought of as little more than a narrow and selfish point of view held by the trading interest, mercantilism was in fact a broad definition and explanation of the world shared by most of Western Europe in the seventeenth and eighteenth centuries.[9] In this sense it was the basic outlook of those who labored to build a dynamic balanced economy of agriculture and business organized on a capitalistic basis within a nationalistic framework.

Depending upon their specific function and power at any given stage in the process, mercantilists argued among themselves over the best means to achieve and maintain such a system—and differed in their estimates of whether or not it had been established—but they agreed on the objective and upon the need to use the state as a tool.

Whether agrarian or urban, therefore, mercantilists were essentially national-ists who strove for self-sufficiency through increased domestic production and a favorable balance (and terms) of trade. Their emphasis on production and the control of export markets and sources of raw materials, rather than on consumption and economic interdependence, led them to fear surpluses as a sign of crisis and failure. Thus they dropped the old feudal restrictions on exports and replaced them with taxes on imports. Their greatest fear was a surplus of goods. In this respect, furthermore, mercantilism was reinforced—albeit in a backhanded and even unintentional way—by the broad ethical outlook of Puritanism (which frowned on luxury), even though mercantilism itself was a secular and almost amoral system. Likewise, the concept of a chosen people, so strong in Puritanism, also strengthened the secular and economic nationalism of mercantilism. Thus mercantilists constantly labored to build a tightly organized and protected national market and to increase their share of the world market. The key points in their program were integration at home and expansion abroad.

In the exuberant confidence of their victory over Britain, Americans tended to assume that each new state could survive and thrive as a mercantile empire unto itself. That attitude was not too surprising, for each of the new states appeared to enjoy the raw materials, labor supply, and trading facilities for a balanced economy. That estimate of the situation was supported and reinforced by the conviction, itself part of the traditional theory, that a state could remain democratic in political and social life only if it were small and integrated, and by the experiences of the colonies in dealing with Great Britain's imperial policy after 1763. Yet the political outlook and faith contradicted certain basic tenets of mercantilism, which Americans also entertained, or assumed.

The first attempt to reconcile the conflict produced the Articles of Confeder-ation. That instrument of government stressed the independence of the states as self-contained units of mercantilism and democratic republicanism, yet also established a central government for the purposes of war and, as in the case of Canada, future expansion. But specific postwar developments, such as the serious recession, the expansionist conflicts between the states, and the difficulties in dealing with other countries in economic affairs, combined to disillusion many Americans with their experiment in particularistic mercantil-ism.

Broadly speaking, the resulting movement toward a stronger central govern-ment grew out of internal and international economic difficulties analyzed and explained with the ideas of mercantilism. By 1785, for example, most of the states, including the agrarian ones, were switching from tariffs for revenue to tariffs for international retaliation and protection. Merchants demanded American navigation acts, artisans agitated for protection of their labor, and agricultural interests wanted help in balancing their political economy.[10] Various groups of Americans who concerned themselves directly with the problem of strengthening the central government—and there were many who were preoccupied with local and immediate difficulties or opportunities—offered several proposals for handling the problem. Centered in New England, the smallest group favored establishing an aristocratic society at home and rejoining the British Empire as a contractual junior partner. Such men were not willing to return to colonial status, but they did favor economic and social reintegration. Most Americans opposed that solution, favoring instead either the delegation of more power to the central government under the Articles of Confederation or the substitution of an entirely new instrument of government.

A letter from James Madison to Thomas Jefferson in the spring of 1786 not only indicates that the agrarian as well as the urban interests favored one or the other of those last two approaches, but dramatizes the fundamental mercantilism of the entire movement. "A continuance of the present anarchy of our commerce," Madison explained, "will be a continuance of the unfavorable balance on it, which by draining us of our metals . . . [will bring our ruin]. In fact, most of our political evils may be traced up to our commercial ones, and most of our moral may to our political."[11]

Against this background, the Constitution appears as an instrument of centralized national government framed in the classic manner by men thinking within the framework of mercantilism and blessed with the physical and human resources for a balanced economy. It provided the foundation for a national system of economics and politics and organized American strength for the struggle with other mercantile empires and for the conquest of less powerful peoples. The latter considerations were essential, for the Founding Fathers resolved the contradiction between the stress on expansion in mercantilism and the emphasis on a small state in existing democratic political theory by developing a theory of their own which held that democratic republicanism could be sustained by just such expansion. James Madison, often called the Father of the Constitution, provided the most striking formulation of this proposition, but Thomas Jefferson, John Adams, and other early leaders either shared or adopted it in one form or another within a reasonably short time.

Taking his cue from David Hume, the Englishman who attacked Montesquieu's argument that democracy was a system that could work only in small states, Madison asserted that a large state offered a much better foundation for republicanism.[12] Institutional checks and balances could help, and were therefore necessary, but they were not enough in and of themselves. "Extend the sphere," he argued, "and you take in a greater variety of parties and interests; you make it less probable that a majority of the whole will have a common motive to invade the rights of other citizens; or if such a common motive exists, it will be more difficult for all who feel it to discover their own strength, and to act in unison with each other. . . "[13]

While it is possible to conclude from Madison's remarks that he had in mind a static conception of such a large state, three considerations would appear to weaken that reading of his thesis. First, Madison used the verb "extend" in its active, unlimited sense. Second, he was stating a general theory, not making an argument in behalf of a given territorial settlement. And third, he advocated and vigorously supported the continued expansion of the United States. It seems more probable, therefore, that Madison was proposing, *as a guide to policy and action in his own time*, the same kind of an argument that Frederick Jackson Turner formulated a century later, when he advanced his frontier thesis which explained America's democracy and prosperity as the result of such expansion.

Madison's theory became the key to an American mercantilism. Merchants and manufacturers who wanted their own empire found it convincing and convenient. And Jefferson's thesis that democracy and prosperity depended upon a society of landholding freemen was a drastically simplified version of the same idea. Edward Everett of Massachusetts captured the essence of the interpretation in his judgment that expansion was the *"principle* of our institutions."[14] Additional support for this interpretation is offered by Madison's later prophecy (in 1828–29) that a major crisis would occur in about a century, when the continent was filled up and an industrial system had deprived most people of any truly productive property. In the event, Madison's fears proved true sooner than he anticipated. For in the crisis of the 1890's, when Americans *thought* that the frontier was gone, they advanced and accepted the argument that new expansion was the best—if not the only—way to sustain their freedom and prosperity.[15]

Madison's original statement of the expansionist thesis was important for two reasons. First, it provided the theoretical basis for an American mercantilism combining commercial and territorial expansion with political democracy. Second, by thus re-emphasizing the idea of empire, and proposing expansion as the key to national welfare, Madison opened the way for a discussion of the basic questions facing American mercantilism. Those issues concerned domestic economic affairs, the kind of expansion that was necessary and desirable, and the means to accomplish such gains while the nation was young and weak.

Washington's Farewell Address formulated a bipartisan answer to the problem of basic strategy. The solution was to build a commercial empire (which included markets for agricultural surpluses) by avoiding political involvement in the European system, meanwhile retaining complete freedom of action to secure and develop a continental empire in the Western Hemisphere. Washington's proposition was classically simple: play from the strength provided by America's basic economic wealth and geographic location in order to survive immediate weakness and emerge as the world power. "If we remain one people, under an efficient government," he promised, "the period is not far off when we may defy material injury from external annoyance . . . when we may choose peace or war, as our interest, guided by justice, shall counsel." Sharing that objective, and quite in agreement with the strategy, Thomas Jefferson summed it all up a bit later in one famous axiom: "entangling alliances with none." And with the enunciation of the Monroe Doctrine, freedom of action became the avowed and central bipartisan theme of American foreign policy.

As a condition of that persuasive agreement, however, several serious conflicts had to be resolved. Perhaps they can be discussed most clearly by defining and considering them within the framework of the gradual defeat and amalgamation of the pro-British and pro-French minorities by a growing consensus in favor of an American mercantilism. Such an approach has the additional value of making it possible to organize the analysis around familiar personalities as symbols of certain ideas, functional groups, and special interests. Let it be posited, therefore, that the following men are key figures in the evolution of an American mercantilism: Timothy Pickering, John Adams, and John Quincy Adams of Massachusetts; Alexander Hamilton of New York; and James Madison, Thomas Jefferson, and John Taylor of Virginia.

In many respects, at any rate, Pickering and Taylor represented the nether fringes of American mercantilism. Pickering trod the trail from reluctant revolutionary to threatening secessionist in the name of a domestic merchant aristocracy functioning as a quasi-independent contractual member of the

British Empire. His ideal was a central government charged with the responsibility (and armed with the power and authority) to establish and sustain a politically and socially stratified society and to provide the economic assistance (especially funded credit) that was necessary for the rationalized operations of overseas correspondents of British mercantilism and for domestic speculative ventures. Though Pickering and his supporters fit the traditional stereotype of mercantilists, they were in fact and function no more than the agents of British mercantilism. They were very successful agents, to be sure, but they did not view or define America in terms of its own mercantilism. Rather did they visualize it as a self-governing commonwealth of the British Empire. Hence it was only very late and with great reluctance, if at all, that they supported the measures necessary for a mercantilist state in America.

At the other extreme, John Taylor developed his program as a variation on a theme first stated by the French physiocrats. He emphasized the primacy of agriculture as narrowly as Pickering stressed the virtue and necessity of the merchant-trader-speculator. Taylor's tirades against funded debts and bank stock, and his soliloquies in praise of the noble farmer, seem alike in their total opposition to the principles of mercantilism. But in other respects his ideas were not so untainted by mercantilism as his rhetoric indicated. As with most other planters, for example, his theory of labor coincided at all essential points with the view held by British mercantilists.[16] So, too, did his conception of the role of western lands in the economy of the seaboard "mother country."

With respect to foreign trade, moreover, Taylor was trapped by the weakness of the physiocrats in that area of economics.[17] Ostensibly free traders, the physiocrats did not favor the navy essential to such a program. Taylor and other American imbibers of the physiocratic elixir awoke to discover that their vision did not correspond to reality. Taylor himself was not very adaptive, and ended his career in attacks on Jefferson and other agrarians who did develop an American mercantilism. But Taylor's position does dramatize the dilemma faced by the agrarian.[18] The contradiction between theory and actuality confronted them with a rather apparent choice: either they could content themselves with slow economic stagnation or they could build an American maritime system, accept dependence upon a foreign naval power, or support an American industry. In that choice lies a key aspect of the rise of a mature American mercantilism; for it developed most consciously and was ultimately practiced most rigorously by the southern agrarians who are often assumed to have been most rabidly antimercantilist. If nothing else, the weakness of their ideal program drove them into mercantilism.

It is particularly important to keep that fact in mind when considering Hamilton, about whom the discussion of American mercantilism has billowed for so long. Joseph Charles was essentially correct in his view that "the standard works on Hamilton evade the main issues which his career raises," and his judgment remains relevant despite the plethora of centennial essays and biographies.[19] The entire question of Hamilton's mercantilism has to be decided with reference to three points: the meaning and significance of the *Report on Manufactures*, his role in the Jay Treaty episode, and his plans to join in the further expansion of the British Empire in the Western Hemisphere. However difficult it may be to pin him down with an alternate characterization, Hamilton simply cannot be considered the fountainhead of American mercantilism unless those aspects of his career can be interpreted within the framework of mercantilist thought and action.

Since the *Report on Manufactures* is often accepted as proof, as well as evidence, of Hamilton's mercantilism, it is convenient to give first consideration to that document. In doing so, it seems wise to recall the chronology of his three state papers on economic affairs. Hamilton was commissioned as Secretary of the Treasury on September 11, 1789; and there followed the manifesto on public credit in January 1790, the report on a central bank in December 1790, and the paper on manufacturing in December 1791. Even the most cursory review of those dates catches the two-year delay between the reports on credit and manufacturers. That interval becomes even more striking when viewed in the context of other events.

It was Madison rather than Hamilton, for example, who gave more attention to protective duties on manufactures during the Constitutional Convention. That is still more illuminating since associations for the promotion of American manufactures had appeared in New York, Boston, Providence, and Baltimore as early as 1785; and resolutions for domestic goods had followed the next year from such additional and widely separated localities as Hartford, Germantown, Richmond, and Halifax (South Carolina). By 1789, furthermore, not only had the anti-Federalists picked up political support from such groups in New England, New York, and Pennsylvania, but the special session of Congress received numerous requests and petitions from various manufacturing societies.[20]

Having passed an emergency revenue bill in the form of tariff legislation, the Congress then *ordered* Hamilton, on January 15, 1790, to prepare a specific report on manufactures. That makes his delay even more noticeable, whatever allowances may be granted for his other duties and the thoroughness of his research. As late as October 1791, moreover, the administration saw no need to increase the tariff of 1789. In matters of chronology, urgency, and emphasis, therefore, it seems clear that Hamilton gave priority to funding the debt and establishing the bank. Those operations represented precisely the needs and objectives of the merchants who were semiautonomous correspondents of British mercantilism, and who were fundamentally opposed to a strong American industry. Their economic, political, and social position would be threatened by a vigorous program of industrialization; for at the very least they would have to make drastic changes in their outlook and actions. Since Hamilton's personal and political position was based on his rapport with that group, it seems relevant to consider whether Hamilton's mercantilism was as thoroughgoing as historians have assumed it was.

In Hamilton's behalf, it can be argued with considerable validity that domestic industry had to have a sound credit system as a cornerstone. But that approach only raises the question of why Hamilton did not present his funding and bank programs as the means to achieve an independent balanced economy. Since he did not, the most relevant explanation would seem to be that Hamilton was in fact a mercantilist who was hamstrung by his political dependence upon the Federalists around Pickering. His association with Tench Coxe would serve to strengthen that analysis.[21] The same argument could then be used to explain why Hamilton delayed his paper on manufactures for almost two years after the Congress had asked for it in January 1790.

The weakest point in that interpretation concerns Hamilton's response to Madison's resolution of January 3, 1794, that "the interests of the United States would be promoted by further restrictions and higher duties in certain cases on the manufactures and navigation of foreign nations employed in the commerce of the United States." Working through William Smith of South Carolina,

Hamilton killed Madison's entire program which was designed to promote commercial and industrial independence. Instead, Hamilton's committee in the House reported in favor of more borrowing and further domestic taxes. For that matter, neither Hamilton nor the Federalist party acted to increase protection after 1792.[22]

The explanation of Hamilton's action which does the most to sustain his reputation as an American mercantilist is not as generous to his standing as a reformed monarchist. For given the broad and vigorous agitation from manufacturing societies for greater protection, Madison's resolutions offered Hamilton a striking opportunity to widen the base of the Federalist party. That would have strengthened his hand against the pro-British group within the party and have enabled him to give substance to the *Report on Manufactures*. If it be said that Hamilton favored domestic excise taxes in preference to domestic manufacturing, then his mercantilism appears even more questionable. A stronger argument could be made by reference to Hamilton's known reservations about democracy, which would account for his refusal to court the manufacturers as a counterweight to the merchants around Pickering.

It may be, however, that Hamilton's vigorous opposition to Madison's resolutions of 1794 derived in considerable part from the fact that Madison's program was aimed at Great Britain. Not only was that true in the immediate, particular sense, but it also was the case in that Madison's proposals pointed toward general economic independence. That approach to the question of Hamilton's mercantilism has the virtue of having considerable relevance to his role in Jay's Treaty. An American mercantilist could explain and defend Hamilton's basic attitude and maneuvers behind Jay's back by one or both of two arguments. First, England had to be courted while the United States built a navy. Second, Hamilton stressed the political side of mercantilism.

Neither of those explanations is very convincing: Hamilton always favored the Army over the Navy, and political mercantilism is such a contradiction in terms that it begs the entire issue. That interpretation becomes even less convincing when asked to account for the fact that at the end of his career Hamilton turned not toward manufacturing but in the direction of becoming a partner in Britain's imperial adventures in Latin America. Indeed, Hamilton's foreign policy does less to settle the question of his mercantilism than to recall the report in 1793 that "the English considered Hamilton, [Rufus] King, and [William] Smith, of South Carolina, as main supports of British interest in America. Hamilton, not Hammond, was their effective minister."[23] Perhaps the most to be said of Hamilton's mercantilism is that it was latent and limited, for his actions belied his rhetoric.

As in many other contexts, it is Madison who emerges as the central figure in the development of an American mercantilism. While there are many illustrations, perhaps his resolutions of January 1794 provide the most illuminating evidence. Once again Charles points the way: "The program with which Madison began the first strategic moves against the Federalists was not one which could be called anti-Federalist, particularist, or States' rights."[24] His plan was to combine landed expansion to the west with support for domestic manufacturing and an independent American commercial policy. Considered at the practical political level, it represented a bid to the growing numbers of dissident Federalists who opposed a one-way relationship with Britain. Some of those men eyed a bull market for domestic manufactures. Others thought of an expansionist foreign policy with the established states cast in the role of "mother country." Madison saw such groups as allies for the anti-Federalists, as well as the building blocks of an American mercantilism.

Madison's conception of an American mercantilism was possibly too comprehensive as well as too premature politically to be adopted by Congress in 1794, though it was extensively debated before being sidetracked by Hamilton and Smith. But it did serve as a keen analysis and program for the growing consensus among anti-Federalists. That drive toward economic independence manifested itself in the Non-Intercourse Bill introduced in the summer of 1794, a move which was defeated only by the vote of Vice-President John Adams. Equally significant is the fact that it was backed by congressmen from Pennsylvania and Delaware as well as by those from southern states. Madison's mercantilism picked up new allies very rapidly, and two subsequent events served as catalysts in the process. Considered in the order of their importance, they were Jay's Treaty and the last stage in the defection of John Adams from High Federalism.

Following so closely upon the narrow defeat of the Non-Intercourse Bill, Jay's Treaty added injury to frustration. The great majority of Americans reacted bitterly and vigorously. Already weakened by deep fissures, the Federalist party cracked open under the ensuing attack. It cost them key leaders in such states as New Hampshire and Pennsylvania and alienated unknown numbers of voters south of the Potomac. As one who had cast the deciding vote against the Non-Intercourse Bill only with great reluctance, John Adams provided temporary leadership for such Federalist dissidents.

Adams strengthened his position even more by refusing to go quietly along to war with France at the bidding of the High Federalists. The differences between Hamilton and Adams were numerous, but perhaps none is so important to an appreciation of the maturing American mercantilism as the contrast between Hamilton's passion for a large army and Adams' emphasis on an American navy. Hamilton's military policy was that of the British nabob in North America, while that of Adams represented American mercantilism. Against that background, and in the context of his deciding vote on the Non-Intercourse Bill of 1794, it is possible to appreciate the full impact of Jay's Treaty on Adams. He made peace with France and forced Pickering out of the cabinet.

Little wonder, then, that Jefferson was willing to give way in favor of Adams. But thanks to Madison, who had been organizing a party as well as projecting a theory and a program, Jefferson became President. Once in power, Jefferson and his supporters were prodded by necessity and spurred by their own visions of empire toward the full development of an American mercantilism. There are several explanations for this phenomenon. Among the most important, one might list the following: the foreign-trade dilemma inherent in physiocratic theory (which was intensified by the wars stemming from the French Revolution); the creative leadership provided by such men as Madison and Albert Gallatin (who made his own *Report on Manufactures* in 1810); the political necessities and expediences of unifying and sustaining a national party; and the maturing thought of Jefferson himself. But wherever one chooses to place the emphasis, the fact remains that the Jeffersonians in action were far more mercantilistic than the Federalists had been—even in theory and rhetoric.

As early as 1791, for that matter, Jefferson began to shift away from the physiocratic dogma of free trade. And by 1793 he concluded his *Report on Commercial Policy* with a series of retaliatory proposals that were as mercantilistic as any he criticized. Perhaps even more significant was his early ambivalence toward manufacturing, which he never condemned outright once and for all. Jefferson disliked cities and the factory system for what he judged their negative impact on politics and morals, and for the conditions and style of life they imposed upon human beings, but he never discounted the importance of home manufacturing and commerce. He could not afford to, either as the leader of agrarians beginning to produce surpluses for sale, or as one who sought and accepted support from the increasing number of urban groups of all classes who preferred an empire of their own to rejoining the British system. Even if Jefferson had not caught the intellectual flaw in physiocratic trade theory, its practical consequences were something he could not avoid. In substance, therefore, the Jeffersonians based their strength and their policies on the mercantilistic program of a balanced economy at home and a foreign policy of expansion.

Their strategy was to exploit the policy of neutrality initiated by Washington and continued by John Adams. To do so, Jefferson ultimately resorted to the intensely mercantilistic policies of the embargo and non-importation against Britain and France. It was with obvious pride that he remarked, in 1809, that those policies "hastened the day when an equilibrium between the occupations of agriculture, manufactures, and commerce, shall simplify our foreign concerns to the exchange only of that surplus which we cannot consume [in return] for those articles of reasonable comfort or convenience which we cannot produce."[25] Not even Madison ever provided a more classic statement of American mercantilism.

Quite in line with Jefferson's recommendations of the 1790's, and his actions between 1800 and 1809, his successors acted vigorously against such weaker opponents as the Barbary Pirates who threatened American trade. On a more general level, Jefferson's argument that American democracy depended upon a surplus of land was but another, even more overtly formulated, version of Madison's theory that extending the sphere was the key to controlling factions. Hence he and his followers initiated and encouraged such expansion wherever they could, as in Florida and to the West; and it was precisely Jefferson's general expansionist outlook which overrode his concern that the Louisiana Purchase was unconstitutional.

The Louisiana Purchase opened the way to apply the tenets of American mercantilism to the entire hemisphere. It also encouraged an explicit American formulation of the expansionist philosophy of history that was implicit in mercantilism. Americans began to call openly and militantly for further expansion whenever and wherever they encountered domestic or foreign difficulties. Indians and Spaniards had to be pushed out of the way or destroyed. Interference with exports had to be stopped, by war if necessary. Canada offered the solution to other domestic economic problems, and should be taken forthwith.

After 1807, when economic troubles appeared at home, that expansionist outlook and program focused on Great Britain as the chief offender against the American Empire. Growing out of an alliance of business and agrarian interests which favored war to relieve immediate difficulties and forestall future crises, the War of 1812 was a classic mercantilist conflict for trade and colonies.[26] The Jeffersonians' earlier economic and maritime warfare, which almost secured the immediate objectives, and which had appeared capable of clearing the way for a general advance, was just as mercantilistic in nature. Though in many ways it failed to attain its avowed objectives, the War of 1812 was in no sense a strategic defeat for American mercantilism. If only in turning Americans to the west and the south, it focused the general spirit of expansion in a new and powerful manner. Perhaps even more significant, the stalemate strengthened the idea of an American System as opposed to the rest of the world. It was in the wake of the War of 1812, after all, that the vapors of Manifest Destiny gathered themselves for an explosion westward to the Pacific.

John Quincy Adams formulated his own concept of Manifest Destiny as early as 1796, when he assured President Washington that the American System would "infallibly triumph over the European system. . . ."[27] Fifteen years later he defined America as "a nation, coextensive with the North American Continent, destined by God and nature to be the most populous and most powerful people ever combined under one social compact."[28] He pushed overseas economic expansion just as vigorously. Even his harshest critics, the High Federalists of New England who wanted to re-enter the British Empire in some form or another, recognized his mercantilism. They called him one of the species of "amphibious politicians, who live on both land and water. . . ."[29]

Both before and after he served as Secretary of State under President James Monroe, Adams devoted his energies to building such an American Empire. His rational program for a dynamic balanced economy at home was too demanding for his countrymen. They grew ever more enamored of a philosophy that assured them that expansion was the way to ease their dilemmas and realize their dreams. Hence they paid little heed to his proposals for domestic development or to his warning that America should go "not abroad in search of monsters to destroy." But to the extent that Adams wanted an empire big enough to sustain such a balanced economy, and to the degree that he partook of the expansionist elixir, he won support and influence. And, indeed, his very presence in the cabinet of Monroe was a symbol of the maturity of American mercantilism. Having broken with the old pro-British party to vote for the Louisiana Purchase and the measures of economic warfare against Europe, Adams became the leader of those business interests which supported territorial as well as commercial expansion.

In timing, authorship, and content, the Monroe Doctrine was the classic statement of mature American mercantilism. Seizing the opportunity presented by the decay of the Spanish Empire, Monroe and Adams moved quickly, decisively, and independently to give substance to Henry Clay's fervent exhortation to "become real and true Americans and place ourselves at the head of the American System."[30] Adams caught the tone and meaning of the doctrine in his famous remark that it was time for America to stop bobbing along as a cock-boat in the wake of the British Empire. Acting in that spirit, he spurned Secretary George Canning's not-so-subtle suggestion that America join England in a joint guarantee of Latin American independence and a pledge against their own expansion in the region. Canning claimed high honors for having brought in the New World to redress the balance of the Old, but one would like to think that Adams enjoyed a hearty chuckle over such ability to put a rhetorical gloss on a policy defeat. For what Canning had done was to block the old empires only to be confronted by the challenge of a mature American mercantilism.

In the negative sense, the Monroe Doctrine was designed to check further European colonization in the Western Hemisphere. But Americans were quite aware of the positive implications of the strategy: it left the United States as the most powerful nation on the scene. America's ultimate territorial and commercial expansion in the New World would be limited only by its energies and its preferences—just as Washington had argued.[31] The negative side of the Monroe Doctrine is the least significant feature about it: the crucial point is that it was, in the minds of its authors, in its language, and in its reception by Americans, the manifesto of an American Empire.

The Monroe Doctrine was the capstone of a system destined to succumb to its own success. For in broad historical perspective, the classic function of mercantilism was to build a system strong enough to survive the application of the principles of Adam Smith. Without an American mercantilism there could have been no Age of Jacksonian Laissez Moi Faire. Perhaps, indeed, the greatest tribute to the leaders of American mercantilism lies in the fact that their handiwork withstood the trauma of a civil war and the sustained shock of unrestrained and irrational exploitation for some seventy years—until it became necessary in the Crisis of the 1890's to undertake the building of a new corporate system.

NOTES

1. Curtis P. Nettels, "British Mercantilism and the Economic Development of the Thirteen Colonies," *Journal of Economic History*, XII (Spring 1952), 105–114; William D. Grampp, "A Re-examination of Jeffersonian Economics," *Southern Economic Journal*, XII (Jan. 1946), 263–282; "On the Politics of the Classical Economists," *Quarterly Journal of Economics*, LXII (Nov. 1948), 714–747; and "The Liberal Elements in English Mercantilism," *ibid.*, LXVI (Nov. 1952), 465–501; Gunnar Myrdal, *The Political Element in the Development of Economic Theory* (London, 1953); Jacob Viner, "Power versus Plenty as Objectives of Foreign Policy in the Seventeenth and Eighteenth Centuries," *World Politics* I, (Oct. 1948), 1–29; Charles Wilson, " 'Mercantilism': Some Vicissitudes of an Idea," *Economic History Review*, 2nd Ser., X (Dec. 1957), 181–188. This essay owes an equal debt to the extensive publications of Merrill Jenson and to his generous and helpful interest in this approach to the era. His keen criticisms and perceptive suggestions were invaluable. It also benefited from the interest and intelligence of James Cooper, Lloyd Gardner, Kent Kreuter, Thomas J. McCormick, Walter La Feber, and Martin Sklar. This article is a foreshortened statement of the first section of a longer three-part essay dealing with the characterization and periodization of American history. Together with the other two portions, "The Age of Laissez Moi Faire, 1828–1896," and "The Age of Corporate Capitalism, 1896–1958," it will be published as *The Contours of American History* by the World Publishing Company.

2. Some readers may feel that the vigor of the subsequent presentation contradicts these caveats. Perhaps they will be reassured by remembering that any tool has to be sharp, though later it may be laid aside out of preference for another.

3. Albert Bushnell Hart, *The Foundations of American Foreign Policy* (New York, 1901), pp. 174–175. The best published study of the early empire outlook is Arthur B. Darling, *Our Rising Empire, 1763–1803* (New Haven, 1940).

4. Gerald Stourzh, *Benjamin Franklin and American Foreign Policy* (Chicago, 1954), p. 54.

5. On Washington see, among others, Charles H. Ambler, *George Washington and the West* (Chapel Hill, 1936), and Curtis P. Nettels, *George Washington and American Independence* (Boston, 1951). Also consult *Letters of Members of the Continental Congress*, ed. Edmund C. Burnett (Washington, 1921), III, 476; Malbone W. Graham, *American Diplomacy in the International Community* (Baltimore, 1948), pp. 9–24; and Max Savelle, "The Appearance of an American Attitude Toward External Affairs, 1770–1775," *American Historial Review*, LII (July 1947), 655–666.

6. *The Revolutionary Diplomatic Correspondence of the United States*, ed. Francis Wharton (Washington, 1889), II, 332.

7. Jedidiah Morse, *The American Geography; or A View of the Present Situation of the United States of America* (Elizabeth Town, 1789), pp. 468–469, quoted in Richard W. Van

Alstyne, "American Conceptions of Empire," a lecture delivered at the University of Chicago, May 5, 1953, copies available from the author.

8. See Léon Dion, "Natural Law and Manifest Destiny in the Era of the American Revolution," *Canadian Journal of Economics and Political Science,* XXIII (May 1957), 227-247, as a supplement to Albert K. Weinberg, *Manifest Destiny* (Baltimore, 1935).

9. Of the immense literature on mercantilism, the following items proved most stimulating: Max Beer, *Early British Economics from the Thirteenth Century to the Middle of the Eighteenth Century* (London, 1938); Philip W. Buck, *The Politics of Mercantilism* (New York, 1942); Edgar S. Furniss, *The Position of the Laborer in a System of Nationalism* (Boston, 1920); E. F. Heckscher, *Mercantilism,* rev. ed., ed. E. F. Soderlund (London, 1955), esp. Vol. II; E. A. J. Johnson, *American Economic Thought in the Seventeenth Century* (London, 1932), and *Predecessors of Adam Smith* (New York, 1937); Ephraim Lipson, *The Economic History of England* (London, 1948-49); Gustav F. von Schmoller, *The Mercantile System and Its Historical Significance* (New York, 1931); and the items cited in note 1.

10. Here see Oliver M. Dickerson, *The Navigation Acts and the American Revolution* (Philadelphia, 1951), on the attitude of the colonists toward the Navigation Acts per se. Then consult Oscar and Mary F. Handlin, *Commonwealth. A Study of the Role of Government in the American Economy: Massachusetts, 1774-1861* (New York, 1947); Louis Hartz, *Economy Policy and Democratic Thought: Pennsylvania, 1776-1860* (Cambridge, Mass., 1948); and Merrill Jensen, *The New Nation. A History of the United States During the Confederation, 1781-1789* (New York, 1950), on the development of an American mercantilism at the state level.

11. Madison to Jefferson, Mar. 18, 1786, *Letters and Other Writings of James Madison. Published by order of Congress* (New York, 1884), I, 226-227.

12. Robert L. Ketchum, "Notes on James Madison's Sources for the Tenth Federalist Paper," *Midwest Journal of Political Science,* I (May 1957), 20-25; Douglass Adair, " 'That Politics May Be Reduced to a Science': David Hume, James Madison, and the Tenth *Federalist,*" Huntington Library Quarterly, XX (Aug. 1957), 343-360.

13. Madison, Federalist No. 10, *The Federalist,* ed. Henry Cabot Lodge (New York, 1900), pp. 58-60.

14. Edward Everett, *Orations and Speeches on Various Occasions* (Boston, 1850-68), I, 210.

15. Here see Charles S. Campbell, Jr., "American Business Interests and the Open Door in China," *Far Eastern Quarterly,* I (Nov. 1941), 43-58; Nancy L. O'Connor, "The Foreign Policy of the Farmers' Movements, 1890-1900," unpubl. masters thesis, University of Oregon, 1957; William A. Williams, "The Frontier Thesis and American Foreign Policy," *Pacific Historical Review,* XXIV (Nov. 1955), 379-395, and "The Large Corporation and the Political Economy of American Foreign Policy: 1890-1958," paper read at the State University of Iowa Conference on Social Sciences, May 1958.

16. Though independently worked out, this analysis is supported by Charles R. Haygood, "Mercantilism and Colonial Slave Labor, 1700-1763," *Journal of Southern History,* XXIII (Nov. 1957), 454-464.

17. Arthur I. Bloomfield, "The Foreign-Trade Doctrines of the Physiocrats," *American Economic Review,* XXVIII (Dec. 1938), 716-735.

18. William D. Grampp, "John Taylor: Economist of Southern Agrarians," *Southern Economic Journal,* XI (Jan. 1945), 255-268, esp. pp. 258, 263, on Taylor's developing opposition to Jefferson.

19. Joseph Charles, *The Origins of the American Party System* (Williamsburg, 1956), pp. 11-12. Also see John C. Livingston, "Alexander Hamilton and the American Tradition," *Midwest Journal of Political Science,* (Nov. 1957), 209-224; Arnold A. Rogow, "Edmund Burke and the American Liberal Tradition," *Antioch Review,* XVII (June 1957), 255-265; James O. Wettereau, "Letters from Two Business Men to Alexander Hamilton on Federal Fiscal Policy, November, 1789," *Journal of Economic and Business History,* III (Aug. 1931), 667-686; Samuel Rezneck, "The Rise and Early Development of Industrial Consciousness in the United States, 1760-1830," *ibid.,* IV (Aug. 1932), 784-811. This approach to Hamilton had been worked out in all essentials prior to the publication of the most recent biographies, and for that reason it was deemed wise to present it in the form in which it was originally cast.

20. This section draws heavily on Charles, *Origins of the American Party System,* and on Vols. I and II of Irving Brant, *James Madison* (Indianapolis and New York, 1941—in

progress). A more detailed account of these early episodes can be found in Vol. I of Edward Stanwood, *American Tariff Controversies in the Nineteenth Century* (Boston, 1903).

21. Here see Rezneck, "The Rise and Early Development of Industrial Consciousness in the United States, 1760-1820"; and Joseph Dorfman, *The Economic Mind in American Civilization, 1606-1865* (New York, 1946), I, 253-256, 290-293.

22. Stanwood, *American Tariff Controversies*, I, 108-110, 120-121; and for considerable insight into the role of Smith of South Carolina, consult Joseph Ernst, "Growth of the South Carolina Commons House of Assembly, 1761-1775," unpubl. masters thesis, University of Wisconsin, 1958.

23. Eugene P. Link, *Democratic-Republican Societies, 1790-1800* (New York, 1941), n. 16, p. 49.

24. Charles, *Origins of the American Party System*, p. 97.

25. Quoted in Grampp, "A Re-examination of Jeffersonian Economics," p. 279.

26. On eastern urban votes for war see Warren H. Goodman, "The Origins of the War of 1812: A Survey of Changing Interpretations," reprinted in *The Shaping of American Diplomacy*, ed. William A. Williams (Chicago, 1956), p. 122.

27. Quoted in Samuel F. Bemis, *John Quincy Adams and the Foundations of American Foreign Policy* (New York, 1949), p. 64.

28. *Ibid.*, p. 180.

29. *Ibid.*, p. 148.

30. *Ibid.*, p. 352; but cf. pp. 364, 127.

31. The traditional neglect of commercial interests and pressures in connection with the formulation and enunciation of the Monroe Doctrine, an approach symbolized in Dexter Perkins, *Monroe Doctrine, 1823-1826* (Baltimore, 1929), is somewhat corrected by Charles L. Chandler, "United States Commerce with Latin America at the Promulgation of the Monroe Doctrine," *Quarterly Journal of Economics*, XXXVIII (May 1924), 466-486. Even more illuminating are Dorothy B. Goebel, "British-American Rivalry in the Chilean Trade, 1817-1820," *Journal of Economic History*, II (Nov. 1942), 190-202; Charles C. Griffin, *The United States and the Disruption of the Spanish Empire, 1810-1822* (New York, 1937); and Arthur Preston Whitaker, *The United States and the Independence of Latin America, 1800-1830* (Baltimore, 1941).

the versatiles

DANIEL J. BOORSTIN

Daniel J. Boorstin is frequently regarded as the dean of the "consensus school" of mainstream historiography. This brief selection from the second volume of his prize-winning analysis of *The Americans* may indicate the reason for the position he holds. It is a rhapsody to the genius of American business and to the new American working class. But Boorstin is not at all sure that the United States really had a working class in the European sense. The first part of his essay portrays the idyllic beauty of American factories. It is, however, never made clear whether the workers gazed upon the same pastoral magnificence and the azure blue of the "Italian sky" that Boorstin describes.

The second part of his essay is a model of the myth of rapid social mobility in America, the classless society. There is nothing about class antagonisms, economic restrictions against universal suffrage, or the rising nativism prevalent even in the eighteenth century. Finally, Boorstin celebrates the "American Standard of Living" which, he recognizes, promoted useless consumption and waste. The factory system, he writes, resulted in the emergence of the unskilled or "the undifferentiated man." But there is no mention of the alienation and dehumanization of this human commodity, a by-product of mass technology and "the American system" which Boorstin idealizes.

ORGANIZING THE AMERICAN FACTORY

By the middle of the 19th century Europeans began to notice an "American System of Manufacturing" quite different from their own. They should have called it more precisely a "New England System," for there was hardly an important manufacturing innovation in the shaping years before the Civil War that did not have its decisive trial in our Northeast.

This New England System was versatility made into a way of production. It grew not from a specialized skill at making particular things—guns or clocks or textiles or boots—but from know-how that could make anything. It was the offspring of ingenuity and lack of skill, of scarce labor and vast markets, of abundant water power and meager raw materials, of private ambition and large-scale cooperation, of commercial enterprise, corporate capital, government subsidy, and happy accident. For the first time it offered a way of planting New England's seafaring agility firmly on the land.

Transforming production by new ways of bringing together some processes and of separating others, the new factory arrangements had a revolutionary simplicity, a simplicity hidden from the custom-blinded Old World. The new

From "The Versatiles," Chapters 4 and 5, *The Americans: The National Experience*, by Daniel J. Boorstin. (New York: Vintage Books, 1967), 20–34. Copyright © 1965 by Daniel J. Boorstin. Reprinted by permission of Random House, Inc.

combining meant simply bringing together the different processes for making a commodity under a single management and under a single roof. This was, properly speaking, the new American factory organization, which is the subject of this [section]. The second feature, a new way of separating the parts of the operation, is the subject of the next [following section].

The system, which later was to have the look of grand invention and bold discovery, began in the casual experiments of men unencumbered by century-accumulated skills and intricate social regulations. If the American Factory System was a triumph of organization and of cooperation, it was also a triumph of naiveté, for its essence was a loosening of habits and of ways of thinking. Ignorance and "backwardness" had kept Americans out of the old grooves. Important innovations were made simply because Americans did not know any better.

Nearly every feature of the American system of manufacturing, from the elements of the new textile machinery to the concept of interchangeable parts, had actually been conceived earlier by Europeans. But while a few Europeans could see the possibilities, their communities kept them powerless to give their ideas a fair trial. Too many had a stake in the older ways. Industrial progress in Europe required extraordinary courage to break the prevailing pattern; in America it required a willingness to try the obvious. American genius was less for invention or discovery than for experiment.

It was no accident that the headquarters of American seafaring adventure became the headquarters of adventure in manufacturing. Both trafficked in the raw materials of remote places; both sold to the world market. The willingness to change from one commodity to another, to invest grandly and then shift investments, to experiment with novel and outlandish products, to try new ports and test new routes—this would also be required of the new manufacturer.

The commerce of the sea had accumulated capital. And successful seafaring merchants had learned to keep a considerable proportion of their capital fluid because New England habits, climate, and landscape had discouraged the amassing of impressive manorial landed estates, or the building of luxurious mansions for descendants. Whoever heard of a New England Mount Vernon, Monticello, Montpelier, or Ashlawn? With the wealth which the Rhode Island Browns and the Massachusetts Tracys, Lees, Cabots, Higginsons, Jacksons, and Lowells had gathered from the sea, they built factories. Nathan Appleton, for example, who made his start as a seafaring merchant and later became a founder of American textile manufacturing, used to keep at least one third of his capital free for new projects and unforeseen opportunities. To this, among other practices, he attributed the success of his factory enterprises while others were failing.

Mastery of the sea, when the sea was highway to the world, meant mastery of sources of raw materials. New England's ability to bring large quantities of cotton from the South or from Egypt, of hides from Argentina or from the Pacific Northwest, enabled her to supply factories making textiles or shoes or almost anything else. And the sea led to all the customers in the world. Lowell's miles of coarse cloth and Lynn's thousands of pairs of cheap shoes would have glutted a local market, but they went profitably thousands of miles overseas to the unclad and unshod in Africa, Asia, and Latin America.

New England also possessed indirect incentives. Her lack of a rich staple crop or of abundant minerals prevented her becoming fixed in traditional ways of profiting from one or two familiar commodities. And New England businessmen handled impartially the cotton of Georgia or of Egypt or of India, the hides of South America, or the iron of England.

Even her political misfortunes pushed New England to experiment with new forms of factory organization. Jefferson's Embargo (1807–09) and the War of 1812 destroyed much of her foreign commerce and forced her to find new investments at home. It was the cities outside New England—Albany, New York, Philadelphia, Baltimore, and others—that lay near river pathways of trade with the western backcountry. Long settled areas of New York State were a barrier between Boston and the growing market on the other side. The principal New England rivers—the Connecticut, Merrimack, Kennebec, and Penobscot— ran northward. In all these ways she was badly located for shifting from foreign to domestic commerce. In New England, then, labor and capital which could no longer go to sea were tempted to other employments at home before making the great leap to the West.

The "backwardness" of the American economy and technology actually made introduction of new factory ways easier. In the highly developed economy of England, for example, the several stages of production had long been sharply defined: each had become an occupation conducted in a different place with its own business customs and plant practices. In the English production of cotton textiles, the spinner, the weaver, the dyer, and the printer each had his separate traditions and thought of himself as engaged in a distinctly separate process. There was a different market for goods at each stage. An elaborate system of exchange governed specialized traders in yarn, woven goods, and dyestuffs. As a result many groups had vested interests in not centralizing or simplifying production. The American contrast was striking. During the colonial period, when there were already extensive manufacturing establishments in England, most crafts in America were still carried on as small family undertakings. Even at the end of the colonial period, a considerable proportion of the manufactures of the northern colonies still came from village craftsmen. Their distance from the city and from fellow craftsmen also kept them free from guilds. Americans were still without large patterns of organization.

In textiles, where the first large-scale factory of the new American type would appear, Americans had stuck with the old system of home industry. During the colonial period, the rural New England family usually spun its own yarn and made its own cloth. The only textile process commonly carried on outside the home was that of "fulling," or finishing woolen cloth, which was done by the village fuller. Most people were clothed in leather, wool, or linen; cotton cloth was still relatively expensive. American colonials who did not weave for themselves purchased woolens made in England or cottons made in Manchester or the Far East.

Before the invention of the steam engine, the principal source of power for English factories had, of course, been water. Where sources of water power had been used for centuries, the coveted rights to every millsite on a stream had long been established, pre-empted, and sub-divided. Any large source had been broken down and distributed among numerous small customary users. In England, therefore, a supply of water power in one place sufficient to run the combined processes of manufacturing was virtually unobtainable in the early 19th century. The custom-bound fragmentation of power had preserved the custom-bound fragmentation of occupations. Early development of steam power at first even reinforced these tendencies. In England the invention of the steam engine and its widespread use for manufacturing before the 1820's made possible any number of small, mobile sources of power. This made it easier than ever to run a small establishment which performed only a single process in making a product.

In "underdeveloped" New England in the early 19th century, all this was different. Before the age of railroads, coal was prohibitively expensive. The steam engine was only slowly adopted for manufacturing and did not generally replace water power until the Civil War. For there were still many streams never before used for water power; their uses had not yet been legally fragmented. A firm building a factory in New England, therefore, could still purchase and control a single large source. For example, when businessmen who had established the pioneer cotton-textile factory at Waltham decided to erect another, they first "set about discovering a suitable water power." They looked for what it would have been folly to seek in England—a large new source that had never been exploited before. "Why don't they buy up the Pawtucket Canal?" Nathan Appleton, one of these businessmen, recalled a friend suggesting. "That would give them the whole power of the Merrimack, with a fall of over thirty feet." This is precisely what they did. "We perambulated the grounds, and scanned the capabilities of the place," Appleton recalled of his visit in November 1821 to the site (then occupied by less than a dozen houses, but soon to become the flourishing city of Lowell), "and the remark was made that some of us might live to see the place contain twenty thousand inhabitants."

New Englanders, then, were understandably tempted to centralize their operations in large units and to bring the several processes under a single roof. At Waltham, Massachusetts, in 1814 there appeared a factory in which all the processes of manufacturing a complex commodity were carried on by the use of power in a single establishment. Here was born the modern factory organization, which would be momentous for the whole human community within a century. It was to stir crucial changes in the relationships between capital and labor, in the nature of cities and countryside, in the position of women and of the family. Directly or indirectly, it would explain many of the distinctions between life in the mid-20th and that in the mid-18th century.

Nothing exotic or unfamiliar was produced at Waltham—simply cotton cloth. Nor were any of the processes there entirely novel. Except for a few improvements by Francis Cabot Lowell in the power loom, jobs now done inside this one large factory were precisely the same ones which before had been dispersed among separate smaller establishments. The essential novelty, as one of the factory's founders explained in his own history of the enterprise, was not the processes applied but rather their organization—"an entirely new arrangement, in order to save labor, in passing from one process to another." The processes had merely been collected and organized so that raw cotton went in one end of the factory and finished cotton cloth came out the other.

The story of this "Boston Manufacturing Company" of Waltham would be frequently repeated in the next few decades in New England. Its moving spirit was Francis Cabot Lowell, who had made his money in the importing and exporting business. A trip to England's Lancashire textile mills had awakened his imagination to the possibilities of similar manufacturing in New England, and the interruption of his seafaring enterprises by the War of 1812 gave him the leisure and the incentive to develop an American counterpart. He had the lucky assistance of Paul Moody, a self-taught inventor who later established the pioneer American factory for the making of textile machinery. Lowell's principal collaborators were his brother-in-law Patrick Tracy Jackson (grandson of a penniless Irish immigrant and son of a prosperous Boston member of the Continental Congress), who had never been to college, but who rose from supercargo on a West Indian merchantman at the age of twenty, to amass a fortune from shipping to both the Indies; and Nathan Appleton (who had been prepared for Dartmouth College but instead went into business at the age of fifteen), a talented organizer. These men were an allegory of New England enterprise.

From the world perspective what was most remarkable about the Waltham factory was less that it was actually operating by 1814 than that so obvious an innovation, a mere combination of old processes, had not occurred to somebody somewhere long before. The world's most advanced form of industrial organization now suddenly appeared in the backwaters of the New World.

European travelers were astonished by the sites of the new American factories. They were accustomed to find factories, like those in England, mired in the stench and congestion of a festering city. The New England factory sprouted on an unspoiled rural landscape. In the 1830's the visiting French economist Michel Chevalier was amazed that the great American factories were "new and fresh like an opera scene." The contrast between these and the factories of her native England struck Harriet Martineau in 1837. True enough, she said, the tourist in America would be irritated to see awesome natural scenery defaced by modern factories. But one should not forget what this meant for American workers.

. . . to have their dwellings and their occupation fixed in spots where the hills are heaped together, and the waters leap and whirl among rocks, rather than in dull suburbs where they and their employments may not annoy the eye of the lover of the picturesque. It always gave me pleasure to see the artisans at work about such places as Glen's Falls, the Falls of the Genessee, and on the banks of some of the whirling streams in the New England valleys. I felt that they caught, or might catch, as beautiful glimpses of Nature's face as the western settler. . . . It is deplorable enough, in this view, to be a poor artisan in the heart of our English Manchester: but to be a thriving one in the most beautiful outskirts of Sheffield is, perhaps, as favourable a lot for the lover of nature as to be a labourer on any soil: and the privileges of the American artisans are like this.

Twenty years later the English traveler, Charles Weld, could still admire the happy by-product of the American backwardness in displacing water power by steam: the common prospect of "a smokeless factory town canopied by an Italian sky." American anachronism—the factory in the wilderness—helped explain not only the peculiarities of the American factory but the many other American opportunities for naive innovations in the custom-bound industrial world.

FROM SKILL TO KNOW-HOW: "A CIRCULATING CURRENT"

The men who made the new factory at Waltham—Francis Cabot Lowell, Nathan Appleton, and Patrick Tracy Jackson—had never before been in a textile venture, nor in any other manufacturing project. It was less their technical knowledge than their boldness, energy, enterprise, versatility, and, above all, their organizing ability that made their epochal innovations possible. In fact, their lack of strong craft traditions actually helps explain why new-style factories first appeared in New England.

During the colonial period, the center of American craftsmanship had been Philadelphia. There one found the best tailors, the best hatmakers, the best shoemakers, the best finished-metal workers, and the best cabinet makers. It was around Philadelphia that the largest number of 18th-century immigrant artisans, especially those from Germany and central Europe, had settled. The two most distinctively "American" craft products—the Pennsylvania rifle (later called the "Kentucky rifle") and the Conestoga wagon (named after Conestoga Township, in Lancaster County; later called the "covered wagon")—were actually the work of Swiss and German craftsmen who had only recently settled in Pennsylvania. In the Philadelphia area were concentrated the skilled textile-craftsmen, the spinners and weavers who turned out fine goods, elegant plaids, and hand-woven fancy designs in small shops.

These traditions of fine craftsmanship seem to have been more a hindrance than an encouragement to innovation. Just as the European industrial revolution did not come first to France, with its great artisan traditions in luxury products, but to England; so the revolutionary American factory first came not to Philadelphia but to New England.

The "American System of Manufacturing" from its very beginning was no triumph of American inventive genius. Almost all the basic inventions that mechanized textile manufacturing came from England. And they had reached America slowly. Take, for example, the machinery for spinning raw cotton into cotton thread. Fully twenty years passed after Richard Arkwright began operating his first cotton-spinning machinery in England before Americans succeeded in copying it—and that was actually a feat of smuggling!

The evidence of American technical backwardness would be less impressive had there not been such strenuous efforts here to devise machinery similar to that used in England. State lotteries had actually been organized to collect prize money for the first inventor; the Massachusetts legislature even offered a subsidy. Despite many such incentives, American efforts failed repeatedly.

Unable to invent their own, Americans made desperate efforts to import or copy samples of English machines. But English laws forbade the export of manufacturing machinery, including models or drawings of them; even the emigration of any skilled workman who might reproduce such machinery abroad was prohibited. And New Englanders seemed to have lost that skill at smuggling which had helped build their economy in colonial days. Tench Coxe, a public-spirited Philadelphian, persuaded some London workmen to make him a set of brass models of Arkwright's patent machinery, but when the models were all crated and ready to leave England, British customs officers discovered them on the dock.

The crucial feat was finally accomplished by an adventurous young Englishman, Samuel Slater, who, at the age of fourteen, had been luckily apprenticed to Jedediah Strutt, partner of Richard Arkwright. Attracted here by American newspaper advertisements for improved cotton machinery, he was only twenty-one when he arrived in New York in 1789. Because of his knowledge of the Arkwright machinery his departure was forbidden by English law, but he left secretly, without even telling his mother. Not daring to take along plans or models, he had committed all the necessary information to his phenomenal memory. Dissatisfied with the unenterprising business methods and the meager sources of waterpower he found in New York, he accepted an invitation from

Moses Brown, the Providence merchant-philanthropist after whom Brown University was named, to set up a cotton mill in Rhode Island. Brown and his son-in-law William Almy saw the opening Slater's skill gave them. They put up the initial capital and gave Slater a half interest in the business. Slater built, entirely from memory, a cotton-spinning frame of twenty-four spindles, which he put into operation. The firm of Brown & Almy prospered from the beginning.

In England itself employers could draw on the large pool of able-bodied paupers and unemployed. From crowded poorhouses they took workers who could not afford to be choosy about their employment. But in New England there were few poorhouses; laborers had more alternatives; land was plentiful, people scarce. As early as 1791, Alexander Hamilton had noted this as an obstacle to American manufacturing. Forty years later, some European travelers like the Frenchman Chevalier still expressed their surprise that American laborers were not forcing down wages by competing against one another for the chance to work. In America, therefore, manufacturing could secure a labor force only by attracting hands from other work or by drawing new workers into the labor market.

Such advocates of manufacturing as Alexander Hamilton had long been concerned lest the new factories disrupt American farm life by attracting away its essential labor. Hamilton himself noted that women and children were the only workers who could be spared from American farms. Brown & Almy's pioneer cotton-spinning factory at Providence, as Moses Brown himself boasted, did not at first take able-bodied men from other work. On the contrary, by drawing on a new source, it produced "near a total saving of labor to the country." The factory's first labor force consisted of seven boys and two girls, all between seven and twelve years of age. Not for long, however, could enough women and children be found to operate even this first cotton-spinning factory at Providence. Slater turned to the familiar English pattern. He attracted whole families to live in tenements or in company houses; under this "family" system every member of a family over seven years of age was employed in the factory. Such arrangements came to prevail in Rhode Island, Connecticut, and southern Massachusetts, where one began to see a factory working-class similar to that whose condition in England in 1844 Friedrich Engels painted so luridly.

In a few places appeared a more peculiarly American way of recruiting a factory work force, a way that fired the American imagination and shaped American notions of social class: perhaps America could have factories without a "factory class." Such a possibility, pure fantasy in England, seemed real enough in America because of the many alternative opportunities for employment, the well-being of the American populace, the cheapness of farming land, and the relative newness and lack of squalor of American cities.

When Francis Cabot Lowell visited England in 1810–12, he admired the Lancashire textile machinery but was horrified by the condition of the new factory class. He and his partners were determined that New England should not pay this price for industrial progress. Nathan Appleton recalled:

The operatives in the manufacturing cities of Europe, were notoriously of the lowest character, for intelligence and morals. The question therefore arose, and was deeply considered, whether this degradation was the result of the peculiar occupation, or of other and distinct causes. We could not perceive why this peculiar description of labor should vary in its effects upon character from all other occupation.

There was little demand for female labor, as household manufacture was superseded by the improvements in machinery. Here was in New England a fund of labor, well educated and virtuous. It was not perceived how a profitable employment has any tendency to deteriorate the character. The most efficient guards were adopted in establishing boarding houses, at the cost of the Company, under the charge of respectable women, with every provision for religious worship. Under these circumstances, the daughters of respectable farmers were readily induced to come into these mills for a temporary period.

This was the "Waltham" or "Lowell" system, sometimes called the Boarding-House System. It had originated in the belief that there would not, and should not, be a permanent factory class in New England. The Waltham and Lowell communities became show places to support the New England businessman's boast that his new system had "rendered our manufacturing population the wonder of the world." When Harriet Martineau, herself the daughter of a Norwich manufacturer, visited them in 1835, she feared that any accurate description would tempt most of England's workers to the New World. Charles Dickens, not known for his sympathy to anything American, toured New England in 1842 and could not restrain his enthusiasm, describing the contrast with the English mill towns as "between the Good and Evil, the living light and deepest shadow."

Happy communities of well-dressed young ladies, living in spacious houses with piazzas and green venetian blinds, spending their spare time in churches, libraries, and lecture halls, were by no means representative of the new industrial life. Not even in America. New England, of course, had its share of callous factory-owners who considered their workpeople part of the machinery, but the hope of establishing factories without a permanent factory class was widespread and vivid.

As late as 1856, Francis Cabot Lowell's nephew, John Amory Lowell, boasted that American factory life was something new under the sun. The factory girl, he said, was not pursuing a lifetime vocation. She was simply spending a few years in a mill to help earn her dower or to provide for the professional education of a brother. "The business could thus be conducted without any permanent manufacturing population. The operatives no longer form a separate caste, pursuing a sedentary employment, from parent to child, in the heated rooms of a factory; but recruited in a circulating current from the healthy and virtuous population of the country." The ideal of a "circulating current" rather than a static class—of men on the move rather than in the groove—grew naturally. It flourished in this world of the undifferentiated man, where the unexpected was usual. The Old World vision of the industrious poor had dissolved. Even more characteristic than the ideal of equality, the vagueness of social classes became an ideal in America.

In the early 19th century, labor was generally better paid in America than in England. But the unskilled laborers profited most from their American situation: in the 1820's, for example, they commanded a wage a third or a half higher here than in England, while the highly skilled were only slightly better off than in England, if at all. Thus the wage premium on artisan skills was much less in America than in England in the decades before the Civil War. The general labor shortage seems, as usual, to have operated most in favor of the least skilled, as did other factors: abundant land, wide geographic and social mobility, general literacy, and the lack of organized guilds. All these factors tended to reduce the social and monetary premium on the acquisition of artisan skills. Why train yourself for a task you hoped and expected soon to leave?

American working men and women, already known the world over for literacy and intelligence, were not noted for specialized skills.

The purpose of the Interchangeable System, Eli Whitney himself explained, was "to substitute correct and effective operations of machinery for that skill of the artist which is acquired only by long practice and experience; a species of skill which is not possessed in this country to any considerable extent." The unheralded Know-how Revolution produced a new way, not only of making things, but of making the machines that make things. It was a simple but far-reaching change, not feasible in a Europe rich in traditions, institutions, and vested skills.

What happened in America in manufacturing was comparable to what had happened here in other fields. The scarcity of legal learning did not lead to a scarcity of laws or lawyers (we soon became the most lawyered and most legislated country in the world), but instead to a new kind of legal profession and a new concept of law; the scarcity of specialized medical learning soon led to a new kind of doctor and a new concept of medicine; and a scarcity of theological learning led to a new kind of minister and a new concept of religion. Similarly, the scarcity of craft skills set the stage for a new nearly craftless way of making things. And this prepared a new concept of material plenitude and of the use and expendability of things which would be called the American Standard of Living.

The Know-how Revolution brought an unexpected new power to make everything, and for nearly everybody! Oddly enough, the finer and more complex the machine to be manufactured, the more effective and more economical would be the new method. With a momentum of its own, this new American way of making things led people to want more and more things, in kinds and quantities never known before.

For all this New England was the center. The system would first be called the "Uniformity System" or the "Whitney System," for the key man was Eli Whitney. Though Europeans called it the "American System," it had not been invented in America nor by Whitney. Jefferson had seen it in France over a decade before, but there, when difficulties were encountered, Frenchmen preferred time-honored skills to uncertain experiments. In England too, Jeremy Bentham, his brother Samuel, and the ingenious Marc Isambard Brunel had contrived a way of mass-producing wooden pulley blocks for the navy in an effort to employ the idle hands of prisoners and dockyard workers. But in England, too, little changed for decades.

The Uniformity System was simplicity itself, yet to imagine it one again had to leave time-honored ruts. The American factory organization described in the [first section] had merely drawn together separate manufacturing processes under a single roof. Whitney's Uniformity System was more novel: it transformed the role of the worker and changed the very meaning of skill. In Europe the making of a complex machine, such as a gun or a clock, had remained wholly in the hands of a single highly skilled craftsman. The gunsmith or clockmaker himself fashioned and put together all the parts of each gun or clock. By immemorial practice, each gun or clock was a distinctive hand-crafted object, bearing the hallmark of its maker. When it needed repair it was returned to its maker or to another gunsmith or clockmaker who shaped and fitted the required piece. Nothing was more obvious than that the production of guns or clocks depended directly on the numbers of qualified gunsmiths or clockmakers.

The new Uniformity System broke down the manufacture of a gun or of any other complicated machine into the separate manufacture of each of its component pieces. Each piece could then be made independently and in large quantities, by workers who lacked the skill to make a whole machine. The numerous copies of each part would be so nearly alike that any one would serve in any machine. If one piece broke, another of its type could be substituted without shaping or fitting.

How Whitney himself came upon so simple and so revolutionary a notion, the greatest skill-saving innovation in human history, we do not know. Perhaps he had first happened on it in his search for a way of mass-producing his cotton gin. The first successful application of the idea on a large scale was in the making of muskets. The occasion was the new nation's need for firearms in the turbulent era of Europe's Napoleonic Wars. In 1798 France, under a revolutionary dictatorship, threatened war against an unprepared United States. Most of the muskets with which Americans had won their Revolution fifteen years before had been made in France or elsewhere in Europe. Since military firearms had not been manufactured in quantity in this country, the nation was, in effect, unarmed. A tightened Naturalization Act and the infamous Alien and Sedition Acts were symptoms of its hysterical insecurity.

In March of 1798, President John Adams warned that diplomacy had failed. Soon thereafter, on May 1, Eli Whitney of Connecticut wrote the Secretary of the Treasury offering his machinery, water power, and workmen (originally collected for manufacturing cotton gins) for the manufacture of muskets. Whitney signed a contract for ten thousand muskets, a fantastic number in those days, to be delivered within twenty-eight months. He was to be paid $134,000, which would have made the average cost per musket only a few dollars above that paid for imports. This was probably the first contract for mass production in the American manner.

It is significant that Whitney was inexperienced in making guns. He had probably never carefully examined the particular Charleville musket he contracted to reproduce. Had he been a skilled gunsmith, had he loved the feel and look of a beautifully crafted and ornamented piece, he might never have dared violate traditional craft standards by agreeing to mass-produce muskets by the thousands. What Whitney had to offer, he well knew, was not skill but know-how: a general organizing competence to make anything.

Whitney used up his time in perfecting his new production method. Fully twenty-eight months, the contract term for delivery of the whole ten thousand, expired without his delivering even one musket. All the while Whitney was building and equipping his new musket factory at Mill Rock outside New Haven. In January, 1801, desperate for cash and in need of moral support against influential people who were writing him off as a charlatan, he went to Washington and there gave a dramatic demonstration that proved to President John Adams, Vice-President Jefferson, and members of the cabinet that his "interchangeable system" really worked. He spread out before them the musket and a supply of its parts. Then he asked them to select any example of each part at random from its pile and to try with their own hands whether any one would fit with any other into a complete working musket lock. The proof was overwhelming. "He had invented moulds and machines for making all the pieces of his lock so exactly equal," Jefferson reported, "that take 100 locks to pieces and mingle their parts and the hundred locks may be put together as well by taking the first pieces which come to hand. . . . good locks may be put together without employing a Smith."

Now Whitney asked for another six months' grace for delivery of the first 500 muskets of his original contract and for two years beyond that to deliver the remainder. He secured everything he asked for, including another $10,000 advance, an agreement by the government to advance an additional $5000 in three months, and a further $5000 upon delivery of each 500 muskets. Although the new agreement trebled the money he received in advance and doubled the time allowed to perform his contract, Whitney was unable—by a large margin— to meet the revised terms. Not until January, 1809, ten years after the date of the first contract, did Whitney deliver the last musket of the agreed ten thousand. He had made a profit of only $2500 on a job which consumed a decade.

But Whitney had finally proved and successfully applied the basic idea of American mass production, without which the American Standard of Living would have been inconceivable. His was a triumph of organization. The original conception was perhaps not his own; other New Englanders were at the same time experimenting along similar lines. Only twenty miles away, at Middletown, Simeon North, whose main business had been manufacturing scythes, signed his first contract with the War Department in 1799 for 500 horse pistols to be delivered within one year. One of his later contracts (in 1813, for 20,000 pistols) provided that "The component parts of pistols are to correspond so exactly that any limb or part of one Pistol may be fitted to any other Pistol of the twenty thousand." Simeon's son, Selah North, is traditionally credited with inventing the filing jig, the matching concave mold which holds the metal so that any workman then necessarily follows the required shape.

Another feature of this story is worth noting. Government subsidy was crucial. The government's great power to invest and to wait for a return on its investment enabled Whitney to build his factory and tool up for mass production. This first great triumph of the American businessman was a government-sponsored and government-aided (but not government-run) venture.

America was already on its way to becoming the land of human salvation and of material waste. New England versatility now shaped at least two great and lasting tendencies in American civilization.

Machines, not men, became specialized. Where labor was scarce, where a man was expected to turn easily from one task to another, his machines had to possess the competence he lacked. Whitney's Interchangeable System, as he himself explained, was "a plan which is unknown in Europe & the great leading object of which is to substitute correct & effective operations of machinery for that skill of the artist which is acquired only by long practice & experience, a species of skill which is not possessed in this country to any considerable extent." Specialized machinery was required for an unspecialized people. "One of my primary objects," wrote Whitney, "is to form the tools so the tools themselves shall fashion the work and give to every part its just proportion." American technology would be an accessory of the undifferentiated man: the versatile, mobile American. New England had led the way.

A premium on general intelligence. In the Old World, to say a worker was unskilled was to say he was unspecialized, which meant his work had little value. In America, the new system of manufacturing destroyed the antithesis between skilled and unskilled. Lack of artisan skill no longer prevented a man from making complex products. Old crafts became obsolete. In America, too, a "liberal"—that is, an unspecialized—education was no longer proof of gentility; it no longer showed its possessor to be liberated from the need for gainful employment. Unspecialized education was useful to all.

English observers in the mid-19th century admired the ease with which American laborers moved about the country, from one job to another. They were amazed at the general freedom from fear of unemployment, at the vagueness of social classes, at the facility of moving up from one class to another. These facts, among others, they said, explained the absence of trade unions and strikes and the willingness of American workers to try new methods. Even the skilled immigrant sooner or later found it hard to stay in his old groove. While neighboring nations in Europe had jealously guarded their techniques from one another, here individual laborers from England, France, and Germany learned from one another and freely mingled their techniques.

The New England system of manufacturing, destined to become the American system, prized generalized intelligence, literacy, adaptability, and willingness to learn. As the machinery of production became larger, more complicated, more tightly integrated, more expensive, and more rigid, working men were expected to be more alert and more teachable. Open minds were more valuable than trained hands. Technicians and industrialists from England noted a new type of workman being created in the United States. The most skilled English mechanics, they regretfully confessed, showed such "timidity resulting from traditional notions, and attachment to old systems, even among the most talented persons, that they keep considerably behind." In the American system, they said, "you do not depend on dexterity—all you want is intellect." Needing a versatile as well as intelligent populace, New Englanders now reshaped the system of education they had founded two centuries earlier to instil dogmatism and singleness of purpose. They were working a similar transformation in their attitude toward law, and through that, toward all the problems of social change.

the mechanics and the Jeffersonians: New York, 1789-1801

ALFRED YOUNG

In contrast to Boorstin's limited vision of the position of workers in American society, Alfred Young explores the issue of developing political parties and emerging factionalism in class terms. The relationship between poverty, class interests, and politics is analyzed, and an early example of class justice (not unlike the "race etiquette" of the post-Reconstruction period) is described. Young also introduces the spectre of nativism that emerged full blown during the 1830s.

The manipulation of class interests by wealthy Republicans to achieve mechanic, or working class, support did not include expanding the suffrage to the less affluent. But the efforts of New York Republicans did serve to bring workers into the political arena as a separate interest group conscious of its status as the working class. And in 1809 a New York court modified the legal restrictions which defined as conspiracy the activities of unions and other combinations of workers who sought higher wages.

In 1789, on the eve of George Washington's inaugural, New York was a solidly Federalist town. In the Congressional election of 1789, the city chose a Federalist by a vote of 2,342 to 373; in the gubernatorial poll it voted against George Clinton, anti-Federalist Governor, 833 to 385.[1] And the mechanics of all ranks were overwhelmingly Federalist. They poured forth to celebrate Washington's inauguration just as they had marched in 1788 to celebrate ratification of the Constitution. They were active in nominating Federalists and they voted Federalist.[2] "Almost all the gentlemen as well as all the merchants and mechanics," Virginia's Senator Grayson observed in 1789, "combined together to turn [George Clinton] out" while the "honest yeomanry" alone supported him.[3] In 1790 anti-Federalists did not even go through the motions of nominating Assembly or Congressional candidates.

From 1789 to 1801 the major thrust of New York City politics was the effort of the anti-Federalists, then the Republicans, to win back the following they enjoyed in the immediate post-war years and establish a new one among the rapidly expanding electorate.[4] Of necessity this was an effort to win support among the mechanics.

For the old anti-Federalist leaders this was a formidable task. George Clinton, the party chieftain and governor since 1777, was an Ulster county lawyer and landholder whose reputation was built on his services in the Revolution as a staunch Whig, wartime governor and foe of Tories.[5] Anti-Federalist political

From Alfred Young, "The Mechanics and the Jeffersonians: New York, 1789-1801," *Labor History*, V (Fall 1964), 247-276.

support came primarily from the independent small farmers of Long Island, the west bank of the Hudson and the upper Hudson valley.[6] In New York City the small circle of Clintonian leaders, while men of lowly origins, were all successful merchants, as their homes in the fashionable part of lower Manhattan attested.[7] John Lamb, for example, was Collector of the Port, a lucrative position.[8] Marinus Willett was the county sheriff;[9] Melancton Smith was busy with various speculations, some of them in William Duer's group.[10] Henry Rutgers was born to wealth which made him one of the city's largest landlords.[11] Only one officer of the General Society of Mechanics and Tradesmen, John Stagg, their old radical Whig compatriot, acted with the Clintonians; while the only artisan in their circle,[12] Ezekiel Robbins, a wealthy hatter, was not even a member of the Mechanics Society.[13] They had, in fact, better connections among merchants than mechanics.

In 1791–92 when the Livingston family defected from the Federalists to form a coalition with the old anti-Federalists, they brought with them no special strength among the mechanics. They were city merchants and lawyers, and owners of tenanted estates in the upper Hudson valley. Indeed before the Revolution, in 1768–69, the Delancey faction had been able to win over mechanics against William Livingston of the famed "whig triumvirate,"[14] and in 1774–76 the radical mechanic factions usually were at loggerheads with conservatives led by Robert R. Livingston (senior and then junior), Philip Livingston and John Jay and William Duane, related to the Livingstons by marriage.[15] The memory of Chancellor Robert R. Livingston's veto of the charter for the General Society of Mechanics in 1785 was even fresher.[16] Moreover Aaron Burr, the young lawyer sent to the United States Senate in 1791 by the Livingstons and Clinton, in 1785 was the only city Assemblyman who had voted against the charter.[17] Thus the loose coalition that became the "republican interest" as far as New York City politics went—the Clintons, the Livingstons, and Burr—were in reality three factions in search of a following.

They found this following in stages in a long uphill battle. Their first victory did not come until the end of 1794 when they won the Congressional seat by a vote of about 1,850 to 1,650.[18] They did not win an Assembly election until 1797, and in the closing years of the decade all the elections were nip and tuck. In the famous "battle of 1800"—the election that determined that the state's electoral votes would be cast for the Jefferson-Burr ticket—the Republicans took the assembly by 3,050 to 2,600 and squeaked through the congressional race 2,180 to 2,090 votes. Not until 1801 did they win a majority of the £100 freeholder electorate privileged to vote for Governor. Thus even at the end of the Federalist era, New York was not quite a safe Republican town; Federalists in defeat retained a sizable following. Analysis of the election returns leads to the conclusion that the mechanics who in 1789 were overwhelmingly Federalist, by 1800–01 were divided: most were Republican; a good number stayed Federalist. The task, then, that confronts the historian is to explain how various segments of the mechanic population left the house of Federalism in response to the successive issues of the 1790s.

I

Through most of Washington's first administration, from 1789 through 1792, the honeymoon of mechanic Federalist and merchant Federalist continued. The sources of Federalist popularity among mechanics were several. Federalists were the party of the Constitution; they also appeared as the party of the Revolution. The Tories in their camp took a back seat; Colonel Alexander Hamilton ran the party and it was not missed that John Laurence, their first Congressman, had married the daughter of the famed "Liberty Boy," Alexander McDougall.[19] Federalists were also the party of George Washington, an object of universal veneration while the city was the nation's capital in 1789-90. "Poor men love him as their own," said a character in a play by the New York dramatist, William Dunlap.[20] The fact that the city was the capital also helped; anti-Federalists complained that the Federalist "electioneering corps" included "the masons, stone cutters, the carpenters and the mortar carriers" employed in refurbishing city hall as Federal Hall.[21]

In drawing up slates at election time Federalists accommodated mechanics. In the 1789 election when mechanics and merchants each nominated an assembly ticket, Hamilton presided over a meeting of delegates from both groups which drew up a satisfactory coalition ticket.[22] Hamilton claimed, with apparent impunity, in Federalist Essay Number 35 that "Mechanics and manufacturers will always be inclined with few exceptions, to give their votes to merchants, in preference to persons of their own professions and trades. Those discerning citizens are well aware that the mechanic and manufacturing arts furnish the materials of mercantile enterprise and industry."[23] But just to make sure, for years Federalists ran one or more leading mechanics, including leaders of the General Society, on their annual assembly ticket.[24]

In their policies in the first Congress, Federalists made good on some of their promises during the ratification controversy. The city's mechanics petitioned for tariff protection at once, pointing out to their brethren that "foreign impor- tations were highly unfavorable to mechanic improvement, nourishing a spirit of dependence, defeating in a degree the purpose of our revolution and tarnishing the luster of our character."[25] Congressman Laurence neatly balanced the interests of his constituency, pleading for higher duties on beer, candles, hemp, and cordage (manufactured by the city's artisans), for lower duties on rum, madeira, and molasses (imported by the West Indies merchants), couching the latter plea on behalf of the poor—"that part of the community who are least able to bear it."[26] Early in 1792 Congress passed another mildly protective tariff bill while the anti-Federalist position was sufficiently blurred for Hamilton to be able to claim that "this faction has never ceased to resist every protection or encouragement to arts and manufactures."[27]

Hamiltonian finance was generally supported in the city as in the state as a whole. Funding drew only a few whimpers of protest in the city; in fact it was John Stagg, the Clintonian mechanic, who helped squelch a petition that appeared among veterans on behalf of Madison's proposals for discrimination.[28] Assumption struck sparks only among the old anti-Federalist foes of "consoli- dation." While Hamilton's "Report on Manufactures" does not seem to have drawn any special accolades from mechanics, his overall performance as Secretary of the Treasury gave him a prestige that outlasted his party's. On his retirement in 1795 a group of building craftsmen offered to build him a house at their own expense,[29] and after his death in 1804 the General Society went into mourning for six weeks.[30]

The first sign of a serious mechanic alienation from the merchants came in 1791, when the General Society's new petition for incorporation was "treated with contemptuous neglect" by the state assembly which in the same session granted a charter to the Bank of New York, the merchants' favorite. Some of the old mechanic consciousness, last apparent in 1785-86 when the charter was first rejected, now revived. "Mechanics," said a writer in Greenleaf's anti-Federalist organ, "those who assume the airs of 'the well born' should be made to know that the mechanics of this city have equal rights with the merchants, and that they are as important a set of men as any in the community."[31] Another man pushed the issue further:

Who will deny that a republican government is founded on democratic principles? . . . That the manufacturing interest, from its nature is, and ever will remain of the democratic denomination, none can deny. Why then incorporate large monied interests, and no democratic ones? Should we not have a wholesome check to the baneful growth of aristocratic weeds among us?[32]

In the Spring elections of 1791 the mechanics refused to go along with the merchants ticket, nominating instead a slate that included one of their officers and two leaders of the burgeoning Tammany Society. Four of their candidates won—"our motley city representatives," Robert Troup called them in his alarmed report to Hamilton.[33] And the following year the mechanics charter sailed through the legislature.

Once chartered, the Society grew from about 200 members in 1792 to about 600 in 1798, most of them master craftsmen. Chartered "only for charitable purposes" as the society regretfully explained, it occasionally made small loans to its members besides acting as a benefit society.[34] And while it eschewed partisan politics, it nonetheless had the effect it anticipated of "uniting us as brethren in common interests."[35]

Mechanics expressed some of this same spirit by flocking into the Tammany Society, described confidentially by its organizer as "a political institution founded on a strong republican basis whose democratic principles will serve in some measure to correct the aristocracy of the city."[36] Founded in 1789, it had 300 members by the Fall of '91; and perhaps 200 more by 1795, among whom mechanics were the most numerous. Its first chief Sachem was William Mooney, an upholsterer and paper hanger.[37] Its leaders stressed its democratic rather than its class character. Tammany "united in one patriotic band," William Pitt Smith of the Columbia faculty exclaimed, " the opulent and the industrious—the learned and the unlearned, the dignified servant of the people and the respectable plebeian, however distinguished by sentiment or by occupation."[38] The organization was not political, and its leadership at first was predominantly Federalist. But the fact that anti-Federalists were active in Tammany and the Assemblymen elected in 1791 were Tammany figures were both omens of its political potential.[39]

The little appreciated "bank war" and "panic" of 1792 brought to a boil such disillusionment with the Federalist honeymoon as then existed.[40] After the Bank of the United States was chartered and a threat of a coalition of its New York branch with the Bank of New York loomed in 1791, there was a movement to charter a third bank led by "the disappointed in the direction of the existing banks," foremost among whom were the Livingstons.[41] While the origins of the venture were speculative, "men of all classes flocked" to subscribe to its stock, as Edward Livingston claimed in extolling its advantages to "persons of small capital" and victims of the lending "favoritism" of the Bank of New York.[42] Hamilton fought the new venture desperately; by March he knew that the "bank mania" was "made an engine to help the governor's

[Clinton's] re-election."[43] In April the "prince of speculators," William Duer, Hamilton's recently resigned Assistant Secretary, collapsed, and the bubble inflated by speculation in the bank stock, securities, and land burst. Duer brought down with him not only leading merchants like the Livingstons but a host of common folk from whom he had borrowed to the hilt: "shopkeepers, widows, orphans, butchers, carmen, gardeners, market women," a businessman recorded, "even the noted bawd Mrs. McCarty." All business, including that of construction, halted; and "the mechanics began to feel the effect of the failures."[44] Small wonder, then, that a mob of about 400–500 threatened Duer's life at the debtor's jail,[45] or that Republicans "made bitter use" of Hamilton's "attachment to Colonel Duer" in the elections.[46] In the gubernatorial poll of 1792 Clinton ran better than he ever had in the city, receiving 603 votes, to 729 for John Jay, or 44 per cent of the total.[47]

In the Congressional election late in 1792 William Livingston—elected previously as a Federalist Assemblyman—offered the Federalists their first national challenge. "That whore in politics," as Hamilton's informant called him,[48] Livingston made a special appeal to the Mechanics Society for support, claiming to be responsible for their charter. He was also identified with an unsuccessful appeal to make New York City's appointive mayor elective.[49] In a cloudy campaign in which party lines were not clearly drawn, Livingston received 700 votes to 1,900 for the successful Federalist, John Watts.[50]

Through these minor political crises, the leaders of the Mechanics Society did not break with the Federalists. They turned down Livingston's plea for support; it was not only "repugnant to their objects to participate in elections," but he was "an improper person."[51] Similarly they refused to endorse Governor Clinton in 1792[52] or Melancton Smith when he successfully sneaked into the Assembly in 1791. In the Spring of 1793 several officers of the Mechanics Society, including Robert Boyd, the radical Whig blacksmith, were still on the Federalist assembly ticket giving the party an easy victory.[53] In short, at the end of the first Washington administration, despite a smouldering discontent with Federalism in the city, mechanics of the substantial sort and mechanics as a whole had not left the house of Federalism.

II

The parting of the ways came in Washington's second term, and the precipitant was Federalist foreign policy. The French Revolution was an initial stimulus in 1793. When the French frigate L'Embuscade did battle with the English man of war Boston off Sandy Hook some nine boatloads of New Yorkers went out to cheer the French victory while on the shore fistfights broke out between "Whig" and "Tory" cartmen.[54] The arrival of Citizen Edmund Genêt prompted the first open mass meeting of the decade and a welcoming committee was formed whose secretary was White Matlack, a well-to-do brewer and iron manufacturer.[55] As a young doctor walked through the poor east side section, he heard "a dram shop full of Frenchmen singing 'Carmagnole.' The next shop I came upon some person was singing 'God Bless Great George' and which immediately procured a parcel of hearty curses upon his majesty from the rest of the company."[56]

Actually it was Britain and not France that proved the real catalyst. By early 1794, because the thin wall of Federalist tariff protection was not holding the line against the competition of British manufactures, craft groups once again dispatched petitions to Congress.[57] Then news of massive British depredations against American ships and of a British threat to renew the Indian war electrified all classes; it brought the possibility of war to the state's unprotected frontier and the city's unprotected harbor. Thus Republican proposals—in Congress, Madison's old bill for discrimination against British shipping; in New York, Governor Clinton's demand to fortify the harbor and the Livingstons' strident cry for war—caught full sail the most violent wave of Anglophobia since the Revolution.[58] At a meeting sponsored by Republicans, White Matlack was the principal speaker and mechanics were so prominent that a Federalist satirist derided the "greasy caps" in a mock epic poem. At each good point made by a speaker, he jibed:

Hats, caps and leathern aprons flew
And puffs of wondrous size and jerkins blue[59]

In the same flurry of patriotism the city's Democratic Society came into being: its leaders were merchants and lawyers; its members, according to one of them, "are composed of and mingle with every class of citizens"; its meetings, according to a Federalist critic, were attended by "the lowest order of mechanics, laborers, and draymen."[60]

A dramatic change in city opinion was apparent in the Spring of 1794 when the Commissioners of Fortifications, headed by Governor Clinton, called for volunteer labor to erect a fort on Governor's Island.[61] For weeks, the Republican paper reported, "hardly a day has passed . . . without a volunteer party of fifty to one hundred" putting in a day's labor.[62] A British visitor described it vividly:

Marching two and two towards the water side . . . a procession of young tradesmen going in boats to Governor's Island to give the state a day's work . . . drums beating and fifes playing . . . with flags flying. Today the whole trade of carpenters and joiners, yesterday the body of masons; before this the grocers, school masters, coopers and barbers; next Monday all the attorneys and men concerned in the law, handle the mattock and shovel the whole day, and carry their provisions with them.[63]

And of course he could have added more: The Democratic Society, Tammany, the General Society of Mechanics, "all the true Republican carpenters," "the patriotic Republican sawyers," "the patriotic sailmakers"—so they called themselves in the papers—the journeymen hatters, cordwainers, peruke makers, hairdressers, tallow chandlers, tanners and curriers; in short, it was the Constitutional parade of 1788 all over again but under different leadership. And there was also something new: the most recent immigrants to the city styling themselves "Irish laborers," "English Republicans," and the "patriotic natives of Great Britain and Ireland."[64]

The Republicans reaped a political harvest quickly. Early in April 1794, Chancellor Robert R. Livingston advised his younger brother, Edward, not to run again for the Assembly. "The mechanics and cartmen" were Federalist; "I find no class of people on which you can depend."[65] A few weeks later in elections held after the work on the fort had just begun, Federalists won but the Republican vote unexpectedly zoomed from a high of 500 in 1793 to a range of 1,200 to 1,400.[66] Then in the Congressional poll of December 1794-January 1795 Edward Livingston risked a race against John Watts, the Federalist incumbent. A lawyer and city resident, a member of the aristocratic Hudson Valley family known as "Beau Ned" (the young dandy),[67] he was presented to the voters as "the poor man's friend," a "good Whig," and "a good Republican and true friend of the French." Watts was described as a "Tory," "a paper man," "an opulent merchant," and "a friend to British measures."[68] The year before, when Livingston ran for the Assembly, he received 214 votes; he now won 1,843 to 1,638.[69]

In this changing climate the General Society of Mechanics and Tradesmen shifted perceptibly. John Stagg, the Clintonian and radical Whig, was returned as President; later he presided at the public meeting at which Livingston was nominated.[70] At its Fourth of July dinner in 1794, the Society toasted "the republican societies of the City of New York"; the following year it accepted an invitation from the Democratic Society for a joint celebration of Independence Day with them, Tammany and the Coopers Society. A committee worked out the details of an observance that was repeated every year thereafter: a parade to a church (militia officers seated in front of the pulpit, the mechanics to the right of the center aisle, the Democrats to the left, Tammany and the Coopers off to either side aisle), a ceremony consisting of the reading of the Declaration of Independence followed by a patriotic oration by a Republican leader.[71] The typical mechanic could now be portrayed in Republican hues: he was, according to a writer in the Republican paper, a hard working man who eschewed high living, opposed the "haughty well born," saved to buy a lot in the suburbs for his old age, and enjoyed a family gathering at home where his children beat time to "Yankee Doodle" and "Carmagnole."[72]

Thus, the first Republican breakthrough came in a revival of "The Spirit of '76." Over the next few years Republicans had great difficulty transferring this new strength, which came on a national issue, to state elections.[73] They were also unable to sustain mechanic Republicanism on national questions, as the vicissitudes of the Jay Treaty fight of 1795–96 illustrated. A "town meeting" protesting the treaty was attended by from 5,000 to 7,000 people. It was held at the noon lunch hour when, according to an irate Federalist, "our demagogues always fix their meetings in order to take in all mechanics and laborers—over whom they alone have influence."[74] The poorer workers were especially noticeable: cartmen with their horses, "the hodmen, and the ash men and the clam men," as were recent immigrants—Scotsmen, Irish, English, and French.[75] When the vote was taken to damn the Treaty, according to one contemporary, "there was not a whole coat" among them. The Livingstons were "supported by a few of the principal citizens, the rest being made up of men of the lower class." Others claimed, however, that the leaders did not have "a majority of the lower class," or that several hundred sided with Hamilton.[76] By the Spring of 1796, after Washington signed the treaty and Republicans in the House threatened to hold up its enforcement, anti-treaty sentiment faded. Playing on the fear of war and threatening economic coercion, Federalists were able to collect some 3,200 signatures on a pro-Treaty petition.[77] Republicans by contrast turned out less than half of the previous year's opponents at a public rally, one-third of whom, a Federalist charged, "as is usually the case were negroes, sweeps, boys, Frenchmen, and curious people." The "merchants and traders," he insisted, and "the substantial mechanics" backed the Treaty.[78]

The claim was probably justified. In the Congressional election at the end of 1796 James Watson, a wealthy merchant, received the Federalist nomination after four others had turned it down because, in Hamilton's words, "he had gotten a strong hold of most of the leading mechanics who act with us."[79] Edward Livingston recovered his lost ground to win a second term by a safe margin of 2,362 to 1,812 votes. But his vote, a contemporary accurately put it, came from wards "chiefly inhabited by the middling and poorer classes of the people."[80] Thus at the end of the second Washington administration the city's working population was split: the Federalists retained a good section of the "substantial mechanics" while the Republicans had the "middling and poorer classes" in an unstable constituency.

III

Republicans did not consolidate this foothold until they mastered the art of exploiting the class antagonisms of the poor, threats to the economic interests of particular crafts, and the aspirations of new immigrants.

Poverty in New York went hand in hand with population growth and economic progress.[81] The city, the worldly-wise La Rochefoucauld observed in 1796, "like all great towns contains at once more riches and more wretchedness than towns less populous and commercial."[82] A petition from one group of workers pointed out that "house rent, fuel, provisions and prices of everything necessary for the support of a family have been rising." In the winter of 1796–97 some 600 unemployed journeymen petitioned for public assistance because many "by reasons of large families" were "in want of sufficient fire and wood."[83] For newcomers housing was the worst problem. The upper-east side near the shore—the seventh ward—was the city's worst slum. As a doctor described it, it had "narrow, crooked, flat, unpaved, muddy alleys" filled with swamps, stagnant water, "little decayed wooden huts," some inhabited by several families; all was wafted by an intolerable stench from garbage piled in the streets, putrefying excrement at the docks, and a tan yard in their midst.[84] Understandably, when a yellow-fever epidemic claimed 700 lives in the summer of 1795, it was here that the toll was heaviest.[85]

Discontent bred of such conditions was ready for political exploitation. By 1795 there were 900 more voters in the £100 electorate for a total of 2,100; but there were 2,300 more 40 shilling renters, or a total of 5,000. Moreover, the poorer voters were concentrated in the newly-built parts of town, the fifth and especially the seventh wards along the East River, and the fourth and especially the sixth to the west along the North (or Hudson) River. In the seventh, known as the "cartman's ward," there were 870 40 shilling voters to 311 £100 voters; in the sixth the proportion was 1,298 to 223. Here was the Republican potential.[86]

The pent-up class feeling erupted in the election of the Spring of '96 which, as Hamilton put it, "in view of the common people . . . was a question between the rich and the poor because of the 'vile affair of whipping Burke and McCredy.' "[87] Thomas Burk and Timothy Crady—Federalists could not get their names straight—were ferrymen, recent Irish immigrants who got into an altercation with Gabriel Furman, an arrogant Federalist alderman of the wealthy first ward. Accused of the crime of "insulting an alderman," they were tried without due process before a court of three aldermen and a Federalist Mayor intent upon making an example of the "impudent rascals," and were sentenced to two months in jail (Burk got twenty lashes as well).

William Keteltas, a young Republican lawyer, took this case of the "oppression of the innocent poor" to the State Assembly, demanding impeachment of the city official.[88] After a Federalist committee exonerated them and Keteltas turned his guns on the Assembly, he was called before the Bar of the House and asked to apologize. He refused and was found guilty of contempt, whereupon the tumultuous crowd that had jammed the Assembly carried him off to jail in a handsome arm chair midst cries of "The Spirit of '76." An issue of class justice had been transformed into one of free speech. After a month of agitation from "the iron gate," Keteltas was released and escorted home by a cheering crowd. That was a Tuesday; on Friday Republicans nominated him as one of their twelve Assembly candidates. When Federalists mocked the "ragamuffins" who paraded for Keteltas, Republicans claimed them as "the men by whose mechanical labours the necessaries and conveniences of life are produced in abundance"; it was "such men as these [who] were the triumphant victors at Breed's Hill, at Saratoga, at Yorktown." The Federalists won, but the Republican slate hit its highest peak thus far.[89]

In the September 1796 municipal elections Republicans for the first time capitalized on local issues. The Common Council was in the hands of conservative Federalist merchants elected by a tiny handful of voters.[90] Republicans railed at the Mayor and Council for dispensing arbitrary justice, failing to curb forestalling in the markets, neglecting to keep the streets clean, and increasing expenditures and taxes. They elected two men, both of whom were disqualified on technicalities, then re-elected one of them, Jacob Delamontagnie, a secretary of the Democratic Society, by an even wider margin.[91]

Early in 1797 Republicans took up the cause of a single craft, the seventy-five members of the Association of Tallow Chandlers and Soap Makers, whose factories the state legislature ordered removed from the city proper to the outskirts of towns—on the grounds that their fumes were a cause of epidemic. The chandlers petitioned the Assembly. The Republican Brockholst Livingston became their counsel, and at their request Dr. Samuel Latham Mitchill, the Columbia scientist and Tammany orator, prepared a pamphlet-length treatise, exonerating the chandlers' "pestilential vapors," blaming the fever on "septic acid vapors," his favorite theory.[92] The chandler issue boiled through March; in April the Republicans nominated Mitchill for the Assembly on a slate that included a tanner, a hatter, a sailmaker, and the two aldermen elected in the wake of the Keteltas affair. Federalists capitulated, endorsing half the Republican ticket, an unheard of event, and Republicans won their first Assembly election of the decade, their vote ranging between 1,600 and 2,100 to a scant 600 to 700 for the Federalists.[93] In 1800 Dr. Mitchill, the tallow chandlers' hero, was the successful Republican candidate to replace Edward Livingston in Congress.

Republicans also won over another group, the cartmen. Numbering more than 1,000 by 1800, they were known for their "quick tempers" and "mistreating their horses." Normally they chafed under the regulations of the city fathers.[94] In the ferryman affair a doggerel verse on broadside reminded the cartmen of their own trouble with Major Richard Varick:

He often sits upon a bench
Much like unto a judge, sir.
And makes the wretch's bosom wrench
To whom he owes a grudge sir.

But now he does a great offense
It is no thing to mock at
He takes away the cartmen's pence
And puts them in his pocket.[95]

By 1798 the cartmen were Republican enough for the Federalists to gerrymander the outlying seventh ward ("the cartmen's ward") out of the city into the Westchester congressional district. In the 1799 Assembly elections Federalist merchants stood at the polls and "used all their influence with the cartmen" with some success.[96] The next year "Independent Cartman" appealed to his brethren not to submit again to such merchant pressure: who will do the work if not us? "Will their puny clerks carry the burdens which we do?"[97] The cartmen resisted and as a result there were only eighteen cartmen in the crowd when Hamilton, in 1801, appeared at a meeting of cartmen and appealed to "my dear fellow citizens."[98]

From the mid-'90s on, Republicans also spoke in clear tones to the city's new immigrants. Federalists were not without experience in dealing with nationality groups politically.[99] But to the French, Scots, English, and especially the Irish recent arrivals who ran up the cost of charity at the alms house, hated England, and allegedly brought in yellow fever, Federalists were cool or hostile.[100] Republicans, by contrast, formed the "Society for the Assistance of Persons Emigrating from Foreign Countries." They turned out en masse to welcome Joseph Priestley and in their press, Irish and Scots could read reports of struggles for liberty in their native lands.[101] Congressman Livingston, during the xenophobia of 1798 to 1800, eloquently opposed the Alien Law, even introducing a petition from Irish aliens of New York, and in the Assembly Aaron Burr fought the proposed constitutional amendment to bar Federal office to naturalized citizens.[102] The political fruits fell accordingly. "The poor Irish and French," one Federalist was convinced, were enough to carry the sixth and seventh wards for Jefferson in 1800.[103]

IV

In the closing years of the decade Republicans also picked up some of the issues that from the 1780s mechanics. For one, they committed themselves to tariff protection. In the General Society a committee headed by the Republican sailmaker, George Warner, drafted a letter lamenting the growth of foreign importations; they were "an influence highly unfavorable to mechanical improvement, nourishing a spirit of dependence, defeating in a degree the purpose of our Revolution, and tarnishing the luster of our national character"—the very language was that used by Federalist mechanics in 1789.[104] In 1801 a mass meeting of "the mechanics and manufacturers of New York City" sent a memorial to Congress beseeching the "protecting hand of government."[105] As the reign of Jefferson approached, "A Song for Hatters" expressed the expectations of other artisans:

Before the bad English Treaty,
Which Jay with that nation has made
For work we need make no entreaty
All Jours were employed at their trade.

Philadelphia she then had a hundred
New York she had fifty and more
In the first scarce the half can be numbered
In the last there is hardly a score. . . .

And what has occasion'd this failing,
And caus'd us to fall at this rate

'Tis the English, whose arts are prevailing
With our Great rulers of state. . . .

When shortly in our constitution
A Republican party will sway
Let us all then throw in a petition
Our grievance to do away. . . .

That our party in Congress may now rule
Let each voter for liberty stir
And not be to England a base tool
When Jefferson aids us and Burr.[106]

Republicans again took up the cause of freer banking facilities. But where the Livingstons' frontal assault of 1792 failed, Aaron Burr in 1799 managed the camouflaged Bank of Manhattan through the legislature with finesse.[107] While the new bank was primarily of concern to aspiring merchants, it is symptomatic of the mechanic interest in credit that some two dozen members of the Mechanics Society were among the charter stock subscribers.[108] The new bank, Republicans boasted, broke the "banking monopoly" and struck a blow at usury, an object of special contempt to many working class patrons of the city's money lenders.[109]

From 1797 on, Republicans also committed themselves clearly to direct representation of master mechanics on their assembly tickets. In 1798 they repeated their success of the previous year by running four artisans on their ticket; in 1799 they ran six new ones. Even the famous all-star slate Aaron Burr assembled for the battle of 1800 had a place on it for George Warner, sailmaker, Ezekial Robbins, hatter, and Phillip Arcularius, tanner.[110]

The inroads Republicans made among mechanics of all types was confirmed by Federalist tactics from 1798–1801. For a while during the "half war" with France and the "reign of terror," Federalists basked in a glow of X.Y.Z. patriotism as some mechanics turned against the Republicans—now the so-called "French party"—just as they had deserted the Federalists in 1794–95 as the British party. It was almost a second honeymoon of mechanic and merchant as the Mechanics Society toasted "Millions for defense, not one cent for tribute," Tammany substituted "Yankee Doodle" for "The Marseillaise," and mechanics paraded en masse in Washington's funeral cortege. But the Federalist attitude to Republican mechanics was by this time fatally ambivalent. Besides threatening mechanics with the loss of their jobs, they beat the nativist drums, challenging naturalized aliens at the polls, and attempted to suppress the city's two Republican papers. At election time when they sought to woo mechanics, Republicans warned about "the avowed despisers of mechanics who may for a few days intermingle with honest men in order to deceive them."[111] Federalists also voted the poor from the alms house and courted free Negroes with promises of office holding and "enormous supplies of home crackers and cheese."[112] And in the election of 1800 when Hamilton was unable to induce men of "weight and influence" to run, he arranged an Assembly slate filled with unknown artisans: a ship chandler, a baker, a bookseller, a potter, a shoemaker, a leather inspector, and spoiled the image only by including Gabriel Furman, "the man who whipped the ferrymen."[113] Federalist tactics thus can only be described as desperate and to no avail. Mechanic interest was unsurpassed in the voting in the Spring of 1800: "all business was suspended, even the workmen deserted the houses they were building";[114] yet Federalists lost the city.

The election returns for 1800 and 1801 indicate that the mechanics were preponderantly Republican yet were divided in their allegiances. The fact that there were two categories of voters—the £100 freeholders alone qualified to vote for Senators and Governor, and the 40 shilling renters allowed to vote only for Assemblymen— enables us to differentiate roughly the voting patterns of various strata of mechanics (see Table 1). First, about two-thirds of the Republican vote— in 1800, about 2,200 of 3,100 votes; in 1801, 2,400 of 3,600 votes—came from the Assembly voters, the 40 shilling renters who in effect were the poorer mechanics, the cartmen, petty tradesmen and journeymen. Secondly, about one-half of the total Federalist vote came from this same group—in 1800, 1,300 of their 2,600 votes; in 1801, 1,100 of 2,150 votes. Thirdly, Republicans also had significant support among the £100 freeholders who included the master craftsmen—43 per cent or 876 voters in 1800, 54 per cent or 1,266 voters in 1801. As a Republican editor proudly pointed out, this refuted the Federalist contention that Jefferson and Burr were supported only by "persons of no property."[115]

TABLE 1. The New York City Elections of 1800 and 1801

| | 1800 | | | | 1801 | | | |
| | Assembly | | Senate | | Assembly | | Governor | |
Ward	Rep.	Fed.	Rep.	Fed.	Rep.	Fed.	Rep.	Fed.
1	172	245	47	130	208	222	82	145
2	200	434	74	213	217	375	112	209
3	250	438	75	185	284	365	104	194
4	412	330	124	179	426	274	145	162
5	458	370	139	147	545	313	170	148
6	814	363	187	108	919	267	289	89
7	786	485	231	164	1052	353	364	145
Total vote	3092	2665	877	1126	3651	2169	1266	1090

Sources: for 1800, *American Citizen*, May 5, 1800; for 1801, *Republican Watch-Tower*, May 6, 1801.

Analysis of the returns by wards confirms this political division among both prosperous and poorer mechanics. In the sixth and seventh wards with the greatest proportion of poor voters and recent immigrants, where Republicans made their greatest effort to get out the vote,[116] they received more than half of their total city vote in 1800 and 1801. Yet Federalists also had a following here, 800 voters in 1800, reduced to 600 the following year. By contrast, the second and third wards at the bottom of Manhattan, the centers of the fashionable wealthy merchant residences,[117] through the entire decade gave the Federalists almost a two to one margin. The fourth and fifth wards, the midtown on both the west and east side, which were probably the most "middling" in the city, divided about evenly between the two parties. In 1802 Republicans confirmed the class basis of their support in the poorer wards when they divided the city into two congressional districts. They created their own safe district by placing the sixth and seventh wards in together with the fourth, giving the first, second, third, and fifth wards to the Federalists in a district which also included Brooklyn and Richmond. Federalists did not even run a candidate in the Republican district, while Republicans ran one in the Federalist area with "no hopes of success."[118]

By 1800-01 Republican support among mechanics, it is reasonable to hypothesize, came from : 1.) master craftsmen and journeymen in many trades, especially the less prosperous ones; 2.) craftsmen as a whole in trades whose interests Republicans espoused, such as tallow chandlers and shoemakers; 3.) craftsmen in those trades most in need of protection from British manufacturers such as hatters and tanners; 4.) cartmen as a whole; 5.) newer immigrants, especially the Irish,[119] French,[120] and to a lesser extent the Scots[121] and English; 6.) mechanics who had been patriots in the Revolution and responded to the revival of the "Spirit of '76."

The numerically smaller following of the Federalists may well have come from 1.) the more "substantial mechanics" in many trades to whom Hamilton's appeal for the Federalists—as the party that brought "unexampled prosperity"—was meaningful;[122] 2.) craftsmen least in need of protection, such as the building trades; 3.) poorer tradesmen most closely dependent on and most easily influenced by merchants, such as the service trades; 4.) American-born mechanics and New England migrants who felt their status threatened by the influx of "foreigners";[123] 5.) new immigrants, anxious to differentiate themselves from their radical countrymen, especially the English;[124] and 6.) mechanics of a loyalist or neutralist background who were made uneasy by the revival of anti-Toryism.

V

The New York Republicans, it should be clear, did not become a labor party. The Clintons, Livingstons, and Burrites, and other merchants, landholders, lawyers, and office holders ruled the party. Moreover, they had the support of a substantial segment of the merchant community, although not the men at the apex of economic power in the city.[125] Nor did the mechanics become even an organized wing of the party, bargaining for nominations as they had with the Federalists early in the decade. Republicans always found a place for a few mechanics on their twelve-man Assembly slate and for many others on their electioneering committees. Mechanics were members, though not leaders, of the Democratic Society and leaders as well as members of the Tammany Society. George Warner, sailmaker, or Matthew Davis, printer,[126] were speakers at the annual Republican celebration of Independence Day; James Cheetham, a former hatter,[127] was influential as an editor and pamphleteer; and early in the 1800s a number of tanners were active enough to win a reputation as the "tannery yard clique" and "the swamp clique." But there was no assertive workingmen's faction among the Repubicans as there would be in the Jacksonian era.[128] And mechanic support was as much the product of the courting by Republican politicians as it was of the demands of the labor movement.

Nor were Republicans put to the severe test of choosing between wage workers and master craftsmen in labor disputes. Republicans, it is apparent, were sympathetic to the craft organizations. They celebrated the Fourth with the Mechanics and Coopers Societies, pleaded the cause of the Association of

Tallow Chandlers, and opposed the use of prison labor to manufacture shoes, an issue close to the hearts of cordwainers.[129] While there were a few strikes late in the decade, there was no trial of "a combination of labor" as "a criminal conspiracy" until 1809–10.[130]

Nonetheless Republican thought was unmistakably shaped by the party's mechanic constituency. There was, to be sure, a tinge of agrarianism to some Republicans: a glorification of the yeomanry among the upstate anti-Federalist leaders; an idealization of the rural virtues in the aristocratic landholder Robert R. Livingston[131] (who signed his newspaper articles "Cato"); a contempt for the hateful city in the poet-editor, Philip Freneau.[132] But, understandably, Chancellor Livingston, who fearfully vetoed the Mechanics Society charter in 1785, praised the aggressive tallow chandlers in 1797 as "those respectable and useful citizens."[133] By the late 1790s, when Republican writers analyzed the political alignment of social classes, they found a place for mechanics in the Republican coalition. The concept might be that "farmers and mechanics & co" were the "laborers, men who produce by their industry something to the common stock of the commodity" opposed by the unproductive classes,[134] or it might be that "farmers, merchants, mechanics and common laboring men" have a "common interest" against "the great landholders and monied men."[135] The General Society of Mechanics and Tradesmen, for its part, found a place for a picture of a plowman on its membership certificate side by side with a house carpenter and a shipwright, all beneath a slogan "By Hammer and Hand All Arts Do Stand."[136]

Perhaps the New York Republican leaders, who were neither agrarian-minded nor commercial-minded in the strict sense, will be best understood as spokesmen for productive capital. Three of the four merchant Presidents of the Democratic Society, for example, invested in such productive ventures as a linen factory, a thread factory, a mine, and spermaceti candle works.[137] Chancellor Livingston, who is well known for promoting the steamboat, also experimented with manufacturing paper and reducing friction in millstones. "Mechanicks is my hobby horse," he told Joseph Priestley.[138] He was the President and Samuel L. Mitchill the Secretary of the Society for the Promotion of Agriculture Arts and Manufactures. Mitchill was also a pioneer in industrial chemistry, and sympathized with the goal of protection for American manufactures. He congratulated Hamilton on his "Report on Manufactures" in 1792; as Republican chairman of the House Committee on Commerce and Manufactures, in 1804 he sponsored a tariff program.[139]

New York Republicans also took up the social reforms favored by their mechanic constituents. Tammany, for example, at one dinner toasted in succession "the speedy abolition" of slavery, "a happy melioration of our penal laws," and "the establishment of public schools."[140] William Keteltas, the hero of the ferrymen's *cause célèbre*—when incarcerated in the debtor's prison—edited a paper, *Prisoner of Hope*, which pleaded the debtor's plight.[141] Edward Livingston, in his first term in Congress, began the reform of the criminal code, a subject that would become a life-long concern.[142] Contrary to the contention of some historians, Republicans also lent active support to abolition.[143] Reform was bi-partisan and several measures came to fruition when John Hay was governor, but the urban Republicans imparted a warm humanitarianism to a frosty anti-Federalism and a crusading egalitarian flavor to the genteel philanthropic humanitarianism of the city's merchants and ministers. Equally important Republican orators instilled the environmentalist concepts of the enlightenment that justified a permanent program of reform.[144]

Neither mechanics nor Republicans made much of an issue of political reform, especially during George Clinton's long tenure as governor from 1777–95. The restrictive suffrage provisions in the state constitution and its unique Council of Appointment and Council of Revision were occasionally discussed but not widely protested.[145] Typically, when Tunis Wortman examined the question of abolishing the property qualification to vote, in his political treatise of 1800, the city's leading democratic theorist contented himself with summarizing the pros and cons and ended by saying the question was "not decided."[146] In 1801, when Republicans sponsored the first constitutional revision convention, they permitted universal male suffrage in the election of delegates, but restricted the convention itself to reforming the Council of Appointment.[147]

After 1801, their mechanic constituency cautiously beckoned the Republicans towards reform on the municipal level where only freeholders of £20 or more were permitted to vote for Aldermen and the Mayor was appointed. For a while Republicans were content to broaden suffrage in their own way. Wortman as county clerk was observed "running to the poll with the books of the Mayor's court under his arm, and with a troop of ragged aliens at his tail." He was also one of the organizers of "faggot voting," a process by which a group of propertyless Republicans were qualified to vote by the joint temporary purchase of a piece of real estate.[148] When the courts ruled out faggot voting, Republicans demanded that the voting qualifications be lowered at least to the 40 shilling leasehold requirement in Assembly elections; they also asked for the elimination of plural voting and voice voting and for the popular election of the Mayor.[149] By 1804 they won all but the last of these demands.[150]

It might be argued that Republicans did more within the framework of the existing political institutions to provide a greater place for mechanics. Like the old anti-Federalists, Republicans were generally distrustful of the wealthy. Unlike the anti-Federalists, who had confidence only in the yeomanry, Republicans included a role for mechanics among the *Means for the Preservation of Public Liberty*, as George Warner entitled his oration. The trouble, as this sailmaker put it, was that "tradesmen, mechanics, and the industrious classes of society consider themselves of too little consequence to the body politic."[151] Republicans defended the right of mechanics to scrutinize political affairs in "self-created" societies and to instruct their representatives at "town meetings." When Federalists mocked such pretensions, Republicans delighted in taunting them with their own epithets, signing their newspaper articles "one of the swinish multitude" or "only a mechanic and one of the rabble." Republicans also upheld the election of mechanics to public office against Federalist scoffers who "despise mechanics because they have not snored through four years at Princeton."[152]

The mechanic vote and viewpoint guaranteed that Republicans, in their political philosophy, would abandon the old anti-Federalist suspicion of the Constitution. For converts from Federalism like the Livingstons there was never any problem. Other Republicans straddled the constitutional question: Keteltas said he was "neither a Federal nor anti-Federal."[153] Wortman, however, was tempted to revert to the old anti-Federalist view, and to indict the Federalists of '98. He began to collect materials for a book that would expose "the secret convention of 1787 and its members . . . , [and the] intrigues and artifices made use of, for the purpose of compelling the adoption of the constitution." But the book that appeared in 1800—Wortman's *Treatise Concerning Political Inquiry and the Liberty of the Press*—was a libertarian disquisition devoted to the Constitution and Bill of Rights.[154] Republicans could hardly have done otherwise, for their mechanic supporters were men who had paraded for the Constitution in 1788 or had since migrated to the new democracy in order to seek its blessings. To George Warner, the sailmaker and soldier, "the same American spirit which animated to the contest of heroes of the Revolution" prevailed in directing the national convention of '87 to the constitutional establishment of "the liberty we at this day enjoy."[155] Thus the city's Republicans, like the mechanics, were both nationalistic and democratic in their outlook.

And now to return to the question posed in the introduction as to the character and continuity of the political conflict between the years 1774 and 1801. Beyond any question, in the 1790s the mechanics were important in New York City politics. Charles Beard's observation that "neither the Republicans nor the Federalists seem to have paid much attention to capturing the vote of the mechanics" was based on inadequate evidence. In the effort to construct the party conflict as one of "agrarianism" v. "capitalism," Beard did not allow a sufficient place for the mechanics to whom even Jefferson referred sympathet- ically as "the yeomanry of the city."[156] Carl Becker's projection of the conflict of the 1760s into the 1790s was misleading in another way. The implication of the continuity of mechanic allegiances—radical Whig to anti-Federalist to Jeffer- sonian—is insupportable. Mechanics who clearly were Federalist in 1788 remained safely Federalist until 1794 and the substantial mechanics a good deal longer, many of them through 1801 and beyond. Mechanics did not always behave as one unified class in politics. Nor can the Republicans be understood as a mechanic party if that was Becker's implication.

And yet Becker's thesis remains attractive. There was an intense struggle in New York City in the 1790s for "who shall rule at home," and if not strictly a class conflict, within it were the elements of a clash between "the privileged and the unprivileged" involving the mechanics as Becker suggested. The plot, dialogue, and even character types of the 1790s bear a striking resemblance to the drama of the pre-Revolutionary era. Once again the battle cry that stirred the mechanics was British policy, the cause was American Independence, and the ideology was patriotism or "the spirit of '76." Other insistent mechanic demands thread through the last three decades of the century: for democratic participation, for social recognition, for protection for American manufactures. The new leaders of the 1790s, the Livingstons, resumed something of their pre- war position as aristocratic republicans at the head of the "popular party." The new mechanics' hero of the late 1790s, William Keteltas, was Alexander McDougall of 1769 all over again, a second "John Wilkes of America." The methods, too, were similar: the town meetings, the popular political societies, the churning printing presses. The symbolism of the July Fourth celebration perhaps completes the picture. Thus Jeffersonian Republicans of New York City, with due allowance for the rhetoric of politics, could claim that they were heirs to "The Spirit of '76" and that the "revolution of 1800" was indeed the consummation of the Revolution of 1776.

NOTES

1. *Greenleaf's New York Journal and Patriotic Register*, Apr. 9, 1789 (hereafter cited as *New York Journal*); [New York] *Daily Advertiser*, Apr. 17, 1789. $N   2. In 1788 Federalist legislative and convention candidates were endorsed at meetings of master carpenters, and at a meeting of "the respectable mechanics and tradesmen," *Daily Advertiser*, Apr. 24, 28, 29, 1788.

3. William Grayson to Patrick Henry, June 12, 1789, W. W. Henry, ed., *Life, Correspondence and Speeches of Patrick Henry* (3 vols., New York, 1891), III, pp. 389–95.

4. For a brief survey, Sidney Pomerantz, *New York, an American City, 1783–1803* (Columbia University Studies in History, Economics and Public Law, No. 442, New York, 1938), chs. 2, 3.

5. E. Wilder Spaulding, *His Excellency George Clinton, Critic of the Constitution* (New York, 1938), chs. 7–12.

6. E. Wilder Spaulding, *New York in the Critical Period, 1783–1789* (New York, 1932), chs. 5, 12. Forrest McDonald, *We the People. The Economic Origins of the Constitution* (Chicago, 1958), pp. 283–300.

7. For the leaders see "Minutes of the Republican Society" (1788), John Lamb Papers, N.-Y. Hist. Soc. and Box 5 of Lamb Papers, *passim*.

8. Isaac Q. Leake, *Memoirs of the Life and Times of General John Lamb* (Albany, 1859), pp. 296–98, 351–55; *American State Papers, Miscellany*, I, pp. 57–58, 60–62, for Lamb's income as collector.

9. Daniel E. Wager, *Col. Marinus Willet: The Hero of the Mohawk Valley* (Utica, 1891), pp. 45–47.

10. Robin Brooks, "Melancton Smith, New York Anti-Federalist, 1744-1798" (unpub. doctoral diss., University of Rochester, 1964), ch. 2.

11. L. Ethan Ellis, "Henry Rutgers," *Dictionary of American Biography*, VIII, pp. 255–56; "Tax Lists or Assessments on the Real and Personal Property" (New York City, June, 1796), Ms., N.-Y. Hist. Soc., in particular for the seventh ward.

12. See Roger Champagne, "The Sons of Liberty and the Aristocracy in New York Politics, 1765–1790" (unpub. doctoral diss., University of Wisconsin, 1960), p. 481. For Stagg on Clinton's election committee, *New York Journal*, Apr. 2, 1789.

13. "Minutes of the General Society of Mechanics and Tradesmen," Dec. 1, 1794, Dec. 23, 1795 (typescript at the office of the Society, New York City); for his house see James Wilson, *Memorial History of the City of New York* (4 vols., New York, 1891-93), III, pp. 150–52.

14. Roger Champagne, "Family Politics versus Constitutional Principles: The New York Assembly Elections of 1768 and 1769," *William and Mary Quarterly*, 3rd ser., XX (1963), 57–79; Milton Klein, "William Livingston: American Whig" (unpub. doctoral diss., Columbia University, 1954), chaps. 13, 15.

15. Becker, *New York, 1763–1776, passim*; Champagne, "Sons of Liberty," chap. 7 and pp. 439–440

16. George Dangerfield, *Robert R. Livingston of New York, 1746–1813* (New York, 1960), p. 197; for the veto, Charles Z. Lincoln (ed.), *Messages From the Governors* (Albany, 1909), II (1777–1822), pp. 228–233.

17. Nathan Schachner, *Aaron Burr: A Biography* (New York, 1937), pp. 84–85.

18. The returns for this and subsequent elections are given below.

19. Charles W. Spencer, "John Laurence," *Dictionary of American Biography*, VI, pp. 31–32.

20. Cited in Martha Lamb, *History of the City of New York* (2 vols., New York, 1880), II, p. 352.

21. "Civis," *New York Journal*, Apr. 9, 1789.

22. Miscellaneous Notes and Memoranda for April, 1789, Alexander Hamilton Papers, N.-Y. Hist. Soc.; for the nominations, *Daily Advertiser*, Apr. 8, ff., 1789.

23. Jacob Cooke, ed., *The Federalist*, Essay 35 (Middletown, Conn., 1961), p. 219.

24. The mechanics elected as Federalist Assemblymen and the year of their election were: 1789: Anthony Post, carpenter and President of the General Society; Francis Childs,

printer of the Federalist *Daily Advertiser* and Vice President of the Society, and Henry Will, pewterer, an incorporator of the Society; 1790: William W. Gilbert, silversmith, and Will; 1791: John Wylley, tailor, and Will; 1792: Gilbert and Wylley; 1793: Robert Boyd, blacksmith, Richard Furman, painter and glazier and Jotham Post, either a druggist or carpenter; 1794: Furman and Post; 1795: Furman, Post and Alexander Lamb, a cartman; 1797: (ticket defeated); 1798: Furman; 1799: John Bogert, iron monger, Jacob Sherred, painter, Anthony Steenback, mason and Anthony Post, carpenter; 1800 and 1801, defeated; see *New York Civil List* (Albany, 1869 edn.), 130–48 for Assemblymen; for identifications, see *New York Directory* (New York, annually) and "Minutes of the General Society of Mechanics and Tradesmen, 1785–1832," *passim*. For a published list of the members of the Society, Thomas Earle and Charles C. Congden, eds., *Annals of the General Society of Mechanics and Tradesmen of the City of New York, 1785–1889* (New York, 1882), appendix.

25. A letter to the Mechanics Society of Boston in "General Society of Mechanics Minutes," at November 18, 1788; the petition is in *American State Papers: Finance* (Washington, 1821), I, pp. 8–9.

26. Joseph Gales and W. C. Seaton, eds., *The Debates and Proceedings in the Congress of the United States, 1789-1824* (42 vols., Washington, 1834–56), 1st Cong., 1st sess., Apr. 14, 1789, pp. 131, 133–34, 150, 153; Apr. 24, pp. 205–06. Hereafter cited as *Annals of Congress*.

27. An unpublished ms. fragment (1794) in Hamilton Papers, Lib. of Congress, Microfilm, also reprinted in Beard, *Economic Origins*, pp. 246–47.

28. *Daily Advertiser*, Feb. 3, 22, 1790. Stagg was active in putting down the movement in the Society of Cincinnati.

29. Griffith J. McRee, *Life and Correspondence of James Iredell* (2 vols., New York, 1857), II, p. 442.

30. Martha Lamb, "The Career of a Beneficent Enterprise," *Magazine of American History*, XX, 2 (Aug., 1889), 94. I have found no evidence of mechanic testimonials in a search through the Hamilton Transcripts, Col. Univ. Lib. I am indebted to Harold Syrett, Editor of The Hamilton Papers, for the opportunity to make use of the transcripts. Nor is there any such evidence in Broadus Mitchell, *Alexander Hamilton, The National Adventure, 1788-1804* (New York, 1962) or in John C. Miller, *Alexander Hamilton, Portrait in Paradox* (New York, 1949).

31. A Friend to Equal Rights, *New York Journal*, Mar. 30, 1791.

32. "Leonidas," *ibid.*, Feb. 22, 1792.

33. For nominations, *New York Journal*, Apr. 13, 16, 1791; *Daily Advertiser*, June 2, 1791; Robert Troup to Alexander Hamilton, June 15, 1791, Hamilton Transcripts, Col. Univ. Lib.

34. "Minutes of the General Society," *passim*. The usual loan was £100 or £150; on Mar. 2, 1796, the society had £500 on loan, on Mar. 7, 1798, £1250.

35. A letter to the Mechanics Society of Providence, *ibid.*, at Nov. 7, 1792. For the charter see *Laws of the State of New York*, 13th sess., ch. 26.

36. John Pintard to Jeremy Belknap, Oct. 11, 1790 cited in Edwin P. Kilroe, *Saint Tammany and the Origins of the Society of Tammany . . .* (New York, 1913), pp. 136–37.

37. Peter Paulson, "The Tammany Society and the Jeffersonian Movement in New York City, 1795–1800," *New York History*, XXXIV (1953), p. 50.

38. William Pitt Smith, "An Oration Before the Tammany Society, May 12, 1790," *New York Magazine or Literary Repository*, I (1790), pp. 290–95, at 294.

39. For the officers see *New York Directory* (1789–1792). Pintard was elected to the Assembly in 1790 and failed in 1791 when William Pitt Smith and Melancton Smith were elected. See *New York Journal*, Apr. 22, 1790, *Daily Advertiser*, June 2, 1791.

40. Alfred Young, "The Democratic Republican Movement in New York State, 1788–1797" (unpub. doctoral diss., Northwestern University, 1958), ch. vii and Joseph S. Davis, *Essays in the Earlier History of American Corporations* (2 vols., Harvard Economic Studies, XVI, Cambridge, Massachusetts, 1917), II, ch. 2.

41. Alexander Macomb to William Constable, Feb. 21, 1792, Constable Papers, N.Y. Pub. Lib.; see also Seth Johnson to Andrew Craigie, Jan. 21, 1792, Craigie Papers, III, No. 70, Amer. Antiq. Soc.

42. Reported in Johnson to Craigie, Jan. 22, 1792, *ibid.*, No. 71; see also "Decius," *New*

York Journal, Feb. 15, 1792 and a spate of articles, Daily Advertiser, Feb. 7-29, 1792, passim.

43. See Alexander Hamilton to William Seton, cashier of the Bank of New York, Jan. 18, 24, Feb. 10, Mar. 19, 21, 1791; the quotation is from James Tillary to Hamilton, Mar. 1, 1792, all in Hamilton Transcripts, Col. Univ. Lib.

44. Johnson to Craigie, Mar. 25, Apr. 18, 1792, Craigie Papers, III, Nos. 72, 76, Amer. Antiq. Soc.; New York Journal, Mar. 28, 1792.

45. Benjamin Tallmadge to James Wadsworth, Apr. 19, 1792, Wadsworth Papers, Conn. Hist. Soc. and ms. fragment [Apr. 1792], N.Y.C. Misc. ms., Box 14, N.-Y. Hist. Soc.

46. James Watson to James Wadsworth, Apr. 3, 1792, Wadsworth Papers, Conn. Hist. Soc. and Johnson to Craigie, Apr. 15, 1792, Craigie Papers, III, No. 75, Amer. Antiq. Soc.

47. Daily Advertiser, June 2, 1792.

48. James Tillary to Hamilton, Jan. 14, 1793, Hamilton Transcripts, Col. Univ. Lib.; for Livingston, Wilson, Memorial History of the City of New York, III, pp. 79-80.

49. Journal of the Assembly of the State of New York, 15th sess., 151; "Atticus," New York Journal, June 17, 1792.

50. New York Journal, Feb. 20, 1793: Livingston was not endorsed by anti-Federalist or Republican leaders either for Congress or for the Assembly the following spring; see Philip Ten Eyck to John B. Schuyler, Apr. 3, 1793, Schuyler Papers, Misc., N.Y. Pub. Lib.

51. "General Society Minutes," Jan. 9, 1793; New York Journal, Jan. 12, 1793.

52. See the election committees in New York Journal, Feb. 25, Mar. 21, 1792.

53. Ibid., May 29, June 1, 1793.

54. Alexander DeConde, Entangling Alliance: Politics and Diplomacy Under George Washington (Durham, N.C., 1958), pp. 269-70.

55. New York Journal, Aug. 7, 10, 1793; Rufus King to Alexander Hamilton, Aug. 3, 1793, Charles King, ed., The Life and Correspondence of Rufus King (6 vols., New York, 1894-1900), I, p. 493.

56. Alexander Anderson, "Diary," Jan. 9, 1794, Ms., Columbiana Col., Col. Univ. Lib.; see also entries for July 31, Aug. 8, 1793.

57. Annals of Congress, 3rd Congress, 1st sess. Petitions were received from the following New York City artisans: manufacturers of hand bellows (Feb. 3, 417), nail manufacturers (Feb. 21, 458), hatters (Mar. 5, 478). From other cities petitions came from manufacturers of metal buttons, tobacco, hemp, nails, paint, bar iron, glass, hats, and hosiery, 482, 1023, 1131, 432, 256, 475, 452, 453, 456, 523, 522. For support for protection from Tammany, see New York Journal, Nov. 27, 1795.

58. DeConde, op. cit., ch. 3. John C. Miller, The Federalist Era, 1789-1801 (New York, 1960), ch. 9.

59. New York Daily Gazette, Mar. 4, 1794; "Acquiline Nimblechops" [pseud.], Democracy, An Epic Poem . . . (New York, 1794), attributed, falsely, I believe, to Brockholst Livingston.

60. William Woolsey to Oliver Wolcott, Jr., Mar. 6, 1794 cited in Eugene P. Link, Democratic Republican Societies, 1790-1800 (Columbia Studies in American Culture No. 9, New York, 1942), 94, "Address . . . by the Democratic Society of New York, May 28, 1794, Broadside, N.Y. Pub. Lib. Of 47 men known to be members of the Society, a very incomplete number, it has been possible to identify them as follows: merchants, 14; craftsmen, 12; public officials, 2; lawyers, 4; teachers, 2; unidentified, 13. For analysis of the comparable Philadelphia society in which 32.8% were craftsmen, see ibid., pp. 71-73.

61. "Proceedings of the Commissioners of Fortifications for the City of New York and its Vicinity," (1794-1795), Ms., N.Y. Hist. Soc.

62. New York Journal, May 10, 1794.

63. Henry Wansey, The Journal of an Excursion to the United States of North America in the Summer of 1794 . . . (Salisbury, Eng., 1796), reprinted in Bayrd Still, ed., Mirror for Gotham (New York, 1956), pp. 65-66. I have changed the order of several sentences.

64. See New York Journal, Apr. 26, 30, May 3, 7, 10, 24, 28, June 18, 21, 1794. See also I. N. P. Stokes, comp., Iconography of Manhattan Isle (6 vols., New York, 1915-1928), V, 1307.

65. Robert R. to Edward Livingston, Apr. 10, 1794, R. R. Livingston Papers, N.-Y. Hist. Soc.

66. New York Journal, June 7, 1794.

67. William Hatcher, *Edward Livingston: Jeffersonian Republican and Jacksonian Democrat* (Baton Rouge, 1940), ch. I; Charles H. Hunt, *Life of Edward Livingston* (New York, 1964), chs. 1-3.

68. William Miller, "First Fruits of Republican Organization: Political Aspects of the Congressional Elections of 1794," *Penn. Mag. Hist. and Biog.*, LXIII (1939), 118-43; Young, *op. cit.*, pp. 616-20.

69. *New York Journal*, Feb. 7, 1795, cf. to returns, *ibid.*, May 29, June 1, 1793.

70. *New York Journal*, Nov. 26, 29, Dec. 3, 1794.

71. *New York Journal*, July 5, 1794; "General Society of Mechanics Minutes," June 3, 24, July 1, 1795 and for the seating arrangements, June 7, 1798.

72. "See to That," *New York Journal*, Dec. 27, 1794.

73. For returns in the 1795 gubernatorial elections, *New York Journal*, June 3, 1795.

74. Benjamin Walker to Joseph Webb, July 24, 1795 in W. C. Ford, ed., *Correspondence and Journals of Samuel Bacheley Webb* (3 vols., New York, 1894), III.

75. Grant Thorburn, *Forty Years' Residence in America . . .* (Boston, 1834), 37-40.

76. Seth Johnson to Andrew Craigie, July 23, 1795, Craigie Papers, III, No. 97, Amer. Antiq. Soc.; "Slash," *New York Journal*, July 25, 1795 for the remark about "not a whole coat"; Benjamin Walker cited in footnote 74.

77. Alexander Hamilton to Rufus King, Apr. 24, 1796, Hamilton Transcripts, Col. Univ. Lib. For pressure by insurance underwriters, "Circular letter by Nicholas Low, Archibald Gracie and Gulian Verplanck, New York, May 3, 1796," Broadside, N.Y. Pub. Lib.

78. William Willcocks, a New York City Federalist Assemblyman, in *Albany Gazette*, May 2, 1796.

79. Hamilton to Rufus King, Dec. 16, 1796, Hamilton Transcripts, Col. Univ. Lib.

80. "Impartial History of the Late Election," *New York Journal*, Dec. 27, 1796; *Argus*, Jan. 20, 1797.

81. Pomerantz, *op. cit.*, 199-225; Morris, *Government and Labor in Early America*, 200 ff.

82. F. A. F. de La Rochefoucauld-Liancourt, *Travels Through the United States of America, in the Years 1795, 1796, 1797* (2 vols., London, 1799), II, p. 205.

83. "Petition of the Repackers of Beef and Pork to the State Legislature, Jan. 24, 1795," Misc., Ms., N.Y.C. No. 86, N.-Y. Hist. Soc.; "Jehosphapet" [New York], *Evening Post*, Jan. 14, 1795; "To the Inhabitants of the City of New York," *Argus*, Jan. 14, 1797.

84. Dr. Elihu Hubbard Smith, "Letters to William Bull . . . on the Fever" in Noah Webster, Jr., comp., *A Collection of Papers on the Subject of Billious Fevers* (New York, 1796), pp. 66-74.

85. Matthew Davis, *A Brief Account of the Epidemical Fevers* (New York, 1796), pp. 58-67 for a list of the dead, 6, 16-17 for housing. For verification, Dr. Richard Bayley, *An Account of the Epidemic Fever* (New York, 1796), 59-60, 122 and *Argus*, Oct. 17, 1795.

86. For the electoral census of 1795 by wards, see Supplement to the *Daily Advertiser*, Jan. 27, 1796.

87. Hamilton to Rufus King, May 4, 1796, Hamilton Transcripts, Col. Univ. Lib.

88. For a full account, Young, *op. cit.*, ch. 20; for a brief account, Pomerantz, *op. cit.*, pp. 263-68.

89. *New York Journal*, Apr. 15, 19, 22, especially "A Dialogue Between an Old Tory and a Young Republican," *ibid.*, Apr. 22.

90. Pomerantz, *op. cit.*, pp. 64-76.

91. In the *New York Journal*, "An Elector," Sept. 20; "A Citizen," Sept. 22; "A Freeholder," Sept. 22; and an editorial paragraph, Sept. 29, 1796; for the contested election, Arthur Peterson, ed., *Minutes of the Common Council of the City of New York* (19 vols., New York, 1917), II, pp. 284-86; Pomerantz, *op. cit.*, pp. 120-22.

92. For the petition, Assembly Papers, Box 5, No. 113, New York State Lib.; for newspaper accounts, *New York Journal*, Feb. 18, 23, Mar. 8, 11, 1797; Samuel L. Mitchill, *The Case of the Manufacturers of Soap and Candles in the City of New York Stated and Examined* (New York, 1797); Mitchill to Robert R. Livingston, June 9, 1797, Misc., Ms., N.-Y. Hist. Soc.; Livingston to Mitchill, July 18, 1797, R. R. Livingston ms., N.Y. State Lib.

93. *New York Journal*, June 4, 1797.

94. Kenneth and Anna M. Roberts, trans. and ed., *Moreau de St. Mary's American Journey (1793-1798)* (New York, 1947), pp. 124-25, and 127, 158-59, 162 for other observations on labor in the city; "Regulations of the Cartmen . . . 1795," Broadside, Lib. of Congress.

95. "The Strange and Wonderful Account of a Dutch Hog" (New York, 1796), Broadside No. 7765, N.Y. State Lib.; Varick was Dutch for hog.

96. Peter Jay to John Jay, May 3, 1799, John Jay Papers, Col. Univ. Lib.

97. "An Independent Cartman," *Republican Watch-Tower*, Apr. 30, 1800 and in the same issue "To the Cartmen of New York," "To the Cartmen," by "Eighteen Hundred," and report of a meeting; "Leonidas," *ibid.*, Mar. 14, 1801 claimed that only 1,150 of 1,500 votes were cast in the 1800 election as a result of threats.

98. "A Cartman," *Republican Watch-Tower*, Apr. 25, 1801.

99. To take the Germans as an example: In 1788 Federalist candidates were endorsed "at a very numerous meeting of Germans" (*Daily Advertiser*, Apr. 28, 1788); in 1790 the German Society, claiming to be rebuffed by the merchants, offered support to the mechanics' ticket if they nominated a German (*New York Gazette*, Apr. 20, 1790).

100. See Alfred Young, "New York City in the Hysteria of 1798 to 1800" (unpub. master's thesis, Col. Univ., 1947), pp. 91-101.

101. "Society for the Assistance of Persons Emigrating From Foreign Countries . . . June 30, 1794," Broadside, N.-Y. Hist. Soc.; for their constitution, *New York Journal* (June 25, 1794), and philosophy, Thomas Dunn, A.M., *A Discourse . . . October 21, 1794 Before the New York Society . . .* (New York, 1794); for Priestley's Welcome, Edgar Smith, *Priestley in America, 1794-1804* (Philadelphia, 1920), pp. 21-40.

102. The *Speech of Edward Livingston on the Third Reading of the Alien Bill* (Philadelphia, 1798) also in *New York Journal*, July 14, 1798; *Annals of Congress*, 5th Congress, 1st Sess., Feb. 12, 1799, p. 2884; Schachner, *Aaron Burr*, 152.

103. Phillip Livingston to Jacob Read, Feb. 23, 1801, reprinted in *Col. Univ. Quart.*, XXIII (June, 1931), p. 200.

104. "General Society of Mechanics Minutes," Jan. 16, Feb. 6, Feb. 20, Mar. 6, Apr. 3, 1799, reprinted in Earle and Congdon, eds., *Annals*, pp. 241-42. The letter was drafted, agreed to, and reconsidered at a special meeting, then rejected. Thus there was a division in the Society on the question which may also account for the first recorded contest for officers, Jan. 4, 1800. The fact that George Warner, an active Republican, was chairman of the drafting committee leaves no doubt as to the Republican position.

105. *American Citizen*, Mar. 19, Mar. 21, Apr. 10, 1801. George Warner was secretary to this committee; another petition was sent to the state legislature requesting bounties for the production of sheep to encourage the wool industries, signed by a number of Republicans, *American Citizen*, Feb. 14, 1801.

106. "A New Song," by J. C. [James Cheetham, hatter and co-editor of the paper], *Republican Watch-Tower*, Feb. 21, 1801; for other evidence of Republican support for manufacturers, Minutes of the Tammany Society, Dec. 1, 1800, Ms., N.Y. Pub. Lib., for a debate; *Argus*, Nov. 27, 1795 for a Tammany toast; *New York Journal*, Apr. 15, 1797, June 8, 1799.

107. Beatrice Rubens, "Burr, Hamilton and the Manhattan Company," *Polit. Sci. Quart.*, LXII (1957), 578-607 and LXIII (1958), 100-125.

108. Bank of Manhattan, *A Collection of 400 Autographs Reproduced in Facsimile from the Signatures of the Original Subscription Book of the Bank of Manhattan* (New York, 1919).

109. *New York Journal*, Jan. 8, Feb. 12, 15, 1800; "Philander," *American Citizen*, Apr. 28, 29, 1800; for a debate, "Minutes of the Tammany Society," Mar. 31, 1800, Ms., N.Y. Pub. Lib.

110. The mechanic candidates on the Republican ticket were: for 1797: Phillip Arcularius, tanner, Ezekial Robbins, hatter, and George Warner, sailmaker; for 1798: Arcularius, Robbins, Arthur Smith, mason, and John Wolfe, boot- and shoemaker; for 1799: Joshua Barker, manager of an air furnace, Ephraim Brasher, goldsmith, John Brower, upholsterer, Matthew Davis, printer, Benjamin North, carpenter, and William Vredenbergh, grocer. For excellent details: Anne B. Seeley, "A Comparative Study of Federalist and Republican Candidates in New York City" (unpublished master's thesis, Col. Univ., 1959). Of 16 Republican candidates of mechanic background nominated over the entire decade Mrs.

Seeley found the tax evaluations of about half of them to be high, e.g., £1200 to 5850 and about half to be low, £100 to 400.

111. *Argus*, Apr. 20, 1799; see James Smith, *Freedom's Fetters. The Alien and Sedition Acts* (Ithaca, N.Y., 1956), pp. 204-220, 385-417; Young, "New York City in the Hysteria of 1798-1800," *passim*.

112. "To a Certain Man," *American Citizen*, Apr. 24, 1801.

113. Matthew L. Davis to Albert Gallatin, Apr. 15, 1800, Gallatin Papers, N.-Y. Hist. Soc.; see also Robert Troup to Rufus King, Mar. 9, 1800, in C. King, ed., *Correspondence of Rufus King*, III, pp. 207-08.

114. Peter Jay to John Jay, May 3, 1800, Jay Papers, Col. Univ. Lib.

115. *American Citizen*, May 4, 1801; see also Aaron Burr to William Eustis, Apr. 28, 1801, Eustis Ms., Mass. Hist. Soc.

116. For 1800 Matthew L. Davis to Albert Gallatin, May 1, 1800, Gallatin Papers, N.-Y. Hist. Soc. Notices of meetings: *American Citizen*, Apr. 22, 25, 1800; Peter Jay to John Jay, May 3, 1800, Jay Papers, Col. Univ. Lib.; John C. Miller, *Alexander Hamilton*, p. 512.

117. Wilson, *Memorial History of New York*, III, 150-52, for a list of 250 homes assessed at over £2000 in 1798; Stokes, *Iconography of Manhattan Island*, V, p. 1374; Beard, *Economic Origins*, pp. 382-87, erred in lumping the first with the second and third; it was more mixed; see "Impartial History of the Late Election," *New York Journal*, Dec. 27, 1796, for comment that remains valid for 1800.

118. Editorial, *American Citizen*, Apr. 30, 1802.

119. For Republican organizations among the Irish: for the United Irishmen of New York, *Time Piece*, July 6, Aug. 30, 1798 and *Argus*, Mar. 18, 1799; for "Republican Irishmen," *American Citizen*, July, 1800, and July 9, 1801; for Hibernian Provident Society, *Republican Watch-Tower*, Mar. 18, 28, 1801; for Hibernian Miltia Volunteers, Link, *op. cit.*, p. 184.

120. For the variety of political opinions among the French see F. S. Childs, *French Refugee Life in the United States: An American Chapter of the French Revolution* (Baltimore, 1946), pp. 70-75; Moreau de St. Mary's *American Journey*, *passim*; for a French newspaper of Republican cast see George P. Winship, "French Newspapers in the United States from 1790 to 1800," *Bibliographic Society of America Papers*, XIV (1920), pp. 134-47.

121. For the Calendonian Society, decidedly Republican, see [New York] *Evening Post*, Dec. 22, 1794; *Argus*, Dec. 3, 1795; *New York Directory for 1796*, unpaged; for a conservative Scot's observations on the "hot characters" among his fellow migrants, Grant Thorburn, *Forty Years' Residence*, pp. 23, 37-40, 92.

122. *New York Commercial Advertiser*, Apr. 11, 1801 and *An Address to the Electors of the State of New York* (Albany, 1801).

123. See the toasts of a "Yankee Fraternity," *Daily Advertiser*, July 10, 1798.

124. For a short-lived Federalist paper founded by a recent English migrant, John Mason Williams, see [New York] *Columbian Gazette* (April 4-June 22, 1799), especially the prospectus, April 6, and valedictory, June 22.

125. Alfred Young, "The Merchant Jeffersonians: New York as a Case Study," (unpub. paper delivered before the Miss. Valley Hist. Ass'n., Apr., 1954).

126. Matthew Davis, while best known as Burr's amanuensis for *Memoirs and Correspondence of Aaron Burr*, was a printer, publisher of the short-lived [New York] *Evening Post* (1795), then co-publisher of [New York] *Time Piece* (1797). He was active in Tammany and the Mechanics Society, was the Independence Day orator in 1800, and the organizer of the Society for Free Debate (1798).

127. James Cheetham, a recent English immigrant and a hatter by trade, became co-editor of *American Citizen* and *Republican Watch-Tower* (1801-ff), a leading pamphleteer and the first biographer of Thomas Paine (1809).

128. Frank Norcross, *History of the New York Swamp* (New York, 1901), 8-11; Lee Benson, *The Concept of Jacksonian Democracy: New York as a Test Case* (Princeton, 1961); Walter Hugins, *Jacksonian Democracy and the Working Class: A Study of the New York Workingman's Movement, 1829-1837* (Stanford, 1960).

129. "A Shoemaker," *American Citizen*, Apr. 23, 1801; "To the Shoemakers," *Republican Watch-Tower*, Apr. 22, 1801; "A Shoemaker to the Journeymen Shoemakers," *ibid.*, Apr. 25; Report of the Commissioners of the Prison, *Albany Register*, Mar. 3, 1801.

130. Richard Morris, "Criminal Conspiracy and Early Labor Combinations in New York," *Polit. Sci. Quart.,* LVII (1937), pp. 51–85.

131. Robert R. Livingston, "Address to the Agricultural Society of the State of New York," *New York Magazine,* VI (Feb., 1795), pp. 95–102.

132. Lewis Leary, *That Rascal Freneau. A Study in Literary Failure* (New Brunswick, N.J., 1931), pp. 260–65, 275.

133. Robert R. Livingston to Samuel L. Mitchill, July 18, 1797, Livingston Ms., N.Y. State Lib.; for the veto see note 16 above.

134. "To Farmers, Mechanics and other Industrious Citizens," *Time Piece,* May 14, 1798.

135. "Strutator," *New York Journal,* Apr. 19, 1797.

136. Lamb, "The Career of a Beneficent Enterprise," *op. cit.;* a membership certificate is on exhibit at the General Society, New York City.

137. Henry Rutgers established a "bleach-field and thread manufactory" (*Daily Advertiser,* May 12, 1791); James Nicholson was chairman of the New York Manufacturing Society (*New York Directory for 1790,* p. 135) and was interested in a textile venture (Joseph Garlick to Nicholson, Mar. 15, 1798, Misc. Ms., Nicholson, N.-Y. Hist. Soc.); Solomon Simpson had an interest in the New York Iron Manufacturing Company, was part owner of a lead mine and a founder of the American Mineralogical Society and co-owner of a spermaceti candle factory (Morris Schappes, "Anti-Semitism and Reaction, 1795–1800," *Pubs. of the American Jewish Hist. Soc.,* XXVIII, Part 2 [Dec., 1948], 115–16).

138. Dangerfield, *op. cit.,* pp. 284–289.

139. Lyman C. Newall, "Samuel Latham Mitchill," *Dictionary of American Biography,* VII, pp. 69–70; Mitchill to Hamilton, Dec. 3, 1792, Hamilton Transcripts, Col. Univ. Lib.; Joseph Dorfman, *The Economic Mind in American Civilization, 1606–1865* (New York, 1946), I, pp. 324–25.

140. *New York Journal,* "Extraordinary" page, Dec. 6, 1794; for the Mechanics Society reform sentiment see "Minutes of the General Society," July 1, 1795.

141. *Forlorn Hope,* Mar. 24–Sept. 13, 1800; for a rival debtor's paper also edited by a Republican, see *Prisoner of Hope,* May 3–Aug. 23, 1800.

142. *Annals of Congress,* 4th Cong., 1st sess., pp. 254–55, 257, 304–07, 1394.

143. See Young, "Democratic Republican Movement," pp. 768–69.

144. Tunis Wortman, *An Oration on the Influence of Social Institutions Upon Morals and Human Happiness . . . before the Tammany Society May 12, 1795* (New York, 1796); and DeWitt Clinton, *An Oration on Benevolence Delivered before the Society of Black Friars . . . November 10, 1794* (New York, 1795).

145. I saw no signs of interest in suffrage reform in the Minutes of the Mechanics or Tammany, the toasts offered at their celebrations or in the expressions of the Democratic Society; for pro universal suffrage articles in *Time Piece:* "On Some of the Principles of American Republicanism," May 5, 1797; "Political Creed," Aug. 21, 1797; "Communication," Oct. 6, 1797; and "Universal Justice," Nov. 10, 1797.

146. Tunis Wortman, *Treatise Concerning Political Enquiry and the Liberty of the Press* (New York, 1800), pp. 195–97.

147. Jabez Hammond, *History of Political Parties in the State of New York* (2 vols., Cooperstown, 1846), I, ch. 6.

148. John Wood, *A Full Exposition of the Clintonian Faction* (Newark, 1802), 20–21; Pomerantz, *op. cit.,* pp. 208, 134.

149. James Cheetham, *Dissertation Concerning Political Equality and the Corporation of New York* (New York, 1800).

150. Pomerantz, *op. cit.,* 133–145; Chilton Williamson, *American Suffrage From Property to Democracy 1760–1860* (Princeton, 1960), pp. 161–64.

151. George Warner, *Means for the Preservation of Public Liberty . . . delivered before the Mechanics, Tammany, Democratic and Coopers Societies, July 4, 1797* (New York, 1797), pp. 12–13.

152. *Argus,* Apr. 8, 1799.

153. "A Dialogue Between 1776 and 1796," *New York Journal,* Jan. 29, 1796.

154. Tunis Wortman to Albert Gallatin, Feb. 12, 1798, Gallatin Papers, N.-Y. Hist. Soc. For

the book see Leonard Levy, *Legacy of Suppression, Freedom of Speech and Press in Early American History* (Cambridge, Mass., 1960), pp. 283–89.

155. Warner, *Means for the Preservation*, pp. 9, 19; in the same pro-constitution vein see Samuel L. Mitchill, *An Address . . . July 4, 1799* (New York, 1800), pp. 7, 20; Matthew L. Davis, *An Oration . . . July 4, 1800* (New York, 1800), 15; for a hint of the old anti-Federalist attitude, George Eacker, *An Oration . . . July 4, 1801* (New York, 1801), pp. 10–11, all delivered before the several societies.

156. Beard, *op. cit.*, p. 466; Jefferson to Thomas Mann Randolph, May 6, 1793, Paul L. Ford, ed., *The Writings of Thomas Jefferson* (10 vols., New York, 1892–1899), VI, p. 241.

Andrew Jackson's Indian policy: a reassessment

F. P. PRUCHA

In the past, Prucha's* article would have been considered a thoroughly standard mainstream interpretation of Indian-white relations. Today, when there is greater sensitivity to the existence of white racism and cultural genocide, his analysis is somewhat of an anomaly. Perhaps the most instructive aspect of his article is that it was published by the most prestigious journal of United States history as recently as December 1969.

Prucha's thesis is that contemporary historians have unfairly condemned Andrew Jackson's Indian policy. In support of that contention, Prucha affirms what the enemies of the Indians have agreed from the beginning: American settlers had a God-given right to Indian lands. Indian claims to their territory, like Indian claims to their own culture and nationality, were absurd. Jackson merely mopped up the situation because his predecessors were too weak to do so.

Finally, Prucha's contention that Jackson's Indian policies enabled the federal government to avoid a "head-on collision with a state" is indeed dubious. A far more plausible interpretation indicates that Georgia's ability to defy the law of the land with impunity encouraged Mississippi and several other states to do likewise. That decision, probably more than either the Kentucky Resolutions of 1799 or South Carolina's tariff nullification of 1832, helped to pave the road toward secession and civil war.

A great many persons—not excluding some notable historians—have adopted a "devil theory" of American Indian policy. And in their demonic hierarchy Andrew Jackson has first place. He is depicted primarily, if not exclusively, as a western frontiersman and famous Indian fighter, who was a zealous advocate of dispossessing the Indians and at heart an "Indian-hater." When he became President, the story goes, he made use of his new power, ruthlessly and at the point of a bayonet, to force the Indians from their ancestral homes in the East into desert lands west of the Mississippi, which were considered forever useless to the white man.[1]

This simplistic view of Jackson's Indian policy is unacceptable. It was not Jackson's aim to crush the Indians because, as an old Indian fighter, he hated Indians. Although his years in the West had brought him into frequent contact with the Indians, he by no means developed a doctrinaire anti-Indian attitude. Rather, as a military man, his dominant goal in the decades before he became

F. P. Prucha, "Andrew Jackson's Indian Policy: A Reassessment," The Journal of American History, LVI (December 1969), 527–539.

*The author is Professor of History in Marquette University.

President was to preserve the security and well-being of the United States and its Indian and white inhabitants. His military experience, indeed, gave him an overriding concern for the safety of the nation from foreign rather than internal enemies, and to some extent the anti-Indian sentiment that has been charged against Jackson in his early career was instead basically anti-British. Jackson, as his first biographer pointed out, had "many private reasons for disliking" Great Britain. "In her, he could trace the efficient cause, why, in early life, he had been left forlorn and wretched, without a single relation in the world."[2] His frontier experience, too, had convinced him that foreign agents were behind the raised tomahawks of the red men. In 1808, after a group of settlers had been killed by the Creeks, Jackson told his militia troups: "[T]his brings to our recollection the horrid barbarity committed on our frontier in 1777 under the influence of and by the orders of Great Britain, and it is presumeable that the same influence has excited those barbarians to the late and recent acts of butchery and murder. . . ."[3] From that date on there is hardly a statement by Jackson about Indian dangers that does not aim sharp barbs at England. His reaction to the Battle of Tippecanoe was that the Indians had been "excited to war by the secrete agents of Great Britain."[4]

Jackson's war with the Creeks in 1813–1814, which brought him his first national military fame, and his subsequent demands for a large cession of Creek lands were part of his concern for security in the West.[5] In 1815, when the Cherokees and Chickasaws gave up their .overlapping claims to lands within the Creek cession, Jackson wrote with some exultation to Secretary of War James Monroe: "This Territory added to the creek cession, opens an avenue to the defence of the lower country, in a political point of view incalculable."[6] A few months later he added: "The sooner these lands are brought into markett, [the sooner] a permanant security will be given to what, I deem, the most important, as well as the most vulnarable part of the union. This country once settled, our fortifications of defence in the lower country compleated, all [E]urope will cease to look at it with an eye to conquest. There is no other point of the union (america united) that combined [E]urope can expect to invade with success."[7]

Jackson's plans with regard to the Indians in Florida were governed by similar principles of security. He wanted "to concentrate and locate the F[lorida] Indians at such a point as will promote their happiness and prosperity and at the same time, afford to that Territory a dense population between them and the ocean which will afford protection and peace to all."[8] On later occasions the same views were evident. When negotiations were under way with the southern Indians for removal, Jackson wrote: "[T]he chickasaw and choctaw country are of great importance to us in the defence of the lower country[;] a white population instead of the Indian, would strengthen our own defence much." And again: "This section of country is of great importance to the prosperty and strength of the lower Mississippi[;] a dense white population would add much to its safety in a state of war, and it ought to be obtained, if it can, on any thing like reasonable terms."[9]

In his direct dealings with the Indians, Jackson insisted on justice toward both hostile and peaceful Indians. Those who committed outrages against the whites were to be summarily punished, but the rights of friendly Indians were to be protected. Too much of Jackson's reputation in Indian matters has been based on the first of these positions. Forthright and hard-hitting, he adopted a no-nonsense policy toward hostile Indians that endeared him to the frontiers-men. For example, when a white woman was taken captive by the Creeks, he declared: "With such arms and supplies as I can obtain I shall penetrate the creek Towns, until the Captive, with her Captors are delivered up, and think myself Justifiable, in laying waste their villiages, burning their houses, killing their warriors and leading into Captivity their wives and children, untill I do obtain a surrender of the Captive, and the Captors."[10] In his general orders to the Tennessee militia after he received news of the Fort Mims massacre, he called for "retaliatory vengeance" against the "inhuman blood thirsty barbar-ians."[11] He could speak of the "lex taliones,"[12] and his aggressive campaign against the Creeks and his escapade in Florida in the First Seminole War are further indications of his mood.

But he matched this attitude with one of justice and fairness, and he was firm in upholding the rights of the Indians who lived peaceably in friendship with the Americans. One of his first official acts as major general of the Tennessee militia was to insist on the punishment of a militia officer who instigated or at least permitted the murder of an Indian.[13] On another occasion, when a group of Tennessee volunteers robbed a friendly Cherokee, Jackson's wrath burst forth: "that a sett of men should without any authority rob a man who is claimed as a member of the Cherokee nation, who is now friendly and engaged with us in a war against the hostile creeks, is such an outrage, to the rules of war, the laws of nations and of civil society, and well calculated to sower the minds of the whole nation against the united States, and is such as ought to meet with the frowns of every good citizen, and the agents be promptly prosecuted and punished as robers." It was, he said, as much theft as though the property had been stolen from a white citizen. He demanded an inquiry in order to determine whether any commissioned officers had been present or had had any knowledge of this "atrocious act," and he wanted the officers immediately arrested, tried by court-martial, and then turned over to the civil authority.[14]

Again, during the Seminole War, when Georgia troops attacked a village of friendly Indians, Jackson excoriated the governor for "the base, cowardly and inhuman attack, on the old woman [women] and men of the chehaw village, whilst the Warriors of that *village* was with me, fighting the battles of our *country* against the common enemy." It was strange, he said, "that there could exist within the U. States, a cowardly monster in human shape, that could violate the sanctity of a flag, when borne by any person, but more particularly when in the hands of a superanuated Indian chief worn down with age. Such base cowardice and murderous conduct as this transaction affords, has not its paralel in history and should meet with its merited punishment." Jackson ordered the arrest of the officer who was responsible and declared: "This act will to the last ages fix a stain upon the character of Georgia."[15]

Jackson's action as commander of the Division of the South in removing white squatters from Indian lands is another proof that he was not oblivious to Indian rights. When the Indian Agent Return J. Meigs in 1820 requested military assistance in removing intruders on Cherokee lands, Jackson ordered a detachment of twenty men under a lieutenant to aid in the removal. After learning that the officer detailed for the duty was "young and inexperienced," he sent his own aide-de-camp, Captain Richard K. Call, to assume command of the troops and execute the order of removal.[16] "Captain Call informs me," he wrote in one report to Secretary of War John C. Calhoun, "that much noise of opposition was threatened, and men collected for the purpose who seperated on the approach of the regulars, but who threaten to destroy the cherokees in the Valley as soon as these Troops are gone. Capt. Call has addressed a letter to those infatuated people, with assurance of speedy and exemplary punishment if they should attempt to carry their threats into execution." Later he wrote that Call had performed his duties "with both judgement, and prudence and much to the interest of the Cherokee-Nation" and that the action would "have the effect in future of preventing the infraction of our Treaties with that Nation."[17]

To call Jackson an Indian-hater or to declare that he believed that "the only good Indian is a dead Indian" is to speak in terms that had little meaning to Jackson.[18] It is true, of course, that he did not consider the Indians to be noble savages. He had, for example, a generally uncomplimentary view of their motivation, and he argued that it was necessary to operate upon their fears, rather than on some higher motive. Thus, in 1812 he wrote: "I believe self interest and self preservation the most predominant passion. [F]ear is better than love with an indian."[19] Twenty-five years later, just after he left the presidency, the same theme recurred; and he wrote: "long experience satisfies me that they are only to be well governed by their fears. If we feed their avarice we accelerate the causes of their destruction. By a prudent exertion of our military power we may yet do something to alleviate their condition at the same time that we certainly take from them the means of injury to our frontier."[20]

Yet Jackson did not hold that Indians were inherently evil or inferior. He eagerly used Indian allies, personally liked and respected individual Indian chiefs, and, when (in the Creek campaign) an orphaned Indian boy was about to be killed by Indians upon whom his care would fall, generously took care of the child and sent him home to Mrs. Jackson to be raised with his son Andrew.[21] Jackson was convinced that the barbaric state in which he encountered most Indians had to change, but he was also convinced that the change was possible and to an extent inevitable if the Indians were to survive.

Much of Jackson's opinion about the status of the Indians was governed by his firm conviction that they did not constitute sovereign nations, who could be dealt with in formal treaties as though they were foreign powers. That the United States in fact did so, Jackson argued, was a historical fact which resulted from the feeble position of the new American government when it first faced the Indians during and immediately after the Revolution. To continue to deal with the Indians in this fashion, when the power of the United States no longer made it necessary, was to Jackson's mind absurd. It was high time, he said in 1820, to do away with the "farce of treating with Indian tribes."[22] Jackson wanted Congress to legislate for the Indians as it did for white Americans.

From this view of the limited political status of the Indians within the territorial United States, Jackson derived two important corollaries. One denied that the Indians had absolute title to all the lands that they claimed. The United States, in justice, should allow the Indians ample lands for their support, but Jackson did not believe that they were entitled to more. He denied any right of domain and ridiculed the Indian claims to "tracts of country on which they have neither dwelt nor made improvements, merely because they have seen them from the mountain or passed them in the chase."[23]

A second corollary of equal import was Jackson's opinion that the Indians could not establish independent enclaves (exercising full political sovereignty) within the United States or within any of the individual states. If their proper status was as subjects of the United States, then they should be obliged to submit to American laws. Jackson had reached this conclusion early in his career, but his classic statement appeared in his first annual message to Congress, at a time when the conflict between the Cherokees and the State of Georgia had reached crisis proportions. "If the General Government is not permitted to tolerate the erection of a confederate State within the territory of one of the members of this Union against her consent," he said, "much less could it allow a foreign and independent government to establish itself there." He announced that he had told the Indians that "their attempt to establish an independent government would not be countenanced by the Executive of the United States, and advised them to emigrate beyond the Mississippi or submit to the laws of those States."[24] "I have been unable to perceive any sufficient reason," Jackson affirmed, "why the Red man more than the white, may claim exemption from the municipal laws of the state within which they reside; and governed by that belief, I have so declared and so acted."[25]

Jackson's own draft of this first annual message presents a more personal view than the final public version and gives some insight into his reasoning. He wrote:

The policy of the government has been gradually to open to them the ways of civilisation; and from their wandering habits, to entice them to a course of life calculated to present fairer prospects of comfort and happiness. To effect this a system should be devised for their benefit, kind and liberal, and gradually to be enlarged as they may envince a capability to enjoy it. It will not answer to encourage them to the idea of exclusive self government. It is impracticable. No people were ever free, or capable of forming and carrying into execution a social compact for themselves until education and intelligence was first introduced. There are with those tribes, a few educated and well informed men, possessing mind and Judgment, and capable of conducting public affairs to advantage; but observation proves that the great body of the southern tribes of Indians, are erratic in their habits, and wanting in those endowments, which are suited to a people who would direct themselves, and under it be happy and prosperous.[26]

Jackson was convinced from his observation of the political incompetence of the general run of Indians that the treaty system played into the hands of the chiefs and their white and half-breed advisers to the detriment of the common Indians. He said on one occasion that such leaders "are like some of our bawling politicians, who loudly exclaim we are the friends of the people, but who, when the[y] obtain their views care no more for the happiness or wellfare of the people than the Devil does—but each procure[s] influence through the same channell and for the same base purpose, *self-agrandisement.*"[27]

Jackson was genuinely concerned for the well-being of the Indians and for their civilization. Although his critics would scoff at the idea of placing him on the roll of the humanitarians, his assertions—both public and private—add up to a consistent belief that the Indians were capable of accepting white civilization, the hope that they would eventually do so, and repeated efforts to take measures that would make the change possible and even speed it along.

His vision appears in the proclamation delivered to his victorious troops in April 1814, after the Battle of Horseshoe Bend on the Tallapoosa River. "The fiends of the Tallapoosa will no longer murder our Women and Children, or disturb the quiet of our borders," he declared. "Their midnight flambeaux will no more illumine their Council house, or shine upon the victim of their infernal orgies. They have disappeared from the face of the Earth. In their places a new generation will arise who will know their duties better. The weapons of warfare will be exchanged for the utensils of husbandry; and the wilderness which now withers in sterility and seems to mourn the disolation which overspreads it, will blossom as the rose, and become the nursery of the arts."[28]

The removal policy, begun long before Jackson's presidency but wholeheartedly adopted by him, was the culmination of these views. Jackson looked upon removal as a means of protecting the process of civilization, as well as of providing land for white settlers, security from foreign invasion, and a quieting of the clamors of Georgia against the federal government. This view is too pervasive in Jackson's thought to be dismissed as polite rationalization for avaricious white aggrandizement. His outlook was essentially Jeffersonian. Jackson envisaged the transition from a hunting society to a settled agricultural society, a process that would make it possible for the Indians to exist with a higher scale of living on less land, and which would make it possible for those who adopted white ways to be quietly absorbed into the white society. Those who wished to preserve their identity in Indian nations could do it only by withdrawing from the economic and political pressures exerted upon their enclaves by the dominant white settlers. West of the Mississippi they might move at their own pace toward civilization.[29]

Evaluation of Jackson's policy must be made in the light of the feasible alternatives available to men of his time. The removal program cannot be judged simply as a land grab to satisfy the President's western and southern constituents. The Indian problem that Jackson faced was complex, and various solutions were proposed. There were, in fact, four possibilities.

First, the Indians could simply have been destroyed. They could have been killed in war, mercilessly hounded out of their settlements, or pushed west off the land by brute force, until they were destroyed by disease or starvation. It is not too harsh a judgment to say that this was implicitly, if not explicitly, the policy of many of the aggressive frontiersmen. But it was not the policy, implicit or explicit, of Jackson and the responsible government officials in his administration or of those preceding or following his. It would be easy to compile an anthology of statements of horror on the part of government officials toward any such approach to the solution of the Indian problem.

Second, the Indians could have been rapidly assimilated into white society. It is now clear that this was not a feasible solution. Indian culture has a viability that continually impresses anthropologists, and to become white men was not the goal of the Indians. But many important and learned men of the day thought that this was a possiblilty. Some were so sanguine as to hope that within one generation the Indians could be taught the white man's ways and that, once they learned them, they would automatically desire to turn to that sort of life. Thomas Jefferson never tired of telling the Indians of the advantages of farming over hunting, and the chief purpose of schools was to train the Indian children in white ways, thereby making them immediately absorbable into the dominant culture. This solution was at first the hope of humanitarians who had the interest of the Indians at heart, but little by little many came to agree with Jackson that this dream was not going to be fulfilled.

Third, if the Indians were not to be destroyed and if they could not be immediately assimilated, they might be protected in their own culture on their ancestral lands in the East—or, at least, on reasonably large remnants of those lands. They would then be enclaves within the white society and would be protected by their treaty agreements and by military force. This was the alternative demanded by the opponents of Jackson's removal bill—for example, the missionaries of the American Board of Commissioners for Foreign Missions.

But this, too, was infeasible, given the political and military conditions of the United States at the time. The federal government could not have provided a standing army of sufficient strength to protect the enclaves of Indian territory from the encroachments of the whites. Jackson could not withstand Georgia's demands for the end of the *imperium in imperio* represented by the Cherokee Nation and its new constitution, not because of some inherent immorality on his part but because the political situation of America would not permit it.

The jurisdictional dispute cannot be easily dismissed. Were the Indian tribes independent nations? The question received its legal answer in John Marshall's decision in *Cherokee Nation v. Georgia*, in which the chief justice defined the Indian tribes as "dependent domestic nations." But aside from the juridical decision, were the Indians, in fact, independent, and could they have maintained their independence without the support—political and military—of the federal government? The answer, clearly, is no, as writers at the time pointed out. The federal government could have stood firm in defense of the Indian nations against Georgia, but this would have brought it into head-on collision with a state, which insisted that its sovereignty was being impinged upon by the Cherokees.

This was not a conflict that anyone in the federal government wanted. President Monroe had been slow to give in to the demands of the Georgians. He had refused to be panicked into hasty action before he had considered all the possibilities. But eventually he became convinced that a stubborn resistance to the southern states would solve nothing, and from that point on he and his successors, John Quincy Adams and Jackson, sought to solve the problem by removing the cause. They wanted the Indians to be placed in some area where the problem of federal versus state jurisdiction would not arise, where the Indians could be granted land in fee simple by the federal government and not have to worry about what some state thought were its rights and prerogatives.[30]

The fourth and final possibility, then, was removal. To Jackson this seemed the only answer. Since neither adequate protection nor quick assimilation of the Indians was possible, it seemed reasonable and necessary to move the Indians to some area where they would not be disturbed by federal-state jurisdictional disputes or by encroachments of white settlers, where they could develop on the road to civilization at their own pace, or, if they so desired, preserve their own culture.

To ease the removal process Jackson proposed what he repeatedly described as—and believed to be—*liberal* terms. He again and again urged the commissioners who made treaties to pay the Indians well for their lands, to make sure that the Indians understood that the government would pay the costs of removal and help them get established in their new homes, to make provision for the Indians to examine the lands in the West and to agree to accept them before they were allotted.[31] When he read the treaty negotiated with the Chickasaws in 1832, he wrote to his old friend General John Coffee, one of the commissioners: "I think it is a good one, and surely the religious enthusiasts, or those who have been weeping over the oppression of the Indians will not find fault with it for want of liberality or justice to the Indians."[32] Typical of his views was his letter to Captain James Gadsden in 1829:

You may rest assured that I shall adhere to the just and humane policy towards the Indians which I have commenced. In this spirit I have recommended them to quit their possessions on this side of the Mississippi, and go to a country to the west where there is every probability that they will always be free from the mercenary influence of White men, and undisturbed by the local authority of the states: Under such circumstances the General Government can exercise a parental control over their interests and possibly perpetuate their race.[33]

The idea of parental or paternal care was pervasive. Jackson told Congress in a special message in February 1832: "Being more and more convinced that the destiny of the Indians within the settled portion of the United States depends upon their entire and speedy migration to the country west of the Mississippi set apart for their permanent residence, I am anxious that all the arrangements necessary to the complete execution of the plan of removal and to the ultimate security and improvement of the Indians should be made without further delay." Once removal was accomplished, "there would then be no question of jurisdiction to prevent the Government from exercising such a general control over their affairs as may be essential to their interest and safety."[34]

Jackson, in fact, thought in terms of a confederacy of the southern Indians in the West, developing their own territorial government which should be on a par with the territories of the whites and eventually take its place in the Union.[35] This aspect of the removal policy, because it was not fully implemented, has been largely forgotten.

In the bills reported in 1834 for the reorganization of Indian affairs there was, in addition to a new trade and intercourse act and an act for the reorganization of the Indian Office, a bill "for the establishment of the Western Territory, and for the security and protection of the emigrant and other Indian tribes therein." This was quashed, not by western interests who might be considered hostile to the Indians, but by men like John Quincy Adams, who did not like the technical details of the bill and who feared loss of eastern power and prestige by the admission of territories in the West.[36]

Jackson continued to urge Congress to fulfill its obligations to the Indians who had removed. In his eighth annual message, in December 1836, he called attention "to the importance of providing a well-digested and comprehensive system for the protection, supervision, and improvement of the various tribes now planted in the Indian country." He strongly backed the suggestions of the commissioner of Indian affairs and the secretary of war for developing a confederated Indian government in the West and for establishing military posts in the Indian country to protect the tribes. "The best hopes of humanity in regard to the aboriginal race, the welfare of our rapidly extending settlements, and the honor of the United States," he said, "are all deeply involved in the relations existing between this Government and the emigrating tribes."[37]

Jackson's Indian policy occasioned great debate and great opposition during his administration. This is not to be wondered at. The "Indian problem" was a complicated and emotion-filled subject, and it called forth tremendous efforts on behalf of the Indians by some missionary groups and other humanitarians, who spoke loudly about Indian rights. The issue also became a party one.

The hue and cry raised against removal in Jackson's administration should not be misinterpreted. At the urging of the American Board of Commissioners for Foreign Missions, hundreds of church groups deluged Congress with memorials condemning the removal policy as a violation of Indian rights; and Jeremiah Evarts, the secretary of the Board, wrote a notable series of essays under the name "William Penn," which asserted that the original treaties must be maintained.[38] It is not without interest that such opposition was centered in areas that were politically hostile to Jackson. There were equally sincere and humanitarian voices speaking out in support of removal, and they were supported by men such as Thomas L. McKenney, head of the Indian Office; William Clark, superintendent of Indian affairs at St. Louis; Lewis Cass, who had served on the frontier for eighteen years as governor of Michigan Territory; and the Baptist missionary Isaac McCoy—all men with long experience in Indian relations and deep sympathy for the Indians.

Jackson himself had no doubt that his policy was in the best interests of the Indians. "Toward this race of people I entertain the kindest feelings," he told the Senate in 1831, "and am not sensible that the views which I have taken of their true interests are less favorable to them than those which oppose their emigration to the West."[39] The policy of rescuing the Indians from the evil effects of too-close contact with white civilization, so that in the end they too might become civilized, received a final benediction in Jackson's last message to the American people—his "Farewell Address" of March 4, 1837. "The States which had so long been retarded in their improvement by the Indian tribes residing in the midst of them are at length relieved from the evil," he said, "and this unhappy race—the original dwellers in our land—are now placed in a situation where we may well hope that they will share in the blessings of civilization and be saved from that degradation and destruction to which they were rapidly hastening while they remained in the States; and while the safety and comfort of our own citizens have been greatly promoted by their removal, the philanthropist will rejoice that the remnant of that ill-fated race has been at length placed beyond the reach of injury or oppression, and that the paternal care of the General Government will hereafter watch over them and protect them."[40]

In assessing Jackson's Indian policy, historians must not listen too eagerly to Jackson's political opponents or to less-than-disinterested missionaries. Jackson's contemporary critics and the historians who have accepted their arguments have certainly been too harsh, if not, indeed, quite wrong.

NOTES

1. Typical examples of this view are Oscar Handlin, *A History of the United States* (2 vols., New York, 1967-1968), I, 445; T. Harry Williams, Richard N. Current, and Frank Freidel, *A History of the United States* (2 vols., New York, l964), I, 392; Thomas A. Bailey, *The American Pageant: A History of the Republic* (3rd. ed., New York, 1966), 269; Dale Van Every, *Disinherited: The Lost Birthright of the American Indian* (New York, 1966), l03; R. S. Cotterill, "Federal Indian Management in the South, 1789-1825," *Mississippi Valley Historical Review*, XX (Dec. 1933), 347.

2. John H. Eaton, *The Life of Andrew Jackson, Major General in the Service of the United States: Comprising a History of the War in the South, from the Commencement of the Creek Campaign, to the Termination of Hostilities Before New Orleans* (Philadelphia, 1817), 18.

3. John Spencer Bassett, ed., *Correspondence of Andrew Jackson* (7 vols., Washington, 1926-1935), I, 188.

4. Andrew Jackson to William Henry Harrison, Nov. 30, 1811, *ibid.*, 210. See also Jackson to James Winchester, Nov. 28, 1811; Jackson to Willie Blount, June 4, July 10, and Dec. 21, 1812; Jackson to Thomas Pinckney, May 18, 1814, *ibid.*, I, 209, 226, 231-32, 250, II, 3-4.

5. For the part played by desire for defense and security in the Treaty of Fort Jackson, see Jackson to Pinckney, May 18, 1814, *ibid.*, II, 2-3, and Eaton, *Life of Jackson*, 183-87. Eaton's biography can be taken as representing Jackson's views.

6. Jackson to James Monroe, Oct. 23, 1816, Bassett, *Correspondence*, II, 261.

7. Jackson to Monroe, Jan. 6, 1817, *ibid.*, 272. See also Jackson to Monroe, March 4, 1817, *ibid.*, 277-78.

8. Jackson to John C. Calhoun, Aug. 1823, *ibid.*, III, 202. See also Jackson's talk with Indian chieftains, Sept. 20, 1821, *ibid.*, 118.

9. Jackson to John Coffee, Aug. 20, 1826; Jackson to Coffee, Sept. 2, 1826, *ibid.*, 310, 312. See also Fred L. Israel, ed., *The State of the Union Messages of the Presidents, 1790-1966* (3 vols., New York, 1966), I, 334.

10. Jackson to Blount, July 3, 1812, Bassett, *Correspondence*, I, 230.

11. General Orders, Sept. 19, 1813, *ibid.*, 319-20.

12. Jackson to David Holmes, April 18, 1814, *ibid.*, 505.

13. Jackson to Colonel McKinney, May 10, 1802, *ibid.*, 62.

14. Jackson to John Cocke, Dec. 28, 1813, *ibid.*, 415.

15. Jackson to Governor of Georgia, May 7, 1818, *ibid.*, II, 369-70.

16. Jackson to Calhoun, July 9, 1820, *ibid.*, III, 29. See also Jackson's notice to the intruders, *ibid.*, 26n.

17. Jackson to Calhoun, July 26, Sept. 15, 1820, *ibid.*, 30-31, 31n.

18. Note this recent statement: "President Jackson, himself a veteran Indian fighter, wasted little sympathy on the paint-bedaubed 'varmints.' He accepted fully the brutal creed of his fellow Westerners that 'the only good Indian is a dead Indian.'" Bailey, *American Pageant*, 269.

19. Jackson to Blount, June 17, 1812, Bassett, *Correspondence*, I, 227-28.

20. Jackson to Joel R. Poinsett, Aug. 27, 1837, *ibid.*, V, 507.

21. See Jackson to Mrs. Jackson, Dec. 19, 1813, *ibid.*, I, 400-01; Eaton, *Life of Jackson*, 395-96.

22. Jackson to Calhoun, Sept. 2, 1820, Bassett, *Correspondence*, III, 31-32. See also Jackson to John Quincy Adams, Oct. 6, 1821; Jackson to Calhoun, Sept. 17, 1821, Walter Lowrie and Walter S. Franklin, eds., *American State Papers: Miscellaneous* (2 vols., Washington, 1834), II, 909, 911-12.

23. Israel, *State of the Union Messages*, I, 310. See also Jackson to Isaac Shelby, Aug. 11, 1818, Bassett, *Correspondence*, II, 388.

24. Israel, *State of the Union Messages*, I, 308-09. Jackson dealt at length with this question in his message to the Senate, Feb. 22, 1831. James D. Richardson, ed., *A Compilation of the Messages and Papers of the Presidents* (11 vols., Washington, 1897-1914), II, 536-41. See also Jackson to Secretary of War [1831?], Bassett, *Correspondence*, IV, 219-20.

25. Draft of Second Annual Message, Series 8, vol. 174, nos. 1409-1410, Andrew Jackson Papers (Manuscript Division, Library of Congress). This statement does not appear in the final version.

26. Draft of First Annual Message, Dec. 8, 1829, Bassett, *Correspondence*, IV, 103-104.

27. Jackson to Robert Butler, June 21, 1817, *ibid.*, II, 299. See also Jackson to Coffee, June 21, 1817; U. S. Commissioners to Secretary Graham, July 8, 1817, *ibid.*, 198, 300.

28. Proclamation, April 2, 1814, *ibid.*, I, 494.

29. Israel, *State of the Union Messages*, I, 310, 335, 354, 386-87.

30. For the development of the removal idea see Annie Heloise Abel, "The History of Events Resulting in Indian Consolidation West of the Mississippi," *Annual Report of the American Historical Association for the Year 1906* (2 vols., Washington, 1908), I, 233-450; Francis Paul Prucha, *American Indian Policy in the Formative Years: The Indian Trade and Intercourse Acts, 1790-1834* (Cambridge, 1962), 224-49.

31. See, for example, Jackson to Coffee [Sept. 1826?], Bassett, *Correspondence*, III, 315-16.

32. Jackson to Coffee, Nov. 6, 1832, *ibid.*, IV, 483.

33. Jackson to James Gadsden, Oct. 12, 1829, *ibid.*, 81.

34. Richardson, *Messages and Papers of the Presidents*, II, 565-66.

35. Jackson to Coffee, Feb. 19, 1832; Jackson to John D. Terrill, July 29, 1826, Bassett, *Correspondence*, IV, 406, III, 308-09.

36. Prucha, *American Indian Policy in the Formative Years*, 269-73.

37. Israel, *State of the Union Messages*, I, 465-66.

38. See the indexes to the *House Journal*, 21 Cong., 1 Sess. (Serial 194), 897–98, and the *Senate Journal*, 21 Cong., 1 Sess. (Serial 191), 534, for the presentation of the memorials. Some of the memorials were ordered printed and appear in the serial set of congressional documents. Jeremiah Evarts' essays were published in book form as [Jeremiah Evarts,] *Essays on the Present Crisis in the Condition of the American Indians; First Published in the National Intelligencer, Under the Signature of William Penn* (Boston, 1829).

39. Richardson, *Messages and Papers of the Presidents*, II, 541.

40. *Ibid.*, III, 294. See the discussion in John William Ward, *Andrew Jackson: Symbol for an Age* (New York, 1955), 40–41.

in pursuit of property: the dispossession of the American Indian

BLANCHE WIESEN COOK

Despite the renewed interest in white-Indian relations, the full story of the cruelty and greed that accompanied every stage of Indian subjugation has yet to be told. Just as we systematically pushed the Indians out of our expansionist path, so we have removed them from our books—except as foils against which to measure the bravery of our pioneers. In the essay that follows, Blanche Wiesen Cook seeks to redress the balance. Sparing no feeling for the racism of those who did not even consider Indians to be human, she indicts the incredible arrogance with which America took possession of the continent. Expansion left in its wake a legacy of brutality and a heritage that exalted the value of property above the cost of human life.

The natives of North America never understood the nature of the white man's greed for land. Land was sacred to the Indians and they did not comprehend private ownership of God's possessions. With much territory already lost through scores of treaties made and broken, Tecumseh, a Shawnee chief, sought to organize a fighting alliance of all Indian tribes from Canada to Florida.

In 1792 the government sent the tribes a message that President George Washington wanted to assure them that it was not his intent to deprive the Indians of their lands and called a peace council with thirteen tribes. At the council the commissioners offered the tribes money for their lands; but the Indians rejected the offer. Tecumseh declared: "Sell land! As well sell air and water. The Great Spirit gave them in common to all. . . ."[1] The Indians had an alternate plan—give the money offered them to the settlers:

Money to us is of no value, and to most of us unknown . . .
We know that these settlers are poor, or they would never have ventured to live in a country which has been in continual trouble ever since they crossed the Ohio. Divide, therefore, this large sum of money which you have offered us among these people; give to each, also, a proportion of what you say you would give to us annually . . . , and we are persuaded they would most readily accept of it in lieu of the lands you sold them. If you add, also, the great sums you must expend in raising the paying armies with a view to force us to yield you our country, you will certainly have more than sufficient for the purpose of repaying these settlers for all their labor. . . .
. . . Our only demand is the peaceable possession of a small part of our once great country

. . . review the lands from whence we have been driven to this spot, we can retreat no farther, because the country behind hardly affords food for its inhabitants. . . .

After the meeting, the commissioners notified the governor of the Northwest Territory that the Indians had "refused to make peace." Major General Anthony Wayne wrote the secretary of war that the western frontiers were endangered and "the dignity and interest of the nation . . . forbid a retrograde maneouvre, or giving up one inch of the ground we now possess. . . ."[2]

Tecumseh's alliance fought Wayne and 3,600 troops all the way to Cincinnati. But the Indians were routed in the Battle of Fallen Timbers in August 1794. Wayne "destroyed every Indian village he could find" and built Fort Wayne, Indiana.[3] The general described one of the villages he leveled: It had "very extensive and highly cultivated fields and gardens. . . . The margins of those beautiful rivers . . . appear like one continued village for a number of miles, . . . nor have I ever before beheld such immense fields of corn in any part of America, from Canada to Florida." But he burned the villages, and all the crops were cut and destroyed.[4]

The war was concluded by the Treaty of Greenville whereby the United States received two-thirds of Ohio to be sold to settlers; much of Indiana and Michigan; and sixteen important areas in the Northwest, including the sites of Detroit, Toledo, Peoria, and Chicago. In return, the Indians got $20,000 and the promise of annuities. Tecumseh refused to attend the council that drew up this agreement and split with the chiefs who agreed to it. But as settlers poured into the territory he, too, left the Ohio country and moved westward to Indiana.

John Randolph of Roanoke pointed out that the Treaty of Greenville provided America with "more land than it could sell or use" for fifty years. Randolph disapproved of "the want of moderation" and the "blind cupidity" which seemed to drive America on and resulted in Indian enmity.[5] But the clamor for yet more territory did not abate. John Quincy Adams, for example, argued that America was growing rapidly and needed to acquire territory for future generations. Governor William Henry Harrison, of the recently organized Indiana Territory, asked if "one of the fairest portions of the globe [was] to remain in a state of nature, the haunt of a few wretched savages, when it seems destined by the Creator to give support to a large population and to be the seat of civilization, of science, and of true religion?"[6]

By 1800, the Treaty of Greenville was violated regularly. Tenskwatawa, the Prophet, and his twin brother Tecumseh (whose real name was Tecumtha which, in Shawnee, means "panther lying in wait") again tried to establish Indian unity to secure their remaining lands.[7] They traveled north and south and as far west as Wisconsin for support. Everywhere Tecumseh went his message was the same:

Are we not being stripped, day by day, of the little that remains of our ancient liberty? . . . Do they not even now kick and strike us as they do their blackfaces? How long will it be before they tie us to a post and whip us and make us work for them in corn fields? . . . Shall we wait for that moment or shall we die fighting before submitting to such ignominy?[8]

But many tribal chiefs insisted that the best way to ensure peace was to continue to submit grievances to the Congress. Shawnee ethics played a certain role in Tecumseh's failure to achieve a strong alliance of all Indians. The two basic rules of the Shawnee were: "Do not kill or injure your neighbor, for it is not him that you injure, you injure yourself." "Do not wrong or hate your neighbor, for it is not him that you wrong, you wrong yourself. Maneto, the Grandmother, the Supreme Being, loves him also as she loves you."[9]

By 1809 there were 20,000 Americans in Indiana campaigning for statehood and still more Indian land. Since much of the Ohio Valley bordered on British territory, the British and the Indians were allied in the tense months before the outbreak of the War of 1812. There were strong pressures on Harrison to prevent a violent confrontation at that time. Harrison therefore agreed to meet with Tecumseh, who repeated the Indian philosophy of land ownership: "No tribe has a right to sell, even to each other; much less to strangers, who demand all, and will take no less . . . . sell a country! why not sell the air, the clouds and the great sea, as well as the earth?"

But Harrison would make no concessions. Although he reported to the War Department the Indian complaint that "Americans had driven them from the seacoast, and would shortly, if not stopped, push them into the lakes," he did not include any plans for conciliation or moderation. In fact, he decided to force the issue. Bypassing Tecumseh altogether, he called a group of old and pacifistic chiefs to Fort Wayne while Tecumseh was recruiting for his alliance in the South. Harrison "mellowed" the chiefs with liquor; pressured and possibly threatened them and, for $7,500 in cash and a promised annuity of $1,750, they ceded three million acres of Indiana, much of which belonged to tribes not even represented at the meeting. Tecumseh was furious and in 1810 his league of Wyandots, Creeks, Choctaws, and a force of 1,100 Sauk, Fox, and Winnebagos mobilized to save their lands.[10]

On November 6, 1811, Harrison decided to smash Tecumseh's village, Prophetown, on the mouth of the Tippecanoe River and be forever free of this threat to his ambition for land and political power. But Tecumseh and most of his warriors were away and after only two days of battle, Harrison moved unopposed into an abandoned Prophetown, burned the buildings, and destroyed possessions and food. Between 25 and 40 Indians were killed; Harrison's forces suffered 61 soldiers dead and 127 wounded. It was not a glorious triumph; but, in the manner of Napoleon returning from Russia, Harrison announced that it had been a splendid victory and wrote to the secretary of war that "the Indians have never sustained so severe a defeat since their acquaintance with the white people." Many believed that he had defeated Tecumseh himself.[11] No matter, the propaganda was good enough to secure Harrison's election to the presidency in 1840, with Tyler too.

Tecumseh was killed in battle in 1812, and with him also died his dream of a united Indian confederacy that would establish a secure Indian nation in America. By 1818 the Indians of the Old Northwest Territory were removed from Ohio, Indiana, and Michigan. By 1833 the secretary of war could announce that "the country north of the Ohio, east of the Mississippi, including the States of Ohio, Indiana, Illinois, and the Territory of Michigan as far as the Fox and Wisconsin Rivers, [was] . . . cleared of the embarrassments of Indian relations. . . ." The Indian residents of these areas were among the first tribes to settle the territory designated and reserved for the Indians of all America in Oklahoma.

Many American statesmen regarded Indians as child-like creatures who lived in a state of innocence that required the protection of a wise and compassionate white father. These statesmen became, in their own eyes at least, the beneficent guardians who knew what was best for their charges. If Indians would listen and learn they might be permitted to live peacefully in a man's world.[12] Thomas Jefferson, for example, viewed the tragedy of Indian removal "with comiseration." In Jefferson's Second Inaugural Address, March 4, 1805, he explained why so many problems between civilized America and the aboriginal nations persisted:

Endowed with the faculties and the rights of men, breathing an ardent love of liberty and independence, and occupying a country which left them no desire but to be undisturbed, the stream of overflowing people from other regions directed itself on these shores; without power to divert or habits to contend against it, they have been overwhelmed by the current or driven before it; now reduced within limits too narrow for the hunter's state, humanity enjoins us to teach them agriculture and the domestic arts; . . . and to prepare them in time for that state of society which to bodily comforts adds the improvement of the mind and morals. We have, therefore, liberally furnished them with the implements of husbandry and house-hold use; we have placed among them instructors in the arts of first necessity, and they are covered with the aegis of the law against aggressors from among ourselves.

But the endeavors to enlighten them on the fate which awaits their present course of life, to induce them to exercise their reason, follow its dictates, and change their pursuits with the change of circumstances have powerful obstacles to encounter; they are combated by the habits of their bodies, prejudices of their mind, ignorance, pride, and the influence of interested and crafty individuals among them who feel themselves something in the present order of things and fear to become nothing in the other. These persons inculcate a sanctimonious reverence for the customs of their ancestors; that whatsoever they did must be done through all time; that reason is a false guide, and to advance under its counsel in their physical, moral or political condition is perilous innovation; that their duty is to remain as their Creator made them. . . . In short, my friends, among them also is seen the action and counteraction of good sense and of bigotry. . . .

Ignorant of or unsympathetic to Indian culture and religion, the paternalistic "friends" of the Indians engineered their destruction. Thomas Jefferson, John Calhoun, James Madison, and William H. Crawford all maintained that their programs were in the Indians' best interest. Although the son of an Indian fighter, Calhoun genuinely "liked" Indians and scandalized Washington social circles by inviting them to formal parties when he was secretary of war under James Monroe. Calhoun believed that Indians should be absorbed into the "mighty torrent of our civilization . . . our laws and manners." Long before the Dawes Act of 1887, he suggested that their tribal lands should be divided up among individual families, their tribal structure should be abandoned, the men should be compelled to learn farming skills and the women "cooking, sewing, and home-making."[13] As his predecessor William Crawford, secretary of war under James Madison, said in 1816: "no man will exert himself to procure the comforts of life unless his right to enjoy them is exclusive."[14]

But Americans wanted a homogeneous society free from the burden of alien Indians; and their assimilation into white man's culture, John Calhoun later concluded, was not in the Indians' best interests. It is difficult to know which came first: Calhoun's recognition that tribal culture was essential to the preservation of Indian life or the false reports of explorer Zebulon Pike that the entire area west of the 95th meridian was an arid wasteland "where the wind had thrown up the sand in all the fanciful forms of the ocean's rolling waves and on which not a speck of vegetable matter existed." At any rate, by 1823 most Americans believed the territory west of the 95th meridian was the great American desert, completely unfit for human habitation; and Calhoun substituted his plea for assimilation with a demand, urged first by Thomas Jefferson, that the Indians be removed to northern Wisconsin or beyond the Mississippi and Missouri rivers. Calhoun considered his policy entirely humane; it would unite all Indian tribes into one great nation where they would be out of the reach of the "sins and diseases of white men." And, to be successful, Calhoun declared, "force . . . must be used to prevent the whites from crossing the boundary line."[15]

James Monroe adopted the policy of his secretary of war. Many tribes were persuaded to leave for money, gifts, and the promise of freedom from white oppression. John Quincy Adams did not pursue this policy, and after several tribes appealed for protection from the harassment of state officials eager for their lands, he sent military support into the states to protect Indian rights. But, in 1830, Andrew Jackson became president and sent the federal troops home.

Removal was championed by Andrew Jackson's secretary of war, the former governor of Michigan Territory, Lewis Cass as an alternative to genocide—or the "utter extinction" of the Indians, which nineteenth century statesmen called "extermination."[16] But in practice the two policies were frequently mixed up. The history of the removal of the Cherokees is the best example of this process.

Cherokee lands were guaranteed by a federal treaty of 1791. But the state of Georgia regarded the treaty as obsolete. By 1828 America's frontier had moved across the Mississippi into Louisiana, Arkansas, and Missouri. Of the eastern tribes only 60,000 Cherokees, Creeks, Choctaws, and Chickasaws remained in the mountain country of Appalachia where Georgia, North Carolina, Tennessee, and Alabama converge. The Cherokee were peaceful farmers who bothered nobody. However, gold was found on their land in 1828 and everybody wanted their property. In 1829 Georgia appropriated all Indian land within the state, declared all Cherokee laws null and void, forbade Indians from testifying in court against whites, and distributed Indian lands to settlers on a lottery system.[17] Georgia's Governor George Gilmer addressed himself specifically to the question of prior treaties made with Indians and dismissed them in the terms of the New England Puritans: they were "expedients by which ignorant, intractable, and savage people were induced without bloodshed to yield up what civilized people had a right to possess by virtue of that command of the Creator . . .—'be fruitful, multiply, replenish the earth, and subdue it.' "[18]

But the Indians of Georgia were entirely civilized by white standards and had multiplied and subdued the earth; the traditional Calvinist argument for conquest was irrelevant. The Cherokees appeared before a Senate investigating committee to explain their situation and report their achievements. In 1790 they had decided to adopt white customs, and by 1825 possessed 22,000 cattle, 7,600 houses, 46,000 swine, 2,500 sheep, 762 looms, 1,488 spinning wheels, 2,948 plows, 10 saw mills, 31 grist mills, 62 blacksmith shops and 18 schools. In one Cherokee district there were 1,000 volumes of "good books." In 1821, after twelve years of study, Sequoya perfected a method of syllabary notation, an Indian alphabet, and printed a Cherokee Bible and weekly newspaper. The tribe also had a written constitution which featured a bicameral legislature, an executive, and a supreme court. Therefore, the Cherokee chiefs concluded, they hoped that they might be allowed to continue to enjoy in peace "the blessings of civilization and Country on the soil of their rightful inheritance":[19]

We have been called a poor, ignorant, and degraded people. We certainly are not rich; nor have we ever boasted of our knowledge, or our moral or moral elevation. But there is not a man within our limits so ignorant as not to know that he has a right to live on the land of his fathers, in the possession of his immemorial privileges, and that this right has been acknowledged and guaranteed by the United States. . .[20]

The Cherokee Removal Act was passed in May 1830 and when the Indians appealed to Andrew Jackson they were informed that the administration considered them "tenants at will," and their residency anywhere was a temporary privilege. Therefore, no treaty needed to be enforced between the white man and the red man, and "the President of the United States has no power to protect them against the laws of Georgia."[21] As President Jackson explained to Congress in December 1830:

What good man would prefer a country covered with forests and ranged by a few thousand savages to our extensive Republic, studded with cities, towns, and prosperous farms, embellished with all the improvements which art can devise or industry execute, occupied by more than twelve million happy people, and filled with all the blessings of liberty, civilization, and religion?[22]

Finally, the Cherokees appealed to the Supreme Court and William Wirt, a former attorney general, and John Sergeant, the former chief counsel of the Bank of the United States, agreed to represent them. Since Georgia could not argue that the Indians had not used and increased the land, they argued that they had no right to use and increase the land. Governor George M. Troup announced that Indians' rights protected in federal treaties were limited to hunting privileges and when they "changed essentially their right . . . for the purpose of tillage . . . , they violated the treaties in their letter and spirit, and did wrong to Georgia." The argument that God wanted land tilled by its occupants was dismissed by Troup. God had destined the earth "to be tilled by the white man and not by the Indian." For the citizens of Georgia and for the Congress of the United States that argument was sufficient to justify removal. As Benjamin Franklin once said: "So convenient a thing it is to be a reasonable creature since it enables one to find or to make a reason for everything one has a mind to do."[23] As for Chief Justice John Marshall, he ruled that the Cherokee nation was in fact a "state" that had been party to federal treaties; but they were only a "domestic dependent nation" and not a "foreign state" whose grievances against one of the United States could appropriately be adjudicated in his Court: "If it be true that wrongs have been inflicted, and that still greater are to be apprehended, this is not the tribunal which can redress the past or prevent the future."[24]

Actually, John Marshall himself had accelerated the movement toward "the future" when, in the 1823 case of *Johnson's and Graham's Lessee* v. *McIntosh* (8 Wheaton 542, 591), he declared that Indians did not possess exclusive sovereignty over their lands despite all the laws and treaties which indicated otherwise:

However extravagant the pretension of converting the discovery of an inhabited country into conquest may appear; if the principle has been asserted in the first instance, and afterwards sustained; if the country has been acquired and held under it; if the property of the great mass of the community originates in it, it becomes a law of the land, and cannot be questioned. However this restriction may be opposed to natural right, and the usages of civilized nations, yet, if it be indispensable to the system under which the country has been settled, and be adapted to the actual condition of the two people, it may, perhaps, be supported by reason, and certainly cannot be rejected by courts of justice.

This was perhaps the first juridical expression in the United States of the doctrine that might makes right; and it was this initial sanction that encouraged Georgia to step up the process of removal.

Justice John Marshall partially reversed himself in 1832 in the case of *Rev. Samuel A. Worcester v. the State of Georgia* (6 Peters 515). Worcester was a missionary who had lived among the Cherokees as one of them. He and two other ministers protested the state policy, and, as citizens of the Cherokee nation, refused to swear an oath of allegiance to Georgia. The three clergymen were chained together and forced to walk twenty-one miles behind a wagon to jail. They were later sentenced to four years at hard labor. But the Supreme Court declared that Indian nations "had always been considered as distinct, independent, political communities, retaining their original natural rights. . . ." The Cherokees, Marshall affirmed, were a nation, or at any rate a "distinct community," and within their boundaries "the laws of Georgia can have no force and [within] which the citizens of Georgia have no right to enter, but with the assent of the Cherokees themselves. . . ." The Cherokees were still considered a "domestic dependent nation," but dependent on the federal government alone.[25] Andrew Jackson's arrogant dismissal, "It is Mr. Marshall's decision, let him enforce it," enabled Georgia to appropriate seven million acres of land. The Indians refused to move for three years.

But General Winfield Scott with 7,000 regular troops and an unaccounted number of civilians eager to occupy the land, invaded the village and, without notice, removed the 1,700 Cherokees in the middle of the winter. Livestock, farm tools, household belongings were all appropriated by the settlers. The Cherokee were first removed to Arkansas and then to Oklahoma. About 100 Indians died each day from cold, hunger, or disease.[26] One eyewitness observed that "even aged females . . . were travelling with heavy burdens attached to their backs, sometimes on frozen grounds . . . , with no covering for their feet."[27] Another observer, Alexis De Tocqueville, noted that "It was the middle of winter, and the cold was unusually severe; the snow had frozen and the sick, with children newly born and old men upon the verge of death. They possessed neither tents nor wagons. . . . I saw them embark to pass the mighty river, and never will that solemn spectacle fade from my remembrance. No cry, no sob, was heard among the assembled crowd; all was silent. Their calamities were of ancient date, and they knew them to be irremediable."[28]

In the north, remnants of the Shawnees, Miamis, Ottawas, Delawares and other tribes were also forcibly removed at this time. All were supposed to settle in the area already occupied by the Plains Indians. In the "permanent Indian frontier," which was to last "as long as grass grows and water runs," the eastern tribes were met with hostility and further deprivation.

But for Andrew Jackson, the final removal of the eastern tribes was an occasion for joy:

The states which had so long been retarded in their improvement by the Indian tribes residing in the midst of them are at length relieved from the evil, and this unhappy race . . . are now placed in a situation where we may well hope that they will share in the blessings of civilization and be saved from that degradation and destruction to which they were rapidly hastening while they remained in the States; . . . the philanthropists will rejoice that the remnant of that ill-fated race has been at length placed beyond the reach of injury or oppression, and that the paternal care of the General Government will hereafter watch over them and protect them.[29]

Jackson's successor, Martin Van Buren, reported to Congress on December 3,

1838, that the removal "had the happiest effects" and the entire expedition had been "just and friendly" with the government "directed by the best feelings for humanity" protecting the Indian throughout.[30]

Lewis Cass, Jackson's secretary of war, was perhaps the most pleased. Cass, the "Father of the West," had been one of the chief architects of Jackson's policy, and one of the most honest about its goals:

It would be miserable affectation to regret the progress of civilization, the triumph of industry and art, by which these regions have been reclaimed, and over which freedom, religion and science are extending their sway. . . .

Cass believed that the removal of the Indian was made inevitable "by the access and progress of the new race of men, before whom the hunter and his game were destined to disappear." After all, he concluded, a "barbarous people . . . cannot live in contact with a civilized community."[31]

One of the few western congressmen to denounce the forced removal of the Indians was Henry Clay. He did not believe the manacled removal of so many Indians was inevitable and feared it involved the very nature of American society. In a speech before the Senate on February 14, 1835, Clay recited a list of outrages committed against the Cherokees as well as fourteen different treaties made and broken within fifty years. Clay's speech is reported to have "brought tears to the eyes of Senators."[32] But it did not alter the situation any more than had his 1818 remonstrance. At that time, Henry Clay was the only congressman to denounce Andrew Jackson when the general had crossed the Florida border, seized two Spanish towns, and murdered several Indian chiefs and two British subjects. In 1818 Clay had demanded that Jackson be rebuked for military insubordination and asked Congress to "remember that Greece had her Alexander, Rome her Caesar, . . . and that if we would escape the rock on which they split we must avoid their errors."[33]

Like Clay, Frances Trollope, a British essayist and visitor to the United States in 1832, was appalled by the Cherokee removal and disgusted by what she considered the colossal arrogance and hypocrisy of Americans:

If the American character may be judged by their conduct [toward the Indians], they are most lamentably deficient in every feeling of honour and integrity. . . . Had I during my residence in the United States, observed any single feature in their national character that could justify their eternal boast of liberality and the love of freedom, I might have respected them. . . . But it is impossible for any mind of common honesty not to be revolted by the contradictions in their principles and practice. They inveigh against the governments of Europe, because, as they say, they favour the powerful and oppress the weak. . . . [But] you will see [the Americans] with one hand hoisting the cap of liberty, and with the other flogging their slaves. You will see them one hour lecturing their mob on the indefeasible rights of man, and the next driving from their homes the children of the soil, whom they have bound themselves to protect by the most solemn treaties.[34]

From 1840 to 1890 the "winning of the West" was accomplished by the most savage methods of occupation, removal, and massacre. Beyond the "permanent Indian frontier," the United States was not an unusable desert, but one of the world's richest areas for gold, silver, oil, and a variety of minerals even more precious—such as uranium. The Indians were safe so long as Americans believed that they now lived on an arid wasteland which no white man could possibly want and where the Indians, perhaps, would not survive. But as soon as it became known that Indians actually thrived on the high grasslands where the earth was rich and black and crops grew in abundance, and on the Great

Plains where vegetation could be made to grow with the care the Indians gave to it and where livestock, buffalo, and horses roamed freely, it became evident that the Indians had been removed to lands quite as valuable as the ones they had been removed from.

When in 1848 gold was found in California, thousands of settlers, vagabonds, and speculators trekked across America. They passed the high grasslands of the Central Plains of Missouri and Iowa, through the Great Plains of Kansas, Nebraska, and Wyoming; many of those from New England went north through the Dakotas, and those from the Carolinas, Georgia, and Alabama crossed south through Oklahoma; and they all passed through the magnificent Rocky Mountain country. Americans traveled west along parallel lines that depended on their point of departure and they observed for themselves the Indian lands, the "Great American Desert," and saw that Zebulon M. Pike had been in error. Here was land many wanted. Entire wagon trains stopped along the way to try out the earth in country that attracted them; and much of it was filled with gold. Prospectors en route to California found gold in Colorado in 1850 and in Rocky Mountain territory in 1858. New hordes of prospectors swarmed across the Plains. Settlers, railroad builders, buffalo hunters, all moved west. Kansas and Nebraska, two vast territories, were organized by the government for settlement and future statehood. The area enveloped all the territory of the Plains Indians. The era of peace was over. In 1858 Minnesota became a state; its western boundary one hundred miles beyond the 95th meridian, the "permanent Indian frontier," which was, said John Calhoun, to have been forcefully protected to ensure the Indians a homeland where they could live in peace for as long as the waters ran into the sea.

NOTES

1. See Alvin M. Josephy, "Tecumseh, The Greatest Indian," *The Patriot Chiefs: A Chronicle of Indian Resistance* (Viking, 1969), pp. 131–173; George Novack, *Genocide Against the Indians: Its Role in the Rise of United States Capitalism* (Pathfinder Press, 1970), p. 10.

2. Helen Hunt Jackson, *A Century of Dishonor* (Harper Torchbooks, 1965 [1881], p. 42.

3. Josephy, p. 145.

4. Wayne quoted in Jackson, pp. 43–44.

5. Randolph quoted in Paul Jacobs, et al. (eds.), *To Serve the Devil: A Documentary Analysis of America's Racial History and Why It Has Been Kept Hidden*, 2 vols. (Vintage, 1971), Vol 1, pp. 24–25.

6. Harrison quoted in Albert K. Weinberg, *Manifest Destiny: A Study of Nationalist Expansionism in American History* (Johns Hopkins University Press, 1935), p. 79.

7. Josephy, p. 137.

8. Tecumseh quoted in Jacobs, pp. xvii–xviii.

9. John Collier, *Indians of the Americas* (Mentor, 1947), p. 106.

10. Josephy, pp. 152–157.

11. *Ibid.*, p. 157.

12. See Michael P. Rogin, "Liberal Society and the Indian Question," *Politics and Society*, 1 (May 1971), 269–312.

13. Calhoun quoted in Margaret L. Coit, *John Calhoun: American Patriot* (Houghton Mifflin, 1950), p. 131.

14. Crawford quoted in William T. Hagan, "Private Property, The Indian's Door to

Civilization," reprinted in Roger L. Nichols and George Adams (eds)., *The American Indian: Past and Present* (Xerox, 1971), p. 203.

15. Ray Allen Billington, *Westward Expansion* (Macmillan, 1960), p. 470; Coit, p. 131.

16. I am indebted to Richard Drinnon of Bucknell University who kindly gave me the manuscript version of his excellent article, "Violence in the American Experience: Winning the West." Subsequently published in *The Radical Teacher* (December 30, 1969); see p. 23.

17. Collier, p. 122.

18. Weinberg, p. 83.

19. Peter Farb, *Man's Rise to Civilization, As Shown by the Indians of North America from Primeval Times to the Coming of the Industrial State* (Avon, 1968), p. 302.

20. From the Memorial of the Cherokee Nation, July 17, 1830, quoted in *Niles Weekly Register*, 38 (August 21, 1830), 454–457.

21. Jackson quoted in Weinberg, pp. 82–83.

22. Jackson quoted in Mary E. Young, "Indian Removal and Land Allotment: The Civilized Tribes and Jacksonian Justice"; reprinted in Nichols and Adams, p. 133.

23. See Weinberg, pp. 86–88.

24. *The Cherokee Nation v. Georgia*, 5 Peters 1 ff. (1831).

25. *Worcester v. Georgia*, 6 Peters 515, 560 (1832).

26. Collier, p. 123.

27. Quoted in Thomas F. Gossett, *Race: The History of An Idea in America* (Schocken Books, 1965), p. 233.

28. De Tocqueville quoted in Farb, p. 305.

29. From Jackson's *Farewell Address*, March 4, 1837, quoted in Francis Paul Prucha, "Andrew Jackson's Indian Policy: A Reassessment," *Journal of American History* 6 (December 1969), 539.

30. Van Buren quoted in Farb, p. 304.

31. Cass quoted in Drinnon, p. 22.

32. For Clay's speech, see *The Congressional Record*, 23d Cong., 2d sess., Vol. II, pp. 289–306. For its effect, see Samuel Eliot Morison, *The Oxford History of the American People* (Oxford University Press, 1965), pp. 450–451.

33. Clement Eaton, *Henry Clay and the Art of American Politics* (Little, Brown, 1957), p. 38.

34. Frances Trollope, *Domestic Manners of the Americans* (Vintage, 1949 [1832]), pp. 221–222.

bibliography

The renewed interest in white-Indian contact has resulted in important new works on American attitudes toward race, power, and the process of social change. See especially the work of Richard Drinnon, who is currently writing a full length study, "Violence in the American Experience: Winning the West," *Radical Teacher* (December 30, 1969); Michael Paul Rogin, "Liberal Society and the Indian Question," *Politics and Society* (May 1971); and Roy H. Pearce, *Savagism and Civilization: A Study of the Indian and the American Mind*, 2nd ed. (Johns Hopkins University Press, 1967). Other valuable histories include Harold Fey and D'Arcy McNickle, *Indians and Other Americans* (Harper & Row, 1970); Mary E. Young, *Redskins, Ruffleshirts and Rednecks* (University of Oklahoma Press, 1971); Loring B. Priest, *Uncle Sam's Stepchildren* (Rutgers University Press, 1942); Edward Spicer, *Cycles of Conquest*(University of Arizona Press, 1967); Wilbur Jacobs, *Indians and Whites: Struggle on the Colonial Frontier* (Scribner, 1972); Wilcomb Washburn, *Red Man's Land/White Man's Law: A Study of the Past and Present Status of the American Indian* (Scribner, 1971); Robert Venables, *Crowded Wilderness: The Indian in American History* (Scribner, 1972); and John Collier, *Indians of the Americas* (Mentor, 1947). See also Alvins Josephy's study of Indian resistance, *The Patriot Chiefs* (Viking, 1958). The most vivid descriptions of Indian removal and warfare are Dee Brown, *Bury My Heart at Wounded Knee: An Indian History of the American West* (Holt, Rinehart and Winston, 1970); Ralph Andrist, *The Long Death: The Last Days of the Plains Indians* (Collier, 1964); and the classic appeal for Indian reform, Helen Hunt Jackson, *A Century of Dishonor* (Harper & Row, 1965 [1881]. Among the best collections of primary and analytical sources are Council on Interracial Books for Children (ed.), *Chronicles of American Indian Protest* (Fawcett, 1971); Wilcomb Washburn (ed.), *The Indian and the White Man* (Anchor, 1964); Roger Nichols and George Adams (eds.), *The American Indian: Past and Present* (Xerox, 1971); and Edward Spicer (ed.), *A Short History of the Indians of the United States* (Van Nostrand, 1969).

For studies that focus on American foreign policy, Indians, and commerce, see Reginald Horsman, *The Frontier in the Formative Years, 1783-1815* (Holt, Rinehart and Winston, 1970); Sidney Lens, *The Forging of the American Empire* (Crowell, 1971); Albert Weinberg, *Manifest Destiny: A Study of Nationalist Expansion in American History* (Johns Hopkins University Press, 1935); William A. Williams, *The Contours of American History* (Quadrangle, 1966); and Stuart Bruchey, *The Roots of American Economic Growth, 1607-1861: An Essay in Social Causation* (Harper & Row, 1965).

For the early political role of workers, see Staughton Lynd, "The Mechanics in New York City Politics, 1774-1788," *Labor History*, 5 (Fall 1964); David Montgomery, "The Working Classes of the Pre-Industrial American City, 1780-1830," *Labor History*, 9 (1968).

Radical works dealing with America's changing economic and political structure during the Jacksonian period have yet to be written. Arthur M. Schlesinger's *The Age of Jackson* (Little, Brown, 1945) won a Pulitzer Prize and is frequently called definitive, but it has almost no analysis of Jackson's attitudes toward Indians, blacks, or workers. John William Ward's *Andrew Jackson: Symbol for An Age* (Oxford University Press, 1962) analyzes the rugged individualist values of Jacksonianism. For other interpretations, see Lee Benson, *The Concept of Jacksonian Democracy* (Princeton, University Press, 1961), and Marvin Meyers, *The Jacksonian Persuasion: Politics and Belief* (Vintage, 1957). For a critique of these works, see Michael A. Lebowitz, "The Jacksonians: Paradox Lost," in Barton Bernstein (ed.), *Towards A New Past: Dissenting Essays in American History* (Vintage, 1969).

slavery, sexism, and nativism
in the nineteenth century

This chapter deals with America's attitudes toward its victims: slaves, recent immigrants, and women. Although we celebrate egalitarian and democratic national values, white chauvinism, sexism, and nativism have dominated the quality of our national life. Only recently have historians begun to deal with this discrepancy.

Slavery as analyzed by white American historians has been almost consistently reflective of the white racist attitudes that permitted the institution to flourish in the first place. For almost fifty years the works of Ulrich B. Phillips were the standard interpretation of slave society. Phillips regarded slavery as the "best school" for the "mass training" of Africans; he considered them inherently inferior and unprepared for the American way of life. In *American Negro Slavery* (1918) and *Life and Labor in the Old South* (1929), he portrayed the stereotypic Sambo: "submissive rather than defiant, light-hearted instead of gloomy, amiable and ingratiating instead of sullen." Professor C. Vann Woodward, writing in 1963, noted that Phillips' work reflects "a paternalistic and indulgent affection toward what he regarded as a childlike and irresponsible people with many endearing traits." As late as 1950, Henry Steele Commager and Samuel Eliot Morison, two distinguished northern professors, compounded the vision: "As for Sambo . . . , there is some reason to believe that he suffered less than any other class in the South from its 'peculiar institution.' "

The major challenge to this interpretation did not appear until 1956 when Kenneth Stampp's *The Peculiar Institution*, a product of the integrationist 1950s, was published. In the preface to his first edition, Stampp announced that he "assumed that the slaves were merely ordinary human beings, that innately Negroes were, after all, only white men with black skins, nothing more, nothing less." This denial of race prejudice is nevertheless a denial of black identity. Stampp, a northern liberal, set out to understand the south and not what slavery did to the slaves. Consequently, they are seen entirely through the eyes of their owners and through the prism of slavery, not as people in their own right. Stampp attempted to destroy the myth of cheerful acquiescence and so emphasized slave resistance, recalcitrance, and rebellion. Since his focus was always on how events affected the planters, in a chapter entirely devoted to slaves who resisted by running away he noted that some slaves were so "determined to make their recapture as costly as possible" they even risked their lives. Is it possible that it never occurred to Stampp that a slave might be more concerned about his or her freedom than about what the flight might cost the owner? But Stampp considered slavery a highly profitable, if peculiar, institution. Once again we are presented with a Sambo stereotype—a sneaky, untrustworthy, and surly kind. Robbed of freedom, slaves resorted to petty larceny—a subject to which Stampp devoted several pages: "Dishonesty, as the master understood the term, indeed seemed to be a common if not inherent trait of southern slaves."

Stampp's insistence that slaves had courage and did resist, although not very much and not very often, was countered by Stanley Elkins' *Slavery: A Problem in American Institutional and Intellectual Life* (1959). Elkins wrote that in fact slaveowners had so much power that slaves were infantilized and helplessly dependent on their masters for whom they felt a "childish attachment." They were also submissive and docile, and the stereotype of 1918 was again blown full, but now with more sophisticated techniques and within a comparative framework, not only internationally comparative but institutionally compar-ative. To Elkins, slavery is abhorrent, a system of oppression analogous, he contended, to the Nazi concentration camp. The real problem with Elkins' thesis is not that the slave system, like all thoroughly dehumanizing systems, oppressed and damaged the people trapped in them, but that Elkins insisted that slaves internalized the damage and were incapable of maturation and development.

Eugene Genovese, a Marxist historian who has written several major works on slavery, has concluded that the Sambo stereotype, as Elkins portrayed that stereotype, existed "wherever slavery existed—to a greater or lesser degree." Despite this observation, Genovese maintains that slavery in the United States enabled the slave to transcend the limitations of his or her environment, since in "purely material terms" it was "probably the best" slave system of all. "American slaves," Genovese affirms in the following article, "were generally fed, clothed, housed, and worked better" than slaves in other countries.

As opposed to Stampp, Genovese asks, "What was done to the slave?" And, as opposed to Elkins, he acknowledges that slaves were and remained whole people. But in affirming the dignity of slaves he romanticizes the conditions of slavery. It is almost as if he were saying that there was nothing broken; nothing fell apart. We are presented with a portrait of a model society in which, for example, the nuclear family flourished (although he contradicts his contention that planters honored slave marriages by observing that families struggled to find each other during Reconstruction). Moreover, Genovese insists: "People, black and white, slave and master, thrown together in the intimacy of the Big House had to emerge loving and hating each other." Lillian Smith, a southern essayist known for her book *Killers of the Dream*, provides an alternative insight into the relationship between slave and master. She contends that black women were dehumanized in the minds of the white men who visited the back-house shack. When children were born of such union they were, according to the white race philosophy, born without souls, "a strange exotic new kind of creature whom they made slaves of and sometimes sold on the auction block."

Perhaps it is an index of our historical bankruptcy that in order to deny the Sambo stereotype it is also deemed necessary to deny the depth of a brutal and dehumanizing system. Regardless of the violent intensity of slavery, slaves did maintain inner autonomy and "assert their own personalities." But the slaver regarded his or her slave as a commodity, as chattel, who existed solely for the benefit of the owner.

David Brion Davis in *The Problem of Slavery in Western Culture* also used the comparative method and in many ways Davis' work is the most sophis-ticated study of all. In an analysis of the western world's major slave systems, he concludes that since the treatment of man as property and without rights was universal, there were very few basic differences between slave cultures. The cruelty of slavery is marked by the simple fact that "slaves were men who are defined as things." Davis asked how one was "to reconcile the brute fact that slavery was an intrinsic part of the American experience with the image of the New World . . . as a paradise which promised fulfillment of man's highest aspirations?" And that was what white American historians set out to do. As a result, they consistently portrayed slavery as "a curious blend . . . of tyranny and benevolence, of antipathy and affection," with much evidence of "kindliness," "contentment," and "mutual loyalty."

Black historians, such as W.E.B. DuBois, Ernest Kayser, and C. L. R. James, set out to do something else, as is made clear by James' article in this chapter. Black historians have, of course, a different perspective and, as the editors of *Freedomways* have frequently observed, white historians tend to ignore or devalue their works, their insights, and their visions. To begin with, black historians do not participate in the Elkins controversy that has for so many years engrossed white historians. The editors of *Freedomways* reviewed a 1971 anthology entirely devoted to Elkins: "the preoccupation of white historians with this phony thesis is really laughable. Why do white historians want to believe this? The slave's job was to get around or escape as much inhuman slavery as he or she could in any way he or she could. His personality, real or faked, stemmed from that drive. Why is this simple concept so hard for white historians to understand?" As black poet Paul Laurence Dunbar wrote:

Why should the world be overwise
In counting all our tears and sighs?
Nay, let them only see us while
We wear the mask.

C. L. R. James once wrote that "the history of the development of ideas . . . are of the greatest value to civilization." To understand the ideological principles behind America's institutions is perhaps a historian's most important task. Referring to Frantz Fanon's *Wretched of the Earth*, which he preferred to call the "Condemned of the World," James concluded that "the work done by Black intellectuals, stimulated by the needs of the Black people, had better be understood by the condemned of the world whether they are in Africa, the United States, or Europe. Because if the condemned of the earth do not understand their pasts and know the responsibilities that lie upon them in the future, all on the earth will be condemned. That is the kind of world we live in." That Genovese called those ideas "Fanon's psychopathic panegyric to violence" is of no particular concern, especially since Genovese is not notably consistent. In another essay he noted that Fanon's prescription for change is "better than none," and "a society which provides no other has no right to complain."

In 1944, when Gunnar Myrdal first published his massive study *The American Dilemma: The Negro Problem and Modern Democracy*, he noted a conflict between "the American Creed," which he accepted as being a liberal and democratic one, and America's attitude toward its black citizens. Aileen Kraditor's work on abolitionists revealed that they recognized so great a disparity between American slavery and the proclaimed American "way of life" as to be evidence of a greater institutional dilemma. It was evidence, in fact, of an America that might institutionally be rotten at the core. Her chapter on women's rights and the abolitionist movement places racism and sexism in the context of the disparity between America's rhetoric and its reality. Garrisonian abolitionists pursued equality for all people—including women— and opposed a government of force because they considered coercion and democratic equality incompatible. But nineteenth century America was not an egalitarian democracy, and blacks, women, and immigrants were outside its contours.

Nineteenth century racists did not limit their prejudices to blacks. Eric Foner describes the situation vividly: American democracy was considered the sole preserve of the "Anglo-Saxon" race. For immigrants to participate in it they would have to "Americanize." The myth of the melting pot is rooted in a desire to burn away other peoples' heritages. A professor of anatomy at the University of Edinburgh, Scotland, Dr. Robert Knox cited America's Know-Nothing riots to prove the inevitability of race war between democratic Protestant Saxons and unruly Catholic Celts. Knox blamed the Roman Catholic victims for the damage done to their churches, their orphanages, and their homes. Celts, he declared, were fanatics who loved "war and disorder" and had "no accumulative habits." Saxons, however, are "the only democrats on the earth, the only race which truly comprehends the meaning of the word liberty." Thomas Gossett reports that Ralph Waldo Emerson was "repelled" by Knox's "wild exaggerations," but considered the work "charged with pungent and unforgettable truths." For Ralph Waldo Emerson, race was all significant: " 'It is race, is it not? that puts the hundred millions of India under the dominion of a remote island in the north of Europe . . . ; that Celts love unity of power, and Saxons the representative principle. . . .' " And, finally, Emerson noted, " 'Race in the negro is of appalling importance.' "

An infinite variety of racial stereotypes have been applied to each succeeding wave of immigrants to land on these shores. As for women, they have been considered useful ancillaries of the men who dominated their lives.

a troublesome property

KENNETH M. STAMPP

The following excerpt from "A Troublesome Property," Chapter Three of Kenneth Stampp's *The Peculiar Institution*, is a liberal-mainstream analysis of those slaves who sought to resist the brutality of servitude by either running away or establishing an alternative moral code. But, Stampp notes, only a small "minority of slaves" could not be humbled by the discipline they received. On the other hand, in a later chapter, entitled "To Make Them Stand in Fear," Stampp explains that because "slaveholders had to manage less-than-perfect slaves, they found that their government never worked perfectly."

According to Dr. Cartwright, there was a second disease peculiar to Negroes which he called *Drapetomania*: "the disease causing negroes to run away." Cartwright believed that it was a "disease of the mind" and that with "proper medical advise" it could be cured. The first symptom was a "sulky and dissatisfied" attitude. To forestall the full onset of the disease, the cause of discontent must be determined and removed. If there were no ascertainable cause, then "whipping the devil out of them" was the proper "preventive measure against absconding."[1]

Though Cartwright's dissertations on Negro diseases are mere curiosities of medical history, the problem he dealt with was a real and urgent one to nearly every slaveholder. Olmsted met few planters, large or small, who were not more or less troubled by runaways. A Mississippian realized that his record was most unusual when he wrote in his diary: "Harry ran away; the first negro that ever ran from me." Another slaveholder betrayed his concern when he avowed that he would "rather a negro would do anything Else than run-away."[2]

The number of runaways was not large enough to threaten the survival of the peculiar institution, because slaveholders took precautions to prevent the problem from growing to such proportions. But their measures were never entirely successful, as the advertisements for fugitives in southern newspapers made abundantly clear. Actually, the problem was much greater than these newspapers suggested, because many owners did not advertise for their absconding property. (When an owner did advertise, he usually waited until his slave had been missing for several weeks.) In any case, fugitive slaves were numbered in the thousands every year. It was an important form of protest against bondage.

Who were the runaways? They were generally young slaves, most of them under thirty, but occasionally masters searched for fugitives who were more than sixty years old. The majority of them were males, though female

From "A Troublesome Property," *The Peculiar Institution: Slavery in the Ante-Bellum South*, by Kenneth M. Stampp. (New York: Vintage Books, 1956), 109–132. Copyright © 1956 by Kenneth M. Stampp. Reprinted by permission of Alfred A. Knopf, Inc.

runaways were by no means uncommon. It is not true that most of them were mulattoes or of predominantly white ancestry. While this group was well represented amoung the fugitives, they were outnumbered by slaves who were described as "black" or of seemingly "pure" African ancestry. Domestics and skilled artisans—the ones who supposedly had the most intimate ties with the master class—ran away as well as common field-hands.

Some bondsmen tried running away only once, or on very rare occasions. Others tried it repeatedly and somehow managed to escape in spite of their owners' best efforts to stop them. Such slaves were frequently identified as "habitual" or "notorious" runaways. While a few of them were, according to their masters, "unruly scoundrels" or "incorrigible scamps," most of them seemed to be "humble," "inoffensive," or "cheerful" slaves. Thus an adver-tisement for a Maryland fugitive stated: he "always appears to be in a good humor, laughs a good deal, and runs on with a good deal of foolishness." A Louisiana master gave the following description of three slaves who escaped from him: the first was "very industrious" and always answered "with a smile" when spoken to; the second, a "well-disposed and industrious boy," was "very timid" and spoke to white men "very humbly, with his hand to his hat"; and the third addressed whites "humbly and respectfully with a smile."[3] Slaves such as these apparently concealed their feelings and behaved as they were expected to—until one day they suddenly made off.

Runaways usually went singly or in small groups of two or three. But some escaped in groups of a dozen or more, and in a few instances in groups of more than fifty. They ran off during the warm summer months more often than during the winter when sleeping out of doors was less feasible and when frost-bitten feet might put an end to flight.

Many fugitives bore the marks of cruelty on their bodies, but humane treatment did not necessarily prevent attempts to escape. More than a few masters shared the bewilderment of a Marylander who advertised for his slave Jacob: "He has no particular marks, and his appearance proves the fact of the kind treatment he has always received." Slaveholders told Olmsted that slaves who were treated well, fed properly, and worked moderately ran away even when they knew that it would cause them hardship and, eventually, severe punishment. "This is often mentioned to illustrate the ingratitude and especial depravity of the African race."[4]

In advertising for a runaway, owners frequently insisted that he had absconded for no cause, or for none that they could understand. A Virginia slave ran off without the excuse "either of whipping, or threat, or angry word"; the slaves Moses and Peter left an Alabama plantation "without provocation." A small Virginia planter recorded in his diary that he had punished a slave woman for running away, because there was "no cause" for it but "badness."[5]

While the North Star was the fugitives' traditional guide, some saw liberty beckoning from other directions. They fled to the British during the American Revolution and the War of 1812, and to the Spanish before the purchases of Louisiana and Florida. At a later date Florida slaves escaped to the Seminole Indians, aided them in their war against the whites, and accompanied them when they moved to the West.[6] At Key West, in 1858, a dozen slaves stole a small boat and successfully navigated it to freedom in the Bahamas.[7] Arkansas runaways often tried to make their way to the Indian country. For Texas slaves, Mexico was the land of freedom, and most of those who sought it headed for the Rio Grande. In Mexico the fugitives generally were welcomed and protected, and in some cases sympathetic peons guided them in their flight.[8]

How often runaways received assistance from free persons residing in the South is hard to determine, but it seems likely that they seldom trusted anyone but fellow slaves. A few white Southerners who opposed slavery gave sanctuary to fugitives or directed them along their routes. Slaveholders sometimes suspected that runaways were being harbored by some "evil disposed person" or "unprincipled white." Now and then free Negroes also gave aid to the less fortunate members of their race. One of them, Richard Buckner, was convicted of assisting slaves to escape from Kentucky and sentenced to two years in prison. Free Negroes who were employed on river boats or on vessels engaged in the coastal trade occasionally concealed slaves who were trying to reach the free states.[9]

Many Southerners were convinced that the slave states were honeycombed with northern abolitionist agents seeking to create discontent among the slaves and to urge them to abscond. While this was an exaggeration, a few Northerners did undertake this hazardous enterprise. In 1849, a Missouri newspaper complained that almost every day slaves were induced "by the persuasions of Abolitionists, to abandon comfortable homes." Supporters of the antislavery movement operated in Kentucky (sometimes disguised as peddlers) and guided hundreds to freedom across the Ohio River. On one occasion three Northerners made an unsuccessful effort to help seventy-eight slaves escape from the District of Columbia by boat down the Potomac River. In 1844, Jonathan Walker, a New Englander, was severely punished for attempting to ferry seven fugitives from Pensacola to the Bahamas. Ten years later, James Redpath, the Massachusetts abolitionist, traveled through the slave states trying to persuade slaves to run away.[10] But the bondsmen generally needed assistance more than persuasion.

Not the least of those who gave assistance to fugitives were former slaves who had themselves escaped and then returned to help others. One of them was Ben, "a stout hearty negro," who absconded from Kentucky but "was not satisfied with letting 'well enough alone.'" Instead he engaged in "running off the 'property' of his late master at every opportunity." When at length Ben was caught, he "fought with the desperation of a man who had once tasted the sweets of liberty"; but he was overpowered and re-enslaved. Harriet Tubman, after twenty-five years in bondage, escaped from her master who lived on the Eastern Shore of Maryland. During the 1850's she returned nineteen times to deliver parties of fugitives.[11] There were others whose careers were less spectacular.

Harriet Tubman was one of the many ex-slaves who served as "conductors" on the famed Underground Railroad. Along its various routes in the Northeast and Northwest they, together with northern free Negroes and sympathetic whites, sheltered the frightened fugitives and sped them on their way.[12] These runaway slaves did much to disturb the consciences of the northern people and to arouse sympathy for those they left behind.

But southern masters were less disturbed about the ultimate consequences than they were about their immediate losses. Moreover, every successful runaway was bound to encourage other slaves to try their luck in the same enterprise. When a Tennessee master learned that several of his bondsmen had escaped to Canada, he vowed that he would recover them if it cost all that they were worth. "I intend going to Canada next spring and if there is no other choice I will kidnap them, or have them at the risk of my life."[13] This was idle talk; his slaves were lost forever.

Only a few of the runaways left records of their feelings at the time they made their break for liberty. One of them, Anthony Chase, the property of a Baltimore widow, composed a priceless document. In 1827, after failing to get permission to purchase his freedom, Chase escaped from the man to whom he was hired. It was to him, rather than to his owner, that Chase penned his personal Declaration of Independence:

> I know that you will be astonished and surprised when you becom acquainted with the unexspected course that I am now about to take, a step that I never had the most distant idea of takeing, but what can a man do who has his hands bound and his feet fettered [?] He will certainly try to get them loosened in any way that he may think the most adviseable. I hope sir that you will not think that I had any fault to find of you or your family[.] No sir I have none and I could of hired with you all the days of my life if my conditions could of been in any way bettered which I intreated with my mistress to do but it was all in vain[.] She would not consent to anything that would melorate my condition in any shape or measure[.] So I shall go to sea in the first vesel that may offer an opportunity and as soon as I can acumulate a sum of money suficient I will remit it to my mistress to prove to her and to [the] world that I dont mean to be dishonest but wish to pay her every cent that I think my servaces is worth. . . . I dont supose that I shall ever be forgiven for this act but I hope to find forgiveness in that world that is to com.

After wishing his former employer "helth and happyness," Anthony Chase, with an unconscious touch of irony, signed himself "your most obedient serv[an]t." [14] And thus another slaveholder was left to meditate upon the folly of placing confidence in the loyalty of slaves.

The bondsmen who protested against bondage by running away or by some form of malingering were a perplexing lot. Since, by all outward appearances, they usually seemed cheerful and submissive, masters could never be sure whether their misdeeds were purposeful or capricious. Their smiling faces were most disarming.

There were some bondsmen, however, who did not smile.

"His look is impudent and insolent, and he holds himself straight and walks well." So a Louisiana master described James, a runaway slave.[15] There were always bondsmen like James. In 1669, a Virginia statute referred to "the obstinacy of many of them"; in 1802, a South Carolina judge declared that they were "in general a headstrong, stubborn race of people"; and in 1859, a committee of a South Carolina agricultural society complained of the "insolence of disposition to which, as a race, they are remarkably liable." An overseer on a Louisiana plantation wrote nervously about the many "outrageous acts" recently committed by slaves in his locality and insisted that he scarcely had time to eat and sleep: "The truth is no man can begin to attend to Such a business with any Set of negroes, without the Strictest vigilance on his part."[16] It was the minority of slaves whom his discipline could not humble (the "insolent," "surly," and "unruly" ones) that worried this overseer—and slaveholders generally. These were the slaves whose discontent drove them to drastic measures.

Legally the offenses of the rebels ranged from petty misdemeanors to capital crimes, and they were punished accordingly. The master class looked upon any offense as more reprehensible (and therefore subject to more severe penalties) when committed by a slave than when committed by a free white. But how can one determine the proper ethical standards for identifying undesirable or even criminal behavior among slaves? How distinguish a "good" from a "bad" slave? Was the "good" slave the one who was courteous and loyal to his master, and who did his work faithfully and cheerfully? Was the "bad" slave the one who would not submit to his master, and who defiantly fought back? What were the limits, if any, to which a man deprived of his freedom could properly go in resisting bondage? How accountable was a slave to a legal code which gave him more penalties than protection and was itself a bulwark of slavery? This much at least can be said: many slaves rejected the answers which their masters gave to questions such as these. The slaves did not thereby repudiate law and morality: rather, they formulated legal and moral codes of their own.

The white man's laws against theft, for example, were not supported by the slave's code. In demonstrating the "absence of moral principle" among bondsmen, one master observed: "To steal and not to be detected is a merit among them." Let a master turn his back, wrote another, and some "cunning fellow" would appropriate part of his goods. No slave would betray another, for an informer was held "in greater detestation than the most notorious thief."[17]

If slaveholders are to be believed, petty theft was an almost universal "vice"; slaves would take anything that was not under lock and key. Field-hands killed hogs and robbed the corn crib. House servants helped themselves to wines, whiskey, jewelry, trinkets, and whatever else was lying about. Fugitives sometimes gained from their master unwilling help in financing the journey to freedom, the advertisements often indicating that they absconded with money, clothing, and a horse or mule. Thefts were not necessarily confined to the master's goods: any white man might be considered fair game.

Some bondsmen engaged in theft on more than a casual and petty basis. They made a business of it and thus sought to obtain comforts and luxuries which were usually denied them. A South Carolina master learned that his house servants had been regularly looting his wine cellar and that one of them was involved in an elaborate "system of roguery." A planter in North Carolina found that three of his slaves had "for some months been carrying on a robbery" of meat and lard, the leader being "a young carpenter, remarkable for smartness . . . and no less worthy for his lamentable deficiency in common honesty."[18]

If the stolen goods were not consumed directly, they were traded to whites or to free Negroes. This illegal trade caused masters endless trouble, for slaves were always willing to exchange plantation products for tobacco, liquor, or small sums of money. Southern courts were kept busy handling the resulting prosecutions. One slaveholder discovered that his bondsmen had long been engaged in an extensive trade in corn. "Strict vigilance," he concluded, was necessary "to prevent them from theft; particularly when dishonesty is inherent, as is probably the case with some of them."[19] Dishonesty, as the master understood the term, indeed seemed to be a common if not an inherent trait of southern slaves.

The slaves, however, had a somewhat different definition of dishonesty in their own code, to which they were reasonably faithful. For appropriating their master's goods they might be punished and denounced by him, but they were not likely to be disgraced among their associates in the slave quarters, who made a distinction between "stealing" and "taking." Appropriating things from the master meant simply taking part of his property for the benefit of another part or, as Frederick Douglass phrased it, "taking his meat out of one tub, and putting it in another." Thus a female domestic who had been scolded for the theft of some trinkets was reported to have replied: "Law, mam, don't say I's wicked; ole Aunt Ann says it allers right for us poor colored people to 'popiate whatever of de wite folk's blessings de Lord puts in our way." Stealing, on the other hand, meant appropriating something that belonged to another slave, and this was an offense which slaves did not condone.[20]

The prevalence of theft was a clear sign that slaves were discontented, at least with the standard of living imposed upon them. They stole food to increase or enrich their diets or to trade for other coveted commodities. Quite obviously they learned from their masters the pleasures that could be derived from the possession of worldly goods; and when the opportunity presented itself, they "took" what was denied them as slaves.

Next to theft, arson was the most common slave "crime," one which slaveholders dreaded almost constantly. Fire was a favorite means for aggrieved slaves to even the score with their master. Reports emanated periodically from some region or other that there was an "epidemic" of gin-house burnings, or that some bondsman had taken his revenge by burning the slave quarters or other farm buildings. More than one planter thus saw the better part of a year's harvest go up in flames.[21] Southern newspapers and court records are filled with illustrations of this offense, and with evidence of the severe penalties inflicted upon those found guilty of committing it.

Another "crime" was what might be called self-sabotage, a slave deliberately unfitting himself to labor for his master. An Arkansas slave, "at any time to save an hour's work," could "throw his left shoulder out of place." A Kentucky slave made himself unserviceable by downing medicines from his master's dispensary (thus showing a better understanding of the value of these nostrums than his owner). A slave woman was treated as an invalid because of "swellings in her arms"—until it was discovered that she produced this condition by thrusting her arms periodically into a beehive. Yellow Jacob, according to his master's plantation journal, "had a kick from a mule and when nearly well would bruise it and by that means kept from work."[22] Another Negro, after being punished by his owner, retaliated by cutting off his right hand; still another cut off the fingers of one hand to avoid being sold to the Deep South.[23]

A few desperate slaves carried this form of resistance to the extreme of self-destruction. Those freshly imported from Africa and those sold away from friends and relatives were especially prone to suicide.[24] London, a slave on a Georgia rice plantation, ran to the river and drowned himself after being threatened with a whipping. His overseer gave orders to leave the corpse untouched "to let the [other] negroes see [that] when a negro takes his own life they will be treated in this manner." A Texas planter bewailed the loss of a slave woman who hanged herself after two unsuccessful breaks for freedom: "I had been offered $900.00 for her not two months ago, but damn her . . . I would not have had it happened for twice her value. *The fates pursue me.*"[25]

Some runaways seemed determined to make their recapture as costly as possible and even resisted at the risk of their own lives. One advertisement, typical of many, warned that an escaped slave was a "resolute fellow" who would probably not be taken without a "show of competent force." When, after a day-long chase, three South Carolina fugitives were cornered, they "fought desperately," inflicted numerous wounds upon their pursuers with a barrage of rocks, and "refused to surrender until a force of about forty-five or fifty men arrived."[26] In southern court records there are numerous cases of runaway slaves who killed whites or were themselves killed in their frantic efforts to gain freedom.

In one dramatic case, a Louisiana fugitive was detected working as a free Negro on a Mississippi River flatboat. His pursuers, trailing him with a pack of "Negro dogs," finally found him "standing at bay upon the outer edge of a large raft of drift wood, armed with a club and pistol." He threatened to kill anyone who got near him. "Finding him obstinately determined not to surrender, one of his pursuers shot him. He fell at the third fire, and so determined was he not to be captured, that when an effort was made to rescue him from drowning he made battle with his club, and sunk waving his weapon in angry defiance."[27]

An effort to break up an organized gang of runaways was a dangerous business, because they were often unwilling to surrender without a fight. The fugitives in one well-armed band in Alabama were building a fort at the time they were discovered. Their camp was destroyed after a "smart skirmish" during which three of them were killed.[28] Such encounters did not always end in defeat for the slaves; some runaway bands successfully resisted all attempts at capture and remained at large for years.

Ante-bellum records are replete with acts of violence committed by individual slaves upon masters, overseers, and other whites. A Texan complained, in 1853, that cases of slaves murdering white men were becoming "painfully frequent." "Within the last year or two many murders have taken place, by negroes upon their owners," reported a Louisiana newspaper. And a Florida editor once wrote: "It is our painful duty to record another instance of the destruction of the life of a white man by a slave."[29]

Many masters owned one or more bondsmen whom they feared as potential murderers. A Georgia planter remembered Jack, his plantation carpenter, "the most notoriously bad character and worst Negro of the place." Jack "was the only Negro ever in our possession who I considered capable of Murdering me, or burning my dwelling at night, or capable of committing any act."[30]

Slaves like Jack could be watched closely; but others appeared to be submissive until suddenly they turned on their masters. Even trusted house servants might give violent expression to long pent up feelings. One "first rate" female domestic, while being punished, abruptly attacked her mistress, "threw her down, and beat her unmercifully on the head and face." A "favorite body servant" of a "humane master who rarely or never punished his slaves" one day became insolent. Unwilling to be disciplined, this slave waylaid his owner, "knocked him down with a whiteoak club, and beat his head to a pumice."[31] Here was another reason why it seemed foolish for a master to put his "confidence in a Negro."

At times these acts of violence appeared to be for "no cause"—that is, they resulted from a slave's "bad disposition" rather than from a particular grievance. But more often they resulted from a clash of personalities, or from some specific incident. For example, a slave who had been promised freedom in his master's will, poisoned his master to hasten the day of liberation. A South Carolina bondsman was killed during a fight with an overseer who had whipped his son. In North Carolina a slave intervened while the overseer was whipping his wife, and in the ensuing battle the overseer met his death.[32]

The most common provocation to violence was the attempt of a master or overseer either to work or to punish slaves severely. An Alabama bondsman confessed killing the overseer because "he was a hard down man on him, and said he was going to be harder." Six Louisiana slaves together killed an overseer and explained in their confession that they found it impossible to satisfy him. Three North Carolina slaves killed their master when they decided that "the old man was too hard on them, and they must get rid of him."[33] During one of these crises an overseer called upon his hands to help him punish an "unmanageable" slave: "not one of them paid the least attention to me but kept on at their work." These encounters did not always lead to death, but few plantations escaped without at least one that might easily have ended in tragedy. "Things move on here in the old Style except that now and then a refractory negro has to be taken of," was the off-hand comment of a planter.[34]

Sometimes a slave who showed sufficient determination to resist punishment managed to get the best of his owner or overseer. A proud bondsman might vow that, regardless of the consequences, he would permit no one to whip him.[35] An overseer thought twice before precipitating a major crisis with a strong-willed slave; he might even overlook minor infractions of discipline.

But an impasse such as this was decidedly unusual; if it had not been, slavery itself would have stood in jeopardy. Ordinarily these clashes between master and slave were fought out to a final settlement, and thus a thread of violence was woven into the pattern of southern bondage. Violence, indeed, was the method of resistance adopted by the boldest and most discontented slaves. Its usual reward, however, was not liberty but death!

NOTES

1. *De Bow's Review*, XI (1851), pp. 331-33.

2. Frederick Law Olmsted, *A Journey in the Back Country* (New York, 1860), p. 476; Newstead Plantation Diary, entry for June 7, 1860; Edwin A. Davis (ed.), *Plantation Life in the Florida Parishes of Louisiana, 1836-1846. As Reflected in the Diary of Bennet H. Barrow* (New York, 1943), p. 165.

3. Baltimore *Sun*, September 25, 1856; New Orleans *Picayune*, March 17, 1846.

4. Baltimore *Sun*, August 1, 1840; Frederick Law Olmstead, *A Journey in the Seaboard Slave States* (New York, 1856), pp. 190–91.

5. Richmond *Enquirer*, August 1, 1837; Mobile *Commercial Register*, November 20, 1837; John Walker Diary, entry for December 16, 1848.

6. Kenneth W. Porter, "Florida Slaves and Free Negroes in the Seminole War, 1835–1842," *Journal of Negro History*, XXVIII (1943), pp. 390–421.

7. Tallahassee *Floridian and Journal*, February 20, 1858.

8. Austin *Texas State Gazette*, September 23, 1854; April 7, June 2, 1855; San Antonio *Ledger*, September 21, 1854; Frederick Law Olmsted, *A Journey Through Texas* (New York, 1857), pp. 323-27; Paul S. Taylor, *An American-Mexican Frontier* (Chapel Hill, 1934), pp. 33–39.

9. Louisville *Democrat*, October 26, 1858; Richmond *Enquirer*, August 3, 1847; Harrison A. Trexler, *Slavery in Missouri 1084–1865*, (Baltimore, 1914), p. 178.

10. St. Louis *Missouri Republican*, November 5, 1849; Lexington *Kentucky Statesman*, June 20, 1854; Baltimore *Sun*, April 18, 19, 21, 1848; Edwin L. Williams, Jr., "Negro Slavery in Florida," *Florida Historical Quarterly*, XXVIII (1950), p. 185; James Redpath, *The Roving Editor: or, Talks with Slaves in the Southern States* (New York, 1859), *passim*.

11. Louisville *Democrat*, October 27, 1857; Sarah H. Bradford, *Scenes in the Life of Harriet Tubman* (Auburn, N.Y., 1869), *passim*.

12. William Still, *The Underground Railroad* (Philadelphia, 1879), *passim*; Wilbur H. Siebert, *The Underground Railroad from Slavery to Freedom* (New York, 1898), *passim*.

13. John P. Chester to Hamilton Brown, September 13, 1837, Hamilton Brown Papers.

14. Anthony Chase to Jeremiah Hoffman, August 8, 1827, Otho Holland Williams Papers.

15. New Orleans *Picayune*, November 4, 1851.

16. John C. Hurd, *The Law of Freedom and Bondage in the United States* (Boston, 1858-62), 1, p. 232; Helen T. Catterall (ed.), *Judicial Cases Concerning American Slavery and the Negro* (Washington, D.C., 1926-37), II, pp. 281-82; *De Bow's Review*, XXVI (1859), p. 107; Moore Rawls to Lewis Thompson, May 9, 1858, Lewis Thompson Papers.

17. W. P. Harrison, *The Gospel Among the Slaves*, (Nashville, 1893), p. 103; *Farmers' Register*, V (1837), p. 302.

18. Hammond Diary, entry for October 16, 1835; William S. Pettigrew to [James C. Johnston], October 3, 1850, Pettigrew Family Papers.

19. William S. Pettigrew to J. Johnston Pettigrew, March 9, 1849, Pettigrew Family Papers; Catterall (ed.), *Judicial Cases, passim*.

20. Frederick Douglass, *My Bondage and My Freedom* (New York, 1855), pp. 189-91; Austin Steward, *Twenty-Two Years a Slave* (Canandaigua, N.Y., 1856), p. 29; Olmsted, *Seaboard*, pp. 116-17; James B. Sellers, *Slavery in Alabama*, (University, Alabama, 1950), p. 257.

21. Davis (ed.), *Diary of Bennet H. Barrow*, p. 131 n.; Rachel O'Conner to David Weeks, June 16, 1833, Weeks Collection; S. Porcher Gaillard Ms. Plantation Journal, entry for May 9, 1856.

22. Helena (Ark.) *Southern Shield*, July 23, 1853; James S. Buckingham, *The Slave States of America* (London [1842]), I, p. 402; Gaillard Plantation Journal, entry for May 9, 1856.

23. Harriet Martineau, *Society in America* (New York, 1837), II, p. 113; Drew, *The Refugee*, p. 178.

24. Ulrich B. Phillips (ed.), *Plantation and Frontier: 1649-1863* (Cleveland, 1910), II, p. 31; Catterall (ed.), *Judicial Cases*, II, pp. 425-26; III, pp. 216-17; Benjamin Drew, *The Refugee* (Boston, 1856), p. 178.

25. Phillips (ed.), *Planation and Frontier*, II, p. 94; John R. Lyons to William W. Renwick, April 4, 1854, William W. Renwick Papers.

26. Petition of William Boyd to South Carolina legislature, November 29, 1858, in South Carolina Slavery Manuscripts Collection.

27. *Feliciana Whig*, quoted in Olmsted, *Back Country*, p. 474.

28. Phillips (ed.), *Plantation and Frontier*, II, pp. 90-91; Bassett, *Plantation Overseer*, pp. 78-79.

29. Austin *Texas State Gazette*, September 3, 1853; Alexandria (La.) *Red River Republican*, April 24, 1852; Pensacola *Gazette*, May 4, 1839.

30. Manigault Plantation Records, entry for March 22, 1867.

31. Rachel O'Conner to A. T. Conrad, May 26, 1836, Weeks Collection; Austin *Texas State Gazette*, September 23, 1854.

32. Martineau, *Society in America*, II, pp. 110-11; Catterall (ed.), *Judicial Cases*, II, pp. 206-207, 434-35.

33. Catterall (ed.), *Judicial Cases*, III, pp. 238-41; Reuben Carnal to Lewis Thompson, June 17, 1855, Lewis Thompson Papers; Hardy Hardison to William S. Pettigrew, February 11, 1858, Pettigrew Family Papers.

34. Taylor, "Negro Slavery in Louisiana," pp. 258-59; Charles L. Pettigrew to William S. Pettigrew, October 9, 1837, Pettigrew Family Papers.

35. Douglass, *My Bondage*, pp. 95, 242-46; William W. Brown, *Narrative of William W. Brown, a Fugitive Slave* (Boston, 1856), pp. 17-18.

American slaves
and their history

EUGENE D. GENOVESE

Eugene Genovese acknowledges the importance of blacks' writing black history, but
justifies his own work by contending that "the history of every people must be written
from without, if only to provide a necessary corrective in perspective."

In the following essay, Genovese rejects the myth of the black matriarchy and
discusses the prevalence of the nuclear family. He also describes the leadership role
of the trusted driver and presents his view of a symbiotic relationship between house
slaves and their owners. Genovese concludes that "the best slaves could do was live,
not merely physically but with as much inner autonomy as was humanly possible."
Within the context of servitude that is an accepted notion. Nonetheless, the limited
range of options is perhaps more the point. If Genovese's tone of equanimity
surprises the reader, it may be explained by his belief that until Elkins' book
appeared, slave history was "about to be drowned in a sea of moral indignation"
created by those historians who occupy "the adolescent recesses of our profession."

There is much to be said for the current notion that blacks will have to write
their own history: Black people in the United States have strong claims to
separate nationality, and every people must interpret its own history in the
light of its own traditions and experience. At the same time, the history of
every people must be written from without, if only to provide a necessary
corrective in perspective; sooner or later the history of every people must flow
from the clash of viewpoints and sensibilities that accompanies both external
and internal confrontation. But for the South there is a more compelling reason
for black and white scholars to have to live with each other. There is simply no
way of learning about either blacks or whites without learning about the other.
If it is true, as I suspect, that the next generations of black scholars will bring a
special viewpoint to Southern history, then their success or failure will rest, in
part, on their willingness to teach us something new about the masters as well
as the slaves. He who says the one, is condemned to say the other.

I should like to consider some debilitating assumptions often brought by
social historians to the study of the lower classes, and to suggest a way of
avoiding the twin elitist notions that the lower classes are generally passive or
generally on the brink of insurrection. We have so many books on slavery in
the Old South that specialists need to devote full time merely to keeping abreast
of the literature. Yet, there is not a single book and only a few scattered articles

on life in the quarters—except of course for such primary and undigested sources as the slave narratives and plantation memoirs. A good student might readily be able to answer questions about the economics of the plantation, the life of the planters, the politics of slavery expansionism, or a host of other matters, but he is not likely to know much about slave life, about the relationship of field to house slaves, or about the relationship between the slave driver or foreman and other slaves. To make matters worse, he may well think he knows a good deal, for the literature abounds in undocumented assertions and plausible legends.

The fact remains that there has not been a single study of the driver—the most important slave on the larger plantations—and only a few sketchy and misleading studies of house slaves. So far as the life of the quarters is concerned, it is enough to note that the notion persists, in the face of abundant evidence, that slaves had no family life to speak of. Historians and sociologists, both white and black, have been guilty of reasoning deductively from purely legal evidence—slave marriages were not recognized by law in the United States—and have done little actual research.

I do not propose to discuss the family in detail here, nor house slaves and drivers for that matter, but I should like to touch on all three in order to illustrate a larger point. We have made a great error in the way in which we have viewed slave life, and this error has been perpetuated by both whites and blacks, racists and antiracists. The traditional proslavery view and that of such later apologists for white supremacy as U. B. Phillips have treated the blacks as objects of white benevolence and fear—as people who needed both protection and control—and devoted attention to the ways in which black slaves adjusted to the demands of the master class. Abolitionist propaganda and the later, and now dominant, liberal viewpoint have insisted that the slave regime was so brutal and dehumanizing that blacks should be seen primarily as victims. Both these viewpoints treat black people almost wholly as objects, never as creative participants in a social process, never as half of a two-part subject.

True, abolitionist and liberal views have taken account of the ways in which slaves resisted their masters by shirking their work, breaking tools, or even rebelling, but the proslavery view generally noted that much too, even if within the context of a different interpretation. Neither has ever stopped to consider, for example, that the evidence might reflect less a deliberate attempt at sabotage or alleged Negro inferiority than a set of attitudes toward time, work, and leisure which black people developed partly in Africa and partly in the slave quarters—a set of attitudes which constituted a special case in a general pattern of behavior associated with preindustrial cultures. Preindustrial peoples knew all about hard work and discipline, but their standards were those of neither the factory nor the plantation and were embedded in a radically different culture. Yet, even such sympathetic historians as Kenneth Stampp, who give some attention to slaves as subjects and actors, have merely tried to show that slaves exercised some degree of autonomy in their responses to the blows or cajoling of their masters. We have yet to receive a respectful treatment—apart from some brief but suggestive passages in the work of W. E. B. Du Bois, C. L. R. James, and perhaps one or two others—of their attempts to achieve an autonomous life within the narrow limits of the slave plantation.[1] We have yet to have a synthetic record of their incessant struggle to escape from the culture as well as the psychological domination of the master class.

In commenting briefly on certain features of family life, house slaves, and drivers, I should like to suggest some of the rich possibilities inherent in an approach that asks much more than "What was done to the slaves?" and, in particular, asks, "What did the slaves do for themselves and how did they do it?" In a more leisurely presentation it would be possible and, indeed, necessary to discuss slave religion, entertainment, songs and dances, and many other things. But perhaps we may settle for a moment on one observation about slave religion.

We are told a great deal about the religious instruction of the slaves, by which it meant the attempt to inculcate a version of Protestant Christianity. Sometimes this instruction is interpreted as a good thing in itself and sometimes as a kind of brainwashing, but we may leave this question aside. Recently, Vincent Harding, following the suggestive probing in Du Bois's work, has offered a different perspective and suggested that the slaves had their own way of taking up Christianity and forging it into a weapon of active resistance.[2] Certainly, we must be struck by the appearance of one or another kind of messianic preacher in almost every slave revolt on record. Professor Harding therefore asks that we look at the slaves as active participants in their own religious experience and not merely as objects being worked on by slaveholding ideologues. This argument may be carried further to suggest that a distinctly black religion, at least in embryo, appeared in the quarters and played a role— the extent and precise content of which we have yet to evaluate—in shaping the daily lives of the slaves. In other words, quite apart from the problem of religion as a factor in overt resistance to slavery, we need to know how the slaves developed a religious life that enabled them to survive as autonomous human beings with a culture of their own within the white master's world.

One of the reasons we know so little about this side of the story—and about all lower-class life—is that it is undramatic. Historians, white and black, conservative, liberal, and radical, have a tendency to look for the heroic moments, either to praise or to excoriate them, and to consider ordinary daily life as so much trivia. Yet, if a slave helped to keep himself psychologically intact by breaking his master's hoe, he might also have achieved the same result by a special effort to come to terms with his God, or by loving a woman who shared his burdens, or even by aspiring to be the best worker on the plantation. We normally think of someone who aspires to be a good slave as an Uncle Tom, and maybe we should. But human beings are not so simple. If a slave aspires to a certain excellence within the system, and if his implicit trust in the generous response of the master is betrayed—as often it must be in such a system—then he is likely to be transformed into a rebel. And if so, he is likely to become the most dangerous kind of rebel, first because of his smashed illusions and second because of the skills and self-control he taught himself while appearing on the scene as an Uncle Tom. The historical record of slavery is full of people who were model slaves right up until the moment they killed their overseer, ran away, burned down the Big House, or joined an insurrection.

So what can be said about the decidedly non-Christian element in the religion of the slave quarters? The planters tell us repeatedly that every plantation had its conjurer, its voodoo man, its witch doctor. To the planters this meant a residue of African superstition, and it is, of course, possible by the 1830s all that remained in the slave quarters were local superstitions rather than a continuation of the highly sophisticated religions originally brought from Africa. But the evidence suggests the emergence of an indigenous and unique combination of African and European religious notions, adapted to the specific conditions of slave life by talented and imaginative individuals, which represented an attempt to establish a spiritual life adequate to the task of linking the slaves with the powerful culture of the masters and yet providing them with a high degree of separation and autonomy.

When we know enough of this story we shall know a good deal about the way in which the culture of an oppressed people develops. We often hear the expression "defenseless slaves," but, although any individual at any given moment may be defenseless, a whole people rarely, if ever, is. It may be on the defensive and dangerously exposed, but it almost invariably finds its own ways to survive and fight back. The trouble is that we keep looking for overt rebellious actions—the strike, the revolt, the murder, the arson, the tool-breaking—and often fail to realize that, in given conditions and at particular times, the wisdom of a people and their experience in struggle dictates a different course and an emphasis on holding together both individually and collectively. From this point of view, the most ignorant of the field slaves who followed the conjurer on the plantation was saying no to the boss and seeking an autonomous existence. That the conjurer may, in any one case, have been a fraud and even a kind of extortionist and, in another case, a genuine popular religious leader is, from this point of view, of little importance.

Let us take the family as an illustration. Slave law refused to recognize slave marriages and family ties. In this respect United States slavery was far worse than Spanish American or Luso-Brazilian. In those Catholic cultures the Church demanded and tried to guarantee that slaves be permitted to marry and that the sanctity of the slave family be upheld. As a result, generations of American historians have concluded that American slaves had no family life and that Cuban and Brazilian slaves did. This judgment will not bear examination. The slave trade to the United States was closed early: no later than 1808, except for statistically insignificant smuggling, and, in fact, for most states it ended decades earlier. The rise of the Cotton Kingdom and the great period of slavery expansion followed the closing of the slave trade. Slavery, in the numbers we are accustomed to thinking of, was a product of the period following the end of African importations. The slave force that was liberated during and after the War for Southern Independence was overwhelmingly a slave force born and raised in this country. We have good statistics on the rate of increase of that slave population, and there can be no doubt that it compared roughly to that of the whites—apart from the fact of immigration—and that furthermore, it was unique among New World slave classes. An early end to the slave trade, followed by a boom in cotton and plantation slavery, dictated a policy of encouraging slave births. In contrast, the slave trade remained open to Cuba and to Brazil until the second half of the nineteenth century; as a result, there was little economic pressure to encourage family life and slave-breeding. In Brazil and Cuba, far more men than women were imported from Africa until late in the history of the respective slave regimes; in the Old South, a rough sexual parity was established fairly early. If, therefore, religion and law militated in favor of slave families in Cuba and Brazil and against them in the Old South, economic pressure worked in reverse. The result was a self-reproducing slave force in the United States and nowhere else, so far as the statistics reveal.

It may immediately be objected that the outcome could have reflected selective breeding rather than family stability. But selective breeding was tried in the Caribbean and elsewhere and never worked; there is no evidence that it was ever tried on a large scale in the South. Abolitionists charged that Virginia and Maryland deliberately raised slaves—not merely encouraged, but actually fostered slave-breeding. There is no evidence. If slave-raising farms existed and if the planters were not complete fools they would have concentrated on recruiting women of childbearing age and used a relatively small number of studs. Sample studies of major slave-exporting countries in Virginia and Maryland show no significant deviations from the parallel patterns in Mississippi or other slave-buying regions.

Now, it is clear that Virginia and Maryland—and other states as well—exported their natural increase for some decades before the war. But this was a process, not a policy; it reflected the economic pressures to supplement a waning income from agriculture by occasional slave sales; it was not incompatible with the encouragement of slave families and, in fact, reinforced it. Similarly, planters in the cotton states could not work their slaves to death and then buy fresh ones, for prices were too high. They had been too high from the very moment the Cotton Kingdom began its westward march, and therefore a tradition of slave-killing never did take root. As time went on, the pressures mounted to provide slaves with enough material and even psychological satisfaction to guarantee the minimum morale needed for reproduction. These standards of treatment—so much food, living space, time off, etc.—became part of the prevailing standard of decency, not easily violated by greedy slaveholders. In some respects the American slave system may have been the worst in the world, as so many writers insist. But in purely material terms, it was probably the best. American slaves were generally fed, clothed, housed, and worked better than those of Cuba, Jamaica, or Brazil.

But the important thing here is that the prevailing standard of decency was not easily violated because the slaves had come to understand their own position. If a master wished to keep his plantation going, he had to learn the limits of his slaves' endurance. If, for example, he decided to ignore the prevailing custom of giving Sunday off or of giving an extended Christmas holiday, his slaves would feel sorely tried and would certainly pay him back with one or another form of wrecking. The slaves remained in a weak position, but they were rarely completely helpless, and by guile, brute courage, and a variety of other devices they taught every master just where the line was he dared not cross if he wanted a crop. In precisely this way, slaves took up the masters' interest in their family life and turned it to account. The typical plantation in the South was organized by family unit. Man and wife lived together with children, and within a considerable sphere the man was in fact the man in the house.

Whites violated black family life in several ways. Many families were disrupted by sales, especially in the upper South, where economic pressures were strong. White men on the plantations could and often did violate black women. Nothing can minimize these injustices. The frequency of sales is extremely hard to measure. Many slaves were troublesome and sold many times over; this inflated the total number of sales but obscured the incidence of individual transfers. The crimes against these black people are a matter of record, and no qualifications can soften their impact. But it is not at all certain that most slaves did not live stable, married lives in the quarters despite the pressures of the market. I do not wish to get into the vexing question of the violation of black women here, but certainly there was enough of it to justify the anger of those who condemned the slave regime on this ground alone. The evidence, however, does not warrant the assumption that a large percentage of black plantation women were so violated. In other words, for a judgment on the moral quality of the regime, this subject is extremely important; for an assessment of the moral life of the slaves, it is much less so.

What the sources show—both the plantation books and letters of the masters, and also the reports of runaway slaves and ex-slaves—is that the average plantation slave lived in a family setting, developed strong family ties, and held the nuclear family as the proper social norm. Planters who often nuclear family as the proper social norm. Planters who often families by sale, would sometimes argue that blacks did not really form deep and lasting attachments, that they lacked strong family sense, that they were naturally promiscuous, and so forth. Abolitionists and ex-slaves would reinforce the prevalent notion by saying that slavery was so horrible, no real family tie could be maintained. Since planters, abolitionists, and ex-slaves all said the same thing, it has usually been taken as the truth. Only it was not.

In the first place, these various sources also say opposite things, which we rarely notice. Planters agonized over the breakup of families and repeatedly expressed regrets and dismay. Often, they went to great lengths to keep families together at considerable expense, for they knew how painful it was to enforce separations. Whether they were motivated by such material considerations as the maintenance of plantation morale or more lofty sentiment is neither here nor there. They often demonstrated that they knew very well how strong the family ties were in the quarters. Planters did everything possible to encourage the slaves to live together in stable units; they recognized that a man was easier to control if he had a wife and children to worry about. The slaves, on their side, behaved variously, of course. Many were, indeed, promiscuous although much of the charge of promiscuity stemmed not so much from actual promiscuity as from sequential polygamy. They did change partners more often than Victorian whites could stomach. (In this respect, they might be considered the great forerunners of the white, middle-class sexual morality of the 1960s.) I stress this side of things—the interest of the master in slave family stability and the effort of the slave to protect his stake in a home, however impoverished —because it is now fashionable to believe that black people came out of slavery with little or no sense of family life. But if so, then we need to know why, during early Reconstruction, so many thousands wandered over the South looking for their spouse or children. We do not know just how many slaves lived as a family or were willing and able to maintain a stable family life during slavery. But the number was certainly great, whatever the percentage, and as a result, the social norm that black people carried from slavery to freedom was that of the nuclear family. If it is true that the black family has disintegrated in the ghettos—and we have yet to see conclusive evidence—then the source will have to be found in the conditions of economic and social oppression imposed upon blacks during recent decades. The slave experience, for all its tragic disruptions, pointed toward a stable postslavery family life, and recent scholarship demonstrates conclusively that the Reconstruction and post-Reconstruction black experience carried forward the acceptance of the nuclear family norm.[3]

Let us consider the role of the male and the legend of the matriarchy. Almost all writers on slavery describe the slave man as "a guest in the house" who could have no role beyond the purely sexual. The slave narratives and the diaries and letters of white plantation owners tell us something else. His position was undeniably precarious and frustrating. If his wife was to be whipped, he had to stand by and watch; he could not fully control his own children; he was not a breadwinner in the usual sense; and, in a word, there were severe restrictions imposed upon the manifestations of what we somewhat erroneously call manliness. But, both masters and ex-slaves tell us about some plantations on which certain women were not easily or often punished because it was readily understood that, to punish the woman, it would be necessary to kill her man first. These cases were the exception, but they tell us at the start that the man felt a duty to protect his woman. If circumstances conspired to prevent his fulfilling that duty, those circumstances often included his woman's not expecting it and, indeed, consoling him about the futility of such a gesture. We cannot know what was said between a man and a woman when they lay down together at night after such outrages, but there are enough hints in the slave narratives to suggest that both knew what a man could do, as well as what he "should" do, especially when there were children to consider. Many scholars suggest that black women treated their men with contempt for not doing what circumstances made impossible. This is a deduction from tenuous assumptions; it is not a demonstrated fact.

Beyond that, the man of the house did do various things. He trapped and hunted animals to supplement the diet in the quarters, and in this small but important and symbolic way he was a breadwinner. He organized the garden plot and presided over the division of labor with his wife. He disciplined his children—or divided that function with his wife as people in other circum-stances do—and generally was the source of authority in the cabin. This relationship within the family was not always idyllic. In many instances, his authority over both wife and children was imposed by force. Masters forbade men to hit their wives and children and whipped them for it; but they did it anyway and often. And there is not much evidence that women readily ran to the master to ask that her husband be whipped for striking her. The evidence on these matters is fragmentary, but it suggests that the men asserted their authority as best they could; the women expected to have to defer to their husbands in certain matters; and that both tried hard to keep the master out of their lives. The conditions were unfavorable, and perhaps many men did succumb and in one way or another became emasculated. But we might also reflect on the ways in which black men and women conspired to maintain their own sense of dignity and their own autonomy by settling things among themselves and thereby asserting their own personalities.

Black women have often been praised—and justly so—for their strength and determination in holding their families together during slavery, when the man was supposedly put aside or rendered irrelevant. It is time, I think, to praise them for another thing they seem to have been able to do in large numbers: to support a man they loved in ways deep enough and varied enough to help him resist the mighty forces for dehumanization and emasculation. Without the support of their women, not many black men could have survived; but with it—and there is plenty of testimony that they often had it—many could and did.

If our failure to see the plantation from the vantage point of the slave quarters has led us to substitute abstractions for research on the slave family, so has it saddled us with unsubstantiated and erroneous ideas on house slaves. According to the legend, house slaves were the Uncle Toms of the system—a privileged caste apart, contemptuous of the field hands, jealous of their place in the affection or at least eye of the white master and mistress, and generally speaking, finks, sellouts, and white man's niggers. Like most stereotypes, this one has its kernel of truth. There were, indeed, many house slaves who fit the description. But we might begin by considering a small fact. Half the slaves in the rural South lived on farms of twenty or fewer slaves; another twenty-five per cent lived on plantations with twenty to fifty slaves. Only twenty-five per cent, in other words, lived on plantations of fifty or more, and of those, the overwhelming majority lived on units of less than one hundred—that is, on units of less than twenty slave families. In short, the typical house slave serviced either a small farm or, at best, a moderate plantation. Only a few lived and worked on plantations large enough to permit the formation of a separate group of house slaves—of enough house slaves to form a caste unto themselves.

Our idea of the fancy-dressed, uppity, self-inflated house slave who despised the field blacks and identified with the whites is a product of the relatively small group who lived in the towns and cities like Charleston, New Orleans, and Richmond. These townhouse slaves and a tiny group of privileged house slaves on huge plantations could and sometimes did form a separate caste with the attributes described in the literature. Certainly, the great planters and their families, who left most of the white-family records that have been relied on as the major source, would most likely have remembered precisely these slaves. Even these blacks deserve a more careful look than they have received, for they were much more complicated people than we have been led to believe. But, the important point is that the typical house slave was far removed from this condition. He, or more likely she, worked with perhaps one to three or four others on an estate too small to permit any such caste formation.

If the typical house slave was an Uncle Tom and a spoiled child of the whites, then we need to be told just why so many of them turn up in the records of runaways. There is abundant evidence from the war years. We hear much about the faithful retainers who held the Yankees off from the Big House, or protected young missus, or hid the family silver. Such types existed and were not at all rare. But they do not appear to have been nearly so numerous as those house slaves who joined the field slaves in fleeing to the Yankee lines when the opportunity arose. The best source on this point is the planters themselves, who were shocked at the defection of their favorite slaves. They could readily understand the defection of the field hands, whom they consid-ered stupid and easily led, but they were unable to account for the flight, sometimes with expressions of regret and sometimes with expressions of anger and hatred, of their house slaves. They had always thought they knew these blacks, loved them, were loved by them, and they considered them part of the family. One day they learned that they had been deceiving themselves and living intimately with people they did not know at all. The house slaves, when the opportunity presented itself, responded with the same range of behavior as did the field slaves. They proved themselves just as often rebellious and independent as they did docile and loyal.

This display of independence really was nothing new. If it is true that house slaves were often regarded as traitors to the black cause during slave rebellions, it is also true that their appearance in those rebellions was not as rare as we are led to believe. A black rebel leader told Denmark Vesey and his followers not to trust the house slaves because they were too tied to the whites, but we ought also note that some of the toughest and most devoted of those leaders in Charleston in 1822 were themselves house slaves. In particular, the great scandal of the event in Charleston was the role played by the most trusted slaves, of the governor of South Carolina. Certainly, the role of the house slave was always ambiguous and often treacherous. But if many house slaves betrayed their fellows, many others collected information in the Big House and passed it on to the quarters. We know how well-informed the field slaves were about movements of Yankee troops during the war; we know that these field slaves fled to the Yankee lines with uncanny accuracy in timing and direction. Probably no group was more influential in providing the necessary information than those very house slaves who are so often denigrated.

The decision of slaves, whether house slaves or not, to protect whites during slave insurrections or other catastrophes, hardly proves them to have been Toms. The master-slave relationship, especially when it occurred in the intimacies of the Big House, was always profoundly ambivalent. Many of the same slaves who protected their masters and mistresses from harm and thereby asserted their own humanity were anything but docile creatures of the whites.

Since most house slaves worked on estates too small for a separate existence, their social life was normally down in the quarters and not apart or with the whites. The sexes were rarely evenly matched in the house, where women predominated, and even when they were, the group was too small for natural pairing off. A large number of house slaves married field hands or, more likely, the more skilled artisans or workers. Under such circumstances, the line between house slaves and field hands was not sharp for most slaves. Except on the really large units, house slaves were expected to help out in the fields during picking season and during emergencies. The average house slave got periodic tastes of field work and had little opportunity to cultivate airs.

There are two general features to the question of house slaves that deserve comment: first, there is the ambiguity of their situation and its resultant ambivalence toward whites; the other is the significance of the house slave in the formation of a distinctly Afro-American culture. The one point I should insist upon in any analysis of the house slave is ambivalence. People, black and white, slave and master, thrown together in the intimacy of the Big House, had to emerge loving and hating each other. Life together meant sharing each other's pains and problems, confiding secrets, having company when no one else would do, being forced to help one another in a multitude of ways. It also meant jointly experiencing, but in tragically opposite ways, the full force of lordship and bondage: that is, the full force of petty tyranny imposed by one woman on another; of expecting someone to be at your beck and call regardless of her own feelings and wishes; of being able to take out one's frustrations and disappointments on an innocent bystander, who would no doubt be guilty enough of something since servants are always falling short of the expectations.

To illustrate the complexity of black slave behavior in the Big House, let us take a single illustration. It is typical in the one sense that it catches the condition of ambiguity and of entwined, yet hostile, lives. Beyond that, it is of course unique, as are all individual experiences. Eliza L. Magruder was the niece of a deceased planter and politician from the Natchez, Mississippi, region and went to live with her aunt Olivia, who managed the old plantation herself. Miss Eliza kept a diary for the years 1846 and 1847 and then again for 1854 and 1857.[4] Possibly, she kept a diary for the intermittent years which has been lost. In any case, she has a number of references to a slave girl, Annica, and a few to another, Lavinia. We have here four women, two white and two black, two mistresses and two servants, thrown together in a single house and forced on each other's company all year long, year after year.

On April 17, 1846, Miss Eliza wrote in her diary more or less in passing, "Aunt Olivia whipped Annica for obstinacy." This unladylike chastisement had followed incidents in which Annica had been "impudent." About a month later, on September 11, Annica took another whipping—for "obstinacy." Miss Eliza appears to have been a bit squeamish, for her tone, if we read it correctly, suggests that she was not accustomed to witnessing such unpleasantness. On January 24, 1847, she confided to her diary, "I feel badly. Got very angry and whipped Lavinia. O! for government over my temper." But the world progresses, and so did Miss Eliza's fortitude in the face of other people's adversity. When her diary resumed in 1854, she had changed slightly: the squeamishness had diminished. Annica had not changed: she had remained her old, saucy self. October 26, 1854: "Boxed Annica's ears for impertinence."

Punctuated by this war of wills, daily life went on. Annica's mother lived in Jackson, Mississippi, and mother and daughter kept in touch. Since Annica could neither read nor write, Miss Eliza served as her helpmate and confidant. December 5, 1854: "I wrote for Annica to her mother." Mamma wrote back in due time, no doubt to Annica's satisfaction, but also to her discomfiture. As Miss Eliza observed on January 25, 1855, "Annica got a letter from her mammy which detected her in a lie. O! that negroes generally were more truthful." So, we ought not to be surprised that Miss Eliza could not write without a trace of the old squeamishness on July 1, 1855, "I whipt Annica."

The impertinent Annica remained undaunted. November 29, 1855: "Aunt Olivia gave Annica a good scolding and made her ask my pardon and will punish her otherwise." Perhaps we should conclude that Annica's atrocious behavior had earned the undying enmity of the austere white ladies, but some doubts may be permitted. On July 24, 1856, several of their neighbors set out on a trip to Jackson, Mississippi, where, it will be recalled, Annica's mother lived. Aunt Olivia, with Miss Eliza's concurrence, sent Annica along for a two-week holiday and provided ten dollars for her expenses. On August 3, Annica returned home in time for breakfast. In the interim Miss Eliza had Lavinia as an object of wrath, for Lavinia had "very much provoked" her by lying and by being impertinent. "Aunt Olivia boxed her ears for it." Lavinia's day of glory did not last; it was not long before Annica reclaimed full possession of the title of the most impudent nigger in the Big House. On September 4, 1856, "Annica was very impertinent, and I boxed her ears." Three days later, wrote Miss Eliza, "I kept Annica in in the afternoon for impudence." The next day (September 8) Miss Eliza told Aunt Olivia about Annica's misconduct. "She reproved her for it and will I suppose punish her in some way." Life traveled on into November, when on the tenth day of the month, "Aunt Olivia whipt Annica for impertinence."

At this point, after a decade of impudence, impertinence, obstinacy, whipping, and ear-boxing, one might expect that Annica would have been dispatched to the cotton fields by women who could not abide her. But she remained in the Big House. And what shall we make of such incidents as that which occurred on the night of December 29, 1856, when poor Annica was ill and in pain? It is not so much that Miss Eliza sat up with her, doing what she could; it is rather that she seemed both concerned and conscious of performing a simple duty. On the assumption that the illness left Annica weak for a while, Miss Eliza of course still had Lavinia. January 30, 1857: "I boxed Lavinia's ears for coming up late when I told her not."

On April 23, 1857, Annica greatly pleased Miss Eliza by making her a white bonnet. But by April 26, Annica was once again making trouble: "Aunt Olivia punished Annica by keeping her in her room all afternoon." And the next day: "Aunt Olivia had had Annica locked up in the garret all day. I pray it may humble her and make further punishment unnecessary."

On August 18, 1857, "Aunt Olivia held a court of enquiry, but didn't find out who ripped my pattern." There is no proof that Annica did it; still one wonders. Two weeks later in Miss Eliza's Sunday school, "Annica was strongly tempted to misbehave. I brought her in however." The entries end there.

Let us suppose the ladies had carried their household into the war years: What then? It would take little imagination to see Annica's face and to hear her tone as she marched into the kitchen to announce her departure for the federal lines. It would not even take much imagination to see her burning the house down. Yet, she had never been violent, and we should not be too quick to assume that she would easily have left the only home she had known as an adult and the women who wrote letters to her mamma, exchanged confidences, and stayed up with her on feverish nights. The only thing we can be sure of is that she remained impudent to the day she died.

What I think this anecdote demonstrates above all is the ambivalence inherent in the Big House relationship and the stubborn struggle for individuality that house slaves, whip or no whip, were capable of. Yet it may also hint at another side and thereby help explain why so many black militants, like so many historians before them, are quick to condemn the whole house-slave legacy as one to be exorcized. The house slaves were, indeed, close to the whites, and of all the black groups they exhibited the most direct adherence to certain white cultural standards. In their religious practices, their dress, their manners, and their prejudices they were undoubtedly the black group most influenced by Euro-American culture. But this kind of cultural accommodation was by no means the same thing as docility or Uncle Tomism. Even a relatively assimilated house slave could and normally did strike back, assert independence, and resist arbitrariness and oppression. We are today accustomed to thinking of black nationalists as "militants" and civil rights integrationists as "moderates," "conservatives," or something worse. Yet, Dr. Martin Luther King, Jr., and his followers were and are militant integrationists, prepared to give up their lives for their people; on the other hand, there are plenty of black nationalists who are anything but militant. The tension between integration and separatism has always rent the black community, but now is has led us to confuse questions of militancy with those of nationalism. In fact, the combinations vary; there is no straight identification of either integrationists or separatists with either militancy or accommodation. Field hands or house slaves could be either docile, "accommodating," or rebellious, and in all probablity most were all at once.

If today the house slaves have a bad press, it is largely because of their cultural assimilationism, from which it is erroneously deduced that they were docile. The first point may be valid; the second is not. LeRoi Jones, for example, in his brilliant book, *Blues People*, argues convincingly that field slaves had forged the rudiments of a distinct Afro-American culture whereas the house slaves largely took over the culture of the whites. He writes primarily about black music, but he might easily extend his analysis to language and other fields. There are clearly two ways of looking at this side of the house-slave experience. On the one hand, the house slaves reinforced white culture in the slave quarters; they were one of the Americanizing elements in the black community. On the other hand, they wittingly or unwittingly served as agents of white repression of an indigenous Afro-American national culture. Of course, both these statements are really the same; it is merely that they differ in their implicit value judgments. But we ought to remember that this role did not reduce the house slave to Uncle Tomism. Rather, it was played out by house slaves who were in their own way often quite rebellious and independent in their behavior. And therefore, even these slaves, notwithstanding their assimilationist outlook and action, also contributed in no small degree to the tradition of survival and resistance to oppression that today inspires the black liberation movement.

If today we are inclined to accept uncritically the contemptuous attitude that some critics have toward the house slave, we might ponder the reflections of the great black pianist, Cecil Taylor. Taylor was speaking in the mid-1960s—a century after slavery—but he was speaking of his own father in a way that I think applies to what might be said of house slaves. Taylor was talking to A. B. Spellman, as reported in Spellman's book, *Four Lives in the Bebop Business*:

> Music to me was in a way holding on to Negro culture, because there wasn't much of it around. My father has a great store of knowledge about black folklore. He could talk about how it was with the slaves in the 1860s, about the field shouts and hollers, about myths of black people. . . . He worked out in Long Island for a State Senator. He was a house servant and a chef at the Senator's sanatorium for wealthy mental wrecks. And actually it was my father more than the Senator himself who raised the Senator's children. . . .
>
> And I really used to get dragged at my father for taking such shit off these people. I didn't dig his being a house servant. I really didn't understand my old man; well, you're my generation and you know the difference between us and our fathers. Like, they had to be strong men to take what they took. But of course we didn't see it that way. So that I feel now that I really didn't understand my father, who was a really lovely cat. He used to tell me to stay cool, not to get excited. He had a way of letting other people display their emotions while keeping control of his own. People used to say to me, "Cecil, you'll never be the gentleman your father was." That's true. My father was quite a gentleman. . . . I wish that I had taken down more about all that he knew about black folklore, because that's lost too; he died in 1961.[5]

We may end with another misunderstood group of slaves —the drivers. These black slave foremen were chosen by the master to work under his direction or that of an overseer and to keep the hands moving. They would rouse the field slaves in the morning and check their cabins at night; would take responsibility for their performance; and often, would be the ones to lay the whip across their backs. In the literature the drivers appear as ogres, monsters, betrayers, and sadists. Sometimes they were. Yet, Mrs. Willie Lee Rose, in her book, *Rehearsal for Reconstruction*, notes that it was the drivers in the Sea Islands who kept the plantations together after the masters had fled the approach of the Yankees, who kept up discipline, and who led the blacks during those difficult days. Now, it is obvious that if the drivers were what they have been reported as having been, they would have had their throats cut as soon as their white protectors had left. In my own research for the war years I have found repeatedly, almost monotonously, that when the slaves fled the plantations or else took over plantations deserted by the whites, the drivers emerged as the leaders. Moreover, the runaway records from the North and from Canada reveal that a number of drivers were among those who successfully escaped the South.

One clue to the actual state of affairs may be found in the agricultural journals for which many planters and overseers wrote about plantation matters.

Overseers often complained bitterly that masters trusted their drivers more than they trusted them. They charged that quite often overseers would be fired at the driver's instigation and that, in general, masters were too close to their drivers and too hostile and suspicious toward their white overseers. The planters did not deny the charges; rather, they admitted them and defended themselves by arguing that the drivers were slaves who had earned their trust and that they had to have some kind of check on their overseers. Overseers were changed every two or three years on most plantations whereas drivers remained in their jobs endlessly. The normal state of affairs was for any given driver to remain in his position while a parade of overseers came and went.

It had to be so. The slaves had to be controlled if production was to be on schedule, but only romantics could think that a whip alone could effect that result. The actual amount of work done and the quality of life on the plantation was the result of a compromise between masters and slaves. It was a grossly unfair and one-sided compromise, with the master holding a big edge, but the slaves did not simply lie down and take whatever came. They had their own ways of foot-dragging, dissembling, delaying, and sabotaging. The role of the driver was to minimize the friction by mediating between the Big House and the quarters. On the one hand he was the master's man: he obeyed orders, inflicted punishments, and stood for authority and discipline. On the other hand, he could and did tell the master that the overseer was too harsh, too irregular; that he was incapable of holding the respect of the hands; that he was a bungler. The slaves generally knew just how much they had to put up with under a barbarous labor system but they also knew what even that system regarded as going too far. The driver was their voice in the Big House as well as the master's voice in the quarters.

Former slaves tell us of drivers who were sadistic monsters, but they also tell us of drivers who did everything possible to soften punishments and to protect the slaves as best they could. It was an impossible situation, but there is little evidence that drivers were generally hated by the field hands. The selection of a driver was a difficult matter for a master. First, the driver had to be a strong man, capable of bullying rather than being bullied. Second, he had to be uncommonly intelligent and capable of understanding a good deal about plantation management. A driver had to command respect in the quarters. It would be possible to get along for a while with a brutal driver who could rule by fear, but generally, planters understood that respect and acquiescence were as important as fear, and that a driver had to do more than make others afraid of him. It was then necessary to pick a man who had leadership qualities in the eyes of the slaves.

The drivers commanded respect in various ways. Sometimes they became preachers among the slaves and got added prestige that way. Sometimes, possibly quite often, they acted as judge and jury in the quarters. Disputes among slaves arose often, generally about women and family matters. If there were fights or bitter quarrels, and if they were called to the attention of the overseer or the master, the end would be a whipping for one or more participants. Under such circumstances, the driver was the natural choice of the slaves themselves to arbitrate knotty problems. With such roles in and out of the quarters, it is no wonder that so many drivers remained leaders during and after the war when the blacks had the choice of discarding them and following others.

Every plantation had two kinds of so-called "bad niggers." The first kind were those so designated by the masters because they were recalcitrant. The second kind were those so designated by the slaves themselves. These were slaves who may or may not have troubled the master directly but who were a problem to their fellow slaves because they stole, or bullied, or abused other men's women. The drivers were in a position to know what was happening in the quarters and to intervene to protect weaker or more timid slaves against these bullies. In short, the drivers' position was highly ambiguous and on balance was probably more often than not positive from the slave point of view. Whatever the intentions of the master, even in the selection of his own foremen—his own men, as it were—the slaves generally were not passive, not objects, but active agents who helped shape events, even if within narrow limits and with great difficulty.

We know that there were not many slave revolts in the South, and that those that did occur were small and local affairs. There were good reasons for the low incidence of rebellion: In general, the balance of forces was such that revolt was suicide. Under such conditions, black slaves struggled to live and to make some kind of life for themselves. If their actions were less bombastic and heroic than romantic historians would like us to believe, they were nonetheless impressive in their assertion of resourcefulness, dignity, and a strong sense of self and community. Had they not been, the fate of black America after emancipation would have been even grimmer than it was. For the most part the best that the slaves could do was live, not merely physically but with as much inner autonomy as was humanly possible.

Every man has his own judgment of heroism, but we might reflect on the kind of heroism alluded to by Cecil Taylor in his moving tribute to his father. There are moments in the history of every people—and sometimes these historical moments are centuries—in which they cannot do more than succeed in keeping themselves together and maintaining themselves as human beings with a sense of individual dignity and collective identity. Slavery was such a moment for black people in America, and their performance during it bequeathed a legacy that combined many negative elements to be exorcized[6] and repudiated with decisive elements of community self-discipline. If one were to tax even the privileged house slaves or drivers with the question, "Where were you when your people were groaning under the lash," they could, if they chose, answer with a paraphrase of the Abbé Sieyès, but proudly and without his cynicism, "We were with our people, and together we survived."

NOTES

1. See, e.g., C. L. R. James, "The Atlantic Slave Trade and Slavery: Some Interpretations of Their Significance in the Development of the United States and the Western World," *Amistad 1* (New York, 1970). Du Bois's writings are full of important ideas and hypotheses. See especially *Black Reconstruction in America* and *Souls of Black Folk.*

2. Vincent Harding, "Religion and Resistance Among Ante-Bellum Negroes, 1800–1860," August Meier and Elliott Rudwick, eds., *The Making of Black America*, 1 (New York, 1969), 179–197.

3. Herbert Gutman has presented several papers to scholarly meetings and is close to completing a major book on the historical development of the black family from slavery to World War I. I am indebted to him for allowing me to see the manuscript in progress and for discussing the data with me.

4. Ms. diary in Louisiana State University library, Baton Rouge, La.

5. A. B. Spellman, *Four Lives in the Bebop Business* (New York, 1966), pp. 49–50.

6. I have discussed some of these negative features in "The Legacy of Slavery and the Roots of Black Nationalism," *Studies on the Left*, 6 (Nov.-Dec., 1966), 3–26. I stand by much of what I wrote there, but the essay is doubtless greatly weakened by a failure to appreciate black slave culture and its political implications. As a result, the political story I tried to tell is dangerously distorted. Still, that legacy of slavishness remains an important part of the story, and I think I identified some of its features correctly. I am indebted to many colleagues and friends for their criticism, without which I could not have arrived at the reconsiderations on which the present essay is based; in particular, the criticism of George Rawick has been indispensable.

the Atlantic slave trade and slavery: some interpretations of their significance in the development of the United States and the western world

C. L. R. JAMES

C. L. R. James, a black Marxist historian, analyzes the significance of slavery to world civilization. Slavery contributed to the industrial revolution and the political revolutions that followed in its wake.

He provides an outstanding three-dimensional portrait of slave life, including a vivid description of the great variety of trades and skills. As opposed to Genovese's contention in the previous article that black men could prove their manhood by bullying their women, James points out that black and white women had to free themselves from servile positions of all kinds. James' enduring contribution is his analysis of the impact of slavery and the role of the planters in shaping "an original American nationality."

Who were the slaves? They came for the most part from West Africa, these slaves who had been stolen and taken from their homes and brought virtually nothing with them, except themselves. The slaves not only could not bring material objects with them, they could not easily bring over their older social institutions, their languages, and cultures. Coming from a large area of West Africa in which dozens upon dozens of distinct peoples lived, with their own languages, social relations, cultures, and religions, these Africans were jumbled together on board the slave ships, "seasoned" by the middle passage, and then seasoned again in their first years in the New World.

For the slave brought himself; he brought with him the content of his mind, his memory. He thought in the logic and the language of his people. He recognized as socially significant that which he had been taught to see and comprehend; he gestured and laughed, cried, and held his facial muscles in ways that had been taught him from childhood. He valued that which his previous life had taught him to value; he feared that which he had feared in Africa; his very motions were those of his people and he passed all of this on to

From C. L. R. James, "The Atlantic Slave Trade and Slavery: Some Interpretations of Their Significance in the Development of the United States and the Western World," *Amistad 1: Writings on Black History and Culture*, edited by John A. Williams and Charles F. Harris (New York: Random House, 1970), 132–164.

his children. He faced this contradictory situation in a context into which he was thrown among people of different African backgrounds. All Africans were slaves, slaves were supposed to act in a specific way. But what was this way? There was no model to follow, only one to build.

The slave from Africa was denied the right to act out the contents of his mind and memory—and yet he *had* to do this. How was this contradiction resolved? What were the new forms created in the context of slavery?

A new community was formed; it took its form in the slave quarters of the plantations and the black sections of the cities. In the United States, this community developed its own Christian church, one designed to meet the needs of slaves and Afro-American freedmen in the New World. It had its own system of communication based on the reality of the plantation. It had its own value system, reflective of the attitudes of African peasants, but at the same time owing its allegiance to dominant American modes. It had its own language patterns, because of the isolation of the plantation system from steady European linguistic influences. West African words and speech patterns were combined with the speech of the eighteenth-century Scotch-Irish.

This black community was the center of life for the slaves; it gave them an independent basis for life. The slaves did not suffer from rootlessness—they belonged to the slave community, and even if they were sold down the river they would find themselves on new plantations. Here, people who shared a common destiny would help them find a life in the new environment.

Each plantation was a self-sufficient unit. The slaves worked at all the skills necessary to maintain the plantation in working order and keep at a minimum the expense of importing necessary items from England. Slave blacksmiths manufactured everything from nails to plowshares. Coopers made the hoops around the tobacco barrels. The clothing the wore was turned out by slave shoemakers, dyers, tanners, and weavers. The slave artisan moved from one task to another as the need arose.

Skilled labor also took the slave off the plantation. Black pilots poled the rafts laden with tobacco from the tributaries of the river to its mouth, where the ship was anchored; black seaman conducted the ferries across Virginia's rivers to transport new settlers. Many planters found it more profitable to hire out their skilled black workmen for seventy-five to two hundred dollars a year. This black craftsman living away from the plantation was allowed seventy-five cents a week as his allowance for food and board. When the colonies engaged in their war with England for independence, all imports from the mother country ceased. Crude factories were started and slaves were used to work them; also, out of the mines they dug lead, a necessary ingredient in the manufacture of bullets.

The tedium of tobacco cultivation was worse than the exhaustion of simple physical labor. Cotton, which succeeded tobacco as the plantation's output, had to be chopped with great care when the young plant had no more than three of four leaves.

Overworked field hands would take off to the nearby weeds or swamps where they would lay out for a time. At night they would steal back to the slave quarters for food and information about what the master intended to do about their absence. In the swamps of the eastern section of North Carolina, runaways were employed by black lumbermen or the poor whites and could raise their own children for a time. The master, who didn't know the hideouts as well as the slaves did, let it be known through a word passed on to the slave quarters that he was prepared to negotiate for less work and no whippings if only his precious laborers would return.

The slaves fought to set their own tempo and rhythm of work. Says Frederick Douglass:

> There is much rivalry among slaves, at time, as to which can do the most work and masters generally seek to promote such rivalry. But some of them were too wise to race each other very long. Such racing, we had the sagacity to see, was not likely to pay. We had times out for measuring each others strength, but we knew too much to keep up the competition so long as to produce an extra-ordinary days work. We knew that if by extra-ordinary exertion, a large quantity of work was done in one day, the fact becoming known to the master, the same would be expected of us every day. This thought was enough to bring us to a dead halt whenever so much excited for the race.

There was very little of the slave's life that he could call his own. In the slave quarters at night there was a lowering of the mask that covered the day's labors. Bantering and mimicry, gossiping and laughter could be unrestrained. House servants regaled other members of the "row"—some of whom had never set foot in the big house—with tales of "master" and "missus," would "take them off" in speech and gesture so faithful that the less privileged would shake with laughter.

Besides the oppression of the master himself, his laws, and his overseers, the slaves were oppressed by their limited knowledge of the world outside the plantation. Masters felt that a slave who learned how to read and write would lose his proficiency at picking worms off tobacco leaves or at chopping cotton, so thoroughly had slavery separated thought and feeling from work. But the capacities of men were always leaping out of the confinements of the system. Always with one eye cocked toward the door, the slaves learned how to read and write, thus they attained that standard—besides the accumulation of money, tobacco, cotton, and lands—by which society judged the standing of its members. The Bible was the most readily available book; its wide and varied use by the slave would have made the founders of Christianity proud. It was a course in the alphabet, a first reader, and a series of lessons in the history of mankind.

The capacities of men were always leaping out of the confinements of the system. Written passes, which slaves were required to carry on their person when away from the plantation, could be made up by those who had learned how to read and write. Deciphering the alphabet opened new avenues to the world. A primary achievement of the slaves as a class is that they fashioned a system of communication—an illegal, underground, grapevine telegraph which would stand the test of an emergency.

When hostilities broke out between the thirteen colonies and the King of England, the British field commander in the South offered freedom to every slave who would enter his army. In Virginia alone, thirty thousand fled their labors; the bitter comment of a slaveholder points up this situation: "Negroes have a wonderful art of communicating intelligence among themselves; it will run several hundred miles in a fortnight." There was such a large proportion of slaves in the state, that South Carolina did not even dare enter the War of Independence for fear of what its laboring force would do. It lost twenty-five thousand nevertheless. Across the South every fifth slave fled toward the British army.

An independent national state was being set up by an American Congress.

The very air became filled with expressed passions of human rights, liberties, dignity, equality, and the pursuit of happiness. One of its effects on the slaves was seen on the night of August 30, 1800. Over one thousand slave rebels gathered some six miles from Richmond, capital city of Virginia, the state which was to produce four of the first five American Presidents. All through the spring of that year the slaves prepared their own arms, including five hundred bullets, manufactured in secret. Each Sunday for months, Gabriel Prosser entered the city, noting its strategic points and possible sources of arms and ammunition. Their plan was to proclaim Virginia a Negro state. If the merchants of Richmond would yield their fortunes to the rebels their lives would be spared and they would be feted at a public dinner.

On the night appointed for the march a heavy rain had fallen, making the road into Richmond impassable. The delay gave the stunned authorities an opportunity to mobilize themselves. Some forty slaves were arrested and put on trial. They revealed no names of other participants. Some estimates placed the extent of the rebellion at ten thousand slaves, others put the figure as high as sixty thousand. The demeanor and remarks of the prisoners on trial—Gabriel: "I have nothing more to offer than what General Washington would have had to offer, had he been taken and put on trial by them. I have adventured my life to obtain the liberty of my countrymen . . ."

In this early period the slave who ran away was most often a skilled craftsman, a man with confidence of making his way in the world. As described by a newspaper advertisement of the day:

Run away from the subscriber's farm, about seven miles from Anapolis, on the 8th instant; two slaves Will and Tom; they are brothers. Will, a straight tall well-made fellow, upwards of six feet high, he is generally called black, but has a rather yellowish complextion, by trade a carpenter and a cooper, and in general capable of the use of tools in almost any work; saws well at the whip saw, about thirty years of age. When he speaks quick he stammers a little in his speech. Tom, a stout well-made fellow, a bright mulatto, twenty-four years of age, and about five feet nine or ten inches high; he is a complete hand at plantation work and can handle tools pretty well . . . they have a variety of clothing, and it is supposed they will not appear abroad in what they wear at home. Will writes pretty well, and if he and his brother are not furnished with passes from others they will not be lost for them, but upon proper examination may be discovered to be forged. These people it is imagined are gone for Baltimore as Tom has a wife there . . .

Except in a general way he could not be sure of the direction of his travels, guiding himself by the stars and by the moss which grew on the shady side of the trees. In earlier days the safest places of concealment were the nearby swamps, the neighboring Indian tribes, and Spanish Florida. The long military arm of the slavocracy eventually reached into all these temporary outposts of freedom and incorporated them into slavery. Then soldiers returning from the War of 1812 brought the news that slavery was outlawed in Canada. The route of flight began to cut across the Kentucky mountain ranges and the Atlantic seacoast.

John Parker, a free black man from Ripley, Ohio, considered it below his dignity to ask any white man how to conduct slaves to freedom; he was responsible for the successful passage of one thousand runaways, but left no memoirs as to how he carried out his work.

In later years the work of the scout took him into the Deep South rather than await the knock on the door. On her expeditions, Harriet Tubman would take the precaution of starting on Saturday night so that they would be well along their journey before they were advertised. Harriet often paid another black person to follow the man who posted the descriptions of her companions and to tear them down. The risks of taking along different types of people in one group had to be considered. Babies were sometimes drugged with paregoric. She sometimes strengthened the faint-hearted by threatening to use her revolver and declaring, ". . . you go on you die . . . dead [N]egroes tell no tales . . ."

As with practical people everywhere, everything was done with the materials at hand. An iron manikin in front of the home of Judge Piatt marked an interrupted station; the judge was hostile to the activity, but his wife was an enthusiastic undergrounder. A flag in the hand of the manikin signaled that the judge was not home and that his house had become a temporary station on the road. For disguise one runaway was provided simply with a gardening tool placed on his shoulder. He marched through town in a leisurely way like a man going to work somebody's garden, left the tool in a selected thicket at the edge of town, and proceeded on his way.

The Underground Railroad in the period of the 1840's grew so saucy that it advertised itself publicly as the only railroad guaranteed not to break down. Multiple routes were the key to the practical success of the railroad. It all came into being after the period of the Founding Fathers had definitively come to an end. The men of education, the leading figures of the Revolution, Washington, Jefferson, Adams, Hancock, Hamilton, Lafayette, and Kosciusko, all expressed opposition to slavery in their private conversations and correspondence. But their chief fear was that pushing antislavery to the fore might permanently divide the country into antagonistic sections.

Washington accurately described the sentiment in certain parts of the country after he himself had lost a slave in New England. "The gentleman in whose care I sent him has promised every endeavor to apprehend him; but it is not easy to do this when there are numbers who would rather facilitate the escape of slaves than apprehend them when they run away."

In the early formation of the Underground Railroad, another group whom the runaway touched with his fire was the Quakers. When they arrived in America to escape persecution, the prosperous trade in slaves corrupted even the most tender of consciences. Not being interested in politics, and prohibited by religious belief from being diverted by the theater, sports, or drink, the Quakers became highly successful businessmen and farmers. The Quakers were prom-inent and influential people and could afford to rely on the letter of the law which in Northern states had declared slavery illegal.

Having established the principle, effective organization for antislavery work came naturally to a group whose life had been drawn tightly together for hundreds of years as a religious sect. By 1820 there were some four thousand fugitive slaves in the Quaker stronghold of Philadelphia and all advertisements for runaways disappeared from Pennsylvania newpapers.

Free blacks, Quakers, and New Englanders, linked up to each other, conducted the Atlantic coast route of Underground Railroad operations. Men of a different stamp initiated a section of the western route. At the turn of the century the back-country farmer of Virginia and the Carolinas suffered much from the poverty of his land. The state legislatures were in the control of coastal planters and their lawyers; new government taxes and old debts magnified his poverty. He freed himself of all these burdens by migrating westward into the wilderness.

The slaves who accompanied this first great tide of migration, which depopulated Virginia of two hundred thousand people, were as scattered as their masters. On the early frontier there was less consciousness of their slave status. They helped in the household chores, building cabins and protecting them from Indian attack. Often they were the boatmen, whose arrival was as welcome in the settlement as the ringing of a postman in a modern apartment house.

The runaway slave heightened the powers of the popular imagination. Here was a figure who not only fled oppressive institutions, but successfully outwitted and defied them. And his flight was to the heart of civilization, not away from it; he was a universal figure whose life was in turn adventurous, tragic, and humorous.

The runaway, freed from the disabilities of slavery, was in the second and third decades of the nineteenth century coming into close contact with another highly specialized group of people—the intellectuals. The thinking of intellectuals is characterized by the fact that they view matters whole and in general, however one-sidedly and abstractly. This jamming up of two diverse elements—the black man who supposedly had no civilization in the range of his existence, and the white intellectual in whom society had placed the whole heritage of civilization—produced those works that reminded people who gave thought to the slave held in bondage that they were themselves intimately bound with him for life.

The antislavery movement was produced by the specific relation of blacks and whites during the first third of the nineteenth century. It is a fantastic phenomenon climaxed by the central phenomenon of all American history, the Civil War. Writers offer various explanations, but after a certain amount of reflection it becomes clear that abolition must be seen as an absolutely necessary stage in making America a distinct civilization, rather than just one more piece of boundaried territory in the mosaic of the world's geography.

Abolition is the great indicator of parallel movements before the Civil War and after. History really moves when the traditionally most civilized section of the population—in this case New Englanders representing the longest American line of continuity with the English tradition of lawful sovereignty—joins as coequals with those without whose labor society could not exist for a day—in this case the plantation chattel. Otherwise, history stays pretty much the same, or worse yet, repeats itself. Such was the case of the independent lay preachers in the Great English Revolution, who joined with the apprentices and day laborers; the French intelligentsia in conjunction with peasants and slum proletarians of royalist France; the Russian intellectuals meeting on certain grounds with factory workers under a Czar. In all these instances history moved forward with lasting impress.

Abolition, itself an important instance of democracy, took upon itself the extension of a certain practice and mode of national behavior. Much of the mode of national behavior was based upon regional considerations—the great potential for abolition was the Southern slave in flight to freedom from plantation labor. Then there was the firmest base of abolition extant, the free black communities of Northern city and town. New York City, for a time, provided heavy financing. Garrison's Massachusetts was becoming an antislavery fortress and the rest of New England followed, in various degrees. Children of New England had settled in the fine agricultural flatlands of Ohio and upstate New York; a momentous development as "free soil" was prepared to clash with slave expansion appetites. Pennsylvania housed an antislavery diffused with Quakerized quietist feelings.

Without the self-expressive presence of the free blacks in the cities, embodying in their persons the nationally traumatic experience of bondage and freedom, antislavery would have been a sentiment only, a movement remote and genteel in a country known as impetuous and volatile. The bulk of subscribers to Garrison's *The Liberator* were blacks in New York, Boston, and Philadelphia. It was the publicity surrounding the revolt of Nat Turner which guaranteed that Garrison, the white advocate of immediate abolition, would become a household word. The independent conventions of free blacks were anterior to the rise of Garrison and his friends. The succession of slave personalities delivered by the Underground Railroad would eventually lead to black political independence from Garrison himself.

Ohio was the scene in the 1840's of the "Hundred Convention"—political life as daily fare, with regional figures turning into nationally representative ones. Douglass, the self-emancipated slave by way of Baltimore; Garrison, who hardly had left New England before except to visit neighboring New York or far-off merrie old England; these two together spoke themselves hoarse and into general exhaustion. This now-settled middle frontier, this venerable Old Northwest, was clamoring to hear about the state of the nation from true figures of national stature, since nothing more was heard from the doughfaces in Congress sitting on the hundreds of thousands of petitions pleading for justice to the slave, and discussing the role of free settlers in a democracy.

Impending war with Mexico was a spur to far-reaching conclusions. The revived National Negro Conventions listened to a proposal for a general strike by the slave laborers of the South, who would act as a human wall barring the United States Army from invading Mexican territory and turning it into a slave planting domain. The proposal lost by one vote.

Sophisticated prejudice tells us that *Uncle Tom's Cabin* by Harriet Beecher Stowe is another vast mistake! In impact and implications marking off the hour and the decade of its arrival it rang true; in universal aspect, clear. The average worker competing with the free black man for a job and a place to live, and wrestling with his prejudices all the while, went to see the play and wept upon his identification with the slave runaway. Where formal government failed on the slavery question, people reached for a government which the Greeks had introduced so very many years earlier: that of popular drama—which the city-state then made sure everyone could see for free—so that whatever they thought of politics they could see, through the form of dramatic representation, principles, conditions, and resolutions, and sense from that emotional experience where a whole society was going. Mere political representation was succeeded by a more intense social reproduction, a more popular accurate representation; in book form, *Uncle Tom's Cabin* circulated more widely through the whole of the nineteenth century than any other, with the sole exception of that book of books, the Bible.

And if it was the running debates with Stephen A. Douglas which elevated Abraham Lincoln from the legislator's semiobscurity to national star-fire, who or what besides abolition had initiated the debate, fixing free discussion of nearly obscured cruelties on a Mississippi cotton field as the nation's prime business; set forth the concrete choices, which no mere election could decide, on the future of mid-nineteenth-century America? And if the abolitionists' method had so elevated Lincoln, what shall we say of their achievement in turning each runaway slave, now threatened with kidnapping under a new and permanent sectional compromise, into a monument either to the American's love of liberty or acquiescence to captivity? Before abolition enabled Lincoln to hallow his name, it inscribed Shadrach and Anthony Burns and Dred Scott onto the heavens for the whole world to read the American future through them.

The leading charge against abolition in the 1850's was aimed at its nearly absolute trust in the uninterrupted processes of civilization. The main critique centered upon Garrison and Phillips' endorsing—before Civil War broke out—the secession of the South, confident that slavery, separated from federal protection, must die.

The Civil War was a corrective of the notorious nineteenth-century optimism which trusted free speech and free press and the industriousness of unchatteled labor to push authoritarianism of every familiar type over that same cliff where the vestiges of feudal relations had been shattered or left to hang for dear life.

Confronted by preslavery compromises which were a source of infinite corruption, abolition gave obeisance to certain eternal principles: themselves corollaries of the civilizing process at a certain stage. Growing transcending morality titled "the higher law" would overwhelm all momentary deviousness, nullify all expedients and prearrangements disguising themselves as pillars of the Federal Union.

Belief in the morality of "the higher law" was hardly an empty absolute, devoid of content and barren of result. It was a driving impetus separating democracy in politics from the growing "hunkerism," mere hankering after public office and governmental seatwarmings which dulled the very sense of social accountability and paled before the historical momentousness of American existence.

The years of Civil War show what might have been done much earlier during the War for Independence itself when this nation was first born, and egalitarian feelings were at a zenith. But then there had been no antislavery organization. The unity of the young nation, monarchies all, had taken a certain turn at the Constitutional Convention and elsewhere, indicating that the semblance of national solidity could be maintained only if the slave kept his back bent to his labor; then North and South, East and West would not divide, and foreign enemies would wait in vain for internal weakness as the signal to spring upon their prey, the New World as distinguished from the old. But national unity excluded the black from independence; national prosperity was guaranteed by subordinating the laborer to his labor. The very existence of abolitionists during the next climactic phase of this very same question—Civil War—simply insured that the slave would not be lost sight of no matter how much the government tried to lose sight of him.

The destruction of the Colonizationists earlier was the main factor staying the hand of the government which wanted to colonize blacks, freed men, even in the midst of, and because of, the tensions of Civil War to avoid disputations as to their American destiny.

On the universal effect of American abolition: it helped free the Russian serf on the other side of the world—but not directly. Indirectly, it is clear enough if we go by stepping-stone geography. Harriet Beecher Stowe's book was banned in Italy as an incitement to the peasantry. But the leading Russian publication of the intellectual exiles translated the whole work as a free supplement for all subscribers. Keep in mind, too, that from the time of Peter the Great, Russia had been trying to make its way through the front door of world civilization. Add to this a fact of international power politics: When England and France threatened to join the South, Russia shifted its weight to the North. In the middle of the Civil War the Russian fleet showed up in New York harbor, a great ball was thrown, and a festive time was had by all. Abolition of serfdom there and of slavery here occurred almost simultaneously.

Something should be said about the white American worker in regard to abolition. Some were antislavery, some were not. Skilled workers, proud of their craft which brought them a measure of independence, were by and large antislavery. The unskilled, fearing possible competition from the blacks, inclined toward neutrality or gave in to caste prejudice. However, skilled or unskilled, the worker in America was an ardent democrat. No matter how much he suspected another man might take his job, he could not develop a great affection for plantation life as the prototype of American life as a whole.

Abolitionists were not only concerned with the rights of blacks, free and slave, they were concerned with their education. The abolitionist created the first integrated education in the United States—including higher education. And when they did not create integrated education they conducted classes and schools for the ex-slaves, schools partially staffed by black teachers. The abolitionists were at the center of the educational reforms and changes of this period in the United States. In schools for Negro children they experimented with improved methods of education.

But more. They fought not only for the emancipation of Negroes and the improvement of the lives of freedmen. They fought for the emancipation of women, their education, and their own self-development. Oberlin College, the first college to accept Negroes in the United States, was also the first college to accept women in the United States, becoming the first co-educational institution of higher learning.

In their struggle for women's rights, a struggle that went on inside and outside of the movement, abolitionists set in motion the liberation of women—and consequently of men. What Margaret Fuller and other great female abolitionists were trying to establish was their right to create relations with men in which they were not in effect the chattel of their husbands through the marriage contract, as slaves were chattel in the grip of property holders.

The abolitionists were involved in a crucial way in the most significant struggles for human emancipation that were going on in the United States: the abolition of capital punishment, prison reform, attacks on established religion in the name of a purified religion, work for the rights of new waves of immigrants and better treatment of American Indians, and the movement to abolish war. Though they often differed among themselves, and were very often confused in the way that people are who are going forward, there is a very direct development from the Declaration of Independence to the abolitionists' efforts to Lincoln's understanding that the Civil War was about whether government of the people, by the people, and for the people would perish from the earth.

It must be said that the slave community itself was the heart of the abolitionist movement. This is a claim that must seem most extraordinarily outrageous to those who think of abolitionism as a movement which required organizations, offices, officers, financiers, printing presses and newspapers, public platforms and orators, writers and petitions. Yet the center of activity of abolitionism lay in the movement of the slaves for their own liberation. The general impact of the abolitionist movement upon the slave communities was profound. It gave the slaves that hope that enabled them to survive and to engage in the day-by-day struggles that won for them that amount of extra room in which to live that made more than mere continued existence possible.

The abolitionist movement led to a change in the climate of American life. The reaction after the American Revolution had led to a period in which a profound pessimism touched the lives of all those who lived by the ideals of the Declaration of Independence, that clarion call for a new birth of freedom for mankind. Abraham Lincoln, a son of the Declaration, had in 1837 felt that all that could be done was to defend the gains of the Revolution, and to hope that in the future gradual forward motion could be made. The work of the abolitionists, of black slaves changed all that. By the end of his life Lincoln could see the path of the Declaration, of human freedom, open once again. This was a mighty achievement for the movement.

The spontaneity and universality of feeling which accompanied the antislavery movement indelibly stamped itself on the opening days of the Civil War. The people arose. When the people arose in the North it was a self-mobilization of men and women. Of the 700,000 total Union Army, half a million were volunteers. This was, perhaps, the last great voluntary war in the history of mankind.

Savor the following words:

. . . So large an army as the government has now on foot was never before known, without a soldier in it but who has taken his place there of his own free choice. But more than this: there are many single regiments whose members, one and another, possess full practical knowledge of all the arts, sciences, professions, and whatever else, whether useful or elegant, is known in the world; and there is scarcely one from which there could not be selected a president, a cabinet, a congress, and perhaps a court, abundantly competent to administer the government itself.

. . . It is worthy to note that while in this, the government's hour of trial, large numbers of those in the army and navy who have been favored with the offices have resigned and proved false to the hand which had pampered them, not one common soldier or sailor is known to have deserted . . .

. . . The greatest honor, and the most important fact of all is the unanimous firmness of the common soldiers and sailors. To the last man, so far as known, they have successfully resisted the traitorous efforts of those whose commands, but an hour before, they obeyed as absolute law.

This is from Lincoln's absolutely sober message to Congress, July 5, 1861.

One of the great underestimations in the whole sphere of historiography is undoubtedly the contribution of the slaves to the making of America as a civilization. Some of the justifications for such an underestimation are quite elementary. It is said that all civilization rests upon city life; the bulk of slave labor was on the countryside. The actual documentary works by which much of early America lived are those of the Anglo-Saxon heritage with some bow to Plutarch and perhaps Rousseau, Montaigne, and Demosthenes. The slaves produced little of this kind of literature. They are therefore to be left on the fringe of the matter.

But a New World view of the old question of slavery induces a greater wisdom. For one thing the triangular trade in sugar, rum, and slaves is an instance of programmed accumulation of wealth such as the world has rarely seen. "American slavery," says one author, "was unique, in the sense that, for symmetry and precision of outline, nothing like it had every previously been seen." The element of order in the barbarism was this: the rationalization of a labor force upon which the whole process of colonization depended had the African at its most essential point. If he had not been able to work or sustain himself or learn the language or maintain cooperation in his social life, the whole question of America as a distinct civilization could never have arisen. We might be then talking about a sort of New Zealand or perhaps Canada.

The native American Indian was migratory in his habits and a hunter in his relation with nature. But the slave had to be an African laborer, a man accustomed to social life, before he could ever become a profitable grower of cotton or tobacco—the vital element required before America could claim that it had salvaged something from the wilderness. Something which could be extended to the point where it would win recognition as a landmark in man's emergence from subservience to any laws of nature. . .

The man who made it possible, and we do not know if he knew he was making it possible, was the transported African. Rationalization of the labor supply was tied in with rationalization of production itself. Planters in Louisiana would weigh the pros and cons of working slaves to death in the hazardous work of the rice paddies as against protecting the slave from excessive labor in order to maintain the interest in him as property. The long letters George Washington wrote on the organization of labor on his plantation represent merely one side. The exchange of letters between Thomas Jefferson and Bejamin Banneker, the surveyor of what was to become Washington, D.C., about the propensities and capacities of black people enslaved and otherwise is the other side of the same phenomenon: the recognition that for reasons both clear and obscure the fate of America had depended upon the blacks as laborers. This was to be argued out in the antislavery movement at a higher level, and in the midst of the Civil War and Reconstruction. It is also a seemingly inescapable fact to everybody, but historians have managed to escape it. That is not altogether a surprise. The writing of history comes about at a period when men think about their activity so as to record it in a more permanent form. To give the slave his actual historical due is to alter one's notion about the course of civilization itself. If, for example, each plantation had to strive to be self-sufficient as a unit, it was the skilled and semi-skilled black who would make it so.

The runaway slave fled to the North without compass or definite point of destination, without being blessed like Columbus by Queen Isabella selling her jewels for the voyage, or like the pilgrims to Plymouth Rock—members of a church soon to make a revolution affecting all of England and Ireland; or like pioneers into the wilderness, trying to set a distance between themselves and civilization. If, as can be later demonstrated, the flight of the runaway slave from the South is seen as setting in motion a whole series of forces, which no other class of people, no mere party or political sect, no church or newspaper could succeed in animating, then the whole configuration of America as a civilization automatically changes before our eyes. The distinguishing feature of the slave was not his race but the concentrated impact of his work on the extensive cultivation of the soil, which eventually made possible the transition to an industrial and urban society.

The triumph of slavery, the negative recognition that the slave received in every work sphere, shows how little the South or skilled workers themselves sometimes could tolerate the black as an artisan. In prebellum America he had to be driven out of trade after trade before the assertion could be demonstrated that the black man is fit for nothing more than brutish labor with its inevitable consequence.

Historically one can now begin almost anywhere to show what civilization meant to the slave as a preliminary to showing what the slaves meant to civilization. The natural form of organization was the work gang during the day and the slave quarters at night. The large scale of cultivation required for a profitable export crop guaranteed social connections for the slave even if he was isolated from the centers of "civilization" by the rural surroundings.

But the first specific form of slave organization was the fraternal association which was organized to accompany to their permanent resting place those caught up in life's mortal coils. Small coins were saved for accomplishing that occasion in at least minimal style. The slave was no more afraid to die than is or was any other mortal; he was fearful of dying unaccompanied by those with whom he had associated in the fullness of his life.

Given a holiday, that is, an occasion, the slave was, like most working humans up to this day, his own person. It was for naught that the defenders of the planter's way of life feared the effect of Fourth of July oratory. They might just as well have feared the Christianity in Christmas. It was not only intellectually that everything universal in sentiment panicked the "peculiar institution." It was the concentration of people all experiencing the un-bridgeable gap between their arduous daily toil and the exceptional holiday from work—with the to-ing and the fro-ing from plantation to plantation, the arrival of guests and the spreading of news—which brought about the system of slave patrollers and written passes across the South.

We are dealing with matters of individual skill and social impulse. Small equivalents of the strike action took place at work. Flight to the neighboring woods, followed by messages trailed back to the work area, showed that the blacks knew above all that, even if despised for race, they were necessary—vital to a labor process geared to the agricultural season. Feigning of illness was a commonplace; indeed, one simple definition of the abolition of slavery is that a man or woman need not go to work when incapacitated. This absenteeism may seem of no great import by itself, but the diaries and records of the slavemasters show it to be a matter of grave concern. Everybody knew what was involved in the work process.

And the blacks knew what was involved in their day of rest. The growth of an autonomous black church draws up a balance sheet on historical Christian-ity. It is not finished yet, but if Christianity, as some assert, brought the principle of personality into a world that knew no such thing, and in the person of a simple carpenter who later recruited an equally simple fisherman and so on, the climax of that primitive church was the mass joining together of a population considered as so much flesh to be traded and hands to be worked and backs to be bent or broken under the lash. To the whites religion may have meant a buttress to conscience. To the blacks it meant a social experience of personality: the black preacher.

In the more practical workings of the plantation, the slave owners themselves discovered that the position of foreman or driver was one which fewer and fewer whites measured up to in personal stature. So that in the decade before the Civil War there was a wholesale increase in the number of black overseers. Though it did not mean that race prejudice on the part of the slave owners had changed one whit, this problem of supervision was proof of the demoralizing effect black laborers had upon those who not only considered themselves superior to the slave's lot but had the weapons and the authority to put their superiority into momentary practice. Most white overseers went even before the slave system fell into the dust of Civil War. And by a healthy process of circularity, the fictional summations of the type, the Simon Legrees of the world, were portrayed with such effectiveness that it stimulated the movement toward that system which produced such monsters wholesale. The important point of the slave's contribution to civilization is that he recognized and did battle with the slavery system every day before, long before, white audiences would stare with horror at the representation on stage or in a book.

There is also the matter of the link-ups of the plantation to the outside world. Blacks were the boatmen and teamsters of that day in the South. They would have been the longshoremen as well, but were driven out. Simply by driving the master's coach around they learned of the outside world and brought back information to the slave community. It was known in some of the deepest haunts of the South that there was some kind of underground which would transport a runaway from one hiding place to another if he would but risk the trip.

Indeed, if by virtue of the brutishness and isolation of his situation the slave were himself a brute, how then could he make contact with such varying and even opposing sections of the population as he did? Harriet Tubman had a rapt listener in the philosopher Ralph Waldo Emerson, and Frederick Douglass in Governor—and later Presidential candidate—William Seward. William Wells Brown could speak to all size groups, from two hundred to two hundred thousand people across Europe. It was not a matter of a dispute about the capacity of the Negro; it was not even the great political debates about the future of America—slave or free. It was something so concrete, so easy to overlook and yet so broad in its consequences: The black man was a social being, in some senses the most highly social product of the United States. This was not necessarily due to skin color, but to the close relation between labor and society that he experienced more than did planters, ethnic immigrants, religious societies, pioneering settlements and their human products, political parties and their candidates.

That link of labor and society took on national and even international proportions. Starting from obscure places which nobody ever heard of or even wanted to hear, it became writ large as the experience of slavery intertwined with everything else—politics, diplomacy, commerce, migration, popular culture, the relation between the sexes, the question of labor and civilization in the future of America as a whole. The black man was not in any popularity contest as to who most represented this new man—this undefined American—who so intrigued the Europeans. He was something more: a self-appointed minister with nothing but experience, social experience, to guide him toward those qualities most universally recognizable in the ordinary people—some of whom are still tied to the land in Europe; some recently incorporated into proliferating industry; some hearkening to the American experience; some settling matters with crowns and courts in their Old World countries. The black man was the supreme example not just of how to rise in the world but of how to raise the world toward his own level. He inherited the Declaration of Independence which the plantation plutocracy mocked. In politics, Frederick Douglass took the Constitution as an antislavery document when his own abolition colleagues,

Wendell Phillips and William Lloyd Garrison, set the match to it. The runaway slave, Dred Scott, threw the Chief Justice of the Supreme Court (and the country as a whole) into confusion on whether slavery was a national or regional issue. The black man was not afraid to declare war on war, for instance the conflict with Mexico over Texas in 1846. He could link himself to movements for temperance in drink or for the right of women to divorce or to the nonpayment of rents by upper New York State farmers.

It was training in social labor which gave blacks the opportunity to increasingly affect all social questions of their day. It was their concrete ability to turn from the faculties used in physical work to the powers of speech and other forms of self-expression which made certain of the ex-slaves the astonishing figures they were. After he drew two hundred thousand people to hear him in Europe, William Wells Brown then returned to a port near the Great Lakes, between America and Canada, to help fugitive slaves across the water, unite families, violating the mere boundaries of national existence. In addition he printed a paper announcing the uniting of families, the successes and sometimes failures of the underground travelers, their adventures and misadventures; and denouncing the "peculiar institution" and all those who would compromise with it, thinking they could thereby escape compromising themselves.

The startling challenge to current notions about civilization was presented by the slaves, as soon as they won the public's ear, on the familiar matter of conscience. The contribution of the blacks was that type of social experience—whether it was lyceum, church, or Underground Railroad—which challenged one set of social institutions with a social impact of a most original kind. Doomed by slavery to impersonality, the ex-slave responded with a personality and personal force that had the most obvious social implications and conclusions. Condemned to seasonal labor, and the rhythm and routine determined thereby, the blacks carried on agitation in and out of season until the body politic came to recognize that the country could no longer survive as it was; could survive only by embarking on an uncharted course of slave confiscation and Southern reconstruction. After having been isolated by slavery in provincial fixity, the runaway traversed national boundaries and oceanic waters. Graded by the abolition movement itself as fit only to tell slavery as an atrocity tale, Frederick Douglass and others insisted on publishing their own political policies. This is a long way from the reflex response to slavery by a disturbed conscience. It is a social impact on all media that distinguishes civilization from barbarism. The impact of the slave labor system upon the South as a distinct region has a number of aspects clearly visible to this day.

The plantation was an organized community that was part of a larger regional configuration, but given the isolation concomitant with the rural character of slave society, the social stamp upon the individual, particularly the slave himself, guaranteed certain results. The internal economic principle of the plantation was self-sufficiency. To the slavemaster this meant insularity: foreign immigation mainly excluded; missionary society activity suspect (including the riding preachers who would as likely as not be antislavery); no lyceum or lecture circuit on any extensive scale; no compulsory elementary or secondary education; little exercise of the faculty of logical speculation. For a break in the routine of plantation life there were visits to the North, often no further than the river port city of Cincinnati; or politics in the state capital or in Washington, D.C., actually a Southern city.

To a large extent, certain of the above characteristics were true of America as a whole, or at least of its western part. Especially the smaller Southern planters had certain characteristics in common with the yeomanry of the American Northwest: the need to create isolated pockets of white habitation in a land belonging to the Indians, the establishment of paths into the wilderness, the harsh life for the women of the family, the back-breaking toil in wresting some socially productive result from the natural surroundings, and the independence of habit and speech that is the inevitable result in people living under these conditions.

The dialectical set of connections of the South to the old Northwest is both genuinely subtle and profound. Both were agrarian areas, with the Mississippi and other rivers serving as the turnstiles to ports and citified places. Other similarities were the suspiciousness toward all those outside the isolated region where one's house and cultivated areas and perhaps hunting grounds were located; the tightness of the family and usually its patriarchal basis; the shortage of monies and credit, such that life frequently remained, generally according to the season, on a subsistence level, with only the holiday season to punctuate with some enjoyment above the everyday standard.

Further, there is the historical connection. All of American settlement, at its origins, proceeded in the same manner for both inland planters and Northern yeomanry, and their pioneering ways continued right up to the Civil War. In that sense Southern rural inhabitants were "these new men," the Americans who so intrigued the European observer often sceptical of America as (1) a civilization and (2) a viable nationality. Thus if the black man has been left out of so many history books, if the controversy over the significance of slavery to the South seemed until very recently a matter of no great moment, it is because a certain aspect of American historical continuity seemed to justify itself and no mere racist conspiracy of silence could accomplish what seems to have been imbedded within that historical aspect. To which must be added the fundamental matter of political organization and the effect of the South on certain basic institutions by which an organized society emerged out of the natural wilderness. The individual planter was conditioned not only by pioneering inland to new territories; he had to become an individualist with a social authority larger than the boundaries of his plantation. The reasons are as follows: The South had been originally colonized by British trading companies licensed by the Crown. The Northern settlements were more likely to be religious colonies or fur-trading outposts. So that from the very start the planter, who had to be in charge of the practical and hazardous work of founding some lasting economic basis in the New World, was thrown into conflict with the concentrated mercantile capitalism of the metropolitan colonizing land. To put it succinctly, the anticapitalist bias of the Southerner was there from the day of his birth. It was no small thing. The former slave—the supposedly emancipated black—became, for lack of credit, a sharecropper. This happened because all of Southern history had prepared somebody for that role, and the people at the bottom of the social ladder fell into it and remained there, some unto this day. To make up for their embattlement as regards the shortage of capital, the Southerners would compensate with (a) their geography, strategically considered, (b) the fixed position of the main section of the laboring force—the slaves—and (c) a type of politics which would guarantee the viability of (a) and (b).

All these things add up to a "nativist" outlook that is not that of country bumpkins, but one characterized by a sophistication that was constantly changing by the very reason of its taking place in a nineteenth- and late eighteenth-century setting that was becoming rapidly modernized. Slavery is a peculiar institution not only because of its horrors but because it was something-unto-itself. The Southern attitude seems so often a matter of temperament—unformed character expressing itself against a general trend in worldly affairs which opposed the fixed investment of wealth in land and human chattel. In other words, the South produced "personality" rather than minds of singular or original power. But the personalities are of a singular and sustaining force: Patrick Henry, Jefferson, Jackson, Calhoun, Clay, Stonewall Jackson, Tom Watson, Huey Long are personae who will interest the public imagination until possibly they are surpassed by the characterization of the lives of the obscure slaves and indigent blacks. This tends to be the ongoing matter of interest in our own day.

There is a material basis for the Southern production of men and women of outstanding temperamental force. (The fictional Scarlett O'Hara or Blanche DuBois convey that the matter is not limited to the male gender.) Despite all geographical rationalizations, the commodity crops—tobacco, rice, sugar, cotton, and hemp—were not limited to the South by climate. The planters were a class capable of taking over matters of national interest; they had warred against nature, against the Indian; they had warred against the blacks on the plantation, against the British, the French, and the Spaniards. Their experience had a certain cast by virtue of the international nature of their products—human flesh and large-scale commodity crops. Such large-scale experiences do not lead to the production of small-minded men. So they participated in the formation of an original American nationality. The historical claim can be substantiated that they produced more figures of national distinction than did, say, by comparison, the robber barons. All this combines to make the controversy about the impact of slavery on American civilization such a pregnant and vital intellectual confrontation.

Certain mundane matters have to be mentioned at lease in a preliminary way. It was the boredom and harshness of plantation life that ensured that not general activity, but politics was the only matter of universal interest and appeal. If the rural character of their life induced in the planters, or at least in some of them, a certain respect for plebeian democracy in other sections of the population, it had to be by the nature of the planter's own setting, an abridged version of popular participation in decision-making. The father of the political party of any mass status in American life was the planter-political philosopher, Thomas Jefferson. The father of popular participation in political office, apart from mere suffrage, was the planter Andrew Jackson. The head of an army having the popular militia as a section of its base was the planter George Washington. Yet the halfway houses to genuine democracy which each of these figures created remain America's bones of contention unto this day.

What of social vision? The early accomplishments of these men corresponded to the formative period of American nationality. They could not go beyond. The results were imbedded in the American mentality but not anywhere in self-generating institutions. The popular militia is now the not-very-progressive National Guard. The political parties resting on mass suffrage are now in a state alternating between paralysis and crisis. The spoils of office distributed to members of the population are now a source of perpetual scandal and parasitism.

The Southern figures of the mid-nineteenth century vacillated between accommodation and hopeless fanaticism. Clay was a genius of the first order. He could never win actual leadership of the country as a whole, though he was persistent and colorful enough to engage the political attentions of his countrymen. Calhoun was a different sort. He sought to make the American Constitution a protector of the South's position in national life, invulnerable to changing national majorities. And of Jefferson Davis it can perhaps best be said that though he failed in the Southern rebellion, he was saved from hanging by the long tradition of Northern-Southern accommodation—a tradition punctured only by the actualities of the Civil War.

Some of the bobbling of the minds of the planters was due to the very fact that they stood on a tripod of vital revolutions in the then-known Western world: the Puritans in 1642, the War for Independence in 1776, and volatile France of 1789. The Clays and Calhouns lived to consider the realities of the continental-wide European Revolution of 1848. Their situation was one of Anglo-Saxon nativism turning against itself. Immigrant New York might celebrate 1848, Puritan New England might relate revolutionary antislavery sentiments to the wars between Cavaliers and Roundheads, the democratic yeomanry of the western territories might enjoy the sight of crowns falling all over Europe. The Southern planters had no comparable frame of reference. They stuck by Constitution and Compromise.

And when that did not last they went to war to protect geography. It was not all that simple. The border states which did not produce commodity crops but which had domestic slaves were the geniuses of accommodation right up to the last moment and beyond. The idyllic notion of domestic servitude, partriarchal chatteldom, originates from those Kentucky, Tennessee, upper Virginia, Maryland, and even Delaware manors. If American politics became entwined with a style of life rather than a manner of thought, we have no difficulties discovering why. In short, the Southern position was that of a provincialism entwined with American nationality as a whole, but defenseless against the universal trends of revolutionary democracy of the nineteenth century.

Nevertheless the effects of the planters were immense: The location of the nation's capital in the borderline South; the creation and manipulation of national political parties; the fielding of armies and the tradition of militant armed conflict; the specialization of the South in politics as maneuver and divagation; the bias in favor of the notion that agricultural wealth was real, and commercial wealth always fraudulent; the sense of the manor not as parasitic but as a center of human community; the assertion that the concreteness of the manorial community was superior to the impersonality of the large Northern city; the impulsiveness of the Southern personality as more appealing than the social discipline seemingly inherent in industry and commerce; the general link-up with the rural-romantic character of America's past—all of this seems irrevocable and untouchable by general intellectual argument.

The only way to deal with it is by taking up its foundations. The Southern planter could engage in politics on a much larger scale than many Northerners or Westerners because he was of a leisure class, born and bred—a commander of the fate of men, women, and children of a different color with a more permanently fixed status. Suckled by a black nurse, attended by black servants, often encouraged to sexual experiments in the slave quarters, accustomed to the sight of blacks caring for all business involving manual labor; encouraged, even inspired, by the succession of Southern Presidents, the ambitious Southerner could see politics, even statesmanship, as destiny's decision, and cast himself in the role of fortune's darling. Futhermore, for the isolated manorial communities, politics was the prime form of social communion, whereas in the North religious revivals swept all before them in periods in between political excitement. In today's parlance, the prebellum white planter gives the impression of having found an early answer to the problems of the "lonely crowd" in the solidity of his native tradition, the fixity of his social status, and the values of an inherent and irrevocable individualism.

The availability and accessibility of having things always at hand extended itself to the vast virgin lands and the supply of slaves. If capital and credit were in short supply, then the curse was on the head of the mercantilists—be they tyrannical Englishmen or grasping Boston Yankees. Social status had taken on an overweening importance; but even greater was the display of public personality—elections as jousting contests, a codified individualism rather than the self-expansive effluvia of the Northern Transcendentalists.

The rationalizations for the Atlantic slave trade and American slavery, whether borrowed from the Bible or the instances of Greece and Rome, raise a compelling challenge to the whole matter of what indeed constitutes a civilization. It is safe to say that the majority of Western scholars seem to have placed a gloss on the manner and the matter of this case.

the woman question

AILEEN S. KRADITOR

After 1837, the issue of woman's rights ripped the abolitionist movement apart. The idea that women might claim a measure of equality, including the right to speak against slavery in public, shocked the majority of men in the antislavery movement. They considered the issue of women's rights extraneous and diversionary and accused Garrisonians who supported the women of ungodliness for encouraging "women to leave their appointed sphere."

The following chapter, taken from Aileen Kraditor's outstanding history of abolitionist tactics and theories, is reminiscent of the storm of controversy which broke over Dr. Martin Luther King's head when he decided to identify the war in Vietnam as part of America's racist problem. Many civil rights activists condemned his endorsement of the peace movement as an "extraneous" issue that would divert attention from the movement for racial equality. Others insisted that the two were inseparable and that the goal was to liberate all humanity from white racism and its international component: violent and imperialist domination.

One of the stranger ironies in American intellectual history appears when the relation between the antebellum movements for Negro rights and women's rights is compared with the relation between those movements in the Progressive Era. In both periods both movements based their claims in part on identical principles of natural rights, justice, and the Declaration of Independence. But the period in which woman suffrage became historically possible coincided with what Rayford Logan has called "the nadir" in the status of the Negro.[1] If the suffragists of 1900 had defended the Southern Negro's right to vote (an impossible supposition in view of their own attitudes on the race question) they would have split the suffrage movement, destroyed its Southern wing, alienated many Northern supporters, and delayed passage of the Nineteenth Amendment.[2] Aside from questions of justice and consistency, the suffragists had to consider the expediency of any position they might adopt on Negro rights. The abolitionists confronted the same problem in their day, but in reverse. Aside from questions of justice and consistency, they had to consider the expediency of any position they might adopt on women's rights in a period in which abolitionism was gaining many converts who would be repelled by anything so absurd as the equality of the sexes. In both periods the convenient divorce of the two causes was facilitated by the fact that most advocates of the more popular reform endorsed the prevailing disapproval of the other. The suffragist leaders of 1900–1920 were too young to have been motivated by a desire for revenge on the Negro's earlier friends for having compromised with public

From "The Woman Question," *Means and Ends in American Abolitionism: Garrison and His Critics on Strategy and Tactics, 1834–1850*, by Aileen S. Kraditor. (New York: Vintage Books, 1969), 39–77. Copyright © 1967, 1969 by Aileen S. Kraditor. Reprinted by permission of Pantheon Books/A Division of Random House, Inc.

opinion on the woman question; the state of public opinion in their own generation and the recurrent tactical problems of all reform movements sufficiently explain the ironic reversal.[3]

Another irony can be seen in the reactions of historians: today few historians reading about the suffragists' accommodation to racism during the "nadir" period would justify it; the suffragists' compromise of their own movement's principles is obvious. Most historians, on the other hand, ridicule that minority of abolitionists who advocated women's rights for having tacked an "extraneous" issue onto the antislavery movement. Since the tactical problems as well as the questions of consistency and principle in the two cases were at least similar, the respective reactions tell as much about the historians' attitudes toward sex equality and race equality, respectively, as about the subjects of their studies, just as the tactical solutions proposed by abolitionists and suffragists reflected their own feelings about the less popular issues at least as much as they reflected their considered judgments on the ideals and needs of their own causes.

It may be argued that the reason why and the manner in which a reformer deviates from his professed principles tell more about what he really means by those principles than his activities in clear support of them. One can study at length the suffragists' speeches between 1900 and 1920 urging wider application of the principles of the hallowed Declaration, but begin to learn what they really meant only when one comes to those passages where the women explained, "But of course this applies only to whites." Then, upon investigating this anomaly, one discovers that "the consent of the governed" must be qualified by restriction of the vote to the "fit," for the sake of social stability and progress, and that fitness was much more common among white Protestant men and women, especially "Anglo-Saxons," than among other segments of the American population.

Before 1837 all abolitionists castigated unmercifully those who applied the Declaration of Independence to themselves but not to Negroes and who preferred the proslavery letter of parts of the Bible to its antislavery spirit. The woman question, precisely because it raised the same questions in regard to the status of women and thus forced some abolitionists to qualify their construction of the Declaration and the Bible, provides an excellent angle from which to study basic abolitionist principles and the ways in which those principles affected tactics.[4]

When Sarah and Angelina Grimké began, in 1837, to lecture on abolitionism to mixed audiences of men and women, they did not see themselves as nineteenth-century Pandoras opening a box of troubles that would in three years help to split the antislavery movement. To some abolitionists the parallel between these gentle Quakers from South Carolina and the woman sent by Zeus to bring calamities to mankind would have seemed uncannily close.[5] Throughout the ensuing controversy, however, the advocates of women's rights insisted that not they but their adversaries within the antislavery societies had created the problem, for those adversaries denounced efforts to tack feminism onto abolitionism when no one had tried to do so. In fact, the abstract question of women's rights, involving the pros and cons of such reforms as the right of women to vote for and become government officials, never did become an issue in the antislavery societies. Historians who state that it did are accepting as real a straw man erected by the conservative abolitionists who knew that the principles the Garrisonians did defend in the organization were more difficult to oppose.

The Grimkés' activity did not mark the entrance of women into the antislavery movement. At the founding convention of the American Anti-Slavery Society in December 1833, women were present, and a few of them spoke, after asking permission to do so.[6] Separate women's clubs were organized within the national society, and their valuable work in circulating petitions and raising money is well known. Even that activity was not unprecedented; women had been encouraged by their churches to engage in organized fund-raising and educational work, also through separate clubs and under the supervision of their pastors or the managers of the all-male missionary and Bible societies. What was unprecedented in the antislavery societies was the unplanned and unforeseen coalescing of the hitherto separate spheres of work of men and women members.

The wall between those spheres began to crumble when and where it did because the most interesting lecturers on slavery, in New England, just happened to be women. As former slaveholders and members of a famous family, the Grimké sisters attracted larger audiences than any Northerner could. Their descriptions of slavery had an authenticity that no others could have except those of former slaves. If the Grimkés had been men, lecturing in New England in 1837, they would have drawn crowds; Angelina, at least, was a far more effective speaker than James G. Birney, also a converted slaveholder. That they happened to be women increased their appeal to a curious public, especially since their talks were announced as being for women only. Inevitably men began to show up at the back of the lecture halls or in the doorways and then to take seats, and it was not long before the sisters found themselves speaking to what were then called "promiscuous assemblies."[7] Despite their shyness and stage fright,[8] they did not feel inhibited by the presence of male auditors.[9] The talks were so successful that the sisters found themselves becoming itinerant lecturers, traveling from town to town usually in response to invitations from ladies' antislavery societies, something women simply did not do in those days.

The Congregational clergy of Massachusetts took alarm and issued the notorious Pastoral Letter, declaring:

When the mild, dependant [sic] influence of woman upon the sternness of man's opinions is fully exercised, society feels the effects of it in a thousand forms. The power of woman is in her dependence, flowing from the consciousness of that weakness which God has given her for her protection. . . . But when she assumes the place and tone of man as a public reformer, our care and protection of her seem unnecessary. . . . If the vine, whose strength and beauty is to lean upon the trellis work and half conceal its clusters, thinks to assume the independence and overshadowing nature of the elm, it will not only cease to bear fruit, but fall in shame and dishonor in the dust.[10]

The sisters never considered stopping their open lectures. They were, after all, obeying what they believed to be a call from God to testify against slavery.[11] The only question was whether they should ignore the ever more frequent clerical denunciations[12] or reply to them and defend the propriety of their activity. Theodore D. Weld, who married Angelina the following year, urged the former course. Later the moderate Garrisonian Lydia Maria Child[13] revealed that she too had believed they should exercise but not defend their right to speak.[14] Garrison and his fellow radical Henry C. Wright[15] agreed with the Grimkés that if they did not defend their course their audiences would dwindle after the novelty of women lecturers had worn off.[16]

The arguments that the ministers used were almost impossible to ignore, aside from their probable effect on the size of the sisters' audiences.[17] First, Saint Paul had said that it was a shame for a woman to speak in church and that wives must be subject to their husbands.[18] Second, the Grimkés' activity defied custom and propriety and would, if large numbers of women followed their example, endanger the family. Inevitably, some abolitionists noticed that both these arguments echoed the principal defenses of Negro slavery.[19]

For many years abolitionists had been hearing tiresome repetitions of quotations from the Bible to justify slavery and Negro inferiority: the patriarchs of the Old Testament had owned slaves, the curse on Ham was bequeathed to his descendants, Saint Paul had returned Onesimus to his master, and so on. The abolitionists, when they could not dispute the interpretations of the cited passages, invariably pointed out that the spirit of the Bible if not always the letter proclaimed the brotherhood and equality of all men.[20]

Ironically, antifeminist abolitionists, who interpreted the Bible allegorically when the issue was slavery, became fundamentalists when the issue was women's rights. Henry Grew of Philadelphia, in a public exchange of letters with Henry C. Wright on the "nonresistance" issue, wrote: "You observe, 'We cannot obey God and man.' Then the Word of God requires an impossibility, for it certainly requires obedience to both. Wives are commanded to obey their husbands, and children their parents. . . ."[21] The Rev. Amos A. Phelps[22] argued that women were unfitted, by physiological nature and divine command, for public life. He dismissed the feminists' citations of exceptional women in the Bible on the ground that those women *were* exceptional; that was the reason they were mentioned. He would not silence those few modern women who displayed unusual talents for public speaking; but when they urged that public life be accepted as proper for any woman, he felt he must protest.[23] Sarah Douglass, a Negro abolitionist, admitted that although she felt humiliated by the subjection of women, she believed it was divinely ordained as punishment for Eve's sin.[24]

To the Grimkés' and their friends it appeared that unless they demonstrated that the biblical arguments used against women's speaking were similar to those used against the Negro's equality, they would be undermining the abolitionist rationale itself. They made some attempts to marshall New Testament verses on their side of the question. Sarah Grimké pointed out that the Scriptures had been translated and interpreted by men. If women were permitted to study Greek and Hebrew and publish their translations, she predicted, they would produce some different readings. Even the standard version, she said, contained verses that could be cited against those who would make woman inferior to man.[25] But the most common reply to the biblical argument was not to match text for text; it was, after all, difficult to "reinterpret" the plain statements of Saint Paul. Far preferable was an appeal to the spirit of the New Testament as a whole, which the defenders of women's rights insisted favored equality of the sexes as well as of the races. As Angelina Grimké explained, all human beings have the same rights because they are all moral beings. To suppose that sex gave a man more rights and responsibilities than a woman "would be to deny the self-evident truth, that 'the physical constitution is the mere instrument of the moral nature.' " Sex, she insisted, had no more to do with rights than did color.

This regulation of duty by the mere circumstance of sex, rather than by the fundamental principle of moral being, has led to all that multifarious train of evils flowing out of the anti-christian doctrine of masculine and feminine virtues. By this doctrine, man has been converted into the warrior, and clothed with sternness, and those other kindred qualities, which, in the eyes of many, belong to his character as a man; whilst woman has been taught to lean upon an arm of flesh, to sit as a doll arrayed in "gold, and pearls, and costly array," to be admired for her personal charms, and caressed and humored like a spoiled child, or converted into a mere drudge to suit the convenience of her lord and master.

There are no men's or women's rights; there are only human rights.[26] The chief way, then, to dispose of the arguments against women's rights was to show that they derived from principles which, if made universal, would undermine abolitionism itself.

The same tactic was used in the customary reply to another argument against the Grimkés' activity, that it was contrary to the usages of civilized society.[27] Wholesale emancipation of the slaves was also opposed on grounds of custom and the need to preserve the social fabric. If abolitionists resorted to similar arguments to condemn women's public lecturing or membership in mixed conventions, how could they consistently advocate such social innovations as Negro freedom and the equality of the races? James Mott of Philadelphia, commenting on the objections that had been made to Abby Kelley's partic- ipation in the recent New England Anti-Slavery Convention, wryly observed:

. . . verily some of our northern gentlemen abolitionists are as jealous of any interference in rights they have long considered as belonging to them exclusively, as the southern slaveholder is, in the right of holding his slaves,—both are to be broken up, & *human* rights alone recognized.[28]

Another circumstance made explicit reply to the argument from custom necessary, in the eyes of the Garrisonian abolitionists. Antislavery propaganda always proclaimed that slaves could not legally marry, that slave families could be and were separated by sale, and that slave women were driven to work in the fields under the lash of brutal drivers, were sold on auction blocks like animals, and were helpless to defend their virtue against masters and overseers. These abolitionists could not forbear to cry hypocrite when cler- gymen who did not denounce these outrages denounced as immoral the public lectures of female abolitionists who were motivated in part by empathy with slave women.[29]

Abolitionists who favored an open defense of the Grimkés' speaking to "promiscuous assemblies" understood that the discussion of woman's sphere would frighten away many people who might otherwise be converted to abolition. They felt that a few people converted to the cause of human rights for all, regardless of sex or color, were more valuable in the long run than many people converted to antislavery alone, especially since antislavery alone could be compatible with racism. And as Garrison's disciple Maria Weston Chapman suggested, "the women whose efforts for the cause could not be hindered by men, were more valuable auxiliaries than the men whose dignity forbade them to be fellow-laborers with women."[30] Their approach to this tactical question was a consistent part of an over-all approach to the problem of weighing short-term losses against long-term gains. How their tactic would have worked out in this instance will never be known; the "woman question," which had begun as an argument over a tactic, very soon became itself a tactic, that is, a weapon that both sides in a different factional dispute used against each other.[31] In any event, Pandora's box was empty. One champion of "human rights for all" preferred a different legend to illustrate her view of what had happened: Mrs. Child wrote of the German wizard who by certain incantations

could cause a broom to become a man, and rapidly bring buckets of water from a neighboring river; and when the required work was completed, another spell transformed him to a broom again. The wizard's apprentice, being one day left with a charge to wash the shop and tools very thoroughly, thought he would avail himself of the service of the broom. He succeeded in repeating the first spell correctly; and to his great joy, saw arms and feet start forth to do his bidding. With supernatural activity, the bewitched household utensil brought water, water, water, till tubs were filled, the floor overflowed, the furniture was deluged. "Stop! stop!" cried the terrified apprentice: "We shall all be drowned, if you don't stop!" But, unfortunately, he had forgotten the backward spell, and the animated tool went on with frightful diligence.

Thus it is with those who urged women to become missionaries, and form tract societies. They have changed the household utensil to a living, energetic being; and they have no spell to turn it into a broom again.[32]

The legends of Pandora and the sorcerer's apprentice agree at several points: the events they describe were irreversible, unforeseen, and productive of cumulative results—and so were the innovations in the status of women abolitionists. But could the two factions not have subordinated their differences on this issue to their common dedication to the cause of antislavery? Each side asked this question and insisted that its proposed answer would serve the common end.

The form in which the woman question became a divisive issue within the AASS was both inevitable and guaranteed to make it insoluble; it arose as a problem in constitutional interpretation. The constitution of the national society stated that all "persons," not slaveholders, who subscribed to the principles of the society and supported it financially were eligible for membership.[33] For the first few years no one thought of defining "persons," and custom determined the respective roles of men and women members. The women organized their own clubs, although nothing in the constitution technically precluded their joining the same clubs as the men. Quarterly and annual meetings of the regional and national associations were open to all members; the conventions were not delegated bodies, and all members present could vote. Under the constitution, could women speak and serve on committees at the conventions? Technically yes, if they were persons, and not even the most inveterate quoter of Saint Paul denied that.

Those who buttressed their view of female propriety by citing the letter of the New Testament contended that the actual words of the constitution were irrelevant, because in December 1833 when it was written no one anticipated that the Grimkés would become public lecturers or that Abby Kelley and other women would be willing to serve on committees.[34] The faction that relied on the spirit of the New Testament replied that the constitution meant precisely what it said. Both sides were, in different senses, "right," and as is clear from the debates, both knew perfectly well that they were carrying on in constitutional terms a debate that really involved much more than the "true" interpretation of the society's charter.[35]

At first the executive committee of the national society tried to localize the growing dispute in Massachusetts between the advocates of women's rights and the clerical remonstrants. It issued a statement from its New York headquarters asking the public not to identify the movement with a few individuals who had unorthodox notions of woman's sphere. It quoted the society's constitution on the qualifications for membership and pointed out that the organization had no authority to interfere with its members' views. And it bravely added that diversity of opinion was a sign of strength, because it showed that abolitionism was not restricted to one sect or party.[36] Garrison took the same position. He published a reply to the Rev. James T. Woodbury, who had announced that he had never "swallowed" Garrison; the editor of *The Liberator* retorted that no one had ever been expected to and that abolitionists were not obliged to accept one another's views on such questions as women's rights.[37]

The first showdown occurred at the annual New—England Anti-Slavery Convention in the spring of 1838, when women were given permission to participate in its proceedings. Several members asked to have their names expunged from the roll of the convention. They spoke through the Rev. Charles T. Torrey[38] in a statement complaining that the convention's action deviated from previous usage and had hurt the cause of the slave by connecting it with a foreign subject and by furnishing a precedent for associating it with other irrelevant topics.[39]

An anonymous "Member of the Convention," in a letter to *The Liberator*, pointed out that the convention had not debated the rights, duties, or status of women in American society. To the slight extent that these subjects had been admitted into the discussion the convention had erred. But, he contended, the real issue in dispute *was* germane: whether women should be allowed to become equal members. Suppose a temperance convention voted to admit anyone who pledged abstinence from liquor, he wrote, and some Negroes claimed seats and some whites objected on the grounds that their admission would be unprecedented, that it was wrong for the races to mix on a basis of equality, and that the innovation would give the association bad publicity and cause other members to resign. Would it not be proper for those on the other side to offer their reasons why Negroes ought to be admitted? Would it not be relevant to the purposes for which the convention had met?[40]

This answered Torrey's objection on the ground of "irrelevance," but it did not meet his objection that the convention's vote admitting women reversed accepted policy in regard to convention membership. To deal with that question, the Garrisonians repeatedly pointed out that the women had come forward of their own accord and that the meetings had had to choose either to silence some members at the behest of others or to accord all members the equal status that the constitution seemed to give them.[41] At the time of the split in the national society, the Massachusetts Anti-Slavery Society's board of managers sent an address to its agents explaining that the organization had tried to deal with the woman-question issue

in a practical, inoffensive, and common sense way. Those members appeared at our meetings, and claimed the right to vote and speak. *Their right was questioned.* . . . . It thus became necessary to settle it. . . . We turned to the constitution of our society. We there found that all persons, who were members of the society, had equal rights in its meetings. Unless, therefore, we were prepared to vote that women are not *persons,* we could not deny them the common privileges of membership. Sparingly as our sisters in the cause have exercised their right to speak, our acknowledging that the right existed is put prominently forward as good cause for breaking up the anti-slavery organization in this State!

If a member disagrees with the constitution, the address went on, he should try to have it amended. If instead he resigns, "we can only say that *he is acting on a narrow principle, that would make all organized effort impossible, or very short-lived,*" because perfect agreement at all times is impossible.

We are astonished to hear it pretended, that if a woman speaks at an anti-slavery meeting, the responsibility is not her own, but rests upon every man in the assembly;—a guilt from which he cannot absolve himself by protesting against it, but only by breaking up the whole anti-slavery organization![42]

The next act in the predictable scenario was staged at the annual meeting of the Massachusetts Anti-Slavery Society in January 1839, where a small minority led by Torrey attempted in vain to deprive women of the right to take part in the meeting.[43] That faction had already determined to withdraw from the society and found their own newspaper, *The Massachusetts Abolitionist.* A few months later the Rev. Amos A. Phelps resigned his positions as corresponding secretary and member of the board of managers of the Massachusetts Society, averring that "The Society is no longer an *Anti-Slavery* Society *simply,* but in its principles and modes of action, has become a *women's-rights, non-government Anti-Slavery Society.*"[44]

Phelps retained his membership in the society, however, and at the New England convention in May he offered a resolution that only men be permitted to participate in the proceedings. The reasons he listed were all technical: that only men had participated in the first two New England conventions; that the first had unanimously resolved that conventions be held annually thereafter and that the board of managers of the Massachusetts Society were to be a standing committee to plan such conventions; that the third New England convention was the first of the series held according to this arrangement; and that the basis of organization of that convention ought therefore to be regarded as the basis upon which all future conventions were to be conducted—that is, men only. Phelps's resolution was defeated, and a large majority approved Wendell Phillips's motion to invite all abolitionists present to participate. The minority thereupon withdrew and on May 27 organized the Massachusetts Abolition Society.[45] The first organizational split had occurred. The Essex County (Massachusetts) Anti-Slavery Society divided immediately afterward, with the seceders, led by the Revs. Charles T. Torrey, Alanson St. Clair, and Daniel Wise, forming a new organization auxiliary to the Massachusetts Abolition Society.[46] Other splits took place, including an unusually bitter one in the Boston Female Anti-Slavery Society.[47]

At about the same time the fight officially spread beyond New England, when the national society at its annual meeting in New York had a test vote on seating the women. The Rev. Nathaniel Colver moved that the roll of delegates be made up of men only, but the convention approved the Garrisonian Ellis Gray Loring's amendment to the resolution, recognizing "all persons, male and female, who are delegates from any auxiliary society, or members of this Society," as members of the convention.[48] After much wrangling and voting, James G. Birney presented a protest on behalf of 123 delegates "against the principle, assumed by a majority of persons representing said Society at its present meeting, that women have the right of originating, debating, and voting on questions which come before said Society, and are eligible to its various offices," on the following grounds. First, the action was contrary to the intent of the society's constitution when originally written. Second, it was contrary to the interpretation of the constitution and the custom of the society since its founding. Third, "it is repugnant to the wishes, the wisdom, or the moral sense of many of the early and present members of said Society, and devoted friends of the cause for which that Society was organized." Fourth, although the majority at the convention favored the participation of women, most abolition-ists, male and female, throughout the country did not. Fifth, "it is rather the expression of local and sectarian feelings, of recent origin, than of those broad sentiments which existed among friends of our great enterprise at its begin-ning." Sixth, the founders of the society recommended separate clubs for women. And seventh, regardless of the dissidents' opinions on women's rights, this action would "bring unnecessary reproach and embarrassment to the cause of the enslaved," because it was contrary to custom. However, added the protest, if such action were a necessary part of the fight to end slavery, the signers would disregard such reproach.[49] The following year, when the national convention voted to appoint Abby Kelley to the business committee, the final division occurred, and the minority founded the American and Foreign Anti-Slavery Society (A & F).[50] The A & F's constitution provided for separate women's societies which were to be represented at conventions by male delegates.

It should be noted that the uproar did not start within the movement; the Pastoral Letter and sermons such as Winslow's on woman's place were the work of nonabolitionists, and the other protests and appeals before 1839 were written by clergymen who were local antislavery leaders or on the periphery of the movement or had only recently joined.[51] In the early stages of the controversy, even the conservative Lewis Tappan could write, "Let Mr Garrison conduct his paper, in his own way, untrammelled," provided there was no official connection between it and any antislavery society, and "Let it be understood that our friends Grimke 'go a warfare at their own charges,' as they in fact do & are not connected with any Anti Slavery Society."[52]

But the woman-question controversy quickly became involved in the religious and political disputes that were to tear the association apart in 1840, and its usefulness as a weapon in those other factional struggles was revealed quite early. The second clerical protest[53] declared that Garrison had done more than encourage women to leave their appointed sphere; he had also denounced certain clergymen for refusing to read notices of abolitionist meetings from their pulpits, had repudiated the institution of the Sabbath, had preached the heresy of "perfectionism," and was working for the overthrow of all organized society. "The great body of abolitionists," continued the protest,

. . . deplore the evils of which we complain. . . . It is but a few only who sanction them. And, in fact, these few are not *properly abolitionists.* . . . That class of men amongst us, whose abolition involves the abolition of the Sabbath and the Christian ministry, are *radicals.* They ought to be designated by this title. Let them go out from amongst us, for they are not of us. They are the prolific fountain of all the evils which retard and injure the cause of abolition.[54]

This statement represented an ominous innovation, for here for the first time some abolitionists laid down an ideological test of membership that would exclude many of their co-workers.

What in fact were the Garrisonians charged with? It is important to note that they were not accused of using official abolitionist platforms or society publications to preach that women ought to have the right to go to the polls, to enter professions, to be admitted to colleges. No paid agent of the society was accused of mixing up "extraneous" topics with his lectures on antislavery, except the extreme radical Henry C. Wright, and his appointment was not renewed.[55] The Liberator, which ran articles on both sides of the issue (with no pretense of neutrality, of course), was never, after 1832, the organ of any society. In 1837 it was financially supported by the Massachusetts Anti-Slavery Society, but even then the agreement made it clear that the paper spoke, not for the society, but only for its editor.[56] Discussions at conventions only occasionally and briefly touched on women's rights in general; the advocates of this cause usually refused to become embroiled in debates on the issue in society meetings, and their policy was the same in regard to all the other heresies Garrison was charged with.[57]

What their opponents were really objecting to, then, was that advocates of women's rights and the other eccentric causes belonged to antislavery societies at all. The conservatives' philosophy of abolitionism required the American Society and its auxiliaries to be *officially* orthodox on all subjects besides antislavery, explicitly repudiating what were then called "ultraisms." Their aim was to show white Northerners that antislavery was respectable and perfectly compatible with conventional views on all other questions. Since they themselves held conventional views on those other questions, they were, from their point of view, fighting to prevent abolition from being publicly portrayed in a false light and from being used as a cover for the propagation of false doctrines. The Garrisonians were developing a theory of abolitionist organization that required complete toleration within the society of members with all sorts of views and therefore a very minimal platform on which all abolitionists could stand regardless of their opinions on other issues and their activities outside the organization. In insisting that women who wanted to participate in antislavery meetings be allowed to do so, they did not suggest that the conservatives resign. The conservatives, on the other hand, tried to read the radicals out of the movement. They had no choice, since the public insisted on considering Garrison and The Liberator spokesmen for abolitionism, despite repeated disclaimers by both sides in the controversy. A Garrisonian-type movement could thus include the conservatives, but the conservatives' type of movement could not include the "ultraists." Before the final split in 1840, the Garrisonians fought for resolutions that represented the least common denominator of abolitionist thinking; the conservatives fought for resolutions that represented the least common denominator of their own group's thinking and would have excluded the women's-rights advocates, nonresistants, and nonvoters.[58]

The Second Clerical Protest had argued frankly for a platform so constructed as to accommodate only those who believed in the divinity of the Sabbath and the Christian ministry, and to exclude "radicals." It did not matter that the "radicals" preached their doctrines only in their own organs and from their own platforms, or that the "radicals" themselves endorsed the formula enunciated in the protest—that they were "associated together *as abolitionists,* for no other object," and would therefore have preferred that the common object be the only test of membership. The test-of-membership issue was only a surface indication that two profoundly divergent conceptions of abolitionism itself had developed and with them two mutually exclusive attitudes toward organization, strategy, and tactics.

In the 1839 annual report of the Massachusetts Anti-Slavery Society, Garrison argued that freedom of discussion was an essential condition for unity. Discussing the movement then under way to form a new antislavery society that would refuse equal status to women and exclude those male abolitionists whose beliefs did not permit them to vote, the report argued that if any test other than principle were set up—that is, if "modes of action" were made tests of membership—the movement would be divided, "and a house divided against itself cannot stand." Such tests, Garrison continued, would lead to rivalries and jealousies; other members would propose new tests, and the abolitionist platform would be narrowed further.[59]

The antislavery movement, he wrote, desired to achieve its goal of abolition by preaching, that is, by means of free speech. Was it "introducing a foreign topic" to allow free speech on the subject of slavery to anyone in the society's meetings? Should the society constitute itself a judge of any person's right to speak for God and humanity? Certainly not, replied Garrison to his own rhetorical question; let each society by majority vote decide who might join and participate, and let the minority in each case abide by the decision and not withdraw.[60] Two things should be noted in this argument. First, freedom of speech was demanded for anyone discussing the subject of slavery, not women's rights, perfectionism, or any of the other "extraneous" topics which the seceders from the 1839 convention accused the radicals of dragging in. That is, Garrison and his supporters would encourage untrammeled discussion of all questions as they related to the struggle against slavery, not the merits of those questions in their own right, and they insisted that such freedom of discussion could be guaranteed only if all understood that no one who was otherwise eligible for membership would be read out of the organization for any position he took on those other questions. And obviously, freedom of discussion on all questions implied freedom of discussion for all persons: a limitation of free speech to certain members would itself have been the adoption of an official position on a mooted question, it would have deprived the meeting of the thoughts of some individuals who might have made valuable contributions, and it would have created an authoritarian atmosphere hostile to the spirit of free exchange of ideas for which Garrison and his friends were contending. The second thing that should be noted is that the last sentence of Garrison's statement paraphrased above urges the dissident minority to remain; Garrison was proposing an antislavery platform broad enough to accommodate those whose quarrels with him on the "extraneous issues" and on political action induced them to declare his abolitionism spurious.

Some of the dissidents felt that Garrison's pleas for unity were as spurious as his abolitionism: they believed he had constructed an antislavery platform too narrow for them to stand on side by side with his faction and then publicly deplored their departure! Others, who never doubted his sincerity, found his platform proscriptive in effect, despite his verbal welcome to all who accepted the basic tenets of the movement: the sinfulness of slavery and the obligation of immediate and unconditional emancipation. The New-York City Anti-Slavery Society, in an "Address to Abolitionists" justifying the 1840 secession, pointed out that many people, identifying the abolitionist movement with a minority of its members, had been deterred from joining, and members considered resigning, to the great joy of the friends of slavery. The society's enemies no longer dreaded an organization that was "resolved into a Quixotic crusade of knights-errant valorously battling for the *rights of women!*" It would be better for the enterprise to dissolve than that its object be "made subservient to paltry disputes for a worthless pre-eminence, or personal partialities for particular theories." The movement must discard all foreign questions. Let all abolitionists leave their favorite doctrines at home and meet as abolitionists, the address proposed; in so doing they would show their diversity on other subjects to be a pledge of the movement's strength. Elizur Wright, Jr., summed up the thesis thus: "It is downright nonsense to suppose that the Anti-Slavery cause can be carried forward with forty incongruous things tacked on to it. You can't drive a three tined fork through a hay mow," but turn it around, he said, and "you can drive in the handle."[61]

Here was a delightful irony: each side accused the other of "sectarianism"! Each side claimed its proposed platform was the "broad" one, on which the greater number of abolitionists could stand united. The conservatives called the AASS sectarian for letting its abolitionism be identified in the public mind with other causes approved by only a small "sect" centered in New England (with some supporters elsewhere, particularly in eastern Pennsylvania)—causes like women's rights, nonresistance, anticlericalism, antisabbatarianism, and nonvoting. The AASS would reply that antislavery was one aspect of a broad struggle for human rights; as such it inevitably brought some women into public activity. Those who wanted to silence them were the sectarians; that is, they tried to have the struggle against slavery conducted according to religious and conventional principles not approved by all abolitionists. In doing so they made those principles issues in the societies.[62] An antislavery society that officially endorsed Saint Paul would be free to take official positions on infant baptism, temperance, and so on indefinitely. The Garrisonians insisted that the antislavery platform must be broad enough to include an abolitionist who agreed with Saint Paul and one who did not. They could work together for the slave only so long as neither attempted to impose his opinions on the other.[63] In effect, then, "sectarianism" meant to the conservatives the belief in false doctrines; it meant to the Garrisonians the refusal to work in a movement with believers in false doctrines.

Gilbert H. Barnes considers Garrison a hypocrite for not pushing his female disciples onto the lecture platform.[64] But Garrison was not a champion of women's rights per se. He championed freedom of speech as a corollary of his broad commitment to human rights; freedom for women to follow the dictates of their own consciences was a further corollary that he gladly accepted. If a woman asked to speak or was willing to serve on a committee he was prepared to defend her right to do so, and he was prepared to vote for her if he considered her, as an individual, qualified for the post she sought. His policy in his own bailiwick was thus perfectly consistent with his tenets.

I think another instance of the same misunderstanding is John L. Thomas's statement:

All of Garrison's reform interests suffered from his inability to bring to them a coherent philosophy. His concern with woman's rights was at best sporadic. He supported the Seneca Falls Convention in 1848 and attended the first woman's rights convention in

Massachusetts in Worcester in 1850. His nonvoting perfectionism, however, made him something less than an enthusiastic supporter of the franchise for women. "I want the women to have the right to vote, and I call upon them to demand it perseveringly until they possess it. When they have obtained it, it will be for them to say whether they will exercise it or not."[65]

There is no contradiction between his approval of woman suffrage and his nonvoting principle.[66] Garrison did have a coherent philosophy that encompassed both. Its core was an insistence that every human being was equally, strictly, individually responsible to God to do his will as revealed in the New Testament. It repudiated governments based on force because force was incompatible with this equality, violated what Garrison interpreted as Christ's prohibition of coercion of any sort, and substituted human for divine authority. He stressed the gospel injunction to be perfectly free of sin as an ideal toward which every individual must strive, each accountable to God for his own sins. An obvious corollary of this philosophy was absolute equality of all mankind, including women and Negroes.[67] He therefore opposed a law that prevented women from deciding whether or not they would vote, just as he opposed laws excluding Negroes from militias, even though he abhorred armies on principle. "We want impartial liberty to prevail," he explained, "and then every one must 'give account of himself to God' for the manner in which he uses it."[68] His view of woman suffrage was thus purely negative; it was the eradication of a positive denial of equality, freedom, and responsibility he was after, not woman suffrage as a good in itself.[69]

Abolitionists who agreed on the question of principle could still, and did, ask Garrison whether tacking a historically premature reform onto one that had a better chance of success did not impede the progress of both. Garrison believed that this challenge begged the question. He and his followers were certain that all good causes helped each other.[70] This would of course follow from a commitment to broad human rights that encompassed all the reforms regardless of their relative "ripeness," especially if conceived in terms of a single divine Truth with many aspects. Real conversion to one was a step toward conversion to that larger commitment. Garrison's experience might be illustrated by a metaphor that pictured the white American of his day as in a dark room. Someone lit a small candle, and in the dim light he could now see where another unlit candle was. Each successive candle he lit would throw more light on everything else in the room, including the candles themselves—the full light being, of course, God's single, all-encompassing Truth, and the candles being the small parts of it that each reform represented.[71] Garrison himself had gone through that experience, since abolitionism had led him to his wider commitment.

Birney, the Tappans, Phelps, and the other antifeminist abolitionists had the simplest conceivable reply: abolitionism, temperance, and certain other reforms were part of God's Truth, but the equality of the sexes was most assuredly not. They could tolerate the vagaries of that lunatic fringe that every movement for change attracts, so long as the public clearly understood that those vagaries were not part of the movement proper. But if the activities of the fringe succeeded in identifying its idiosyncratic demands with the cause, it must be repudiated so that potential recruits would not be frightened away or the nature of the movement itself distorted.[72]

In addition to the Garrisonian and the antifeminist positions on the woman question, there was a third position, that of abolitionists who favored sex equality but believed that issue ought to be played down so as to enable the movement to recruit the many people who were ready for abolitionism but not yet enlightened enough to accept women's rights. Once those people had become active in the slave's behalf, that activity would help prepare them for the next step toward the wider cause of human rights. This was the view of Theodore D. Weld. A champion of absolute equality of the sexes, he repeatedly encouraged the Grimké sisters to lecture publicly to "promiscuous assemblies," stressing that as Southerners they could do ten times more for the cause of the slave than any Northern woman, but that

> Any women of your powers will produce as much effect as you on the north in advocating the rights of *free* women (I mean in contradistinction to *slave* women). . . . Now can't you leave the *less* work to others who can do it *better* than you, and devote, consecrate your whole bodies, souls and spirits to the *greater* work which you can do far better and to far better purpose than any body else. Again, the abolition question is most powerfully preparative and introductory to the *other* question. By pushing the former with all our might we are most effectually advancing the latter. By absorbing the public mind in the greatest of all violations of rights, we are purging its vision to detect other violations.[73]

Therefore he urged them to stress in their lectures the fundamental principle of human rights, secure in the knowledge that they would be helping to advance the cause of women's rights without explicitly advocating it. Further, the public's prejudices against women's lecturing would be dissipated more effectively and quickly by repeated exposures to the practice than by polemics on the theory of sex equality. Weld's difference with Garrison on this issue was thus only tactical.

This was not so in the cases of the Quaker poet John Greenleaf Whittier, of Massachusetts, and Elizur Wright, Jr., corresponding secretary of the AASS. Neither could see the larger issue involved. Whittier, an active abolitionist, wrote both private and public letters pleading with Garrison, the Grimkés, and others not to intrude the "irrelevant" and relatively minor grievances of white women into the struggle against the greater crime of slavery.[74] Wright refused to take the argument seriously: "I think the tom-turkies ought to do the gobbling, I am opposed to hens' crowing, and surely, as a general rule, to female-preaching." But, he added, if some women insisted on acting the part of men they should be permitted to do so; nature would assert itself in the end.[75] Whittier and Wright were among those anti-Garrisonians who founded the A & F, which segregated its women members. Weld refused for that reason to join.[76]

But what about the Birneys, Tappans, and Phelpses, those abolitionists whose attitudes toward women were undistinguishable from those of most nonabolitionists? Both the Garrison faction and those who shared Weld's sentiments would have preferred that a formula be found whereby all could work together in the AASS despite their differences. But the conservatives were no more willing to accept Weld's than Garrison's solution, for Weld and Garrison agreed that women must be accorded equal status in the organization. Garrison, for his part, never considered relinquishing that demand. The very experiences that the abolition movement had undergone by late 1837, when the issue arose, provided him with a cogent reason: abolitionists had had to fight constantly for the freedom to advocate their cause, and in the course of the battle had learned, and proclaimed, that free speech and slavery could not coexist for long in any society; one must sooner or later destroy the other, and the spirit that would cut off free speech *was* the spirit of slavery.[77] Garrison saw his task within the organization as parallel to the task of the abolitionists in American society—to liberate thought, to create an atmosphere in which all issues could be discussed freely.[78] He tried to keep the subject of women's rights out of the society's meetings but insisted on his right to discuss it in his paper, and he was convinced that his opponents could conscientiously accept (though not approve of) women's equal status in the organization as a technically correct interpretation of the constitution. When they refused to make that minimum concession, he was certain their action was part of a larger plot to discredit him. The history of the later disputes over religious questions and political action, with which the women's rights issue became entangled, suggests the plot did not exist solely in his imagination.

NOTES

1. Rayford W. Logan, The Negro in American Life and Thought: The Nadir, 1877–1901, (New York, 1954).

2. See Aileen S. Kraditor, The Ideas of the Woman Suffrage Movement, 1890–1920 (New York, 1965), Ch. 7.

3. I do not mean to imply that the two movements were comparable in all respects or that a struggle for the vote can be equated with a struggle for freedom.

4. Keith E. Melder, "The Beginnings of the Women's Rights Movement in the United States, 1800–1840," Ph.D. dissertation, Yale University, 1964, has an extremely detailed and perceptive discussion of the relation of the woman question to abolitionism, especially in Chs. 2 through 6. I read this work after I completed this [paper], but made no substantive changes because his sources coincide almost exactly with mine and our generalizations concur on all but a few minor points. Melder's dissertation deals with the events within the abolitionist movement involving the woman question in far greater detail than is appropriate here. My discussion will recount those events only insofar as they throw light on abolitionist thinking on the goals, strategy, and tactics of abolitionism.

5. The Grimké sisters, Angelina Emily (1805–1879) and Sarah Moore (1792–1873), were born in Charleston to a famous slaveholding family. Their father's distinguished career included membership in his state's constitutional ratifying convention and the posts of senior associate justice of the state and speaker of the South Carolina house of representatives. Their maternal grandfather had been governor of North Carolina, and their two brothers also attained fame, one as a philanthropist and the other as a jurist in Ohio. In 1819 Sarah became a Quaker and eventually converted Angelina, and the sisters moved to Philadelphia. Angelina became an abolitionist in 1834 and two years later converted Sarah to the cause. In 1837 they traveled about New England lecturing for abolition, at their own expense; they were not official agents of the AASS. In 1838 Angelina married Theodore Dwight Weld, and both women retired from public activity, Sarah living thereafter with her sister's family.

6. The "Address of the American and Foreign Anti-Slavery Society" (the anti-Garrisonian "new organization" formed in 1840 by seceders from the AASS), published in The Liberator, June 19, 1840, emphasized that the women had asked permission to speak, and it argued that that showed they had not been considered regular members. See also William Goodell, Slavery and Anti-Slavery, p. 453; [Wendell P. Garrison and Francis J. Garrison], William Lloyd Garrison, 1805–1879: The Story of His Life Told by His Children (hereafter referred to as Garrisons, Garrison), I (1805–1835) (New York, 1885), 413. It should not be inferred that the issue of women's rights had never arisen before this time. In fact, at the 1836 convention of the Massachusetts Anti-Slavery Society, Dr. Charles Follen made an eloquent plea for equality of the sexes. See Fourth Annual Report of the Board of Managers of the New-England Anti-Slavery Society (Boston, 1836), pp. 52–53.

The report does not indicate that any dissent was made. After the controversy arose the following year, however, most proponents of women's rights refrained from making such speeches at society meetings.

7. An excellent account of the episode is in Eleanor Flexner, *Century of Struggle: The Woman's Rights Movement in the United States* (Cambridge, Mass., 1959), pp. 45–50.

8. They mention their shyness in several letters, one of which is Angelina E. Grimke to Amos A. Phelps, August 17, [1837], Phelps Papers, BPL.

9. This and other details about the lectures can be found in a series of letters from Angelina Grimké to Jane Smith throughout 1837, in the Weld Papers, UM; they constitute a sort of diary, with summaries of the lectures, the reactions and sizes of the audiences, and the sisters' thoughts concerning their mission. Only one of these letters is in the published *Weld-Grimké Letters*.

10. *The Liberator*, August 11, 1837.

11. They express this conviction in many letters. An unusually interesting one is Sarah M. Grimké to Amos A. Phelps, August 3, 1837, Phelps Papers, BPL. See also Sarah M. Grimke to Henry C. Wright, August 27, 1837, Anti-Slavery Letters, BPL.

12. Garrison published them all. See "Appeal of Clerical Abolitionists on Anti-Slavery Measures," *The Liberator*, August 11, 1837; "Appeal of Abolitionists of the [Andover] Theological Seminary," *ibid.*, August 25, 1837; "Protest of Clerical Abolitionists, No. 2," *ibid.*, September 8, 1837; "Abolition Women," a lecture by the Rev. Albert A. Folsom of Hingham, *ibid.*, September 22, 1837. From this time on, through 1840, *The Liberator* frequently printed letters on all sides of the woman question. The Andover Appeal and the Protest No. 2 berated Garrison and his supporters mainly for perfectionism and anti-institutionalism. Women's-rightisism was included simply as one of her heresies.

13. Mrs. Child (1802–1880) had been a successful novelist before her conversion to abolitionism, when she sacrificed her lucrative career to publish the pamphlet *An Appeal in Favor of That Class of Americans Called Africans* (1833). After the anti-Garrisonians withdrew from the AASS in 1840, taking the official organ, *The Emancipator*, with them, the society founded a new paper, *The National Anti-Slavery Standard*, and from 1841 to 1842 Mrs. Child was its editor.

14. "Letter from Mrs. Child, on the Present State of the Anti-Slavery Cause," *The Liberator*, September 6, 1839. See also "Speaking in the Church," *ibid.*, July 23, 1841. This editorial by Mrs. Child is reprinted from *The National Anti-Slavery Standard*.

15. Wright (1797–1870), a former hatmaker and Congregational preacher, joined the New-England Anti-Slavery Society in 1835 and became a traveling agent for the AASS. When the Grimkés began their lecture tour he made himself their unofficial booking agent. His alleged incompetence and undisputed radicalism caused the society to transfer him to Pennsylvania and then drop him from its roster of agents. He was an even more uncompromising pacifist than Garrison and provoked the ire of the conservatives by his numerous heretical articles in *The Liberator*.

16. Angelina Grimké to Theodore D. Weld and John G. Whittier, August 20, 1837, Gilbert H. Barnes and Dwight L. Dumond, eds., *The Letters of Theodore Dwight Weld, Angelina Grimké and Sarah Grimké* (Magnolia, Mass., 1965), I, 428. See also Anne Warren Weston to Lucia Weston, n.d., but evidently in September 1840, Weston Papers, BPL: commenting on a lecture tour in Connecticut by Abby Kelley, a Quaker abolitionist from Massachusetts, Miss Weston wrote that one minister had "preached a sermon at her from the text 'Notwithstanding I have a few things against thee because thou sufferest that woman Jezebel *which calleth herself a prophetess*, to teach, & to seduce my servants to commit fornication.' He called her by name applying this verse to her, said every thing he could to attack her character: that 'she was travelling up & down by night & by day, always with men & never with women—' Not a woman in the town but was afraid to speak to her tho' they had known her well."

17. The abolitionist ministers probably were particularly anxious to show that abolitionism did not imply women's-rightism, in view of such statements as that of the Rev. Albert A. Folsom, that neglect of her domestic duties was an inevitable result of a woman's conversion to abolitionism (the speech is in *The Liberator*, September 22, 1837). Statements such as Folsom's were also calculated to reduce the size of the Grimkés audiences and no doubt provided an additional motive for the Grimkés, Garrison, and other abolitionists who favored women's rights to use the podium and the printing press

to show not only that female abolitionists did not neglect their duties but also that public work in behalf of the slave was itself a duty of a Christian woman.

18. I Cor. 14:34–35; Ephesians 5:22–24. Other favorite New Testament verses were I Timothy 2:11–12 and I Peter 3:I.

19. See, for example, letter to the editor from Henry C. Wright, *The Liberator*, May 22, 1840. Wright contended that the spirit that said women should work separately in their own societies was the same spirit that would send Negroes to Liberia. He quoted Lewis Tappan to the effect that it was "contrary to the usages of civilized society" for women to act in organizations with men, and he cited the opinions of the Revs. Amos A. Phelps and C. W. Denison that such integration would be contrary to the gospel. Wright observed that both arguments were used to keep Negroes in slavery or segregated. The same arguments appear in an editorial by Oliver Johnson immediately preceding Wright's letter, and in "Address of the Executive Committee of the American Anti-Slavery Society to the Abolitionists of the United States," *ibid.*, July 31, 1840.

20. Caroline L. Shanks, "The Biblical Anti-Slavery Argument of the Decade 1830–1840," *Journal of Negro History*, XVI (April 1931), 150.

21. *The Liberator*, May 24, 1839.

22. Phelps (1805–1847), after graduation from Yale, was a Congregationalist minister in Massachusetts until 1834, when he became general agent of the New-England Anti-Slavery Society. He became corresponding secretary of that organization in 1838 but resigned the following year. Phelps broke with Garrison during the controversy over the status of women in the AASS. In 1839 he returned to preaching, although for a short time a few years later he edited *The Abolitionist*, the organ of the anti-Garrisonian Massachusetts Abolition Society.

23. *The Liberator*, February 26, 1841. In 1837 Phelps, always a conservative on religious and social questions, had criticized the clerical remonstrants for causing unnecessary dissension within the movement (see his letter as general agent of the Massachusetts Society, *ibid.*, August 18, 1837, and his letter to John G. Whittier, August 17, 1837, Phelps Papers, BPL). But later, when the controversy over the woman question became involved in the general factionalism, he made his conservative views public and joined the anti-Garrison group.

24. Sarah Douglass to Charles K. Whipple, April 26, 1841, Anti-Slavery Letters, BPL.

25. *The Liberator*, October 6, 1837, reprinted from *The New England Spectator*. A long excerpt from this document is reprinted in Aileen S. Kraditor, ed., *Up from the Pedestal: Selected Writings in the History of American Feminism* (Chicago, 1968).

26. "Letters to Catherine E. Beecher, No. XII," *The Liberator*, October 13, 1837. See Kraditor, ed., *Up from the Pedestal*.

27. See, for example, the protest of those members of the AASS national convention of 1839 who withdrew because women were permitted equal status with men in the convention and on its committees (*Sixth Annual Report of the Executive Committee of the American Anti-Slavery Society* [New York, 1839], pp. 44–47).

28. James Mott (husband of Lucretia Mott, the pioneer feminist) to Anne Warren Weston, June 7, 1838, Weston Papers, BPL. See also resolution passed by the Providence Ladies' Anti-Slavery Society at its quarterly meeting in October 1837, in which the ladies expressed their gratitude, as women, to the pioneers in the cause of emancipation, in Europe and America, for helping them discern their own rights "by means of the full light which their benevolent efforts have shed on the equality of the rights of man" (*The Liberator*, November 3, 1837).

29. See, for example, Oliver Johnson's editorial, *ibid.*, August 11, 1837 (Johnson was editor pro tem in Garrison's absence), and a resolution of the Bristol County Anti-Slavery Society at its annual meeting in New Bedford, Mass., as reported *ibid.*, October 27, 1837.

30. Maria Weston Chapman, *Right and Wrong in Massachusetts* (Boston, 1839), pp. 12–13. Mrs. Chapman (1806–1885) was Garrison's chief female supporter, a nonresistant and feminist leader in the Boston Female Anti-Slavery Society, and writer of its reports entitled *Right and Wrong in Boston*. After the 1840 split in the AASS she became a member of the executive committee of the national organization. Upon David Lee Child's resignation as editor of the *Standard*, in 1844, Mrs. Chapman was one of the editorial committee of three that replaced him (the others were Edmund Quincy and Sidney Howard Gay).

31. For this reason the remark by Gilbert H. Barnes in *The Anti-Slavery Impulse, 1830–1844* (New York, 1933), p. 158, is debatable: "The net result of the woman's rights controversy was to reduce the antislavery influence of the Grimké sisters' agency and to retard materially the actual progress of woman's emancipation." But numerous letters in *The Liberator* show that many people were stimulated to think about the question for the first time, that many women abolitionists who had already harbored forbidden thoughts of female emancipation were emboldened to pursue those thoughts further than they would have dared to otherwise, and that some male abolitionists pondered the analogies that had been suggested between Negro rights and women's rights. The exclusion of women from membership at the 1840 World's Anti-Slavery Convention in London was, as is well known, the incident that induced Elizabeth Cady Stanton and Lucretia Mott to organize the first women's-rights convention, and the effort to seat them at the London convention was a direct outgrowth of the controversy.

32. Lydia Maria Child, in *The National Anti-Slavery Standard*, as reprinted in *The Liberator*, July 23, 1841.

33. *First Annual Report of the American Anti-Slavery Society*, back cover.

34. For the antifeminists' construction of the constitution, see Lewis Tappan to Theodore D. Weld, May 26, 1840, Tappan Papers, LC; protest of 123 members of the 1839 national convention, printed in *Sixth Annual Report of the Executive Committee of the American Anti-Slavery Society*, pp. 44–47, especially points 1 and 2 on p. 45; "Address of the American and Foreign Anti-Slavery Society," *The Liberator*, June 19, 1840.

35. One is reminded of the debate over Lincoln's constitutional powers during the Civil War; of course the Constitution did not anticipate a civil war, and so both sides were in a sense right—and wrong.

36. "To the Public," signed by Elizur Wright, Jr., corresponding secretary, in behalf of the executive committee, reprinted from *The Emancipator*, official organ of the AASS, in *The Liberator*, September 1, 1837.

37. Both statements are *ibid.*

38. Torrey (1813–1846) was a Yale graduate, Massachusetts pastor, lecturer for the Massachusetts Anti-Slavery Society, and corresponding secretary of the Andover Anti-Slavery Society when it was formed in 1835. In 1844 he was arrested in Baltimore for having helped some fugitive slaves escape, and was sentenced to six years in prison, where he died of tuberculosis.

39. *The Liberator*, June 8, 1838.

40. *Ibid.*, July 6, 1838. See also ninth resolution passed at the 1839 annual meeting of the Essex County Anti-Slavery Society, reported *ibid.*, June 21, 1839; and "Address to the Abolitionists of Massachusetts," signed by Francis Jackson and Garrison, president and secretary respectively of the Massachusetts Anti-Slavery Society, *ibid.*, July 19, 1839. One Garrisonian who was certainly guilty of the conservatives' charges was Maria Weston Chapman. Her most serious breach of the principle asserted by the "Member of the Convention" was in the annual report of the Boston Female Anti-Slavery Society for 1837, which she wrote. It includes a long argument for sex equality, including biblical citations. Unlike the Grimkés' articles, this was an official antislavery-society document. Five leaders of Mrs. Chapman's organization recorded their dissent from "some portions" of the report. See *Right and Wrong in Boston, No. 3* (Boston, 1837), pp. 3, 74–75. This incident was exceptional, however.

41. See, for example, Oliver Johnson, *The Liberator*, July 27, 1838.

42. *Ninth Annual Report of the Board of Managers of the Mass. Anti-Slavery Society* (Boston, 1841), p. 16. Italics in original. On this one point, the violently anti-Garrisonian Joshua Leavitt, editor of *The Emancipator*, agreed. See "The Woman Question," *The Emancipator*, May 23, 1839.

43. *The Liberator*, February 1, 1839.

44. *Ibid.*, May 3, 1839. The copy of the original letter, dated April 30, 1839, in Phelps Papers, BPL, differs slightly in punctuation.

45. Letter to the editor from Phelps, now recording secretary of the new society, *The Liberator*, June 14, 1839. Since Phelps was one of those who had strong objections, on religious and physiological grounds, to women's public activity (see his letter *ibid.*, February 26, 1841), the purely technical arguments in his resolution provoke speculation whether his action was not a tacit admission that if he had given his real reasons he

would have dragged into the meeting an extraneous issue which had not been introduced by his opponents. Phelps's manuscript letters reveal a hot temper and impulsiveness. Certainly if the women's-rights issue itself had come before the meeting he would have fought it out on its own terms.

46. *Ibid.*, June 21, 28, and July 5, 1839.

47. *Ibid.*, November 1, 5, 22, and December 6, 1839; *Address of the Massachusetts Female Emancipation Society to the Women of Massachusetts*, a circular with a letter written on the same sheet: M. V. Ball to the English abolitionist Elizabeth Pease, May 6, 1840, in Anti-Slavery Letters, BPL. Miss Ball presents the anti-Garrison version of what happened. The other side is presented in Maria Weston Chapman to Elizabeth Pease, April 20, 1840, in the same collection. See Henry B. Stanton to Elizur Wright, Jr., April 11, 1839, Wright Papers, LC: "The Boston Female Soc. had a meeting yesterday, to fight a new edition of the Quarterly meeting of the Mass. Soc. Mrs. Chapman roared like a *female bull!* A motion was made to pledge $500 to the Am. Soc.—She moved to amend by pledging, $1000 to the Mass. Soc.—'The debate took a wide range'—caps, ribbons, tapes, needles, curls & flounces flew at each other most furiously. Mrs. Shipley moved to amend the amendment by striking out *Mass.* & inserting *Amer.* Mrs. Chapman fired a whole broadside of non-resistance into this proposition." And more. Stanton (1805–1887) deserves to be better known in his own right rather than merely as the husband of the leading feminist Elizabeth Cady Stanton. He was one of the "Lane Rebels," the group of students at Lane Theological Seminary in Cincinnati who under the leadership of Theodore Weld engaged in a series of revival-debates on slavery in 1834 that resulted in the conversion of most of the students to abolitionism, and withdrew en masse from Lane when the trustees attempted to prevent their antislavery activities. Stanton was AASS agent for Rhode Island, 1834–1836, and organized the state antislavery society. He was one of the most articulate anti-Garrisonians from the late 1830s on, and later became active in the Massachusetts Liberty party.

48. Barnes, on p. 159 of *The Anti-Slavery Impulse*, states: "Among the regularly constituted delegates a majority was against the measure; but the women insisted upon casting their ballots for the resolution in advance of their right to do so, and their votes gave it a majority." The reference to "regularly constituted delegates" is misleading; the constitution gave rank-and-file members the right to attend and vote at conventions, and such members had done so in all previous conventions. The phrase "in advance of their right to do so" prejudges the issue. Colver's and Loring's motions could be regarded as attempts to clarify the constitution, and according to the Garrisonians, women members had always had the right that Loring's motion merely stated explicitly. Or, the vote could be interpreted as a referendum of all constituitonally defined members to decide which of those members were to act in the society's meetings. By stating that woman had no right to vote on the issue, Barnes transforms into the constitutional ground of the vote the issue that the vote was to decide. Admittedly, I am doing the same when I say the women did have the right to vote. The point is, of course, that the issue could not be settled this way.

49. *Sixth Annual Report of the Executive Committee of the American Anti-Slavery Society*, pp. 27–30, 44–47.

50. This was the convention that Garrison "packed" with his boatload of disciples from New England. Barnes discusses Garrison's stratagem on pp. 169–70 of *The Anti-Slavery Impulse*, but his animus against Garrison causes him to distort what happened. He devotes most of three paragraphs to the chartering of a boat, the fact that in Lewis Tappan's words, "a large part of the town of Lynn" responded to Garrison's appeal for passengers, and the consequent vote by which the convention confirmed Miss Kelley's appointment to the business committee. He dismisses in one sentence the efforts of the Tappan faction to rig the convention its way. But see Henry B. Stanton to Amos A. Phelps, dated "Saturday," and written on the blank pages of a circular from the British and Foreign Anti-Slavery Society dated February 15, 1840, Phelps Papers, BPL. See also comment by Lydia Maria Child in letter to Ellis Gray Loring, May 17, 1840], Child Papers, NYPL, concerning "a very extensive and active agitation on the part of the Ex. Committee. The degree of diligence and tact manifested would exceed your belief. No opportunity . . . has been omitted in this region [central Massachusetts], to preoccupy the minds of the people against the Massachusetts Board. *Every* minister, influential deacon, or active sectarian, for miles and miles and miles around, has been furnished with the N. York side of the case, without any chance of hearing the Mass. side. Private letters *innumerable* have been written in every direction, especially by Phelps. . . . Nothing is more observable in all

these transactions than the efforts at secresy [sic]." Cf. Barnes's statement (p. 279, n. 22) that the Executive Committee restricted its activities to general appeals to attend the convention to secure a majority. Perhaps this statement reflects the inadequacy of his research into manuscript materials. For private efforts to right other conventions, see C. T. Torrey to Edwin F. Clarke, March 7, 1840, Miscellaneous Slavery Collection, NYHS, and A. St. Clair to Phelps, March 30, 1839, Phelps Papers, BPL, among others. The Garrisonians' activities were well publicized. *The Liberator*, April 24, 1840, reprinted from *The Emancipator* a letter from Garrisonian James S. Gibbons to Joshua Leavitt, editor of *The Emancipator*, urging "all abolitionists" to come to the New York convention to help save the society. An anti-Garrisonian appeal for a large turnout appeared in a Connecticut paper and was reprinted in *The Liberator*, May 1, 1840. The May 8 issue had an article describing the special travel arrangements; it said that in view of the many statements proposing dissolution of the society or change of the constitution to eliminate the clause permitting rand-and-file members to vote at conventions, the friends of the old organization ought to go en masse, for if they did not, it would be understood by all that the cause was languishing.

51. Leaders like Birney and the Tappans seem to have been embarrassed by the furious attacks of the clerics. Certainly Elizur Wright and Henry B. Stanton were. Birney and the Tappans, and other leaders who were conservative on the woman question, found ample opportunities for public attacks on Garrison on other questions, although once the innovations in women's activities had evoked the public outcry, they were willing to use them or countenance their use in their factional struggles with Garrison. The nonresistance and nonvoting issues. . .were more important to them. Arthur Tappan signed a statement by the A & F that the same abolitionists who favored women's rights were those who denied the obligation to yield obedience to civil government; Birney at the London Convention used the same tactic in his effort to prevent the seating of women delegates, although the "no human government" theory had no bearing on the question at issue (*The Liberator*, June 19, July 24, 1840).

52. Tappan to Amos A. Phelps, August 22, 1837, Phelps Papers, BPL. Lewis Tappan (1788–1873), along with his partner and older brother, Arthur, was a wealthy New York merchant, a Presbyterian, and an active worker for benevolent and religious causes. When Garrison was jailed for libeling a proslavery merchant in Baltimore in 1829, it was Arthur Tappan who paid his fine. But Lewis was the more active abolitionist of the two, one of the leaders of the conservative "New York group," and broke with Garrison over the latter's various heresies in the late 1830s. After the AASS schism in 1840, Tappan became active in the A & F.

53. See footnote 12 above.

54. *The Liberator*, September 8, 1837.

55. Lewis Tappan to Amos A. Phelps, August 22, 1837, and Elizur Wright, Jr., to Phelps, September 12, 1837, Phelps Papers, BPL; Charles C. Burleigh to James M. McKim, November 13, 1837, Anti-Slavery Letters, BPL.

56. Garrison to Anna E. Benson, February 4, 1837, Garrison Letters, BPL; "To the Public," signed by Francis Jackson and Nathaniel Southard, president and recording secretary respectively of the Massachusetts Anti-Slavery Society, *The Liberator*, September 8, 1837; "Our Cause," *ibid.*, November 3, 1837; *Fifth Annual Report of the Board of Managers of the Massachusetts Anti-Slavery Society* (Boston, 1837), p. xxxvi.

57. It need hardly be pointed out that they energetically used other media to propagate their views. Sarah Grimké advocated women's rights in some of her public lectures (see Angelina E. Grimké to Jane Smith, July 27, [1837], Weld Papers, UM). She wrote fifteen "Letters on the Equality of the Sexes, and the Condition of Woman. Addressed to Mary S. Parker, President of the Boston Female Anti-Slavery Society"; *The Liberator* serialized them in the issues of January 5, 12, 26, February 2, 9, 16, 1838. Starting in the issue of June 23, 1837, *The Liberator* printed Angelina Grimké's "Letters to Catherine Beecher," some of which dealt with the woman question; see letters 11 and 12, issues of September 29 and October 13, 1837. See also letter by Sarah Grimké in *The New England Spectator* (a religious paper violently hostile to Garrison and women's rights, and the paper which originally published many of the clerical assaults on Garrison) as reprinted in *The Liberator*, October 6, 1837, under the title "Province of Woman. The Pastoral Letter." Selections from these essays by both Grimkés may be found in Kraditor, ed., *Up from the Pedestal*.

58. See [Kraditor, *Means and Ends in American Abolitionism*] pages 124, 129–30.

59. Extracts from the Seventh Annual Report of the Massachusetts Anti-Slavery Society," *The Liberator*, February 1, 1839. This part of the report dealt mainly with the question of political tests and only incidentally with the woman question and religion. It will therefore be discussed at greater length in Chapter 5. Garrison's prediction came true. The impotence of the Massachusetts Abolition Society and the A & F was due to several circumstances one of which was internal dissension, especially over political action. As for religious sectarianism, see St. Clair to Phelps, June 21, 1839, Phelps Papers, BPL: discussing the proposed leadership of the Massachusetts Abolition Society, St. Clair marked this section "Confidential": "Dont have any more congregationalists on the Executive Committee. There are already jealousies among some of the Baptists who are with us, on account of the preponderating *number!* of that denomination. I think it best by all means to wait till we know what Baptists will go with us, before filling the vacancies in the Committee. It will be extremely injurious to have any suspicion a particular denomination has a controling [sic] influence entertained by any other sect."

Published announcements of newly formed executive committees, lists of sponsors of mass meetings, and such must be interpreted with caution; often the lists were published before the individuals on them had been asked if they would serve. The Phelps Papers, BPL, for example, contain several letters written in summer 1839 by men who had seen their names listed as officers of the new society and who wrote to Phelps to decline the honor.

60. "The 'Woman Question,' " *The Liberator*, February 1, 1839. This article was a continuation of the extracts from the report.

61. "Address to Abolitionists from the New York City Anti-Slavery Society," signed by John Jay, chairman of the executive committee, May 8, 1840, Chapman Papers, BPL; Elizur Wright, Jr., to Amos A. Phelps, September 5, 1837, Phelps Papers, BPL. Wright (1804–1885) was a Connecticut-born Yale graduate who was teaching mathematics at Western Reserve College when he became converted to abolitionism. He was a corresponding secretary of the AASS from 1833 to 1839 and then became editor of the newly founded organ of the Massachusetts Abolition Society, *The Abolitionist*. In the 1840s he was active in support of the Liberty party, although poverty and the needs of a large family forced him to devote much time to efforts to sell copies of his translation of La Fontaine's fables. In 1845 Wright started a life insurance company for teetotalers, and between that time and 1850 he edited his own paper, the Boston *Chronotype*.

62. Lydia Maria Child, who thought it preferable for women to do their abolitionist duty and not talk about women's rights, wrote that the advocates of women's rights had *not* forced the issue into society meetings; on the contrary, even *The Liberator* had not entered the controversy except when Garrison felt he had to defend the Grimkés against the attacks. If a clergyman thought it wrong for a woman to speak in public, he had a right to his opinion, she said. "I should agree with the Massachusetts Society that it would be a monstrous violation of freedom to request or advise him to withdraw from the society because some of his views seemed likely to retard the progress of the cause." She went on to say that those on the other side insisted on introducing a foreign topic when they objected, in the meetings, to women's participation, and that the society very properly replied that it did not meddle with that subject and would take no action on it. Women, she wrote, had been regular dues-paying members from the start, and the society did not prescribe their mode of action any more than that of other members ("Letter from Mrs. Child, on the Present State of the Anti-Slavery Cause," *The Liberator*, September 6, 1839). The fight over the propriety of prescribing modes of action turned out to be a preliminary skirmish for the more important battle on political action which, when it came, was fought in exactly the same way.

63. Although the Garrisonians tried to follow this policy before the organizational split, they tended more and more to relax it as time went on. Supporters of Garrison, especially those whose opinions were more "ultra" than his, did mix up extraneous issues with abolitionism after it had become clear that there was no chance of keeping the AASS platform board (by their definition of the term).

64. *The Anti-Slavery Impulse*, p. 160: Garrison and his followers "consistently opposed the enlistment of New England women in the public agitation." Barnes offers no evidence, and I know of none, to support this statement. It is true that Garrison did not encourage such enlistment; he accepted the women's own convictions of their duty. Barnes's evidence is doubtful in several places, on this topic. On p. 156 he mentions Angelina

Grimké's asking the Boston abolitionists to have her name added to the list of speakers at a hearing of a Massachusetts legislative committee in early 1838. Barnes: " 'They all flinched,' wrote Angelina, 'except F. Jackson.' Scorning to deal further with 'Abolitionists who were only right in the *abstract* on Woman's rights and duties,' Angelina applied to the chairman of the legislative committee herself, who courteously appointed a time for her to speak. After it was arranged that she should appear, the Boston abolitionists decided to approve it." Barnes's footnote on p. 271 cites Angelina to Weld, February 11, 1838. The relevant portion is in Barnes and Dumond, eds., *Weld-Grimké Letters*, II, 538–39, where she writes that she asked S. Philbrick (with whose family the sisters were boarding) to tell the abolitionists, when he went into Boston, that she was willing to speak. Then, after the comment on abolitionists who favored women's rights only in the abstract: "they all flinched as I understand except F. Jackson. . . ." Barnes presents hearsay as direct testimony and does not indicate by ellipsis the omission of "as I understand." The footnote adds that "the tardy approval by the Boston abolitionists" is in Sarah Grimké to Gerrit Smith, February 16, 1838. The only relevant part of that letter is a paragraph on p. 551, *ibid.*, in which Sarah states that they had written to the chairman asking permission to testify, had received it, and rejoiced that God had found them worthy to plead for the slave. There is not a word on the Boston abolitionists in the letter. In any case, we are not given the Bostonians' own reasons for their hesitation. Barnes gives Henry B. Stanton credit for first suggesting, half in earnest and half in jest, that Angelina testify, and accurately cites the letter in which she reports the suggestion (Angelina to Weld, February 11, 1838). His footnote praises Stanton at length as a champion of women's rights. He does not, however, mention the letter Sarah wrote the very next day, complaining of Stanton's having left Boston before the hearing: "Brother Stanton we think is deserting in a time of need. . . . Somehow he seems not to give his cordial approbation to Angelina's having an opportunity to address the Committee . . ." (*ibid*, p. 541).

65. *The Liberator: William Lloyd Garrison* (Boston, 1963), pp. 372–73.

66. Lucretia Mott, for one, explicitly linked them: "Far be it from me to encourage women to vote, or to take an active part in politics in the present state of our government. Her right to the elective franchise, however, is the same, and should be yielded to her, whether she exercise that right or not. Would that man, too, would have no participation in a government recognizing the life-taking principle. . . . But when, in the diffusion of light and intelligence, a convention shall be called to make regulations for self-government on Christian principles, I can see no good reason why women should not participate in such assemblage, taking part equally with man." "Discourses by Lucretia Mott. Discourse on Woman, Delivered Twelfth Month 17th, 1849," in Anna D. Hallowell, ed., *James and Lucretia Mott, Life and Letters* (Boston, 1884), p. 500. Garrison would have agreed with this entire statement.

67. See his statement at a women's rights convention in New York in 1853, as quoted in Elizabeth Cady Stanton and others, eds., *The History of Woman Suffrage* (New York, 1881), I, 549: "I have been derisively called a 'Woman's Rights Man.' I know no such distinction. I claim to be a Human Rights Man, and wherever there is a human being, I see God-given rights inherent in that being whatever may be the sex or complexion."

68. Editorial commenting on "Right of Suffrage to Women," reprinted from *The New York Tribune* in *The Liberator*, January 11, 1850. The *Tribune* had expressed the same opinion as Thomas and had coyly suggested that Garrison, Phillips, and their friends were not asking women to vote; they were asking that women "have the right to *refuse to vote*." In his reply, Garrison pointed out that the editor of the *Tribune* was a Whig; "yet, anxious as he is to have that party in the ascendant, we presume he would protest against the exclusion of Democrats from the ballot-box . . . because it would be a blow struck at human freedom and equality."

69. This may be inferred from the wording, for instance, of two resolutions he offered at the 1842 Non-Resistance Society convention, as reported in *The Liberator*, October 18, 1842: first, that the federal and state constitutions were "based on usurpation, inasmuch as they proscribe one half of the people, on account of their sex, from the exercise and enjoyment of what are called civil and political rights"; and second, that "friends of human rights" ought to petition their state legislatures to abolish "all those laws which make any distinction, in regard to rights and immunities, on account of sex." (Incidentally, this call for woman suffrage appeared almost six years before the Seneca Falls convention. Garrison was, of course, wrong in believing the U.S. Constitution prevented women from

voting. It never did. Even the word "male" did not appear in it until the Fourteenth Amendment was added in 1868.) The suffragist Alice Stone Blackwell was perhaps reflecting her New England abolitionist heritage when she explained, a generation later, that although she opposed any property test for voting, she would welcome a law to give the vote to all taxpayers regardless of sex rather than the law then in force that specifically barred women. Such a change would remove a positive discrimination against one part of the population (*Woman's Journal*, May 21, 1903).

70. A few expressions of this conviction among his followers are: Angelina E. Grimké's note at the end of Sarah M. Grimké to Henry C. Wright, August 27, 1837, Anti-Slavery Letters, BPL; Sarah M. Grimké to Amos A. Phelps, August 3, 1837, Phelps Papers, BPL; Abby Kelley to Garrison, October 20, 1837, as quoted in Garrisons, *Garrison*, II, 174n; and especially Henry C. Wright's letter in *The Liberator*, October 13, 1837. Cf. Elizur Wright, Jr., to Garrison, November 6, 1837, in Garrisons, *Garrison*, II, 179: "You say, 'Truth is *one*, and not conflictive or multitudinous.' True; but the *people* are conflictive, and moreover they cannot receive and unitedly act upon more than one great truth at once." Lest it be inferred that only the Garrisonians believed all truths helped one another and that all non-Garrisonians favored tactical preferences among them, cf. James G. Birney to Gerrit Smith, June 1, 1846, Dumond, ed., *Birney Letters*, II, 1021–22. Arguing in favor of the Liberty party's broadening its platform to include many reform planks and disagreeing with Smith's assertion that inclusion of the other planks would be "premature," Birney wrote that abolitionists should not fear to tell all the truths they knew; each one supported the others. He asked: When, reading the Bible, we learn a truth we have not understood before, does it weaken or strengthen those we did know before? "So, of emancipation. Does a republican, economical, and free government . . . conflict with emancipation?" Of course not. . . . The issue between Garrisonians and other abolitionists would seem, then, to be not abolition alone versus universal reform but different notions of what universal reform entailed.

71. This metaphor is my own. See Garrison's own explanations in "The Grandeur of our Cause," *The Liberator*, May 23, 1845; "Our New Volume," *ibid.*, January 2, 1846; "The Annual Meeting at New-York," *ibid.*, April 22, 1842; "The Second Reformation—'Come-Outerism'—The Clergy and the Church," *ibid.*, December 22, 1843.

72. Louis Filler, in *The Crusade against Slavery*, p. 130, remarks: "In assessing the harm Garrison and his associates may or may not have done the antislavery movement, it must be recalled that their opponents in the antislavery societies also offended elements of the public with irrelevant opinions. The Tappans, for example, with their rigid sabbatarian principles and anti-Catholic bias, outraged as many citizens as did Garrison—in some cases, many more." It need hardly be noted that a demonstration that the Tappans outraged public opinion does not help one to assess the harm that Garrison may have done the movement. More important, however, is that Filler in my opinion misses the point: I strongly doubt if the Tappans' irrelevant opinions outraged nearly as many *potential abolitionists* as did Garrison's antisabbatarianism and defense of women's rights. Anti-Catholicism and sabbatarianism were quite respectable with the evangelical Protestants among whom the abolitionists exerted their main efforts at conversion. (On p. 132 Filler does remark that the Tappan school of abolitionists had a more "conventional" sort of antislavery movement in mind.) To Garrison's opponents the main task of the movement was to win as many recruits as possible as soon as possible, and this could be done only by leaving those recruits in undisturbed possession of all their other beliefs. The task was certainly agreeable to those abolitionists who shared those other beliefs. To the Garrisonians, that brand of abolitionism was worthless, even to the slave; such recruits would betray their abolitionism when it conflicted with their selfish interests and especially with their political loyalties. The task of the movement was, therefore, to free the public mind of its ideological shackles and bring about, as far as possible, a deep commitment to all human rights. That commitment would ensure the individual's fidelity to principle, for any prejudices incompatible with it would be dropped, and the individual would not be tempted to betray the cause in any test situations. Therefore I question Filler's judgment that the reason the Tappans' prejudices "did not breach antislavery unity" was that those prejudices "were peripheral" whereas Garrison's advocacy of women's participation was not. From Garrison's viewpoint (the viewpoint of which Filler is a champion), the Tappans' sabbatarianism was not a peripheral issue; it was in fact part of an authoritarian philosophy that fostered the proslavery spirit in the nation at large and the proscriptive spirit in the antislavery movement.

73. Weld to Sarah and Angelina Grimké, August 15, 1837, *Weld-Grimké Letters*, I, 426–27. See also Weld to Sarah and Angelina Grimké, August 26, 1837, *ibid.*, p. 433.

74. Whittier to Abby Kelley, March 8, 1841, Stephen S. and Abby Kelley Foster Papers, AAS; Whittier to Sarah and Angelina Grimké, August 14, 1839, *Weld-Grimké Letters*, I, 424; "Rights of Women in Anti-Slavery Conventions—The Question Fairly Stated," a letter to the editor from "A Member of the Convention," *The Liberator*, July 6, 1838, quoting and discussing a letter from Whittier in *The Pennsylvania Freeman*; "Woman's Rights," *The Liberator*, July 27, 1838 (the last third of this article, in the "Miscellaneous" section of the paper, is a reprint from *The Pennsylvania Freeman* of a Whittier article in which he rejected the argument that the admission of women to equal status in antislavery meetings involved the free-speech issue, and he declared that abolitionists should not turn away from their main task "to discuss irrelevant matters of minor importance," or "to turn universal reformers, and with the abolition banner floating over our heads, 'run a muck' at every thing which we may conceive to be erroneous in religion, morals, and politics." As time went on Whittier's language became more bitter and sarcastic. In a letter printed in *The Pennsylvania Freeman* and copied into *The Liberator*, November 27, 1840, he commented on those American abolitionists who had tried to have women recognized as delegates to the London Anti-Slavery Convention. He ridiculed, among other things, "our 'platform' on which men and women lose their distinctive character, and become 'souls without sex,' " and later in the article referred scornfully to "our Yankee doctrines of equality, or sexless democracy."

75. The letter continues, "I have no sympathy with the *terrors* of certain *male women* who quote Paul at the top of their lungs, as if our friend Theodore's wife [Angelina Grimké Weld] or Abby Kelly [sic] were about to wrest from them their diploma of manhood forever & aye—but I have just no doubt at all that Paul & propriety are both on their side in the *argument*. Paul, if I understand him, however, did no less than hint that his instructions for the regulation of women might without much danger have been left to *nature herself*. And whatever was the confidence of the Apostle in the correctness of his views of propriety, I think he must have been too much of a gentleman to choke a woman with authority, as as too *wise a man*." (Elizur Wright, Jr., to Amos A. Phelps, July 11, 1838, Phelps Papers, BPL; a copy is in Wright Papers, LC.) William Goodell was another prominent abolitionist who thought the innovation "harmless and unimportant" (letter to the editor, *The Liberator*, July 17, 1840).

76. See Barnes, *The Anti-Slavery Impulse*, pp. 160, 176, and 274n. Barnes's quotations from Whittier give the impression that Whittier's position was similar to Weld's. The passages cited in note 74 above, however, prove that he did not endorse full equality of the sexes. (The Wright Papers, LC, and the Phelps Papers, BPL, which contain the letters cited in note 75, are not among the few manuscript collections listed in Barnes's bibliography.) I do not contend that Whittier, Wright, or others such as Stanton and Leavitt whom Barnes links with them, were as hostile to women's rights as Birney, Tappan, and Phelps. But the question may legitimately be asked whether one who sincerely believes a certain reform desirable will support an organization that actively exerts its influence against it. Weld's advice to the Grimkés was calculated to advance the cause of women's rights, but Whittier's advice was to ignore it as unimportant, and Wright's view was that the exercise of those rights was a harmless deviation from scripture and nature. Their respective positions were, I think, accurately reflected in their attitudes toward the A & F. Nevertheless, Barnes lumps all these men together in his effort to demonstrate that the sincere advocates of sex equality were not in the Garrison camp.

77. See Russel B. Nye, *Fettered Freedom: Civil Liberties and the Slavery Controversy 1830–1860* (East Lansing, Mich., 1949), *passim*.

78. Cf. Henry B. Stanton to Elizur Wright, Jr., February 9, 1839, Wright Papers, LC. Stanton thanked Wright for some articles sent to *The Massachusetts Abolitionist* (The anti-Garrison paper recently founded), but explained that the editors had deleted part of one of them because it would provoke a reply by Garrison, which "we could not publish; & then the cry of 'proscription'–'gagism' " would be raised. "We understand the game. They mean to embarrass us. The plan is to send us articles about non-government, womens rights, perfection, &c, &c, &c, & then, if we excluded them cry out, 'ay, *you are oppossed*[sic] *to free discussion, are you!*' Bah. As tho. I was obliged to stand all day & hear a man talk nonsense. Ours is not a free discussionist, but an abolitionist journal." On Stanton's own position on the woman question the evidence is ambiguous. See documents cited in note 64 above. The evidence on his vote on admitting women at the London

Convention is conflicting. See Garrison to his wife, June 29, 1840, Garrison Letters, BPL, and Wendell Phillips to Oliver Johnson, in *The Liberator*, July 24, 1840; both say Stanton voted to admit the women. But "Mr. Stanton and the Woman Question," *ibid.*, December 4, 1840, reprinted from *The National Anti-Slavery Standard*, cites both Birney and Stanton as denying he so voted. See also Stanton to Elizur Wright, Jr., [December 2 (?), 1839], Wright Papers, LC: Stanton wrote that he did not split with the AASS on the woman question, that on that issue the AASS was in the right, and that he deplored the A & F's having "made everything to turn" on that question.

the republicans and nativism

ERIC FONER

In 1835 the first organized opposition to immigrants appeared under such names as American-Republican, Native-American, the Order of United Americans, and finally the American Party, the name officially adopted by the "Know-Nothings" in 1854. Their stated philosophy was not nativism but Americanism; their goal was to preserve the principle of nationality. In the following chapter, Eric Foner analyzes the tension within the antislavery political parties and explores the role that nativism played in the emergence of power realignments and the coming of the Civil War. He also explores the tensions between immigrants and abolitionists. Many Protestant Republican Know-Nothings were also abolitionists who despised the new immigrants not only because the "Papists" were frequently on relief, but because they supported slavery.

But in the 1850s nativist tensions diminished as the Republicans identified "free labor" as their essential ideology. The free labor of an open society, Republicans believed, would not only prevent the formation of a permanent lower working class but would ensure northern domination of the West and its continued economic expansion. Since the free labor concept demanded large numbers of immigrants, Republicans could not afford to be nativist.

Although the United States has long pictured itself as an asylum for the oppressed peoples of the world, anti-immigrant movements have displayed a striking tenacity in American politics. The nativist outbreaks of the 1790's, 1850's, and 1920's were but extreme versions of a recurrent pattern, which reflects the underlying tensions of a heterogeneous society. In recent years, a growing number of historians have become convinced that the ethnic and cultural diversity of American society, and not the differing ideologies or platforms of the major parties, have been the major determinants of American political alignments. Studies of modern state and presidential elections have demonstrated that immigrants and Catholics are much more likely to vote Democratic than native-born Protestants, and such findings have also appeared in analyses of nineteenth century voting behavior.[1] Of course astute political observers in the 1850's were hardly unaware of the ethnic dimensions of northern politics. Even Carl Schurz, who hoped to attract German voters to Republicanism, acknowledged that his party was composed "chiefly of . . . the native American farmers," while "the strength of our opponents lies mainly in

From "The Republicans and Nativism," *Free Soil, Free Labor, Free Men: The Ideology of the Republican Party Before the Civil War* by Eric Foner. (New York: Oxford University Press, 1970), 226–237. Copyright © 1970 by Eric Foner. Reprinted by permission of Oxford University Press, Inc.

the populous cities, and consists largely of the Irish and uneducated mass of German immigrants. . . ."[2]

Some historians have taken these ethno-political divisions to mean that party programs and ideologies are largely political window-dressing, having little to do with the way people vote. Samuel P. Hays, for example, argues that party ideologies never reflect the major concerns of grass-roots voters, and that on the local level ethno-cultural issues are much more effective in mobilizing electoral support than such national questions as the tariff and trusts (and presumably, slavery). Similarly, Lee Benson's pioneering study of New York voting behavior in the Jacksonian era, while by no means minimizing the role of ideology, concludes that such ethnic groups as native-born Protestants and immigrant Irish Catholics voted in different parties as one expression of the deep antipathy they felt for one another in view of their antithetical systems of value and ways of life. According to the ethnic analysis of politics, nativism and temperance, not anti-slavery, were responsible for the political upheavel of the 1850's. Or, as Hays puts it, all three movements were outgrowths of the same cultural impulse, evangelical Protestantism, and all reflected the cultural consciousness of native-born Protestant voters. Together, Hays says, they "produced both a sharp realignment of voting behavior and a cultural unity for the Republican party."[3] The implication is that the Republican party was as much a vehicle for anti-Catholic and anti-foreign sentiment as for anti-slavery.

There is no question that Republicanism was in part an expression of the hopes and fears of northern native-born Protestants. As Benson points out, the Whig-Republican view that the state should have broad powers to regulate the economic life of the nation had important moral implications as well. Reform movements such as temperance and anti-slavery, which proposed to use state power to attack moral evils, appealed to New England Protestants because of their tradition of "moral stewardship," what one historian calls their "zeal for making others act correctly." According to Clifford S. Griffin, this attitude stemmed from the Calvinist tradition that there was a moral aristocracy on earth, whose duty it was to oversee the moral conduct of others and remove sin from the world. The Yankee followers of the Republican party felt this mission particularly threatened by the waves of immigrants, mostly Catholics, who poured into the country in the 1840's and 1850's. Moreover, as Will Herberg has observed, perhaps the only cement which has bound American Protestants together has been their fear and hatred of Rome.[4] Many Republicans made it clear that they shared this traditional feeling and considered the United States a part of the world Protestant community. "American civilization," said George William Curtis, "in its idea, is historically, the political aspect of the Reformation. America is a permanent protest against absolutism. . . ." The Catholic Church to these Republicans represented tyranny, while Protestantism meant liberty. Anti-slavery, said the Massachusetts radical E. L. Pierce, was merely a reflection of the general principle of liberty and equal rights expressed in the Declaration of Independence. "It is the principle," he continued, " which sustained the States of Holland, when they bade defiance to the tides of the ocean, the rage of the Inquisition, and the colonial power of Spain." Similarly, John P. Hale and other Republicans opposed the annexation of Cuba not only on anti-slavery grounds, but because the Cuban population was largely Catholic and the American system of government could "only be maintained . . . on the principle of Protestant liberty." For men like Hale, American democracy was not a historical accident—it sprang logically from the fact that the early settlers had been Anglo-Saxon Protestants. "The people made this government, and not the government the people," wrote Charles Francis Adams, and he believed that an influx of a different people, schooled in the traditions of absolutism, would undermine American institutions.[5]

Many Republicans shared the nativist outlook which Milton Gordon has termed "Anglo-conformity," and which demands the complete renunciation by immigrant groups of their Old World cultural ancestry, and an unqualified commitment to assimilation into the dominant Anglo-Saxon culture of the United States. Its ideal of American society is the melting pot, rather than a pluralist culture in which divergent ethnic groups live in more or less segregated enclaves. Ante-bellum American society, however, was far from reflecting the melting pot ideal. Studies of a number of northern cities have concluded that immigrants tended to live in their own communities, and instead of desiring assimilation, they consciously strove to re-establish European traditions and values in the United States.[6] The refusal of immigrants to give up their cultural ancestry was a major complaint of nativists, shared by many Republicans who opposed the more extreme anti-foreign program. The Springfield *Republican*, for example, explained in 1854 that while it opposed "organized opposition to any portion of our population," it agreed that "it is good policy to Americanize everything resident in America." The New York *Times* put it more bluntly. The way for immigrants to escape nativist attacks, it declared, was to assimilate fully into American culture:[7]

There is one duty we would earnestly urge upon the plain good sense and just feeling of our adopted citizens. It is the duty of thoroughly *Americanizing* themselves. . . . They should imbue themselves with American feelings. They should not herd themselves together for the preservation of the customs, habits, and languages of the countries from which they came.

These Republicans did not demand that immigrants give up all their values and beliefs as the price for acceptance in America. They believed that a "protestant toleration of all creeds and opinions" ought to be observed. But they did insist that the clannishness and self-segregation of immigrant groups come to an end, so that the United States could be "one harmonious and homogeneous people."[8]

There were several other reasons, however, why many Republicans found nativist ideas attractive. Political nativism gave expression to the widespread concern among native-born citizens about the increasing political participation and power of foreigners. It was only natural that such feelings were especially pronounced among Whigs and, later, Republicans, because immigrants were generally absorbed into the urban political machines of the Democratic party and voted overwhelmingly for Democratic candidates. Federal law prescribed a five-year naturalization period before immigrants could attain citizenship, but in some Democratic states even this waiting period was waived, and resident aliens who declared their intention to become citizens were given the vote.[9] Whigs and Republicans strongly believed that the immigrants' increasing political power was being wielded by the Catholic Church and the Democratic bosses, especially since they thought foreigners were "by education and custom . . . more submissive to the voice of authority" than native-born Americans. Nativists charged that unscrupulous Democratic politicians obtained fraudulent naturalization papers for foreigners, and then herded them to the polls to vote the straight Democratic ticket. It was a major demand of the Know-Nothing party, and of many Republicans as well, that a system of voter registration be established to prevent these frauds and "secure the purification of the ballot-box."[10]

Because the political power of the immigrants was concentrated in the large towns and cities, the nativist reaction was most pronounced there. But rural anti-slavery men had their own reasons for resenting the political power of foreigners. Many Republicans were advocates of temperance legislation, while German and Irish immigrants were known to enjoy a good drink, and regularly voted against prohibition legislation. Even more important, anti-slavery men were outraged by immigrant opposition to the anti-slavery movement. Nowhere was this more apparent than in Massachusetts, whose Irish immigrants were products of a culture characterized by hostility to reformism and deep respect for class distinctions. The pro-slavery attitudes of Boston's Irish were notorious, and Free Soilers attributed their electoral defeats in large measure to the Irish vote. Then in 1853, after the anti-slavery men had succeeded in drafting a new constitution substantially reducing the political power of conservative Boston, the document was defeated at the polls by the Irish vote.[11] When the Know-Nothing movement emerged in 1854, one political observer declared that it was "controlled in great measure by Free Soilers, who have been much outraged by the movement of the Catholics against the Constitution." "The Catholic press upholds the slave power," declared a Boston Free Soil organ. "These two malign powers have a natural affinity for each other."[12]

Another cause of Republican resentment against immigrants was that many blamed the newcomers for the social ills of the large cities. In the 1850's, large numbers of immigrants were dependent on local and state authorities for relief—in New York City in 1860, 80 per cent of the paupers were foreign-born—and immigrants were disproportionately represented in crime statistics. In view of the free labor attitude toward the native-born poor, it is hardly surprising that Republican spokesmen exhibited a lack of compassion for the poverty of immigrants. Most of them, said the Philadelphia *North American*, were unwilling to work and had come to this country "to steal or beg a living" as best they could.[13] In an era when eastern cities were plagued by expanding slums, increasing poverty, and rising crime rates, many Republicans feared that the influx of immigrants was threatening to destroy the free labor ideal of an open society. Frederick Law Olmsted, for example, concluded after visiting the South that economic opportunity was far greater for the northern poor than for the southern, but he warned that in its large cities the North seemed to be "taking some pains to form a permanent lower class"—exactly the class which Republicans claimed did not exist in free labor society. In terms of the free labor outlook, the poverty of the immigrants marked them as somehow inferior to the Yankees, who dominated the economic life of the North even in areas where immigrants were preponderant. George R. Taylor has commented upon the "discipline, sobriety, and reliability," which Yankees—both factory workers and business leaders—displayed, and on their "spirit of achievement." These qualities, many Republicans believed, were sorely needed by the immigrants, particularly the Irish. As E. Pershine Smith, a New York politician and disciple of Henry Carey, wrote, he preferred German immigrants to the Irish, because the Irish tended to be employed as wage earners while the Germans "become either artisans or cultivators of their own land at once."[14]

There were thus several areas of convergence between the Republican free labor outlook and nativism. Yet in assessing the political impact of nativism, one must also recall that many Republicans who shared nativist suspicions regarding Catholics and immigrants, and who supported the temperance cause, strenuously opposed the emergence of nativism as a political movement. Two powerful elements in the Republican party, the radicals and the followers of William H. Seward, had compelling ideological reasons for combating nativism influence. The radical Republicans viewed the upsurge of nativism exactly as they viewed other political events of the 1840's and 1850's; their first concern was how it would affect the anti-slavery cause. In one respect they did welcome the new movement, for the nativist upsurge of 1854–55 helped accomplish what the radicals themselves had long desired—the break-up of one or both of the major national parties. Samuel Gridley Howe, for example, declared that "the demolition of the two corrupt old organizations is a great good," in spite of the "selfish, narrow, and inhumane" nature of the nativist program.[15] Yet few radicals had even this much to say for the Know-Nothings. Those who had participated in the Liberty and Free Soil parties had long believed that the nation should cordially welcome immigrants and had always opposed efforts to abridge their rights.[16] Gamaliel Bailey, editor of the radical *National Era*, was merciless in his condemnation of nativism in 1854 and 1855, even though it cost him many subscribers, particularly in Massachusetts and Connecticut. Know-Nothingism, he declared, was "inconsistent with the fundamental principles of civil and religious liberty, as embodied in our free institutions." In 1854 all the leading Senate radicals voted in favor of Salmon P. Chase's motion allowing immigrants to benefit from the homestead act.[17]

Equally important in the radicals' opposition to nativism was their calculation of the movement's effect on the political fortunes of anti-slavery. Basically, anti-slavery men considered Know-Nothingism an unfortunate aberration which diverted attention from the anti-slavery cause and divided its adherents. "But for this ill-timed and distracting crusade against the Pope and the foreigners," said George Julian in 1855, "Freedom was bound to have taken possession of the government at the close of this execrable administration." In Illinois, Lyman Trumbull, not a radical but a sincere anti-slavery man, agreed that Know-Nothingism and temperance were irritating "side issues," preventing the formation of a united anti-administration party based on the slavery question.[18] The radicals believed that despite abuses of immigrants' political power, the demands of the Know-Nothings were excessive and unjustified, while the real danger to liberty—the Slave Power—was ignored by them. "Neither the Pope nor the foreigners ever can govern the country or endanger its liberties," wrote Charles A. Dana of the New York *Tribune* after the election of 1856, "but the slavebreeders and slavetraders *do* govern it. . . ." Indeed, some radicals went so far as to describe the whole Know-Nothing movement as a southern plot to cripple the anti-slavery movement just at the moment of its greatest chance for success. The goal of the radicals for over a decade had been to make anti-slavery the focal point of national politics. They were not willing to let Know-Nothingism stand in their way.[19]

The struggle against nativism within the Republican party also drew strength from the position of William H. Seward, perhaps the party's single most popular leader. Seward had long been involved in a bitter struggle with New York nativists, dating from his proposal as governor of New York to appropriate public money for Catholic parochial schools. There have been many interpretations of Seward's motives, some historians viewing his plan as merely an effort to attract Catholic voters to the Whig party, and others crediting him with purely humanitarian motives.[20] There is no question that Seward had long believed that a major weakness of the Whig party had been its overt or covert hostility to foreigners, and that he did hope the school plan would gain support among immigrant voters. But the conservative Whigs of New York City rejected Seward's plans, and many refused to vote for him in 1840 because of his association with the Catholics. In 1844, Seward blamed Henry Clay's loss of New York on "the jealousy of the Whig party or a portion of it, against foreigners and Catholics. . . ."[21] And in the 1850's he bitterly attacked the Know-Nothing party, and sought to dissociate the Republican movement from nativism. For their part, the nativists opposed Seward at every point of his career, although the political magician Thurlow Weed was able to engineer Seward's re-election to the Senate in 1855 by a legislature with a large Know-Nothing contingent. Seward, of course, was quite willing to see the Republican party accept the votes of nativists, but he insisted that no concessions on either anti-slavery or the rights of foreigners be made to attract their support.[22]

Yet even more important than these political considerations was the fact that the encouragement of immigration and the widest possible dispersal of public education were vital parts of Seward's outlook on American society. Seward believed that the combined influences of universal public education, economic expansion, and the influx of immigrant labor would help secure the free labor ideal of social mobility and a steadily improving standard of living for Americans. He also viewed rapid expansion of the labor force as a necessary ingredient in his plans for an American empire. Seward's attitude toward immigrants was purely assimilationist—he accepted the image of America as both a melting pot and an asylum for the oppressed of the Old World, and believed that nativism would only delay social integration. His program of aid to Catholic education, he explained, was intended to facilitate assimilation. "I desire to see the children of Catholics educated as well as those of Protestants," he wrote in 1840, "not because I want them Catholics, but because I want them to become good citizens." Moreover, Seward believed that nativism was incompatible with the essential principles of democracy, which demanded that all subjects of a government be treated equally by the laws. American government, he declared, was founded upon "the rightful political equality of all the members of the state," but the Know-Nothings rejected this principle by attempting "to exclude a large and considerable portion of the members of the state from participation in the conduct of its affairs."[23] Seward's instinct for political power and the problems of governance led him to perceive the essential weakness of nativism in a democracy. No party, he recognized, could govern successfully if it excluded an important segment of the citizenry from meaningful participation in the processes of government.

Seward's attitude toward Know-Nothingism points up the fact that the nativist goal of restricting immigration ran counter to two cardinal objectives of the free labor ideology—free labor control of the western territories, and continuing northern economic expansion. The first consideration was illustrated by the steady southern opposition to homestead legislation in the 1850's and by the South's insistence that such legislation be limited to citizens. For both northerners and southerners believed that the settlement of immigrants in the West would erect an effective barrier against the extension of slavery. Immigrants of all political affiliations demonstrated their preference for life in a free labor society by refusing to settle in the South. When Seward hurled his famous challenge to the South on the eve of the passage of the Kansas-Nebraska bill, forecasting a contest between free and slave labor for control of the territories, he based his confidence in northern victory on the steady stream of immigrants who were making their way westward.[24]

The second contradiction between free labor and nativism was summed up by the New York *Tribune* in 1853: "We have five million acres and need at least one thousand million inhabitants to cultivate them. So we need not dread immigration, but may freely welcome its increasing influx." Economic development, so vital an element of the free labor social outlook, was in large measure dependent upon the continued availability of immigrant labor. "Strike out what the Irishman has done for America," said the Springfield *Republican*, "and the country would be set back fifty years in the path of progress."[25] Indeed, during the Civil War, when the manpower needs of the Union army created a labor shortage in the North, Seward used all the resources of the State Department to induce unemployed European workmen to emigrate to the United States, and the Republican Congress passed an act encouraging immigration. The Republican national platform of 1864 went so far as to extol immigrants for their previous contributions to the nation's economic growth, reaffirmed the historic role of the United States as an asylum for the oppressed of all nations, and endorsed a "liberal and just naturalization policy, which would encourage foreign immigration."[26] The needs of the Union and the northern economy thus took precedence over any lingering nativist sentiments. The conflict over nativism in the Republican party was a prolonged and sometimes bitter one, but in a sense, the Republican party's rejection of nativism during the 1850's and 1860's was inherent in its free labor ideology.

NOTES

1. Walter Dean Burnham, "Party Systems and the Political Process," in *The American Party Systems*, eds., William N. Chambers and Walter Dean Burnham (New York, 1967), 285; Lee Benson, *The Concept of Jacksonian Democracy* (Princeton, 1961), 165ff.; Paul Lazarsfeld, Bernard Berelson, and Hazel Gaudet, *The People's Choice* (2nd ed.: New York, 1948), 22; David S. Sparks, "The Birth of the Republican Party in Iowa, 1854-1856," *IJH*, LIV (April 1956), 19; Michael F. Holt, "Forging a Majority: The Formation of the Republican Party in Pittsburgh, Pennsylvania, 1848-1860" (unpublished doctoral dissertation, Johns Hopkins University, 1967), 464-65; Thomas A. Flinn, "Continuity and Change in Ohio Politics," *Journal of Politics*," XXIV (August 1962), 542; *Walter Dean Burnham*, "American Voting Behavior and the 1964 Election," *Midwest Journal of Political Science*, XII (February 1968), 25-26.

2. Joseph Schafer, ed., *Intimate Letters of Carl Shurz, 1841-69* (Madison, 1928), 180,

3. Samuel P. Hays, "Political Parties and the Community-Society Continuum," in *The American Party Systems*, eds., Chambers and Burnham, 155, 158, 161-62; Samuel P. Hays, "History as Human Behavior," *IJH*, LVII (July 1960), 195-97; Benson, *Concept*, 165-78, 322-23. Cf. Joel H. Silbey, ed., *The Transformation of American Politics, 1840-1860* (Englewood Cliffs, 1967), 3-4.

4. Benson, *Concept*, 180, 199-200, 206; Clifford S. Griffin, *Their Brothers' Keepers: Moral Stewardship in the United States, 1800-1865* (New Brunswick, 1960), x-xiii, 5, 21; Seymour M. Lipset, "Religion and Politics in the American Past and Present," in *Religion and Social Conflict*, eds., Robert Lee and Martin E. Marty (New York, 1964), 75, 108.

5. Charles E. Norton, ed., *Orations and Addresses of George William Curtis* (3 vols.: New York, 1894), I, 51; Boston *Daily Traveler*, in Charles Francis Adams Diary, October 28, 1858, Adams Papers, MHS; *Congressional Globe*, 35 Congress, 2 Session, Appendix, 165-66; [Charles Francis Adams], "The Reign of King Cotton," *Atlantic Monthly*, VII (April 1861),

453. Cf. Boston *Evening Telegraph*, October 3, 1854, January 23, 1855; *Ohio State Journal*, November 14, 1856.

6. Milton M. Gordon, *Assimilation in American Life* (New York, 1964), 85-98; Oscar Handlin, *Boston's Immigrants* (Cambridge, 1959), 161-76; Oscar Handlin, "Immigration in American Life: A Reappraisal," in *Immigration and American History*, ed., Henry Steele Commager (Minneapolis, 1961), 13; Holt, "Forging a Majority," 22-24; Joseph Schafer, "The Yankee and the Teuton in Wisconsin," *WisMH*, VII (1923-24), 156-58.

7. Springfield *Republican*, March 31, 1854; New York *Times*, June 23, 1854. Cf. *Liberator*, August 31, 1860; New York *Times*, April 7, 1852, December 6, 1854; Maldwyn A. Jones, *American Immigration* (Chicago, 1960), 156.

8. Boston *Atlas and Daily Bee*, July 15, 1858; Philadelphia *North American and United States Gazette*, June 5, 1857.

9. Carl F. Brand, "History of the Know-Nothing Party in Indiana," *IndMH*, XVIII (1922), 56-57; Jones, *American Immigration*, 141-43, 153-55; Holt, "Forging a Majority," 213-14; Schafer, "Yankee and Teuton," 159-61; Thomas J. Curran, "Know-Nothings of New York State" (unpublished doctoral dissertation, Columbia University, 1963), 97; Kenneth Stampp, *Indiana Politics During the Civil War* (Indianapolis, 1949), 9.

10. *Address of His Excellency Nathaniel P. Banks, to the Two Branches of the Legislature of Massachusetts, January 7, 1859* (Boston, 1859), 9; "Speech of Daniel Ullmann, Esq.," news clipping, August, 1858, Daniel Ullmann Papers, NYHS. Cf. C. Maxwell Myers, "The Rise of the Republican Party in Pennsylvania, 1854-1860" (unpublished doctoral dissertation, University of Pittsburgh, 1940), 36.

11. Benjamin F. Wade to William Schouler, May 3, 1855, William Schouler Papers, MHS; William G. Bean, "Party Transformation in Massachusetts with Special Reference to the Antecedents of Republicanism 1848-1860" (unpublished doctoral dissertation, Harvard University, 1922), 174-79, 195-223; William G. Bean, "An Aspect of Know-Nothingism— The Immigrant and Slavery," *SAQ*, XXIII (October 1924), 319-24; Boston *Commonwealth*, November 22, 1853; Handlin, *Boston's Immigrants*, 125-41; Joseph R. Gusfield, *Symbolic Crusade: Status Politics and the American Temperance Movement* (Urbana, 1963), 6, 55-56.

12. James W. Stone to Charles Sumner, March 15, 1854, Charles Sumner Papers, Houghton Library, Harvard University; Boston *Commonwealth*, June 24, 1854.

13. Jones, *American Immigration*, 133; Philadelphia *North American and United States Gazette*, November 20, 1855. Cf. New York *Times*, March 20, 1852, January 20, 1858; *Congressional Globe*, 35 Congress, 1 Session, 1005, 36 Congress, 1 Session, Appendix, 174; New York *Tribune*, March 16, 1853; Cleveland *Leader*, November 16, 1857.

14. Douglas T. Miller, *Jacksonian Aristocracy: Class and Democracy in New York, 1830-1860* (New York, 1967), 128-54; Frederick Law Olmsted, *A Journey in the Back Country* (New York, 1863), 416; George R. Taylor, "The National Economy Before and After the Civil War," in *Economic Change in the Civil War Era*, eds., David T. Gilchrist and W. David Lewis (Greenville, Del., 1965), 18-19; E. Pershine Smith to Henry C. Carey, March 11, 1858, Carey Papers, HSPa.

15. Samuel Gridley Howe to Horace Mann, November 14, 1854, Samuel Gridley Howe Papers, Houghton Library, Harvard University. Cf. John G. Palfrey to Giddings, December 20, 1854, Giddings Papers; Giddings to Palfrey, November 27, 1854, John G. Palfrey Papers, Houghton Library, Harvard University.

16. Joel Goldfarb, "The Life of Gamaliel Bailey Prior to the Founding of the *National Era*; the orientation of a Practical Abolitionist" (unpublished doctoral dissertation, University of California at Los Angeles, 1958), 309-11; *National Era*, February 8, 1849, April 1, 1852; Kirk Porter and Donald B. Johnson, comps., *National Party Platforms 1840-1956* (Urbana, 1956), 19.

17. Gamaliel Bailey to Charles Francis Adams, January 23, 1855, Adams Papers; *National Era*, November 30, 1854; *Congressional Globe*, 33 Congress, 1 Session, 1740.

18. George W. Julian to E. A. Stansbury, September 14, 1855, Giddings-Julian Papers, LC; Mildred C. Stoler, "The Influence of the Democratic Element in the Republican Party of Illinois and Indiana, 1854-1860" (unpublished doctoral dissertation, Indiana University, 1938), 98. Cf. Sumner to Howe, January 13, 1855, Sumner Papers; George W. Julian, *Speeches on Political Questions* (New York, 1872), 122.

19. Charles A. Dana to Henry C. Carey, November 27, 1856, Carey Papers; New York

Tribune, September 3, 1856; J. Robert Lane, *A Political History of Connecticut During the Civil War* (Washington, 1941), 46.

20. For various interpretations, see John W. Pratt, "Governor Seward and the New York City School Controversy, 1840–1842," *NYH*, XLII (October 1961), 351–64; Vincent P. Lannie, "William Seward and Common School Education," *HEdQ*, IV (September 1964), 181–92; Vincent P. Lannie, "William Seward and the New York School Controversy, 1840–1842: A Problem in Historical Motivation," *HEdQ*, VI (Spring 1966), 52–71; Glyndon G. Van Deusen, "Seward and the School Question Reconsidered," *JAH*, LII (September 1965), 313–19.

21. Allan Nevins, ed., *The Diary of Philip Hone* (2 vols.: New York, 1927), I, 509; George E. Baker, ed., *The Works of William H. Seward* (5 vols.: Boston, 1853–84), III, 389; William H. Seward to Henry Clay, November 7, 1844, Seward to Christopher Morgan, June 12, 1843, William H. Seward Papers, Rush Rhees Library, University of Rochester.

22. Baker, ed., *Seward Works*, II, 267, IV, 244, 284; Frederick Seward, ed., *Seward at Washington* (2 vols.: New York, 1891), I, 264, 269; E. Pershine Smith to Carey, June 14, 1854, Carey Papers. Cf. Thomas J. Curran, "Seward and the Know-Nothings," *NYHSQ*, LI (April 1967), 141–59, and the comment of the New York *Evening Post* when Seward was re-elected to the Senate with Know-Nothing votes: "With the example of Seward's re-election, one need not be surprised if the vote of the Know-Nothings is cast for Pope Pius at the next election" (February 3, 1855).

23. Baker, ed., *Seward Works*, I, 56, 198–99, 322; III, 14, 480, 489–99; IV, 284; Benson, *Concept*, 104; New York *Tribune*, June 7, 1853; Glyndon G. Van Deusen, *William Henry Seward* (New York 1967), 205–06.

24. Baker, ed., *Seward Works*, IV, 471. Cf. Boston *Commonwealth*, June 24, 1854; *Congressional Globe*, 35 Congress, 1 Session, 1044, 1980; New York *Evening Post*, November 15, 1858; Roy M. Robbins, *Our Landed Heritage, The Public Domain, 1776–1936* (Princeton, 1942), 176.

25. New York *Tribune*, September 29, 1853; Springfield *Republican*, July 10, 1857. Cf. Arnold W. Green, Henry Charles Carey, Nineteenth Century Sociologist (Philadelphia, 1951), 127; Henry C. Carey, The Harmony of Interests, Agricultural, Manufacturing, and Commercial (New York, 1856), 229.

bibliography

Countless books have been written about slavery and the institutionalization of American racism. Of particular value are Winthrop Jordan, *White Over Black: American Attitudes Toward the Negro, 1550-1812* (Penguin Books, 1968); Lerone Bennett, Jr., *Before the Mayflower: A History of the Negro in America, 1619-1964* (Penguin Books, 1966); Robert S. Starobin, *Industrial Slavery in the Old South* (Oxford University Press, 1970); Eugene Genovese, *The Political Economy of Slavery* (Pantheon, 1965); Eugene Genovese, *The World the Slave Holders Made* (Pantheon, 1969); W.E.B. DuBois, *The Suppression of the African Slave Trade to the United States, 1638-1870* (Schocken Books, 1969, [1896]; John Hope Franklin, *From Slavery to Freedom: A History of Negro Americans* (Knopf, 1967).

The controversy stimulated by Stanley Elkins' analysis of the slave personality has been collected by Ann J. Lane (ed.), *The Debate Over Slavery: Stanley Elkins and His Critics* (University of Illinois Press, 1971). For an analysis of the ways in which blacks have hidden their feelings from whites, see Hortense Powdermaker, "The Channeling of Negro Aggression," *American Journal of Sociology*, 48 (May 1943). See also Herbert Aptheker, *American Negro Slave Revolts* (International Publishers, 1963); and Martin E. Dann (ed.), *The Black Press, 1827-1890* (Putnam, 1971).

For abolitionism, anti-abolitionism, and the origins of contemporary racism, see Leon Litwack, *North of Slavery: The Negro in the Free States, 1790-1860* (University of Chicago Press, 1961); Lorman Ratner, *Powder Keg: Northern Opposition to the Anti-Slavery Movement, 1831-1840* (Basic Books, 1968); Sylvan S. Tomkins, "Psychology of Commitment: The Constructive Role of Violence and Suffering for the Individual and for His Society," in Martin Duberman (ed.), *Antislavery Vanguard* (Princeton University Press, 1965); John Demos, "The Antislavery Movement and the Problem of Violent Means," *New England Quarterly* (December 1964); Margaret Shortreed, "The Antislavery Radicals: From Crusade to Revolution, 1840-1868," *Past and Present*, (November 1959); Aileen Kraditor, *Means and Ends in American Abolitionism: Garrison and His Critics on Strategy and Tactics* (Pantheon, 1967); Hans L. Trefousse, *The Radical Republicans: Lincoln's Vanguard for Racial Justice* (Knopf, 1969); James McPherson, *The Struggle for Equality: Abolitionists and the Negro in the Civil War and Reconstruction* (Princeton University Press, 1964); Willie Lee Rose, *Rehearsal for Reconstruction: The Port Royal Experiment* (Bobbs-Merrill, 1964); La Wanda and John Cox, *Politics, Principle, and Prejudice: Dilemma of Reconstruction America* (Free Press, 1963); and W.E.B. DuBois, *Black Reconstruction in America, 1860-1880* (Atheneum, 1969 [1935]).

It is not possible to understand the costs of white racism to black people without knowing something about African history and culture. See the works of Basil Davidson: *The Lost Cities of Africa* (Little, Brown, 1959); *The African Past: Chronicles From Antiquity to Modern Times* (Grosset and Dunlap, 1967); and *The African Slave Trade: Precolonial History, 1450-1850* (Little, Brown, 1961); and Yosef ben-Jochennan, *Black Man of the Nile* (Alkebu-Lan Books, African-American Heritage Series, 1970).

Excellent sources for further study include the following historiographical essays: Ernest Kaiser, "In Defense of the People's Black and White History and Culture," *Freedomways* (1970), Parts I, II, and III; Kaiser, "The History of Negro History," *Negro Digest* (February 1968); Robert Starobin, "Racism and the American Experience," *Radical America* (March-April 1971), which is a revision of "The Negro: A Central Theme in American History," *Journal of Contemporary History* (April 1968).

Most works on nativism deal with the "new immigrants" who arrived after Reconstruction (see *Past Imperfect*, Vol. II, Chapter 1). The traditional study of the early period, Ray Billington's *The Protestant Crusade, 1800-1860* (Macmillan 1938), is somewhat dated. Parts of John Higham, *Strangers in the Land: Patterns of American Nativism, 1860-1925* (Atheneum, 1970 [1955]), and Barbara Miller Solomon, *Ancestors and Immigrants* (Harvard University Press, 1956) are relevant to the early period. See especially John Higham, "Another Look at Nativism," *Catholic Historical Review*, 44 (July 1958); Oscar Handlin,

288

Boston's Immigrants (Harvard University Press, 1959); David Brion Davis, "Some Themes of Counter-Subversion: An Analysis of Anti-Masonic, Anti-Catholic, and Anti-Mormon Literature," *Mississippi Valley Historical Review*, 47 (September 1960); Clifford S. Griffin, *Their Brothers' Keepers: Moral Stewardship in the United States, 1800–1865* (Rutgers University Press, 1960).

Serious work on women in American society has just begun. Gerda Lerner has masterfully filled one of the deepest chasms with *Black Women in White America, A Documentary History* (Pantheon, 1972), which includes slave narratives and an excellent bibliography. See also Gerda Lerner, *The Grimké Sisters From South Carolina: Rebels Against Slavery* (Houghton Mifflin, 1969); Alma Lutz, *Crusade for Freedom: Women in the Anti-Slavery Movement* (Beacon Press, 1968); Eleanor Flexner, *Century of Struggle: The Woman's Rights Movement in the United States* (Harvard University Press, 1959). For a vision of how women were supposed to behave and were trained to believe they should be, see Barbara Welter, "The Cult of True Womanhood, 1820–1860," *American Quarterly*, 18 (Summer 1966). Another view of this theme is presented in Ann F. Scott, *The Southern Lady: From Pedestal to Politics, 1830–1920* (University of Chicago Press, 1970). For additional works, see the excellent bibliographical essay by Ann D. Gordon, Mari Jo Buhle, and Nancy E. Schrom, "Women in American Society: An Historical Contribution," *Radical America* (July–August 1971).

ABOUT THE AUTHORS

Blanche Wiesen Cook received her Ph.D. from Johns Hopkins University in 1968. She is currently Assistant Professor of History at John Jay College, City University of New York and has been a member of its faculty since 1968. Her areas of specialization are U.S. history, American and British peace movements, and violence and social change in the United States. Dr. Cook is the senior editor of Garland Library of War and Peace and has written articles for the *Journal of American Studies*.

Alice Kessler Harris, Ph.D., Rutgers University, 1968, is Assistant Professor of History at Hofstra University and has been a member of its faculty since 1968. She previously taught at Douglass College. Her areas of current academic interest are labor history and immigrant history. Dr. Harris also served in an advisory capacity on the Academic Freedom Committee of the American Civil Liberties Union.

Ronald Radosh received his Ph.D. from the University of Wisconsin in 1967. He is currently Associate Professor of History at Queensborough Community College and on the faculty of the Graduate Center, City University of New York. Dr. Radosh's areas of specialization include twentieth century United States, American labor and radical history, and U.S. foreign policy. He is the author of *America: From World War II Through 1970, Conservative Critics of the American Empire,* and *American Labor and United States Foreign Policy*.

A NOTE ON THE TYPE

The text is set in Melior, a typeface designed by Hermann Zapf and issued in 1952. Melior, like Times Roman, was created specifically for use in a newspaper. With this functional end in mind, Zapf nonetheless chose to base the proportions of its letterforms on those of the Golden Section. The result is a typeface of unusual strength and surpassing sublety.

This book was composed by Volt Information Sciences, Inc., N.Y. Printed and bound by Von Hoffmann Press, Inc., St. Louis, Missouri.